STUDENT ATLAS OF

World Politics

Eighth Edition

John L. Allen
University of Wyoming

 **Higher Education**

Boston   Burr Ridge, IL   Dubuque, IA   New York   San Francisco   St. Louis
Bangkok   Bogotá   Caracas   Kuala Lumpur   Lisbon   London   Madrid   Mexico City
Milan   Montreal   New Delhi   Santiago   Seoul   Singapore   Sydney   Taipei   Toronto

The McGraw·Hill Companies

Higher Education

STUDENT ATLAS OF WORLD POLITICS, EIGHTH EDITION

Published by McGraw-Hill, a business unit of The McGraw-Hill Companies, Inc., 1221 Avenue of the Americas, New York, NY 10020. Copyright © 2008 by The McGraw-Hill Companies, Inc. All rights reserved. Previous edition(s) 1991–2006. No part of this publication may be reproduced or distributed in any form or by any means, or stored in a database or retrieval system, without the prior written consent of The McGraw-Hill Companies, Inc., including, but not limited to, in any network or other electronic storage or transmission, or broadcast for distance learning.

Some ancillaries, including electronic and print components, may not be available to customers outside the United States.

Student Atlas® is a registered trademark of the McGraw-Hill Companies, Inc.
Student Atlas is published by the **Contemporary Learning Series** group within the McGraw-Hill Higher Education division.

✪ This book is printed on recycled, acid-free paper containing 10% postconsumer waste.

1 2 3 4 5 6 7 8 9 0 QPD/QPD 0 9 8 7

MHID 0-07-337972-7
ISBN 978-0-07-337972-2
ISSN 1524-4556

Managing Editor: *Larry Loeppke*
Production Manager: *Faye Schilling*
Senior Developmental Editor: *Susan Brusch*
Editorial Assistant: *Nancy Meissner*
Production Service Assistant: *Rita Hingtgen*
Permissions Coordinator: *Lori Church*
Senior Marketing Manager: *Julie Keck*
Marketing Communications Specialist: *Mary Klein*
Marketing Coordinator: *Alice Link*
Project Manager: *Jane Mohr*
Design Specialist: *Tara McDermott*
Senior Administrative Assistant: *DeAnna Dausener*
Senior Operations Manager: *Pat Koch Krieger*
Cover Designer: *Maggie Lytle*

Compositor: *Carlisle Publishing Services*
Cartography: *Carto-Graphics, Hudson, WI*
Cover Image: *© Parvinder Sethi*

We would like to thank Digital Wisdom Incorporated for allowing us to use their Mountain High Maps cartography software. This software was used to create maps 99, 102, 105, 108, 111, 113, 115, 117, 120, 123, 124, 126, and 127.

Library in Congress Cataloging-in-Publication Data
I. World politics—1991—Atlases. II. International relations—Atlases.
909.82

www.mhhe.com

A Note to the Student

International politics is a drama played out on a world stage. If the events of and subsequent to September 11, 2001—the worldwide "war on terrorism," the specific regional military actions in Afghanistan and Iraq, the resulting civil war in Iraq, the transit bombings in London and Madrid, the Hezbollah-Israeli conflict in Lebanon—have taught us anything, it is that the drama is very real and the stage is indeed a worldwide one. We are not isolated from events that transpire in other parts of the world; our boundaries do make us secure; and we ignore the conditions of political, economic, cultural, and physical geography outside those boundaries at our great peril. The maps in this atlas serve as the stage settings for the various scenes in this drama; the data tables are the building materials from which the settings are created. Just as the stage setting helps bring to life and give meaning to the actions and words of a play, so can these maps and tables enhance your understanding of the vast and complex drama of global politics, including the emergence of global terrorism as a political instrument. Use this atlas in conjunction with your text on international politics or international affairs. It will help you become more knowledgeable about this international stage as well as the actors.

The maps and data sets in the *Student Atlas of World Politics*, eighth edition, are designed to introduce you to the importance of the connections between geography and world politics. In many instances, the data sets have been used to produce the patterns that you see on the maps. But where the data may represent absolute values (at least as reported by individual countries), the maps are generalizations based on the data. The maps are not perfect representations of reality—no maps ever are—but they do represent "models," or approximations of the real world, that should aid in your understanding of the world drama.

You will find your study of this atlas more productive in relation to your study of international politics if you examine the maps on the following pages in the context of five distinct analytical themes:

1. Location: Where Is It? This involves a focus on the precise location of places in both absolute terms (the latitude and longitude of a place) and in relative terms (the location of a place in relation to the location of other places). When you think of location, you should automatically think of both forms. Knowing something about absolute location will help you to understand a variety of features of physical geography, since such key elements are often so closely related to their position on the earth. But it is equally important to think of location in relative terms. The location of places in relation to other places is often more important in influencing social, economic, and cultural characteristics than are the factors of physical geography. Certainly the relative location of the World Trade Center was crucial to the identification of the WTC as both a symbolic and actual center of economic activity—and this identification played an important role in its selection as a target for terrorist action. Equally, both the relative and absolute location of Baghdad play an important role in the ongoing struggle to create a politically stable Iraq.

2. Place: What Is It Like? This encompasses the political, economic, cultural, environmental, and other characteristics that give a place its identity. You should seek to understand the similarities and differences of places by exploring their basic characteristics. Why are some places with similar environmental characteristics so very different in economic, cultural, social, and political ways? Why are other places with such different environmental characteristics so seemingly alike in terms of their institutions, their economies, and their cultures? The place characteristics of parts of the world American students have known little about (like Afghanistan and Iraq) have now emerged as vital components of our necessary understanding of the implementation of military and political strategies.

3. Human/Environment Interactions: How Is the Landscape Shaped? This theme focuses on the ways in which people respond to and modify their environments. On the world stage, humans are not the only part of the action. The environment also plays a role in the drama of international politics. But the characteristics of the environment do not exert a controlling influence over human activities; they only provide a set of alternatives from which different cultures, in different times, make their choices. Observe the relationship between the basic elements of physical geography such as climate and terrain and the host of ways in which humans have used the land surfaces of the world. To know something of the relationship between people and the environment in the arid parts of the Old World is to begin to understand the nature of political, economic, and even religious conflicts between the inhabitants of those regions and others. The ongoing unrest in the Darfur region of Sudan or military conflict in the Congo Basin are at least partly attributable to the interaction between people and their environment.

4. Movement: How Do People Stay in Touch? This examines the transportation and communication systems that link people and places. Movement or "spatial interaction" is the chief mechanism for the spread of ideas and innovations from one place to another. It is spatial interaction that validates the old cliché, "the world is getting smaller." We find McDonald's restaurants in Tokyo and Honda automobiles in New York City because of spatial interaction. And the spread of global terrorism is, first and foremost, a process of spatial interaction. Advanced transportation and communication systems have made possible such

events as transpired in New York City in September 2001, or in Iraq in May 2003, and have transformed the world into which your parents were born. And the world that greets your children will be very different from your world. None of this would happen without the force of movement or spatial interaction.

5. Regions: Worlds Within a World. This theme, perhaps the most important for this atlas, helps to organize knowledge about the land and its people. The world consists of a mosaic of "regions" or areas that are somehow different and distinctive from other areas. The region of Anglo-America (the United States and Canada) is, for example, different enough from the region of Western Europe that geographers clearly identify them as two unique and separate areas. Yet despite their differences, Anglo-Americans and Europeans share a number of similarities: common cultural backgrounds, comparable economic patterns, shared religious traditions, and even some shared physical environmental characteristics. Conversely, although the regions of Anglo-America and Southwestern Asia (the "Middle East") are also easily distinguished as distinctive units of the Earth's surface with some shared physical environmental characteristics, the inhabitants of these two regions have fewer similarities and more differences between them than is the case with Anglo-America and Western Europe: different cultural traditions, different institutions, different linguistic and religious patterns. An understanding of both the differences and similarities between regions like Anglo-America and Europe on the one hand, or Anglo-America and Southwest Asia on the other, will help you to understand much that has happened in the human past or that is currently transpiring in the world around you. At the very least, an understanding of regional similarities and differences will help you to interpret what you read on the front page of your daily newspaper or view on the evening news report on your television set.

Not all of these themes will be immediately apparent on each of the 129 maps and 14 tables in this atlas. But if you study the contents of *Student Atlas of World Politics*, eighth edition, along with the reading of your text and think about the five themes, maps and tables and text will complement one another and improve your understanding of global politics. As Shakespeare said, "All the world's a stage." Your challenge is now to understand both the stage and the drama being played on it.

A Word about Data Sources

At the very outset of your study of this atlas, you should be aware of some limitations of the maps and data tables. In some instances, a map or a table may have missing data. This may be the result of the failure of a country to report information to a central international body (like the United Nations or the World Bank). Alternatively, it may reflect shifts in political boundaries, internal or external conflicts, or changes in responsibility for reporting data have caused certain countries (for example, those countries that made up the former Yugoslavia) to delay their reports. It is always our wish to be as up-to-date as is possible; earlier editions of this atlas were lacking more data than this one and subsequent versions will have still more data, particularly on the southeastern European countries, the independent countries formerly part of the now-defunct Soviet Union, or on African and Asian nations that are just beginning to reach a point in their economic and political development where they can consistently report reliable information. In the meantime, as events continue to restructure our world, it's an exciting time to be a student of international events!

John L. Allen
University of Wyoming

What's New in This Edition

The Student Atlas of World Politics, eighth edition, reflects current political, economic, demographic, and environmental change in every part of the world. This edition is substantially enlarged from its predecessor and is the most comprehensive version yet of a book that has long been a standard in the field. Here, in one volume, are 100 thematic maps, 24 reference maps rich in details of physical and political geography, and 14 data tables of valuable and current data relevant to international political issues and affairs. A number of new thematic maps highlight the impact of demographic stresses on political stability at a global scale. New maps have also been added in the political, economic, demographic, and environmental sections of the atlas. The section on current hotspots or "flashpoints" has been enlarged to include a number of up-to-date areas of actual or potential conflict.

The tables include the latest available country-by-country data on a wide array of political, military, economic, demographic, and environmental issues.

This unique combination of maps and data makes the atlas an invaluable pedagogical tool. It also serves to introduce students to the five basic themes of spatial analysis:

- Location: Where is it?
- Place: What is it like?
- Human-Environment Interaction: How is the landscape shaped?
- Movement: How do people stay in touch?
- Regions: How is the surface of the world arranged and organized?

We have also added an introductory section, "Introduction: How to Read an Atlas." This should help students to evaluate and interpret map data more easily.

Concise and affordable, this up-to-date *Student Atlas of World Politics* is suitable for any course dealing in current world affairs.

About the Author

J ohn L. Allen is emeritus professor of geography at both the University of Connecticut and the University of Wyoming. He taught at the University of Connecticut from 1967 to 2000, when he moved to the University of Wyoming as professor and chair of the Department of Geography. He retired from service at the University of Wyoming in 2007. He is a native of Wyoming and received his bachelor's degree (1963) in International Studies and his master's degree (1964) in Political Science from the University of Wyoming. In 1969 he received his Ph.D. in Geography from Clark University. His areas of special interest include human attitudes toward environmental systems, the impact of contemporary human activities on landscapes, and the historical geography of human-environment interactions. Dr. Allen is the author and editor of many scholarly books and articles as well as several other student atlases, including the best-selling *Student Atlas of World Geography*.

Acknowledgments

The author wishes to recognize with gratitude the advice, suggestions, and general assistance of the following reviewers:

Robert Bednarz
Texas A & M University

Gerald E. Beller
West Virginia State College

Kenneth L. Conca
University of Maryland

Femi Ferreira
Hutchinson Community College

Paul B. Frederic
University of Maine at Farmington

James F. Fryman
University of Northern Iowa

Michael Gold-Biss
St. Cloud State University

Herbert E. Gooch III
California Lutheran University

Lloyd E. Hudman
Brigham Young University

Edward L. Jackiewicz
Miami University of Ohio

Artimus Keiffer
Indiana University–Purdue University at Indianapolis

Richard L. Krol
Kean College of New Jersey

Jeffrey S. Lantis
The College of Wooster

Robert Larson
Indiana State University

Mark Lowry II
United States Military Academy at West Point

Max Lu
Kansas State University

Taylor E. Mack
Mississippi State University

Kenneth C. Martis
West Virginia University

Calvin O. Masilela
West Virginia University

Patrick McGreevy
Clarion University

Tyrel G. Moore
University of North Carolina at Charlotte

David J. Nemeth
The University of Toledo

Emmett Panzella
Point Park College

Daniel S. Papp
University System of Georgia

Lance Robinson
United States Air Force Academy

Jefferson S. Rogers
University of Tennessee at Martin

Barbara J. Rusnak
United States Air Force Academy

Mark Simpson
University of Tennessee at Martin

Jutta Weldes
Kent State University

Table of Contents

Unit III   Population, Health, and Human Development   65

Unit IV   The Global Economy   93

Unit VIII   World Countries: Data Tables   159

Unit IX   Geographical Index   218

Introduction: How to Read an Atlas

The Coordinate System

An atlas is a book containing maps which are "models" of the real world. By the term "model" we mean exactly what you think of when you think of a model: a representation of reality that is generalized, usually considerably smaller than the original, and with certain features emphasized, depending on the purpose of the model. A model of a car does not contain all of the parts of the original, but it may contain enough parts that it is recognizable as a car and can be used to study principles of automotive design or maintenance. A car model designed for racing, on the other hand, may contain fewer parts but would have the mobility of a real automobile. Car models come in a wide variety of types containing almost anything you can think of relative to automobiles that doesn't require the presence of a full-size car. Since geographers deal with the real world, virtually all of the printed or published studies of that world require models. Unlike a mechanic in an automotive shop, we can't roll our study subject into the shop, take it apart, and put it back together. We must use models. In other words, we must generalize our subject, and the way we do that is by using maps. Some maps are designed to show specific geographic phenomena, such as the climates of the world or the relative rates of population growth for the world's countries. We call these maps "thematic maps," and Units I through VI of this atlas contain maps of this type. Other maps are designed to show the geographic location of towns and cities and rivers and lakes and mountain ranges and so on. These are called "reference maps" and they make up many of the maps in Unit VII. All of these maps, whether thematic or reference, are models of the real world that selectively emphasize the features that we want to show on the map.

In order to read maps effectively—in other words, in order to understand the models of the world presented in the following pages—it is important for you to know certain things about maps: how they are made using what are called *projections;* how the level of mathematical proportion of the map or what geographers call *scale* affects what you see; and how geographers use *generalization* techniques such as simplification and symbols where it would be impossible to draw a small version of the real world feature. In this brief introduction, then, we'll explain to you three of the most important elements of map interpretation: projection, scale, and generalization.

Map Projections

Perhaps the most basic problem in *cartography,* or the art and science of map-making, is the fact that the subject of maps—the earth's surface—is what is called by mathematicians "a non-developable surface." Since the world is a sphere (or nearly so—it's actually slightly flattened at the poles and bulges a tiny bit at the equator), it is impossible to flatten out the world or any part of its curved surface without producing some kind of distortion. This "near sphere" is represented by a geographic grid or co-ordinate system of lines of latitude or *parallels* that run east and west and are used to measure distance north and south on the globe, and lines of longitude or *meridians* that run north and south and are used to measure distance east and west. All the lines of longitude are half circles of equal length and they all converge at the poles. These meridians are numbered from 0 degrees (Prime or Greenwich Meridian) east and west to 180 degrees. The meridian of 0 degrees and the meridian of 180 degrees are

halves of the same "great circle" or line representing a plane that bisects the globe into two equal hemispheres. All lines of longitude are halves of great circles. All the lines of latitude are complete circles that are parallel to one another and are spaced equidistant on the meridians. The circumference of these circles lessens as you move north or south from the equator. Parallels of latitude are numbered from 0 degrees at the equator north and south to 90 degrees at the North and South poles. The only line of latitude that is a great circle is the equator, which equally divides the world into a northern and southern hemisphere. In the real world, all these grid lines of latitude and longitude intersect at right angles. The problem for cartographers is to convert this spherical or curved grid into a geometrical shape that is "developable"; that is, it can be flattened (such as a cylinder or cone) or is already flat (a plane). The reason the results of the conversion process are called "projections" is that we imagine a world globe (or some part of it) that is made up of wires running north-south and east-west to represent the grid lines of latitude and longitude and other wires or even solid curved plates to represent the coastlines of continents or the continents themselves. We then imagine a light source at some location inside or outside the wire globe that can "project" or cast shadows of the wires representing grid lines onto a developable surface. Sometimes the basic geometric principles of projection may be modified by other mathematical principles to yield projections that are not truly geometric but have certain desirable features. We call these types of projections "arbitrary." The three most basic types of projections are named according to the type of developable surface: cylindrical, conic, or azimuthal (plane). Each type has certain characteristic features: they may be *equal area* projections in which the size of each area on the map is a direct proportional representation of that same area in the real world but shapes are distorted; they may be *conformal* projections in which area may be distorted but shapes are shown correctly; or they may be *compromise* projections in which both shape and area are distorted but the overall picture presented is fairly close to reality. It is important to remember that all maps distort the geographic grid and continental outlines in characteristic ways. The only representation of the world that does not distort either shape or area is a globe. You can see why we must use projections—can you imagine an atlas that you would have to carry back and forth across campus that would be made up entirely of globes?

Cylindrical Projections

Cylindrical projections are drawn as if the geographic grid were projected onto a cylinder. Cylindrical projections have the advantage of having all lines of latitude as true parallels or straight lines. This makes these projections quite useful for showing geographic relationships in which latitude or distance north-south is important (many physical features, such as climate, are influenced by latitude). Unfortunately, most cylindrical-type projections distort area significantly. One of the most famous is the Mercator projection. This projection makes areas disproportionately large as you move toward the pole, making Greenland, which is actually about one-seventh the size of South America, appear to be as large as the southern continent. But the Mercator projection has the quality of conformality: landmasses on the map are true in shape and thus all coastlines on the map intersect lines of latitude and longitude at the proper angles. This makes the Mercator projection, named after its inventor, a sixteenth-century Dutch cartographer, ideal for its original purpose as a tool for navigation—but not a good projection for attempting to show some geographical feature in which areal relationship is important. Unfortunately, the Mercator projection has often been used for wall maps for schoolrooms and the consequence is that generations of American school children have been "tricked" into thinking that Greenland is actually larger than South America. Much better cylindrical-type projections are those like the Robinson projection used in this atlas that is neither equal area nor conformal but a compromise that portrays the real world much as it actually looks, enough so that we can use it for areal comparisons.

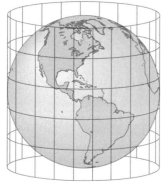

The Mercator Projection

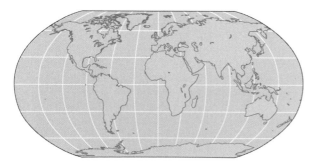

The Robinson Projection

Conic Projections

Conic projections are those that are imagined as being projected onto a cone that is tangent to the globe along a standard parallel, or a series of cones tangent along several parallels or even intersecting the globe. Conic projections usually show latitude as curved lines and longitude as straight lines. They are good projections for areas with north-south extent, like the map of Europe to the right, and may be either conformal, equal area, or compromise, depending on how they are constructed. Many of the regional maps in the last map section of this atlas are conic projections.

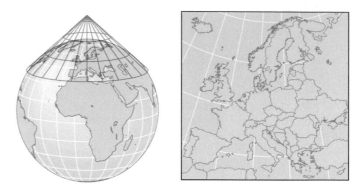

Conic Projection of Europe

Azimuthal Projections

Azimuthal projections are those that are imagined as being projected onto a plane or flat surface. They are named for one of their essential properties. An "azimuth" is a line of compass bearing, and azimuthal projections have the property of yielding true compass directions from the center of the map. This makes azimuthal maps useful for navigation purposes, particularly air navigation. But, because they distort area and shape so greatly, they are seldom used for maps designed to show geographic relationships. When they are used as illustrative rather than navigation maps, it is often in the "polar case" projection shown here where the plane has been made tangent to the globe at the North Pole.

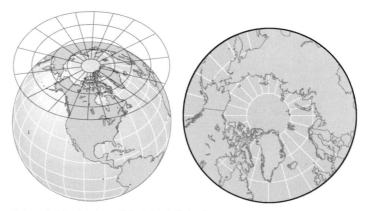

Azimuthal Projection of the North Polar Region

Map Scale

Since maps are models of the real world, it follows that they are not the same size as the real world or any portion of it. Every map, then, is subject to generalization, which is another way of saying that maps are drawn to certain scales. The term *scale* refers to the mathematical quality of *proportional representation,* and is expressed as a ratio between an area of the real world or the distance between places on the real world and the same area or distance on the map. We show map scale on maps in three different ways. Sometimes we simply use the proportion and write what is called a *natural scale* or representative fraction: for example, we might show on a map the mathematical proportion of 1:62,500. A map at this scale is one that is one sixty-two thousand five-hundredth the size of the same area in the real world. Other times we convert the proportion to a written description that approximates the relationship between distance on the map and distance in the real world. Since there are nearly 62,500 inches in a mile, we would refer to a map having a natural scale of 1:62,500 as having an "inch-mile" scale of "1 inch represents 1 mile." If we draw a line one inch long on this map, that line represents a distance of approximately one mile in the real world. Finally, we usually use a graphic or linear scale: a bar or line, often graduated into miles or kilometers, that shows graphically the proportional representation. A graphic scale for our 1:62,500 map might be about five inches long, divided into five equal units clearly labeled as "1 mile," "2 miles," and so on. Our examples here show all three kinds of scales.

The most important thing to keep in mind about scale, and the reason why knowing map scale is important to being able to read a map correctly, is the relationship between proportional representation and generalization. A map that fills a page but shows the whole world is much more highly generalized than a map that fills a page but shows a single city. On the world map, the city may appear as a dot. On the city map, streets and other features may be clearly seen. We call the first map, the world map, a *small-scale* map because the proportional representation is a small number. A page-size map showing the whole world may be drawn at a scale of 1:150,000,000. That is a very small number indeed—hence the term *small-scale* map even though the area shown is large. Conversely, the second map, a city map, may be drawn at a scale of 1:250,000. That is still a very small number but it is a great deal larger than 1:150,000,000! And so we'd refer to the city map as a *large scale* map, even though it shows only a small area. On our world map, geographical features are generalized greatly and many features can't even be shown at all. On the city map, much less generalization occurs—we can show specific features that we couldn't on the world map—but generalization still takes place. The general rule is that the smaller the map scale, the greater the degree of generalization; the larger the map scale, the less the degree of generalization. The only map that would not generalize would be a map at a scale of 1:1 and that map wouldn't be very handy to use. Examine the relationship between scale and generalization in the four maps on this page.

Map 1 Small Scale Map of the United States

Map 2 Map of the Northeast

Map 3 Map of Southeastern New England

Map 4 Large Scale Map of Boston, MA

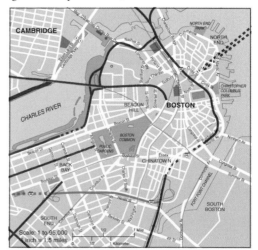

Generalization on Maps

A review of the four maps should give you some indication of how cartographers generalize on maps. One thing that you should have noticed is that the first map, that of the United States, is much simpler than the other three and that the level of *simplification* decreases with each map. When a cartographer simplifies map data, information that is not important for the purposes of the map is just left off. For example, on the first map the objective may have been to show cities over 1 million in population. To do that clearly and effectively, it is not necessary to show and label rivers and lakes. The map has been simplified by leaving those items out. The final map, on the other hand, is more complex and shows and labels geographic features that are important to the character of the city of Boston; therefore, the Charles River is clearly indicated on the map.

Another type of generalization is *classification*. Map 1 on the previous page shows cities over 1 million in population. Map 2 shows cities of several different sizes and a different symbol is used for each size classification or category. Many of the thematic maps used in this atlas rely on classification to show data. A thematic map showing population growth rates (see Map 40) will use different colors to show growth rates in different classification levels or what are sometimes called *class intervals*. Thus, there will be one color applied to all countries with population growth rates between 1.0 percent and 1.4 percent, another color applied to all countries with population growth rates between 1.5 percent and 2.1 percent, and so on. Classification is necessary because it is impossible to find enough symbols or colors to represent precise values. Classification may also be used for qualitative data, such as the national or regional origin of migrating populations. Cartographers show both quantitative and qualitative classification levels or class intervals in important sections of maps called *legends*. These legends, as in the samples that follow, make it possible for the reader of the map to interpret the patterns shown.

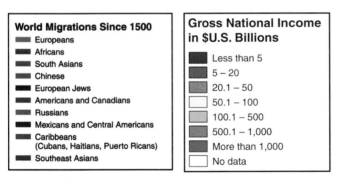

Map Legends

A third technique of generalization is *symbolization* and we've already noted several different kinds of symbols: those used to represent cities on the preceding maps, or the colors used to indicate population growth levels on Map 40. One general category of map symbols is quantitative in nature, and this category can further be divided into a number of different types. For example, the symbols showing city size on Maps 1 and 2 on the preceding page can be categorized as *ordinal* in that they show relative differences in quantities (the size of cities). A cartographer might also use lines of different widths to express the quantities of movement of people or goods between two or more points.

The color symbols used to show rates of population growth can be categorized as *interval* in that they express certain levels of a mathematical quantity (the percentage of population growth). Interval symbols are often used to show physical geographic characteristics such as inches of precipitation, degrees of temperature, or elevation above sea level. The following sample, for example, shows precipitation.

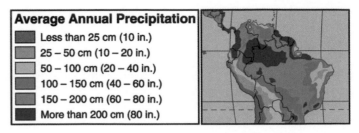

Interval Symbols

Still another type of mathematical symbolization is the *ratio* in which sets of mathematical quantities are compared: the number of persons per square mile (population density) or the growth in gross national product per capita (per person). The following map shows GDP change per capita.

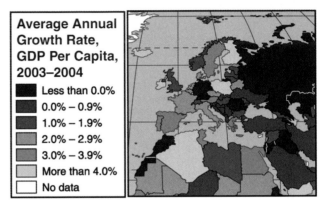

Ratio Symbols

Finally, there are a vast number of cartographic symbols that are not mathematical but show differences in the kind of information being portrayed. These symbols are called *nominal* and they range from the simplest differences such as land and water to more complex differences such as those between different types of vegetation. Shapes or patterns or colors or iconographic drawings may all be used as nominal symbols on maps.

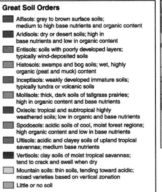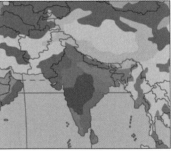

Nominal Symbols

The final technique of generalization is what cartographers refer to as *interpolation*. Here, the maker of a map may actually show more information on the map than is actually supplied by the original data. In understanding the process of interpolation it is necessary for you to visualize the quantitative data shown on maps as being three dimensional: *x* values provide geographic location along a north-south axis of the map; *y* values provide geographic location along the east-west axis of the map; and *z* values are those values of whatever data (for example, temperature) that are being shown on the map at specific points. We all can imagine a real three-dimensional surface in which the *x* and *y* values are directions and the *z* values are the heights of mountains and the depths of valleys. On a topographic map showing a real three-dimensional surface, contour lines are used to connect points of equal elevation above sea level. These contour lines are not measured directly; they are estimated by interpolation on the basis of the elevation points that are provided.

It is harder to imagine the statistical surface of a temperature map in which the *x* and *y* values are directions and the *z* values represent degrees of temperature at precise points. But that is just what cartographers do. And to obtain the values between two or more specific points where *z* values exist, they interpolate based on a class interval they have decided is appropriate and use *isolines* (which are statistical equivalents of a contour line) to show increases or decreases in value. The following diagram shows an example of an interpolation process. Occasionally interpolation is referred to as *induction.* By whatever name, it is one of the most difficult parts of the cartographic process.

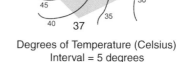

Degrees of Temperature (Celsius)
Interval = 5 degrees

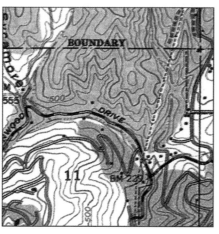

Interpolation

And you thought all you had to do to read an atlas was look at the maps! You've now learned that it is a bit more involved than that. As you read and study this atlas, keep in mind the principles of projection and scale and generalization (including simplification, classification, symbolization, and interpolation) and you'll do just fine. Good luck and enjoy your study of the world of maps as well as maps of the world!

Unit I

The Contemporary World

Map 1 World Political Boundaries

Scale: 1 to 125,000,000

| 0 | 1000 | 2000 Miles |

| 0 | 1000 | 2000 | 3000 Kilometers |

Note: All world maps are Robinson projection.

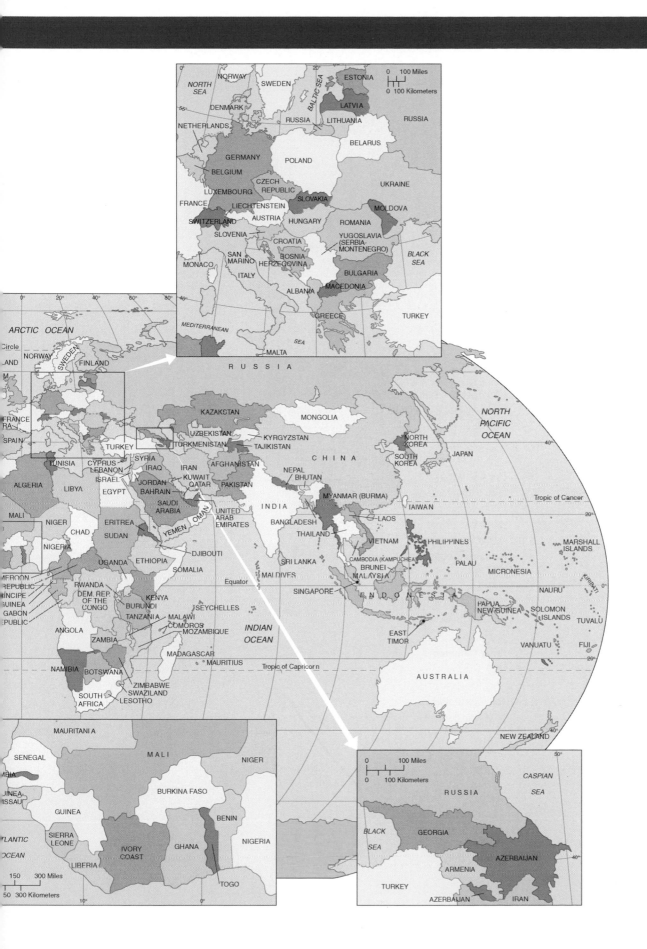

Map 2 World Climate Regions

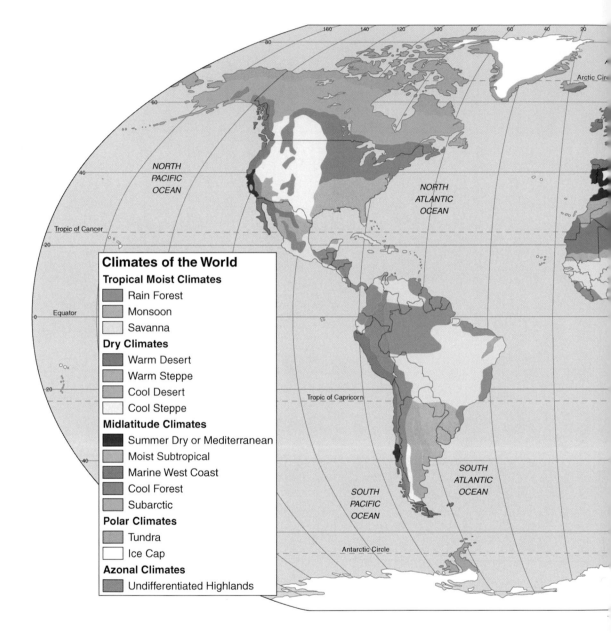

Climates of the World

Tropical Moist Climates
- Rain Forest
- Monsoon
- Savanna

Dry Climates
- Warm Desert
- Warm Steppe
- Cool Desert
- Cool Steppe

Midlatitude Climates
- Summer Dry or Mediterranean
- Moist Subtropical
- Marine West Coast
- Cool Forest
- Subarctic

Polar Climates
- Tundra
- Ice Cap

Azonal Climates
- Undifferentiated Highlands

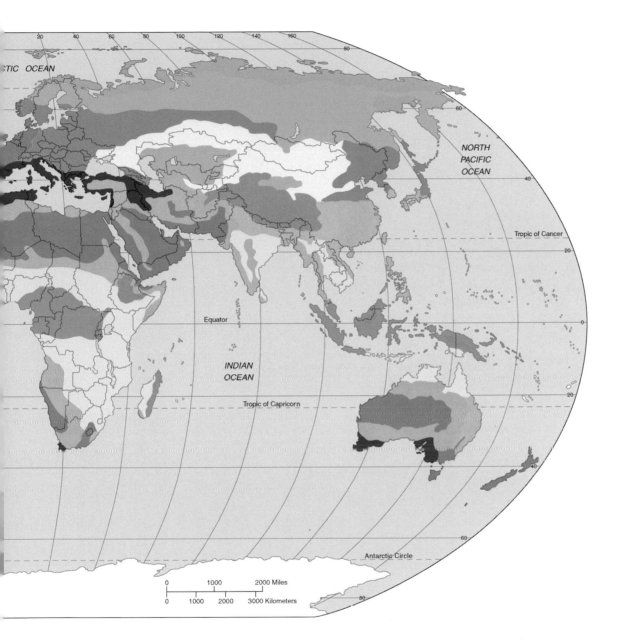

Of the world's many physical geographic features, climate (the long-term average of such weather conditions as temperature and precipitation) is the most important. It is climate that conditions the types of natural vegetation patterns and the types of soil that will exist in an area. It is also climate that determines the availability of our most precious resource: water. From an economic standpoint, the world's most important activity is agriculture; no other element of physical geography is more important for agriculture than climate.

Map 3 World Topography

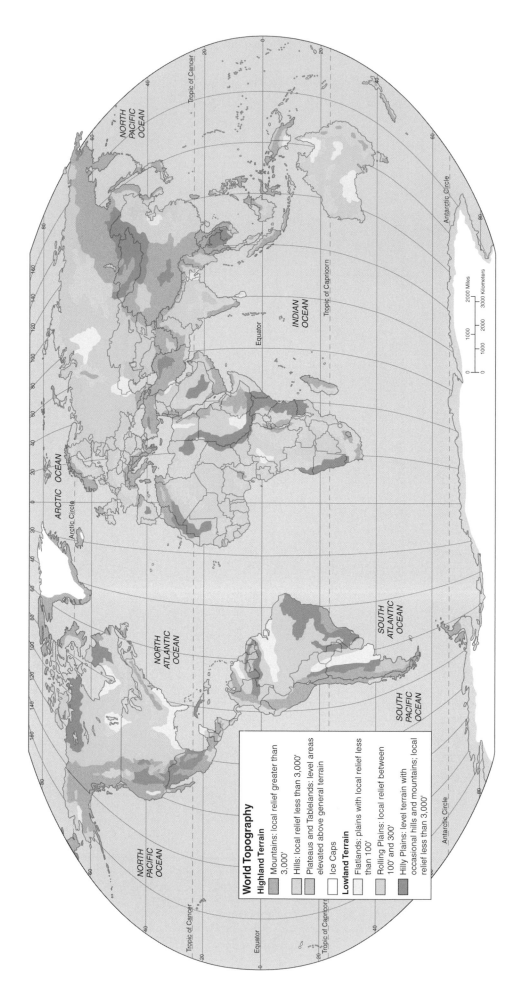

World Topography

Highland Terrain
- Mountains: local relief greater than 3,000'
- Hills: local relief less than 3,000'
- Plateaus and Tablelands: level areas elevated above general terrain
- Ice Caps

Lowland Terrain
- Flatlands: plains with local relief less than 100'
- Rolling Plains: local relief between 100' and 300'
- Hilly Plains: level terrain with occasional hills and mountains; local relief less than 3,000'

Second only to climate as a conditioner of human activity—particularly in agriculture and in the location of cities and industry—is topography or terrain. It is what we often call *landforms*. A comparison of this map with the map of land use (Map 6) will show that most of the world's productive agricultural zones are located in lowland regions. Where large regions of agricultural productivity are found, we tend to find urban concentrations and, with cities, industry. There is also a good spatial correlation between the map of landforms and the map showing the distribution and density of the human population (Map 7). Normally, the world's

landforms shown on this map are the result of extremely gradual primary geologic activity, such as the long-term movement of crustal plates (sometimes called continental drift). This activity occurs over hundreds of millions of years. Also important is the more rapid (but still slow by human standards) geomorphological or erosional activity of water, wind, and glacial ice, and waves, tides, and currents. Some landforms may be produced by abrupt or cataclysmic events, such as a major volcanic eruption or a meteor strike, but these are relatively rare and their effects are usually too minor to show up on a map of this scale.

Map 4 World Ecological Regions

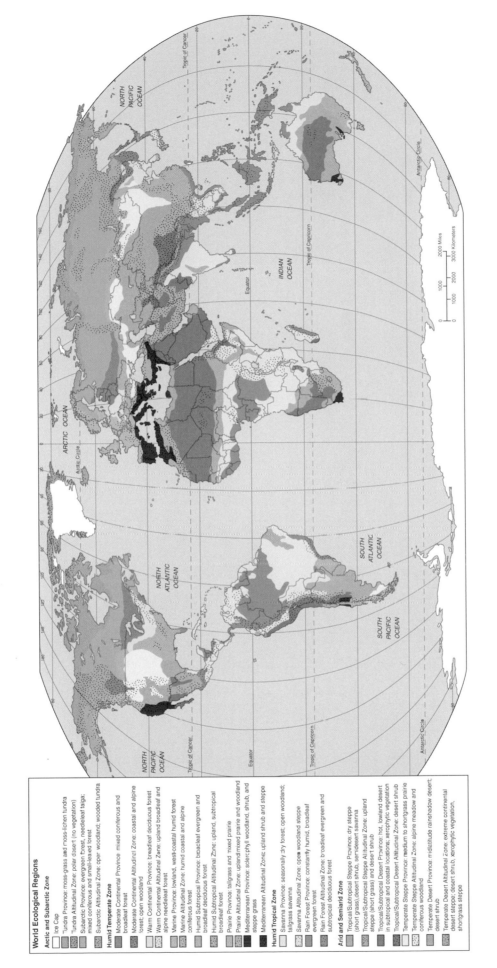

World Ecological Regions

Arctic and Subarctic Zone
- Ice Cap
- Tundra Province: moss-grass and moss-lichen tundra
- Tundra Altitudinal Zone: polar desert (no vegetation)
- Subarctic Province: evergreen forest, needleleaf taiga; mixed coniferous and small-leaved forest
- Subarctic Altitudinal Zone: open woodland; wooded tundra

Humid Temperate Zone
- Moderate Continental Province mixed coniferous and broadleaf forest
- Moderate Continental Altitudinal Zone: coastal and alpine forest; open woodland
- Warm Continental Province: breadleaf deciduous forest
- Warm Continental Altitudinal Zone: upland broadleaf and alpine needleleaf forest
- Marine Province: lowland, west-coastal humid forest
- Marine Altitudinal Zone: humid coastal and alpine coniferous forest
- Humid Subtropical Province: breacleaf evergreen and broadleaf deciduous forest
- Humid Subtropical Altitudinal Zone: upland, subtropical broadleaf forest
- Prairie Province: tallgrass and mixed prairie
- Prairie Altitudinal Zone: upland mixed prairie and woodland
- Mediterranean Province: sclerophyll woodland, shrub, and steppe grass
- Mediterranean Altitudinal Zone: upland shrub and steppe

Humid Tropical Zone
- Savanna Province: seasonally dry forest; open woodland; tallgrass savanna
- Savanna Altitudinal Zone: open woodland steppe
- Rain Forest Province: constantly humid, broadleaf evergreen forest
- Rain Forest Altitudinal Zone: broadleaf evergreen and subtropical deciduous forest

Arid and Semiarid Zone
- Tropical/Subtropical Steppe Province: dry steppe (short grass), desert shrub, semidesert savanna
- Tropical/Subtropical Steppe Altitudinal Zone: upland steppe (short grass) and desert shrub
- Tropical/Subtropical Desert Province: hot, lowland desert in subtropical and coastal locations; xerophytic vegetation
- Tropical/Subtropical Desert Altitudinal Zone: desert shrub
- Temperate Steppe Province: medium to shortgrass prairie
- Temperate Steppe Altitudinal Zone: alpine meadow and coniferous woodland
- Temperate Desert Province: midlatitude rainshadow desert; desert shrub
- Temperate Desert Altitudinal zone: extreme continental desert steppe; desert shrub, xerophytic vegetation, shortgrass steppe

Ecology is the study of the relationships between living organisms and their environmental surroundings. Ecological regions are distinctive areas within which unique sets of organisms and environments are found. Within each ecological region, a particular combination of vegetation, wildlife, soil, water, climate, and terrain defines that region's habitability, or ability to support life, including human life. Like climate and landforms, ecological relationships are crucial to the existence of agriculture, the most basic of our economic activities, and important for many other kinds of economic activity as well.

Map 5 World Natural Hazards

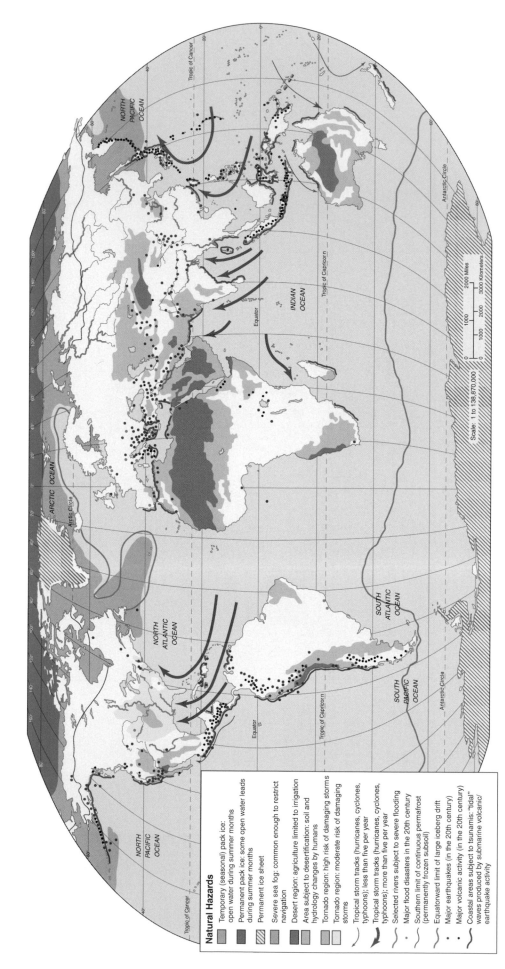

Natural Hazards

- Temporary (seasonal) pack ice: open water during summer months
- Permanent pack ice: some open water leads during summer months
- Permanent ice sheet
- Severe sea fog: common enough to restrict navigation
- Desert region: agriculture limited to irrigation
- Area subject to desertification: soil and hydrology changes by humans
- Tornado region: high risk of damaging storms
- Tornado region: moderate risk of damaging storms
- Tropical storm tracks (hurricanes, cyclones, typhoons); less than five per year
- Tropical storm tracks (hurricanes, cyclones, typhoons); more than five per year
- Selected rivers subject to severe flooding
- Major flood disasters in the 20th century
- Southern limit of continuous permafrost (permanently frozen subsoil)
- Equatorward limit of large iceberg drift
- Major earthquakes (in the 20th century)
- Major volcanic activity (in the 20th century)
- Coastal areas subject to tsunamis: "tidal" waves produced by submarine volcanic/earthquake activity

Unlike other elements of physical geography, natural hazards are unpredictable. There are certain regions, however, where the probability of the occurrence of a particular natural hazard is high. This map shows regions affected by major natural hazards at rates that are higher than the global norm. Persistent natural hazards may undermine the utility of an area for economic purposes. Some scholars suggest that regions of environmental instability may be regions of political instability as well.

Map **6** Land Use Patterns of the World

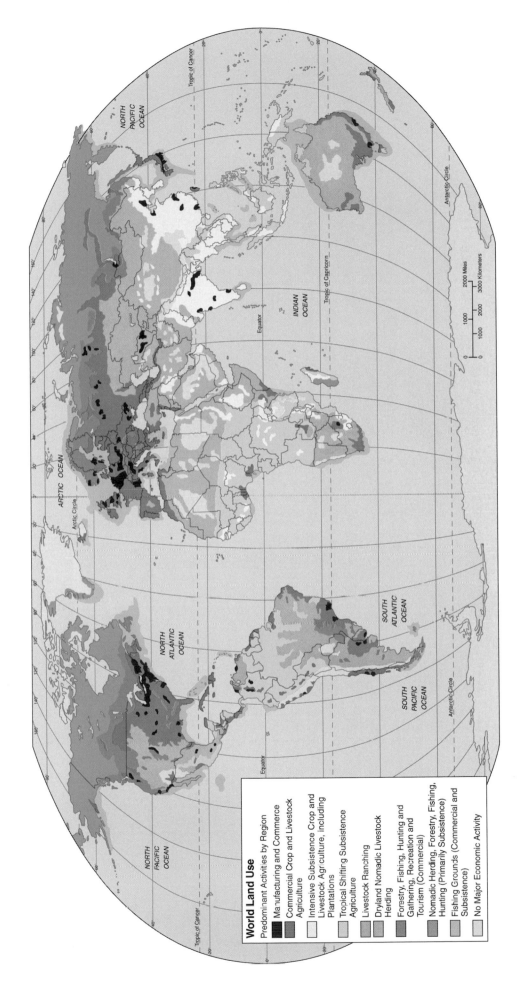

Many of the major land use patterns of the world (such as urbanization, industry, and transportation) are relatively small in area and are not easily seen on maps, but the most important uses people make of the earth's surface have more far-reaching effects. This map illustrates, in particular, the variations in primary land uses (such as agriculture) for the entire world. Note the differences between land use patterns in the more developed countries of the middle latitude zones and the less developed countries of the tropics.

Map 7 World Population Density

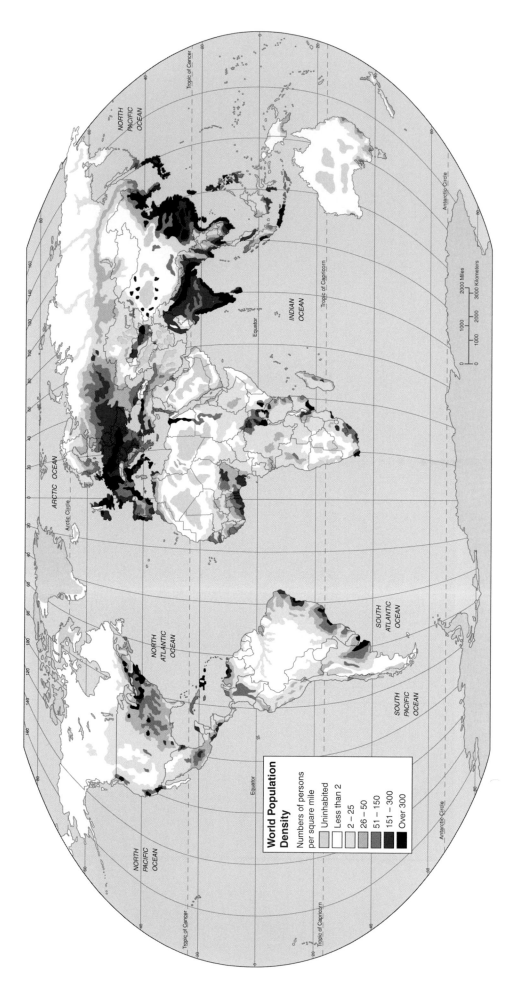

No feature of human activity is more reflective of environmental conditions than where people live. In the areas of densest populations, a mixture of natural and human factors has combined to allow maximum food production, maximum urbanization, and maximum centralization of economic activities. Three great concentrations of human population appear on the map—East Asia, South Asia, and Europe—with a fourth, lesser concentration in eastern North America (the "Megalopolis" region of the United States and Canada). One of these great population clusters—South Asia—is still growing rapidly and is expected to become even more densely populated during the twenty-first century. The other concentrations are likely to remain about as they now appear. In Europe and North America, this is the result of economic development that has caused population growth to level off during the last century. In East Asia, population has also begun to grow more slowly. In the case of Japan and the Koreas, this is the consequence of economic development; in the case of China, it is the consequence of government intervention in the form of strict family planning. The areas of future high density (in addition to those already existing) are likely to be in Middle and South America and Africa, where population growth rates are well above the world average.

Map 8 World Religions

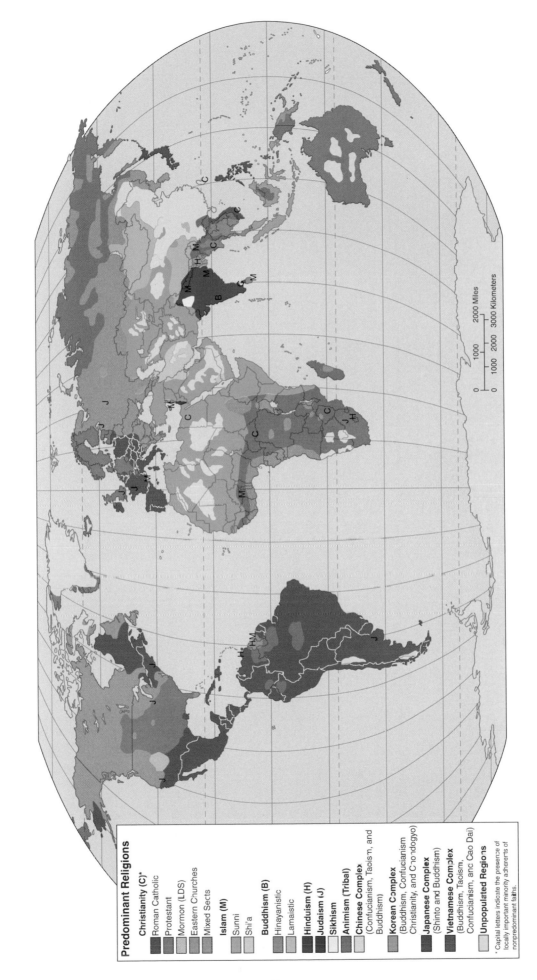

Predominant Religions

Christianity (C)*
- Roman Catholic
- Protestant
- Mormon (LDS)
- Eastern Churches
- Mixed Sects

Islam (M)
- Sunni
- Shi'a

Buddhism (B)
- Hinayanistic
- Lamaistic

Hinduism (H)

Judaism (J)

Sikhism

Animism (Tribal)

Chinese Complex
(Confucianism, Taoism, and Buddhism)

Korean Complex
(Buddhism, Confucianism Christianity, and Ch'ondogyo)

Japanese Complex
(Shinto and Buddhism)

Vietnamese Complex
(Buddhism, Taoism, Confucianism, and Cao Dai)

Unpopulated Regions

* Capital letters indicate the presence of locally important minority adherents of nonpredominant faiths.

Religious adherence is one of the fundamental defining characteristics of culture. A depiction of the spatial distribution of religions is, therefore, as close as we can come to a map of cultural patterns. More than just a set of behavioral patterns having to do with worship and ceremony, religion is an important conditioner of how people treat one another and the environments that they occupy. In many areas of the world, the ways in which people make a living, the patterns of occupation that they create on the land, and the impacts that they make on ecosystems are the direct consequence of their adherence to a religious faith.

Map 9 World Languages

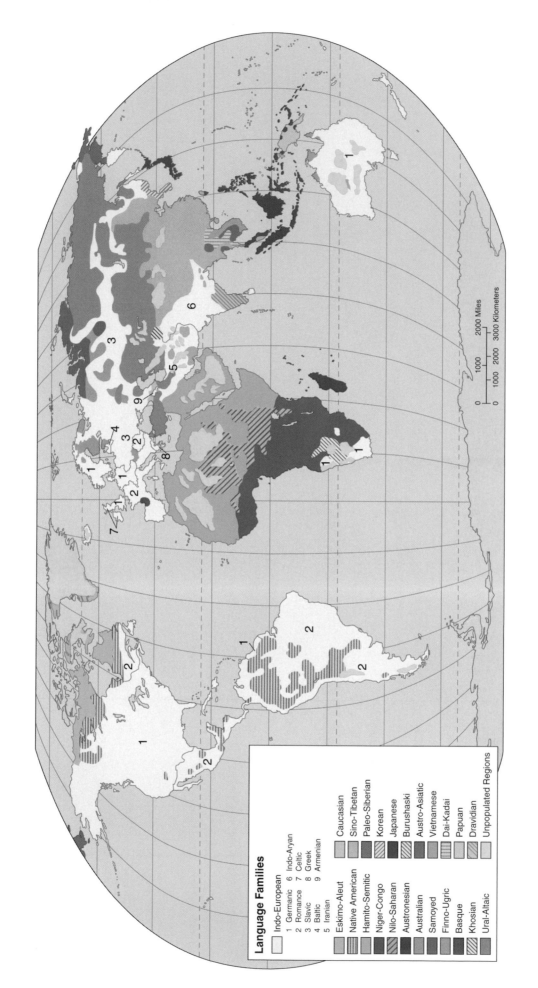

Language Families

Indo-European

1 Germanic   6 Indo-Aryan
2 Romance   7 Celtic
3 Slavic   8 Greek
4 Baltic   9 Armenian
5 Iranian

Eskimo-Aleut
Native American
Hamito-Semitic
Niger-Congo
Nilo-Saharan
Austronesian
Australian
Samoyed
Finno-Ugric
Basque
Khosian
Ural-Altaic

Caucasian
Sino-Tibetan
Paleo-Siberian
Korean
Japanese
Burushaski
Austro-Asiatic
Vietnamese
Dai-Kadai
Papuan
Dravidian
Unpopulated Regions

Like religion, language is an important defining characteristic of culture. It is perhaps the most durable of all cultural traits. Even after centuries of exposure to other languages or of conquest by speakers of other languages, the speakers of a specific tongue will often retain their own linguistic identity. As a geographic element, language helps us to locate areas of potential conflict, particularly in regions where two or more languages overlap.

Many, if not most, of the world's conflict zones are areas of linguistic diversity. Language also provides clues that enable us to chart the course of human migrations, as shown in the distribution of Indo-European languages. And it helps us to understand some of the reasons behind important historical events; linguistic identity differences played an important part in the disintegration of the Soviet Union.

-12-

Map 10 World External Migrations in Modern Times

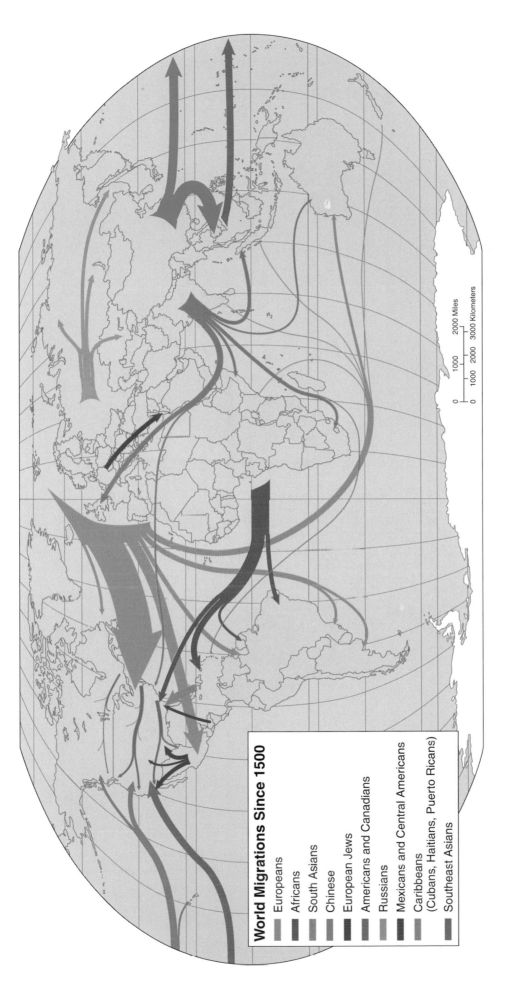

World Migrations Since 1500

- Europeans
- Africans
- South Asians
- Chinese
- European Jews
- Americans and Canadians
- Russians
- Mexicans and Central Americans
- Caribbeans (Cubans, Haitians, Puerto Ricans)
- Southeast Asians

Scale:
0 1000 2000 Miles
0 1000 2000 3000 Kilometers

Migration has had a significant effect on world geography, contributing to cultural change and development, to the diffusion of ideas and innovations, and to the complex mixture of people and cultures found in the world today. Internal migration occurs within the boundaries of a country; external migration is movement from one country or region to another. Over the last 50 years, the most important migrations in the world have been internal, largely the rural-to-urban migration that has been responsible for the recent rise of global urbanization. Prior to the mid-twentieth century, three types of external migrations were most important: voluntary, most often in search of better economic conditions and opportunities; involuntary or forced, involving people who have been driven from their homelands by war, political unrest, or environmental disasters, or who have been transported as slaves or prisoners; and imposed, not entirely forced but which conditions make highly advisable. Human migrations in recorded history have been responsible for major changes in the patterns of languages, religions, ethnic composition, and economies. Particularly during the last 500 years, migrations of both the voluntary and involuntary or forced type have literally reshaped the human face of the earth.

Unit II

States: The Geography of Politics and Political Systems

Map 11 Political Boundary Types

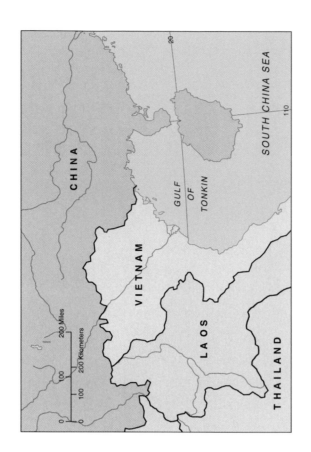

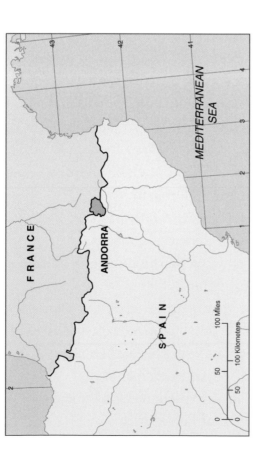

Antecedent: Antecedent boundaries are those that existed as part of the cultural landscape before the establishment of political territories. The boundary between Spain and France is the crest of the Pyrenees Mountains, long a cultural and linguistic barrier and a region of sparse population that is reflected on population density maps even at the world scale.

Subsequent: Subsequent boundaries are those that develop along with the cultural landscape of a region, part of a continuing evolution of political territory to match cultural region. The border region between Vietnam and China has developed over thousands of years of adjustment of territory between the two different cultural realms. Following the end of the Vietnam War, a lengthy border conflict between Vietnam and China suggests that the process is not yet completed.

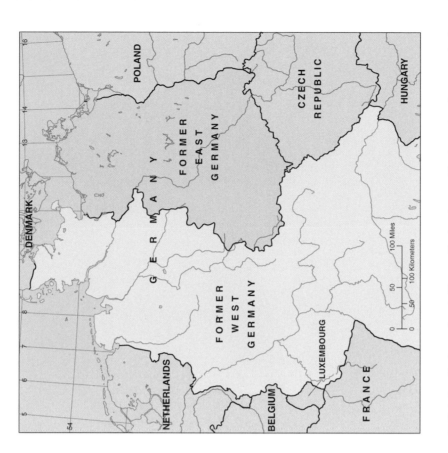

Relict: A relict boundary is like a relict landscape. The boundary between the former North and South Vietnam, along the Ben Hai River, is an example of a relict boundary. So too is the dividing line between the former Federal Republic of Germany (West Germany) and the German Democratic Republic (East Germany). Germany has been unified since 1990, with reintegration of the former Communist East into the West German economy happening progressively and more rapidly than expected. Nevertheless, there are still significant and visible differences between the urban German west and the rural east, between a progressive and modern economic landscape and a deteriorating one.

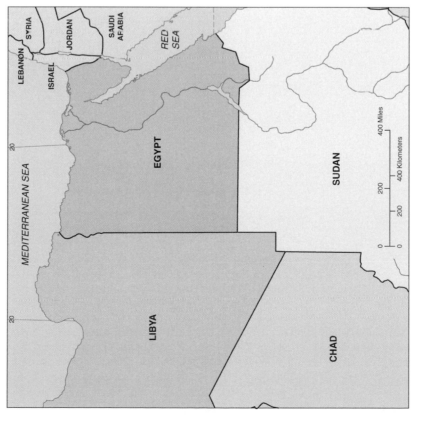

Superimposed: Superimposed boundaries are drawn arbitrarily across a uniform or homogenous cultural landscape. These boundaries often result from the occupation of territory by an expansive settlement process (see, for example, many of the boundaries of the western states in the United States) or from the process whereby colonial powers divided territory to suit their own needs rather than those of the indigenous population. The borders of Egypt, Libya, and Sudan meet in the center of a uniform cultural and physical region, artificially dividing what from a natural and human perspective is unified.

Map 12   Political Systems

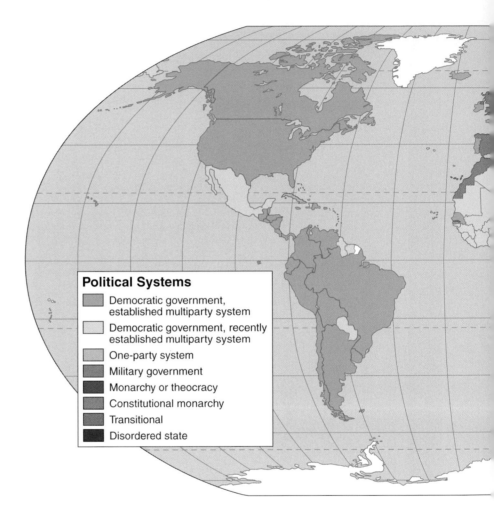

Political Systems

- Democratic government, established multiparty system
- Democratic government, recently established multiparty system
- One-party system
- Military government
- Monarchy or theocracy
- Constitutional monarchy
- Transitional
- Disordered state

World political systems have changed dramatically during the last decade and may change even more in the future. The categories of political systems shown on the map are subject to some interpretation: established multiparty democracies are those in which elections by secret ballot with adult suffrage are and have been long-term features of the political landscape; recently established multiparty democracies are those in which the characteristic features of multiparty democracies have only recently emerged. The former Soviet satellites of eastern Europe and the republics that formerly constituted the USSR are in this category; so are states in emerging regions that are beginning to throw off the single-party rule that often followed the violent upheavals of the immediate postcolonial governmental transitions. The other categories are more or less obvious. One-party systems are states where single-party rule is constitutionally guar-

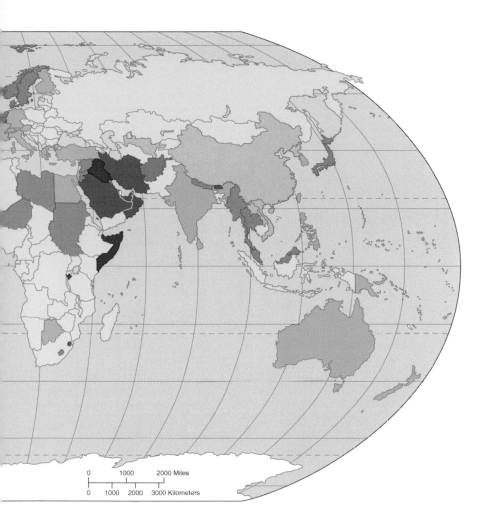

```
0      1000      2000 Miles
0   1000   2000   3000 Kilometers
```

anteed or where a one-party regime is a fact of political life. Monarchies are countries with heads of state who are members of a royal family. In a constitutional monarchy, such as the U.K. and the Netherlands, the monarchs are titular heads of state only. Theocracies are countries in which rule is within the hands of a priestly or clerical class; today, this means primarily fundamentalist Islamic countries such as Iran. Military governments are frequently organized around a junta that has seized control of the government from civil authority; such states are often technically transitional, that is, the military claims that it will return the reins of government to civil authority when order is restored. Finally, disordered states are countries so beset by civil war or widespread ethnic conflict that no organized government can be said to exist within them.

Map 13   The Emergence of the State

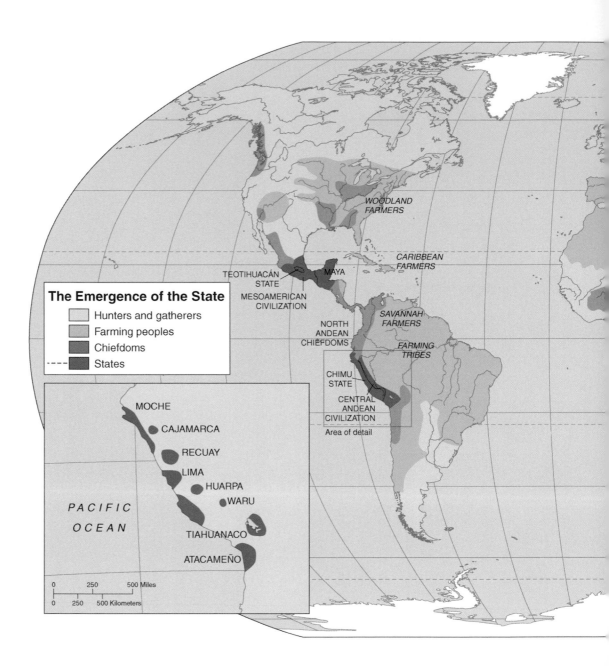

The Emergence of the State

- [ ] Hunters and gatherers
- [ ] Farming peoples
- [ ] Chiefdoms
- [ ] States

WOODLAND FARMERS

CARIBBEAN FARMERS

TEOTIHUACÁN STATE

MAYA

MESOAMERICAN CIVILIZATION

NORTH ANDEAN CHIEFDOMS

SAVANNAH FARMERS

FARMING TRIBES

CHIMU STATE

CENTRAL ANDEAN CIVILIZATION

Area of detail

MOCHE

CAJAMARCA

RECUAY

LIMA

HUARPA

WARU

TIAHUANACO

ATACAMEÑO

PACIFIC OCEAN

0   250   500 Miles

0   250   500 Kilometers

Agriculture is the basis of the development of the state, a form of complex political organization. Geographers and anthropologists believe that agriculture allowed for larger concentrations of population. Farmers do not need to be as mobile as hunters and gatherers to make a living, and people living sedentarily can have larger families than those constantly on the move. Ideas about access to land and owner-ship also change as people develop the social and political hierarchies that come with the transition from a hunting-gathering society to

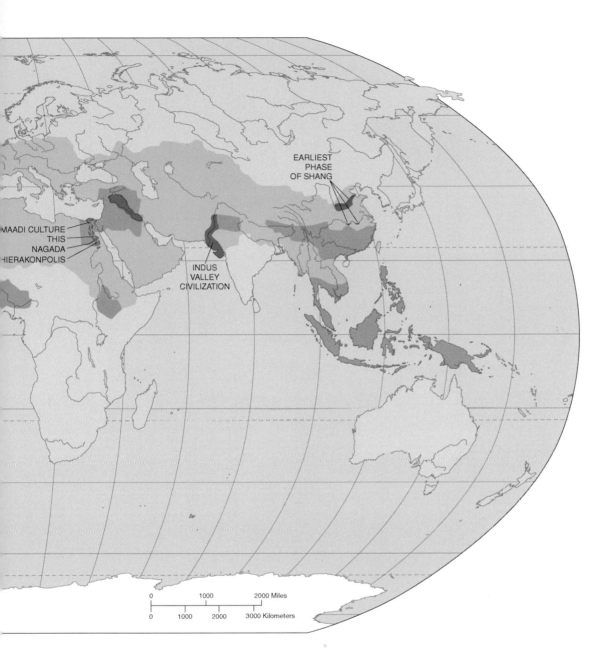

EARLIEST
PHASE
OF SHANG

MAADI CULTURE
THIS
NAGADA
HIERAKONPOLIS

INDUS
VALLEY
CIVILIZATION

0   1000   2000 Miles

0   1000   2000   3000 Kilometers

an agricultural one. Social stratification based on wealth and power creates different classes or groups, some of whom no longer work the land. An agricultural surplus supports those who perform other functions for society, such as artisans and craftspeople, soldiers and police, priests and kings. Thus, over time, egalitarian hunters and gatherers shifted to state-level societies in some parts of the world. The first true states are shown in the rust-colored areas of this map.

Map 14   Organized States and Chiefdoms A.D. 1500

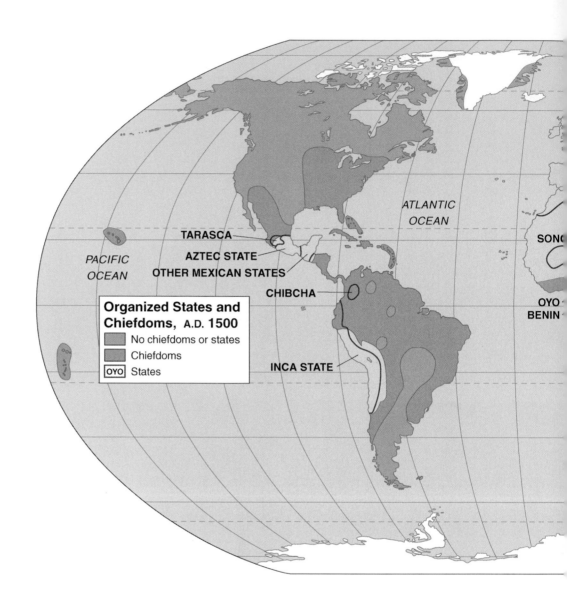

As Europeans began to expand outward through exploration and settlement from the late fifteenth to the eighteenth centuries, it was inevitable that they would find the complex political organizations of chiefdoms and states in many different parts of the world. Both chiefdoms and states are large-scale forms of political organization in which some people have privileged access to land, power, wealth, and prestige. Chiefdoms are kin-based societies in which wealth is distributed from upper to lower classes. States are organized on the basis of socio-

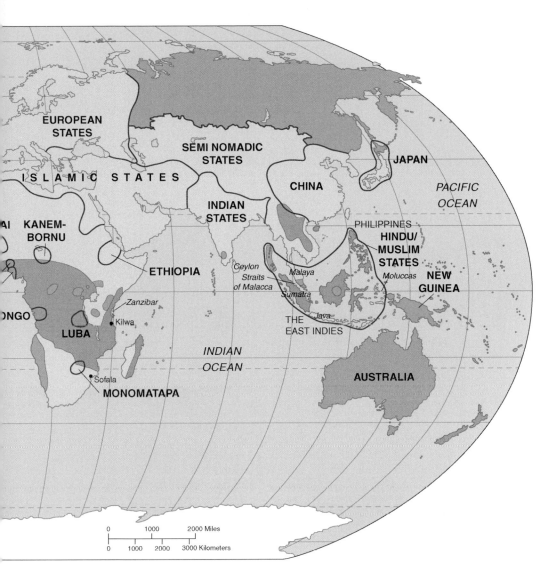

economic classes, headed by a centralized government that is led by an elite. States in non-European areas included, just as they did in Europe, full-time bureaucracies and specialized subsystems for such activities as military action, taxation, operation of state religions, and social control. In many of the colonial regions of the world after the fifteenth century, Europeans actually found it easier to gain control of organized states and chiefdoms because those populations were already accustomed to some form of institutionalized central control.

Map 15   European Colonialism, 1500–2000

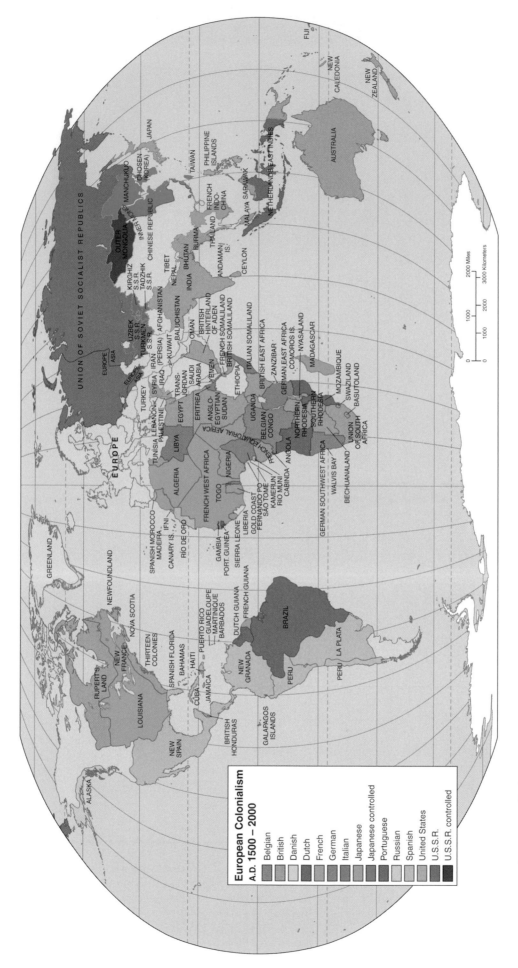

European nations have controlled many parts of the world during the last 500 years. The period of European expansion began when European explorers sailed the oceans in search of new trading routes and ended after World War II when many colonies in Africa and Asia gained independence. The process of colonization was very complex but normally involved the acquisition, extraction, or production of raw materials (including minerals, forest products, products from the sea, agricultural products, and animal furs/pelts) from the areas being controlled by the European colonial power in exchange for items

of European manufacture. The concept of colonial dependency implied an economic structure in which the European country obtained raw materials from the colonial country in exchange for those manufactured items upon which populations in the colonial areas quickly came to depend. The colors on this map represent colonial control at its maximum extent and do not take into account shifting colonial control. In North America, for example, "New France" became British territory and "Louisiana" became Spanish territory after the Seven Years' (French and Indian) War.

-24-

Map 16 Federal and Unitary States

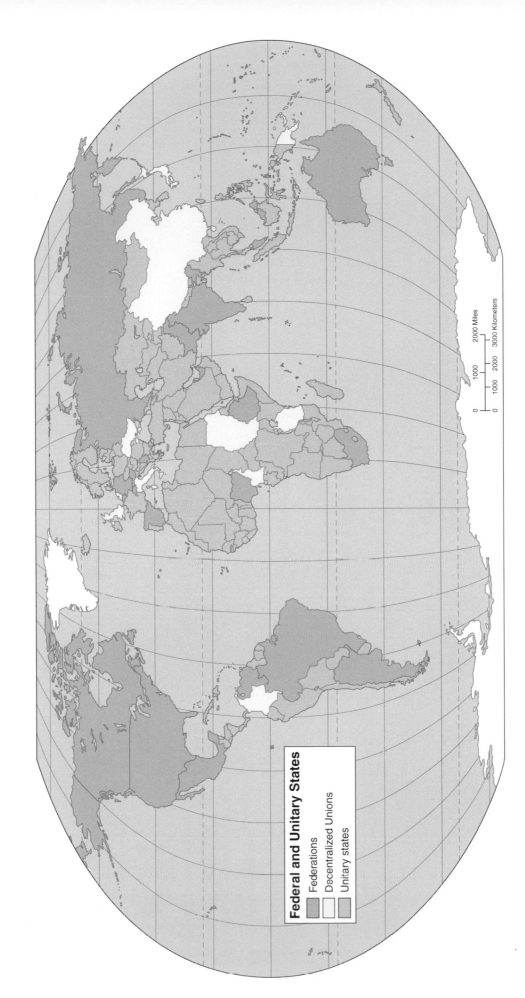

Federal and Unitary States

- Federations
- Decentralized Unions
- Unitary states

0 1000 2000 Miles
0 1000 2000 3000 Kilometers

Countries vary greatly in the degree to which the national government makes a l decisions or certain matters are left to governments of subdivisions. In federal states, each subdivision (state, province, and so on) has its own capital, and certain aspects of life are left to the subdivis ons to manage. For example, in the United States, motor vehicle and marriage/divorce laws are powers for states rather than the federal government. Federal systems are suited to large countries with a diversity of cultures. They easi y accommodate new territorial subdivisions, which can take their places among those already a part of the country. In unitary states, major decisions come from the national capital, and subdivisions administer those decisions. Unitary systems are best suited to small states with relatively homogeneous ethnic and cultural makeup. Some countries, the decentralized unions, have a mix of systems—for example, provinces that follow the dictates of the central government but other subdivisions that have more autonomy.

Map 17 Sovereign States: Duration of Independence

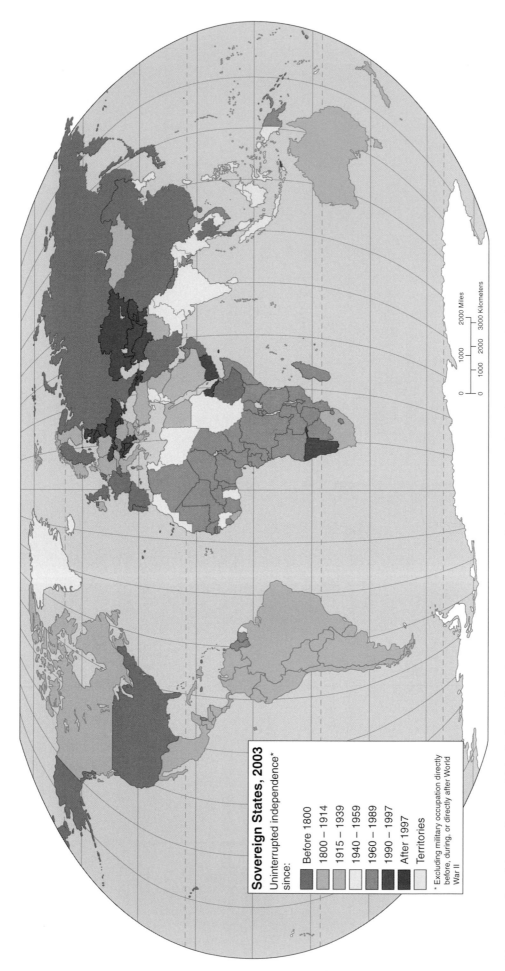

Sovereign States, 2003

Uninterrupted independence*
since:

- Before 1800
- 1800 – 1914
- 1915 – 1939
- 1940 – 1959
- 1960 – 1989
- 1990 – 1997
- After 1997
- Territories

* Excluding military occupation directly before, during, or directly after World War II

Most countries of the modern world, including such major states as Germany and Italy, became independent after the beginning of the nineteenth century. Of the world's current countries, only 27 were independent in 1800. (Ten of the 27 were in Europe; the others were Afghanistan, China, Colombia, Ethiopia, Haiti, Iran, Japan, Mexico, Nepal, Oman, Paraguay, Russia, Taiwan, Thailand, Turkey, the United States, and Venezuela). Following 1800, there have been five great periods of national independence. During the first of these (1800–1914), most of the mainland countries of the Americas achieved independence. During the second period (1915–1939), the countries of Eastern Europe emerged as independent entities. The third period (1940–1959) includes World War II and the years that followed, when independence for African and Asian nations that had been under control of colonial powers first began to occur. During the fourth period (1960–1989), independence came to the remainder of the colonial African and Asian nations, as well as to former colonies in the Caribbean and the South Pacific. More than half of the world's countries came into being as independent political entities during this period. Finally, in the last few years (1990–1997), the breakup of the existing states of the Soviet Union, Yugoslavia, and Czechoslovakia created 22 countries where only 3 had existed before.

Map 18 Political Realms: Regional Changes, 1945–2003

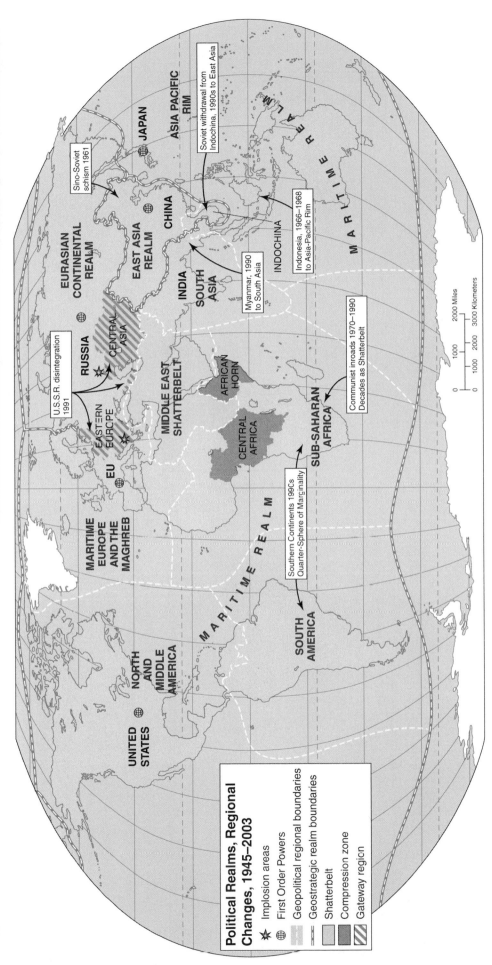

Political Realms, Regional Changes, 1945–2003

☆	Implosion areas
⊕	First Order Powers
	Geopolitical regional boundaries
	Geostrategic realm boundaries
	Shatterbelt
	Compression zone
	Gateway region

Map labels: UNITED STATES · NORTH AND MIDDLE AMERICA · MARITIME EUROPE AND THE MAGHREB · EU · EASTERN EUROPE · RUSSIA · CENTRAL ASIA · EURASIAN CONTINENTAL REALM · EAST ASIA REALM · CHINA · JAPAN · ASIA PACIFIC RIM · SOUTH ASIA · INDIA · INDOCHINA · MIDDLE EAST SHATTERBELT · AFRICAN HORN · CENTRAL AFRICA · SUB-SAHARAN AFRICA · SOUTH AMERICA · MARITIME REALM

Callout boxes: Sino-Soviet schism 1961 · Soviet withdrawal from Indochina, 1990s to East Asia · U.S.S.R. disintegration 1991 · Myanmar, 1990 to South Asia · Indonesia, 1966–1968 to Asia-Pacific Rim · Communist inroads 1970–1990 Decades as Shatterbelt · Southern Continents 1990s Quarter-Sphere of Marginality

Scale: 0 1000 2000 Miles · 0 1000 2000 3000 Kilometers

The Cold War following World War II shaped the major outlines of today's geopolitical relations. The Cold War included three phases. In the first, from 1945–1956, the Maritime Realm established a ring around the Continental Eurasian Realm in order to prevent its expansion. This phase included the Korean War (1950–1953), the Berlin Blockade (1948), the Truman doctrine and Marshall Plan (1947), and the founding of NATO (1949) and the Warsaw Pact (1955). Most of the world fell within one of the two realms: the Maritime (dominated by the United States) or the Eurasian Continental Realm (dominated by the Soviet Union). The Soviet Union sought to establish a ring of satellite states to protect it from a repeat of the invasions of World War II. The United States and other Maritime Realm states, in turn, sought to establish a ring of allies around the Continental Realm to prevent its expansion. South Asia was politically independent, but under pressure from both realms. During the second phase (1957–1979), Communist forces

from the Continental Eurasian Realm penetrated deeply into the Maritime Realm. The Berlin Wall went up in 1961, Soviet missiles in Cuba ignited a crisis in 1962, and the United States became increasingly involved in the war in Vietnam (late 1960s). The Soviet Union sought increased political and military presence along important waterways including those in the Middle East, Southeast Asia, and the Caribbean. These regions became especially dangerous shatterbelts. The third phase (1980–1989) saw the retreat of Communist power from the Maritime Realm. China, after ten years of radical Communism and chaos of the Cultural Revolution (1966–1976), broke away from the Continental Eurasian Realm to establish a new East Asian realm. Soviet influence declined in the Middle East, Sub-Saharan Africa, and Latin America. In 1989 the Berlin Wall fell, and Eastern Europe began to establish democratic governments. In 1991 the Soviet Union broke apart as its constituent republics became independent states.

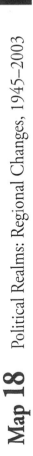

Map 19 European Boundaries, 1914–1948

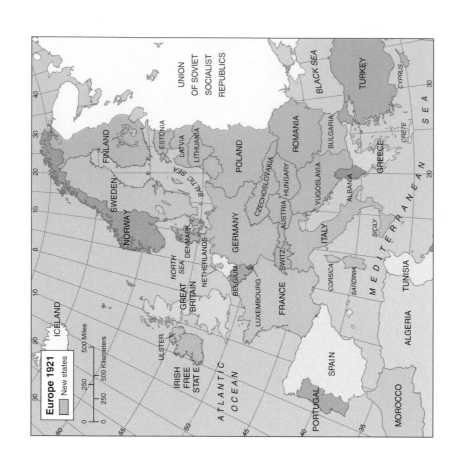

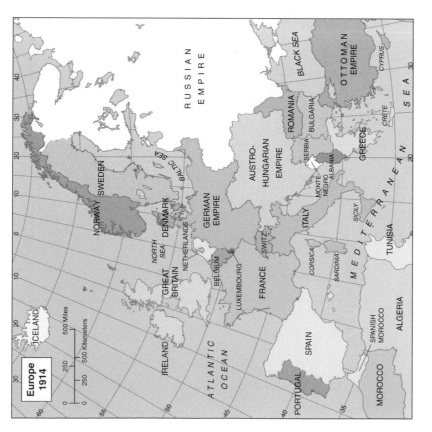

In 1914, on the eve of the First World War, Europe was dominated by the United Kingdom and France in the west, the German Empire and the Austro-Hungarian Empire in central Europe, and the Russian Empire in the east. Battle lines for the conflict that began in 1914 were drawn when the United Kingdom, France, and the Russian Empire joined together as the Triple Entente. In the view of the Germans, this coalition was designed to encircle Germany and its Austrian ally, which, along with Italy, made up the Triple Alliance. The German and Austrian fears were heightened in 1912–14 when a Russian-sponsored "Balkan League" pushed the Ottoman Turkish Empire from Europe, leaving behind the weak and mutually antagonistic Balkan states Serbia and Montenegro. In August 1914, Germany and Austria-Hungary attacked in several directions and World War I began. Four years later, after massive loss of life and destruction, the central European empires were defeated. The victorious French, English, and Americans (who had entered the war in 1917) restructured the map of Europe in 1919, carving nine new states out of the remains of the German and Austro-Hungarian empires and the westernmost portions of the Russian Empire which, by the end of the war, was deep in the Revolution that deposed the czar and brought the Communists to power in a new Union of Soviet Socialist Republics.

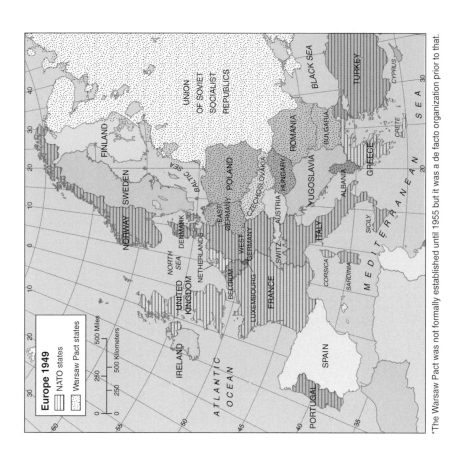

Europe 1949

- NATO states
- Warsaw Pact states

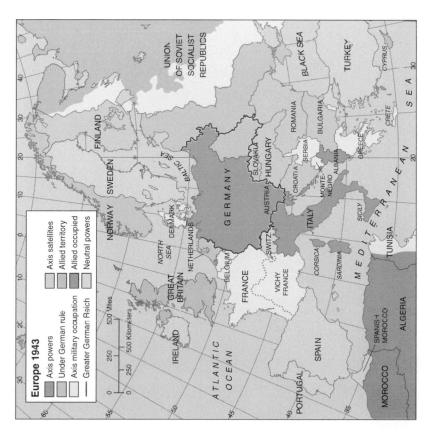

Europe 1943

- Axis powers
- Under German rule
- Axis military occupation
- Greater German Reich
- Axis satellites
- Allied territory
- Allied occupied
- Neutral powers

When the victorious Allies redrew the map of central and eastern Europe in 1919, they caused as many problems as they were trying to solve. The interval between the First and Second World Wars was really just a lull in a long war that halted temporarily in 1918 and erupted once again in 1939. Defeated Germany, resentful of the terms of the 1918 armistice and 1919 Treaty of Versailles and beset by massive inflation and unemployment at home, overthrew the Weimar republican government in 1933 and installed the National Social ist (Nazi) party led by Adolf Hitler in Berlin. Hitler quickly began making good on his promises to create a "thousand year realm" of German influence by annexing Austria and the Czech region of Czechoslovakia and allying Germany with a fellow fascist state in Mussolini's Italy. In September 1939 Germany launched the lightning-quick combined infantry, artillery, and armor attack known as *der Blitzkrieg* and took Poland to the east and, in quick succession, the Netherlancs, Belgium, and France to the west. By 1943 the greater German Reich extended from the Russian Plain to the

Atlantic and from the Black Sea to the Baltic. But the Axis powers of Germany and Italy could not withstand the greater resources and manpower of the combined United Kingdom–United States–USSR–led Allies and, in 1945, Allied armies occupied Germany. Once again, the lines of the central and eastern European map were redrawn. This time, a strengthened Soviet Union took back most of the territory the Russian Empire had lost at the end of the First World War. Germany was partitioned into four occupied sectors (English, French, American, and Russian) and later into two independent countries, the Federal Republic of Germany (West Germany) and the German Democratic Republic (East Germany). Although the Soviet Union's territory stopped at the Polish, Hungarian, Czechoslovakian, and Romanian borders, the eastern European countries (Poland, East Germany, Czechoslovakia, Hungary, Romania, Yugoslavia, Albania, and Bulgaria) became Communist between 1945 and 1948 and were separated from the West by the Iron Curtain.

*The Warsaw Pact was not formally established until 1955 but it was a de facto organization prior to that.

Map 20   An Age of Bipolarity: The Cold War ca. 1970

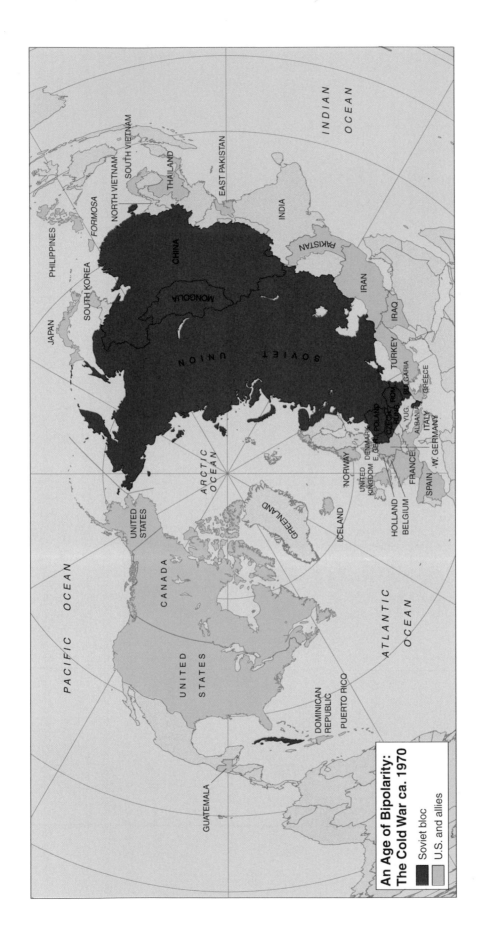

An Age of Bipolarity: The Cold War ca. 1970

Soviet bloc

U.S. and allies

Following the Second World War, the world was divided into two armed camps led by the United States and the Soviet Union. The Soviet Union and its allies, the Warsaw Pact countries, feared a U.S.-led takeover of the eastern European countries that became Soviet satellites after the war and the replacing of a socialist political and economic system with a liberal one. The United States and its allies, the NATO (North Atlantic Treaty Organization) countries, equally feared that the USSR would overrun western Europe. Both sides sought to defend themselves by building up massive military arsenals. The United States, adopting an international geopo-litical strategy of containment, sought to ring the Soviet Union with a string of allied countries and military bases that would prevent Soviet expansion in any direction. The levels of spending on military hardware contributed to the devolution of the Soviet Union, and the obsolescence of alliances and military bases in an age of advanced guidance and delivery systems made the U.S. military containment less necessary. Following a peak in the early 1960s, the cold war gradually became less significant and the age of bipolar international power essentially ended with the dissolution of the USSR in 1991.

Map 21 Europe: Political Changes, 1989–2005

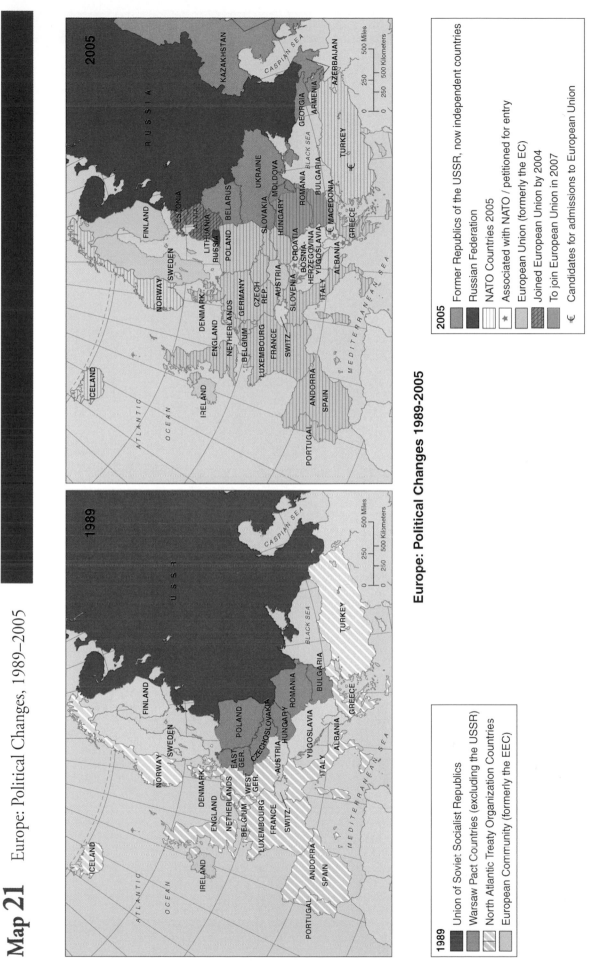

Europe: Political Changes 1989-2005

During the last decade of the twentieth century, one of the most remarkable series of political geographic changes of the last 500 years took place. The bipolar East-West structure that had characterized Europe's political geography since the end of the Second World War altered in the space of a very few years. In the mid-1980s, as Soviet influence over eastern and central Europe weakened, those countries began to turn to the capitalist West. Between 1989, when the country of Hungary was the first Soviet satellite to open its borders to travel, and 1991, when the Soviet Union dissolved into 15 independent countries, abrupt change in political systems occurred. The result is a new map of Europe that includes a number of countries not present on the map of 1989. These countries have emerged as the result of reunification, separation, or independence from the former Soviet Union. The new political structure has been accompanied by growing economic cooperation.

-31-

Map 22   The European Union, 2005

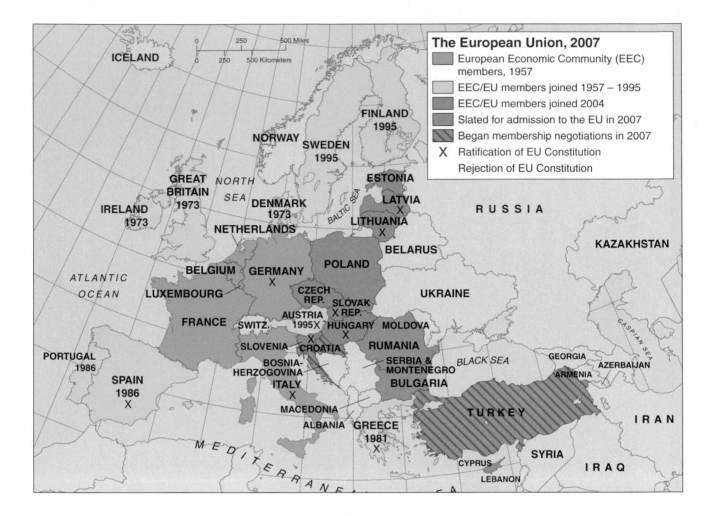

The European Union, 2007

- European Economic Community (EEC) members, 1957
- EEC/EU members joined 1957 – 1995
- EEC/EU members joined 2004
- Slated for admission to the EU in 2007
- Began membership negotiations in 2007
- X   Ratification of EU Constitution
- Rejection of EU Constitution

After World War II, a number of European leaders became convinced that the only way to secure a lasting peace between their countries was to unite them economically and politically. The first attempts at this were made in 1951, when the European Coal and Steel Community (ECSC) was set up, with six members: Belgium, West Germany, Luxembourg, France, Italy and the Netherlands. The ECSC was such a success that, within a few years, these same six countries decided to go further and integrate other sectors of their economies. In 1957 they signed the Treaties of Rome, creating the European Atomic Energy Community (EURATOM) and the European Economic Community (EEC). The member states set about removing trade barriers between them and forming a "common market." The original six member countries were joined in the common market of the EEC by Denmark, Ireland and the United Kingdom in 1973, followed by Greece in 1981, and Spain and Portugal in 1986. In 1992 the 12 countries of the EEC signed The Treaty of Maastricht, which introduced new forms of co-operation between the member state governments—particularly in defense and legal systems—and created the European Union (EU). The original 12 EU members were joined by Austria, Finland and Sweden in 1995. In 2004, 10 new members joined the EU: Cyprus, the Czech Republic, Estonia, Hungary, Latvia, Lithuania, Malta, Poland, Slovakia and Slovenia. Bulgaria and Romania are expected to be admitted to membership in 2007; Croatia and Turkey began membership negotiations in 2005. The EU has meant the dropping of trade barriers and labor migration barriers among member countries, along with economic and political cooperation in a number of areas. The adoption of the Euro in 2002 as the common currency of the majority of EU countries is expected to aid in the integration of the European economy. The major issue for the European Union is the ratification of a constitution, which must be unanimously adopted. As of June 2007, 18 countries had ratified the constitution, 7 have postponed ratification, and 2 have rejected. The European Council is meeting to attempt the development of a new document. However, the economic components of the EU will remain unchanged.

Map 23 The Geopolitical World at the Beginning of the Twenty-First Century

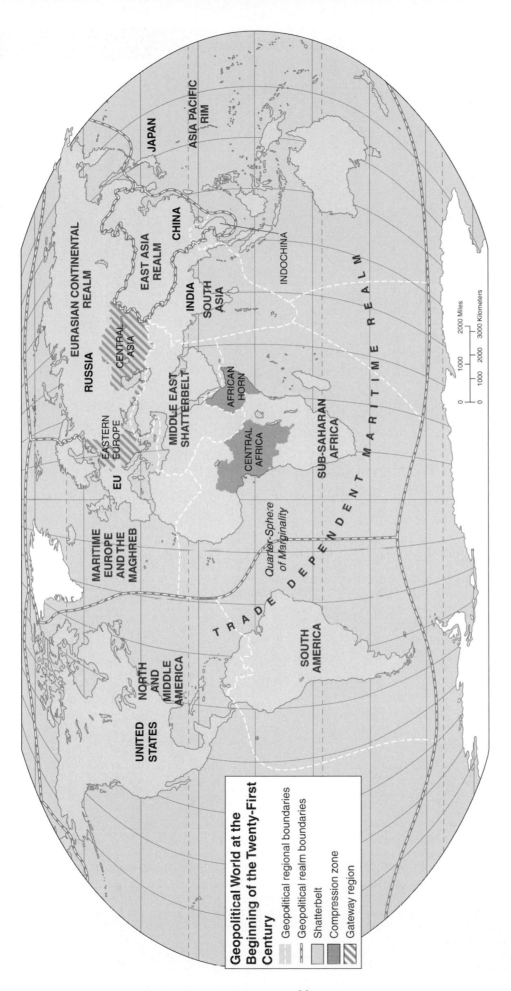

Geopolitical World at the Beginning of the Twenty-First Century

Geopolitical regional boundaries
Geopolitical realm boundaries
Shatterbelt
Compression zone
Gateway region

In the geostrategic structure of the world, the largest territorial units are realms. They are shaped by circulation patterns that link people, goods, and ideas. Realms are shaped by maritime and continental influences. Today's Atlantic and Pacific Trade-Dependent Maritime Realm has been shaped by international exchange over the oceans and their interior seas as mercantilism, capitalism, and industrialization gave rise to maritime-oriented states and to economic and political colonialism. The world's leading trading and economic powers are part of this realm. The Eurasian Continental Realm, centered around Russia, is inner-oriented, less influenced by outside economic or cultural forces, and politically closed, even after the fall of Communism. Expansion of NATO in Europe

has increased its feeling of being "hemmed in." East Asia has mixed Maritime and Continental influences. China has traditionally been continental, but reforms that began in the late 1970s increased the importance of its maritime-oriented southern coasts. Even so, its trade volume is still low, and it maintains a hold on inland areas like Tibet and Xinjiang. Realms are subdivided into regions, some dependent on others, as South America is on North America. Regions located between powerful realms or regions may be shatterbelts (internally divided and caught up in competition between Great Powers) or gateways (facilitating the flow of ideas, goods, and people between regions). Compression zones are areas of conflict, but they are not contested by major powers.

-33-

Map 24   The Middle East: Territorial Changes, 1918–Present

TERRITORIAL CHANGES IN THE MIDDLE EAST, WORLD WAR I TO PRESENT

- Ottoman Empire to World War I
- British control
- French control
- Kurdish homelands
- International boundaries in 1994

The Middle East, encompassing the northeastern part of Africa and southwestern Asia, has experienced a turbulent history. In the last century alone, many of the region's countries have gone from being ruled by the Turkish Ottoman Empire, to being dependencies of Great Britain or France, to being independent. Having experienced the Crusades and colonial domination by European powers, the region's predominantly Islamic countries are now resentful of interference in the region's affairs by countries with a European and/or Christian heritage. The tension between Israel (settled largely in the late nineteenth and twentieth centuries by Jews of predominantly European background) and its neighbors is a matter of European–Middle Eastern cultural stress as well as a religious conflict between Islamic Arab culture and Judaism.

Map 25 Africa: Colonialism to Independence, 1910–2002

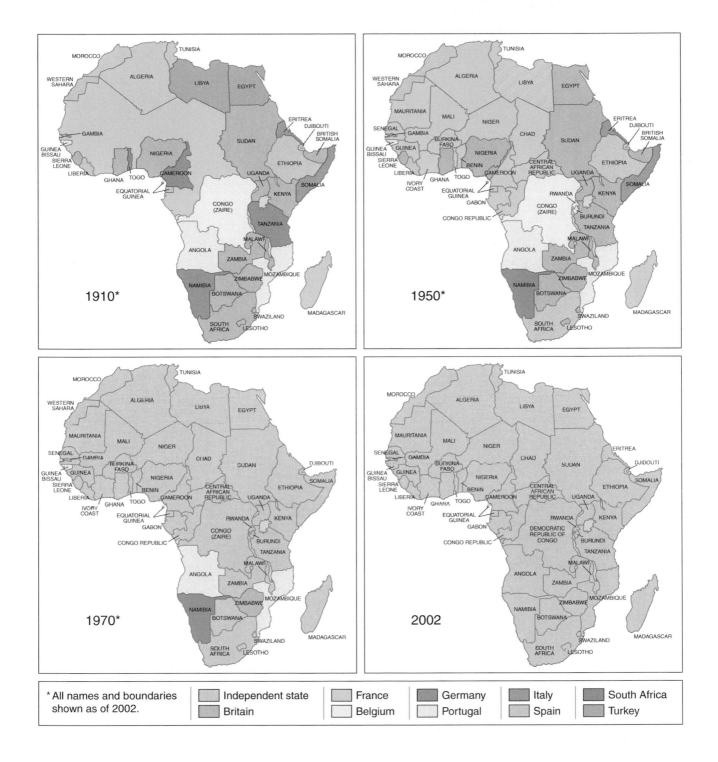

1910*

1950*

1970*

2002

* All names and boundaries shown as of 2002.

Independent state	France
Britain	Belgium

Germany	Italy
Portugal	Spain

South Africa	Turkey

In few parts of the world has the transition from colonialism to independence been as abrupt as on the African continent. Unlike the states of Middle and South America, which generally achieved independence from their colonial masters in the early nineteenth century, most African states did not become independent until the twentieth century, often not until after World War II. In part because they retain borders that are legacies of their former colonial status, many of these recently created African states are beset by internal problems related to tribal and ethnic conflicts.

Map 26   South Africa: Black Homelands and Post-Apartheid Provinces

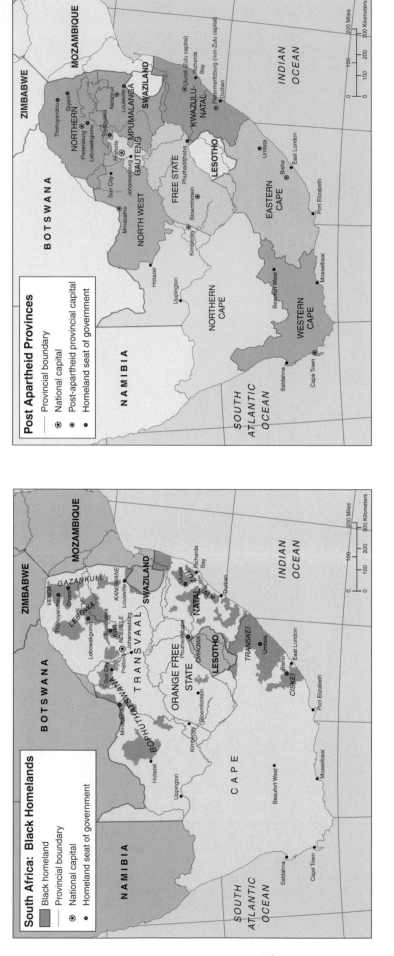

South Africa: Black Homelands

- Black homeland
- — Provincial boundary
- ⊛ National capital
- • Homeland seat of government

Post Apartheid Provinces

- — Provincial boundary
- ⊛ National capital
- ⊙ Post-apartheid provincial capital
- • Homeland seat of government

After their defeat by the British in the Boer War (1899–1902), the Dutch-descended Afrikaners negotiated with the British for greater powers in South Africa. Eventually, they became the most powerful group and imposed "separate development" or *apartheid* on the country. African (and other minority) populations would live completely separated from white South Africans. Millions were forced to relocate to the ancestral areas, where "homelands" that would be declared "independent" were set up for them. The amounts and quality of the land were completely insufficient to support the populations assigned

to them, and many of the "homelands" were fragmented as well. Thousands of black Africans flocked to the black "townships" around major cities, looking for work. Here, they were foreigners in their own land. After the fall of *apartheid* in 1994, the "homelands" were abolished, and South Africa's political geography was reorganized, with each new province centered around its dominant ethnic group. These provinces now serve as subdivisions within the country without restrictions by race or ethnicity on where people can live. This organization was important in the peaceful transfer to majority rule.

-36-

Map 27   Asia: Colonialism to Independence, 1930–2002

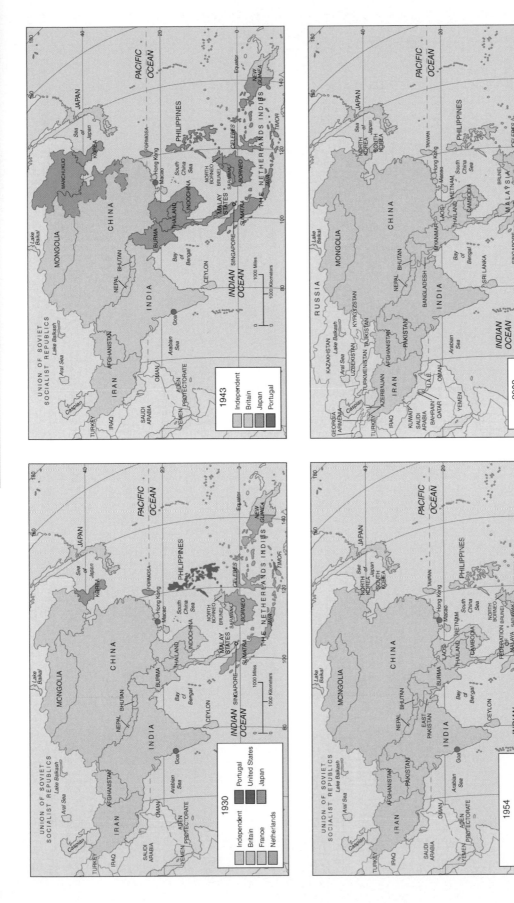

Asian countries, like those in Africa, have recently emerged from a colonial past. With the exception of China, Japan, and Thailand, virtually all Asian nations were until not long ago under the colonial control of Great Britain, France, Spain, the Netherlands, or the United States. For a short period of time between 1930 and 1945, Japan itself was a colonial power with considerable territories on the Asian main-

land. The unraveling of colonial control in Asia, particularly in South and Southeast Asia, has precipitated internal conflicts in the newly independent states that make up a significant part of the political geography of the region. The last vestiges of European colonialism in Asia disappeared with the cession of Hong Kong (1997) and Macao (1999) to China.

Map 28 Global Distribution of Minority Groups

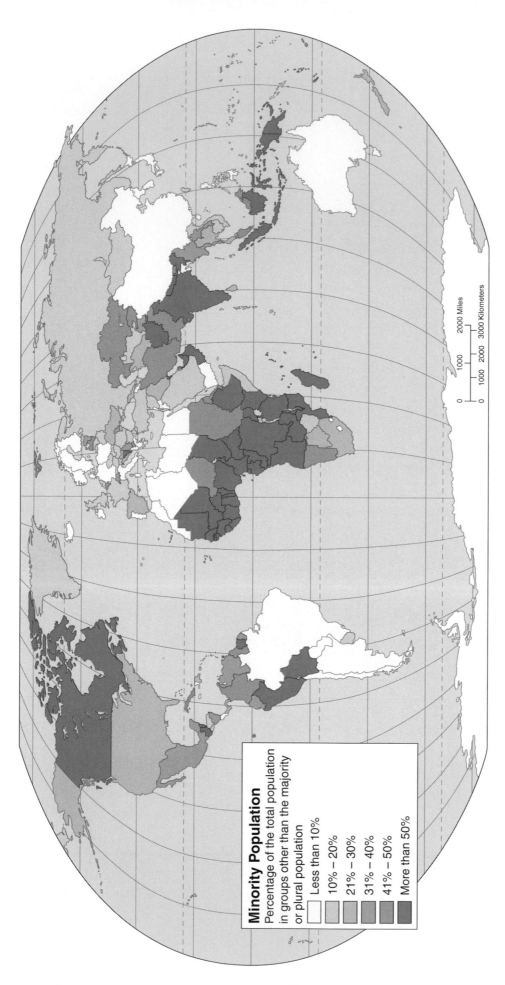

Minority Population
Percentage of the total population
in groups other than the majority
or plural population

Less than 10%
10% – 20%
21% – 30%
31% – 40%
41% – 50%
More than 50%

2000 Miles
1000   2000   3000 Kilometers
0   1000   2000

The presence of minority ethnic, national, or racial groups within a country's population can add a vibrant and dynamic mix to the whole. Plural societies with a high degree of cultural and ethnic diversity should, according to some social theorists, be among the world's most healthy. Unfortunately, the reality of the situation is quite different from theory or expectation. The presence of significant minority populations played an important role in the disintegration of the Soviet Union; the continuing existence of minority populations within the new states formed from former Soviet republics threatens the viability and stability of those young political units. In Africa, national boundaries were drawn by colonial powers without regard for the geographical distribution of ethnic groups, and the continuing tribal conflicts that have resulted hamper both economic and political development. Even in the most highly developed regions of the world, the presence of minority ethnic populations poses significant problems: witness the separatist movement in Canada, driven by the desire of some French-Canadians to be independent of the English majority, and the continuing ethnic conflict between Flemish-speaking and Walloon-speaking Belgians. This map, by arraying states on a scale of homogeneity to heterogeneity, indicates areas of existing and potential social and political strife.

Map 29 Linguistic Diversity

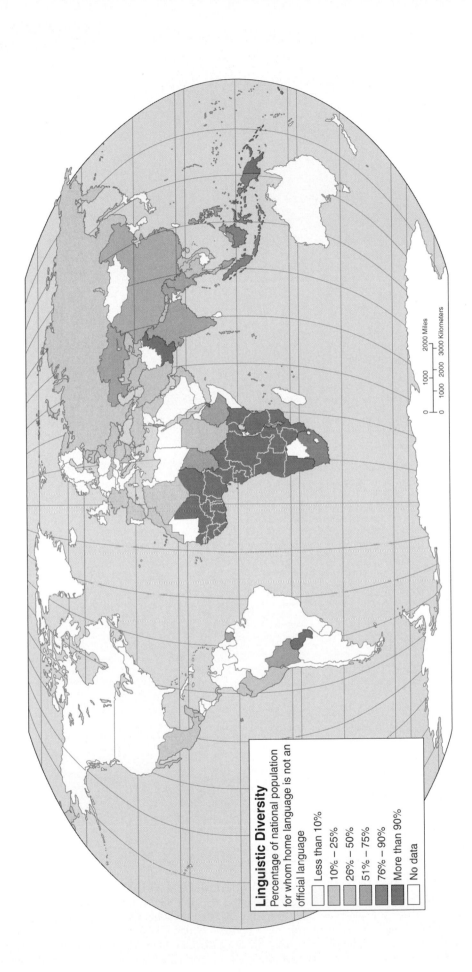

Linguistic Diversity

Percentage of national population for whom home language is not an official language

- Less than 10%
- 10% – 25%
- 26% – 50%
- 51% – 75%
- 76% – 90%
- More than 90%
- No data

Of the world's approximately 5,300 languages, fewer than 100 are official languages, those designated by a country as the language of government, commerce, education, and information. This means that for much of the world's population the language that is spoken in the home is different from the official language of the country of residence. The world's former colonial areas in Middle and South America, Africa, and South and Southeast Asia stand out on the map as regions in which there is significant disparity between home languages and official languages. To complicate matters further, for most of the world's population, the primary international languages of trade and tourism (French and English) are neither home nor official languages.

Map **30** International Conflicts in the Post–World War II World

	Conflict[1]	Start Date	Major Belligerent Countries[2] (in alphabetical order)	
1	Palestine	1948	Egypt Iraq Israel	Jordan Lebanon Syria
2	Korean	1950	China North Korea South Korea United Nations: United States and 11 other countries	
3	Soviet-Hungarian	1956	Hungary	Soviet Union
4	Sinai	1956	Egypt France	Israel United Kingdom
5	Sino-Indian	1962	China	India
6	Kashmir	1965	India	Pakistan
7	Vietnam	1965	Australia North Vietnam South Korea	South Vietnam United States
8	Six-Day	1967	Egypt Israel	Jordan Syria
9	Soviet-Czech	1968	Czechoslovakia	Soviet Union
10	Football	1969	El Salvador	Honduras
11	Indo-Pakistani	1971	India	Pakistan
12	Yom Kippur	1973	Egypt Israel	Syria
13	Cyprus	1974	Cyprus	Turkey
14	Ogaden	1977	Ethiopia	Somalia
15	Cambodian-Vietnamese	1978	Cambodia China	Vietnam
16	Ugandan-Tanzanian	1978	Tanzania	Uganda
17	Afghanistan	1979	Afghanistan	Soviet Union
18	Persian Gulf	1980	Iran	Iraq
19	Angola	1981	Angola Cuba	South Africa
20	Falklands	1982	Argentina	United Kingdom
21	Saharan	1983	Chad	Libya
22	Lebanon	1987	France Israel Lebanon	Syria United States
23	Panama	1989	Panama	United States
24	Persian Gulf	1990	Iraq United Nations: United States and 7 other countries	
25	Yugoslavia	1990	Bosnia-Herzegovina	Croatia Serbia
26	Peruvian-Ecuadorian	1995	Ecuador	Peru
27	Albania	1995	Albania	Yugoslavia (Serbia-Montenegro)
28	Rwanda	1995	Burundi	Rwanda
29	East Timor	1995	Indonesia	New Guinea insurgency
30	Cameroon	1996	Cameroon	Nigeria
31	Northern Iraq	1996	Iraq	Kurdish insurgency
32	Eritrea	1997	Eritrea	Yemen
33	Iraq	1998	Great Britain Iraq	United States
34	Kosovo	1999	Albania NATO	Yugoslavia
35	Democratic Republic of the Congo	1998	Angola Chad Dem. Rep. of Congo	Namibia Uganda Zimbabwe
36	Chechnya	1999	Chechnya	Russia
37	"War on Terrorism"	2001	Afghanistan (Taliban) al-Qaeda organization Great Britain	United States Others
38	Iraq	2003	Great Britain Iraq	United States
39	Lebanon	2006	Israel Lebanon	Hiz'ballah

[1] "Conflict" implies at least 1,000 battle deaths.
[2] "Belligerent" implies country supplied at least 5% of the combat troops in the conflict.

International Conflicts in the Post–World War II World

✵ Area of conflict

The Korean War and the Vietnam War dominated the post–World War II period in terms of international military conflict. But numerous smaller conflicts have taken place, with fewer numbers of belligerents and with fewer battle and related casualties. These smaller international conflicts have been mostly territorial conflicts, reflecting the continual readjustment of political boundaries and loyalties brought about by the end of colonial empires, and the dissolution of the Soviet Union. Many of these conflicts were not wars in the more traditional sense, in which two or more countries formally declare war on one another, severing diplomatic

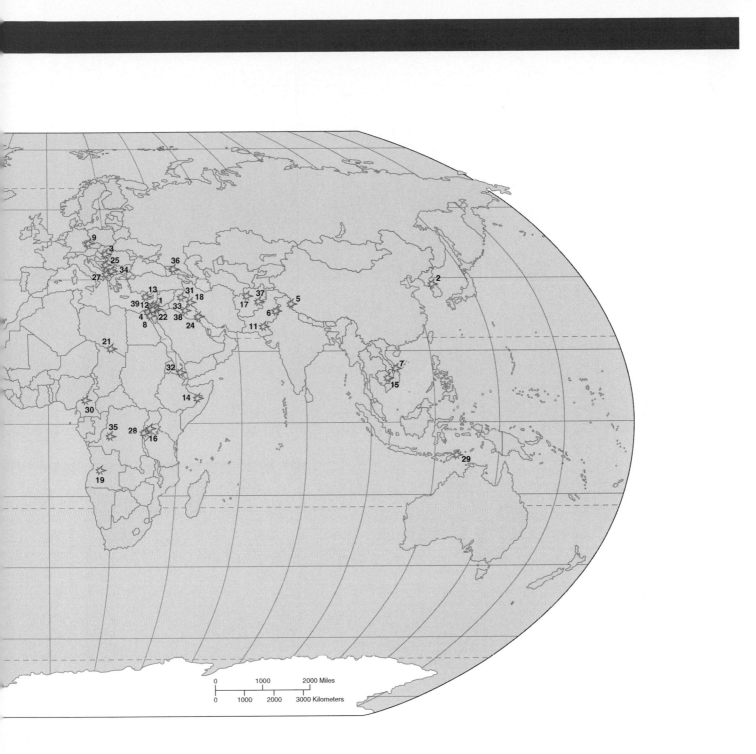

ties and devoting their entire national energies to the war effort. Rather, many of these conflicts were and are undeclared wars, sometimes fought between rival groups within the same country with outside support from other countries. The aftermath of the September 11, 2001, terrorist attacks on the United States indicate the dawn of yet another type of international conflict, namely a "war" fought between traditional nation-states and non-state actors.

Map 31 World Refugees, 2005

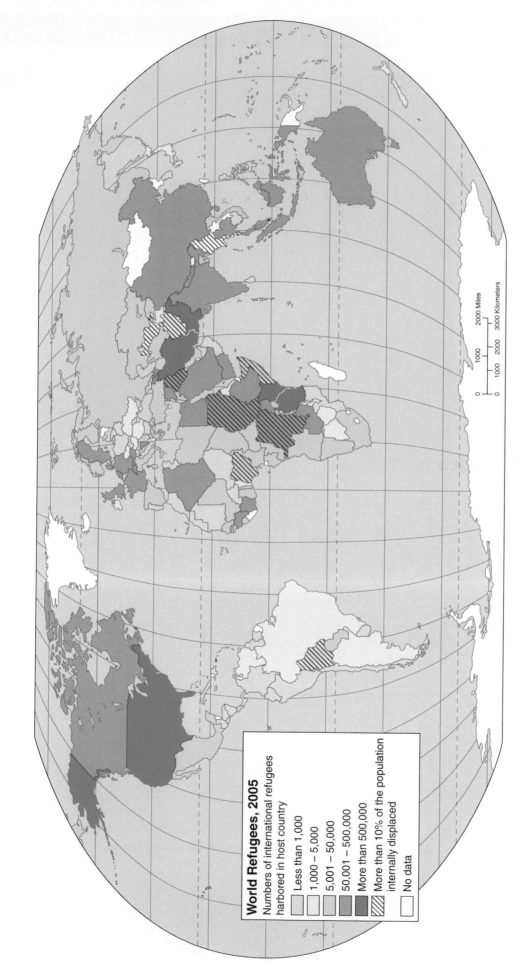

World Refugees, 2005

Numbers of international refugees harbored in host country

- Less than 1,000
- 1,000 – 5,000
- 5,001 – 50,000
- 50,001 – 500,000
- More than 500,000
- More than 10% of the population internally displaced
- No data

0   1000   2000   3000 Kilometers

0   1000   2000 Miles

Refugees are persons who have been driven from their homes, normally by armed conflict, and have sought refuge by relocating. The most numerous refugees have traditionally been international refugees, who have crossed the political boundaries of their homelands into other countries. This refugee population is recognized by international agencies, and the countries of refuge are often rewarded financially by those agencies for their willingness to take in externally displaced persons. In recent years, largely because of an increase in civil wars, there have been growing numbers of internally displaced persons—those who leave their homes but stay within their country of origin. There are no rewards for harboring such internal refugee populations.

Map **32** Post–Cold War International Alliances

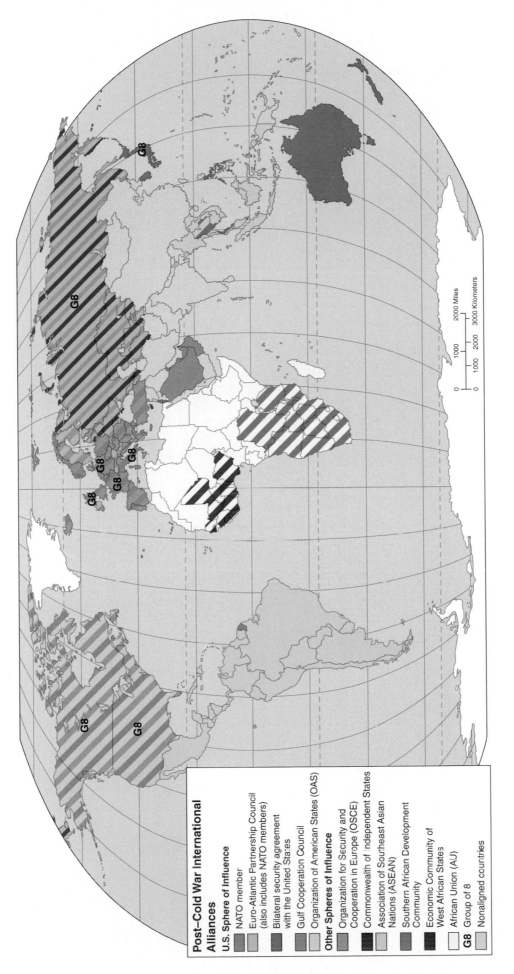

Post–Cold War International Alliances

U.S. Sphere of Influence
- NATO member
- Euro-Atlantic Partnership Council (also includes NATO members)
- Bilateral security agreement with the United States
- Gulf Cooperation Council
- Organization of American States (OAS)

Other Spheres of Influence
- Organization for Security and Cooperation in Europe (OSCE)
- Commonwealth of Independent States
- Association of Southeast Asian Nations (ASEAN)
- Southern African Development Community
- Economic Community of West African States
- African Union (AU)
- **G8** Group of 8
- Nonaligned countries

When the Warsaw Pact dissolved in 1992, the North Atlantic Treaty Organization (NATO) was left as the only major military alliance in the world. Some former Warsaw Pact members (Czech Republic, Hungary, and Poland) have joined NATO and others are petitioning for entry. The bipolar division of the world into two major military alliances is over, at least temporarily, leaving the United States alone as the world's dominant political and military power. But other international alliances, such as the Commonwealth of Independent States (including most of the former republics of the Soviet Union), will continue to be important. It may well be that during the first few decades of the twenty-first century economic alliances will begin to overshadow military ones in their relevance for the world's peoples.

-43-

Map 33　Flashpoints, 2006

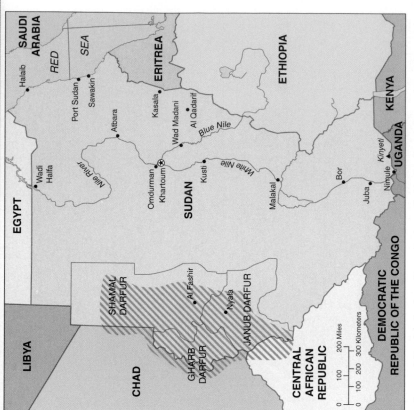

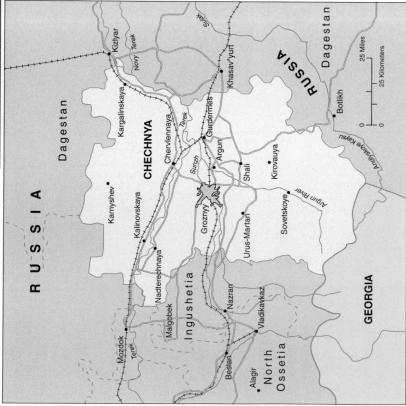

Sudan and Darfur Region: Since Sudan achieved independence from Great Britain in 1956, military regimes favoring Islamic-oriented governments have dominated national politics. These regimes have embroiled the country in a civil war for nearly all of the past half-century. These wars have been rooted in the attempts of northern economic, political, and social interests dominated by Muslims to control territories occupied by non-Muslim, non-Arab southern Sudanese such as the Dinka tribal groups. Since 1983, the war and war- and famine-related effects have resulted in more than 2 million deaths and over 4 million people displaced. The current ruling regime is a mixture of military elite and an Islamist party that came to power in a 1989 coup. Some northern opposition parties have made common cause with the southern rebels and entered the war as part of an anti-government alliance. Peace talks gained momentum in 2002–2003 with the signing of several accords, including a cease-fire agreement. However, conflicts have continued to persist in the 3 Darfur provinces of western Sudan adjacent to the border with Chad and the Central African Republic where government-backed Muslim militia have attacked and killed tens of thousands of non-Muslim tribal peoples. In 2005 and 2006, areas of conflict spilled over the borders of Sudan to involve both Chad and the Central African Republic. The Darfur region is relatively water-rich and forested in a country that is chiefly desert and is therefore desired by Muslim pastoral groups from the north for settlement purposes. International organizations have labeled the conflict in Darfur as "genocide" against the non-Muslim populations.

Chechnya: The area in southern Russia known as the Caucasus Region is home to a large variety of non-Russian ethnic groups; many are Muslim and resent centuries of Russian domination and Soviet-era totalitarianism. After the Soviet Union disintegrated in 1991, several of these ethnic groups began agitating for more autonomy from Moscow or for outright independence. One of the more vocal groups with a history of opposition to Moscow's rule were the Chechens. The Chechens declared themselves a sovereign nation in 1991 and by 1994 relations between the breakaway government in Chechnya and the Russian government had drastically deteriorated. In December of that year, Russian forces attacked Chechnya, beginning the first of two (1994–96 and 1999–present) full-scale military conflicts that have also crept into the neighboring Russian autonomous area of Dagestan, itself largely Muslim. In the mid- and late 1990s Russia experienced several terrorist attacks in cities throughout the nation, which the Russian government attributed to Islamic extremists supporting Chechen independence. As a result, a second round of the conflict began in August 1999 with a full-scale Russian military assault on Dagestan and Chechnya. This assault is ongoing and continues to face intense resistance, with heavy casualties on both sides. In 2003 and 2004 Chechen rebels increased their pressure with urban terrorist activities in Russian cities, including Moscow. Although conflicts between Russian and Chechnyan forces decreased in intensity in 2005–2007, there were continuing terrorist incidents, including the bombing of a school building that killed numerous children.

-44-

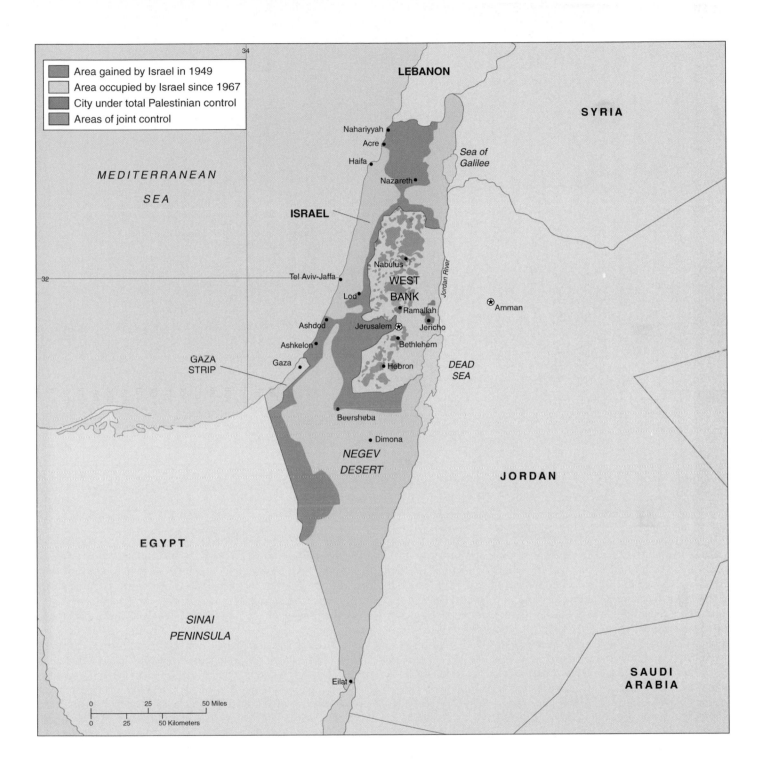

Area gained by Israel in 1949
Area occupied by Israel since 1967
City under total Palestinian control
Areas of joint control

34

LEBANON

SYRIA

MEDITERRANEAN

SEA

Nahariyyah
Acre
Haifa

Sea of
Galilee

ISRAEL

Nazareth

32

Nabulus

WEST
BANK

Tel Aviv-Jaffa

Lod

Ramallah

Jordan River

Amman

Ashdod

Jerusalem

Jericho

Ashkelon

Bethlehem

GAZA
STRIP

Gaza

Hebron

DEAD
SEA

Beersheba

Dimona

NEGEV
DESERT

JORDAN

EGYPT

SINAI
PENINSULA

Eilat

SAUDI
ARABIA

0   25   50 Miles

0   25   50 Kilometers

Israel and Its Neighbors: The modern state of Israel was created out of the former British Protectorate of Palestine, inhabited primarily by Muslim Arabs, after World War II. Conflict between Arabs and Israeli Jews has been a constant ever since. Much of the present tension revolves around the West Bank area, not part of the original Israeli state but taken from Jordan, an Arab country, in the Six-Day War of 1967. Many Palestinians had settled this part of Jordan after the creation of Israel and remain as a majority population in the West Bank region today. Israel has established many agricultural settlements within the region since 1967, angering Palestinian Arabs. For Israel, the West Bank is the region of ancient Judea and this region, won in battle, will not be ceded back to Palestinian Arabs without protracted or severe military action. The West Bank, inhabited by nearly 400,000 Israeli settlers and 4 million Palestinians, is also the location of most of the suicide bombings carried out by Islamic militant groups from 2001 to 2007.

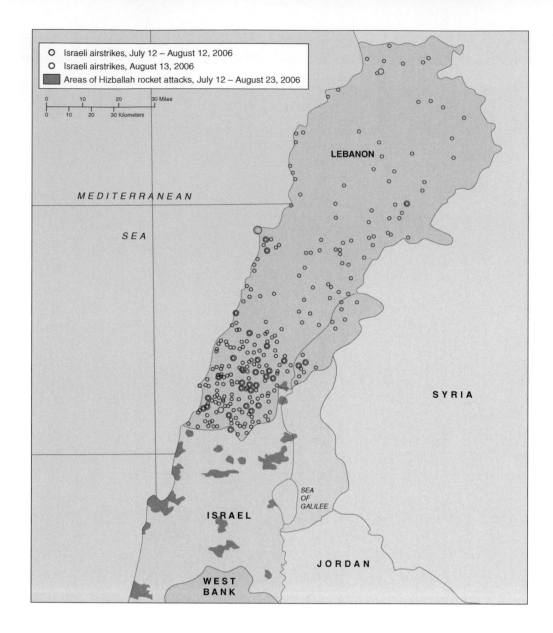

Legend:
○ Israeli airstrikes, July 12 – August 12, 2006
○ Israeli airstrikes, August 13, 2006
▪ Areas of Hizballah rocket attacks, July 12 – August 23, 2006

0   10   20   30 Miles
0   10   20   30 Kilometers

MEDITERRANEAN

SEA

LEBANON

SYRIA

SEA
OF
GALILEE

ISRAEL

JORDAN

WEST
BANK

Lebanon-Israel: Following a devastating civil war between 1976 and 1991, Lebanon's Muslim majority (about 53%) and Christian minority (about 35%) agreed to rebuild its political institutions via a "blueprint for national reconciliation." In this, the Lebanese established a more equitable political system, particularly by giving Muslims a greater voice in the political process while institutionalizing sectarian divisions in the government. Lebanon's neighbor, Syria, intruded into Lebanese territory with military forces and, in response, Israel occupied a good part of southern Lebanon until 2000. Israeli withdrawal left many areas of Lebanon under Syrian control until the passage of a United Nations resolution in 2004, calling for Syria to withdraw from Lebanon and end its interference in Lebanese affairs. This encouraged the Lebanese government to oppose Syria's presence in Lebanon. In February 2005, the assassination of a popular former prime minister led to the "Cedar Revolution," massive demonstrations in Beirut against the Syrian presence. In April 2005, Syria finally withdrew the remainder of its military forces from Lebanon. In May–June 2005, Lebanon held its first legislative elections since the end of the civil war free of foreign interference, and the nation began rebuilding its formerly thriving economy. Most militias were disbanded,

and the Lebanese Armed Forces extended authority over about two-thirds of the country. Unfortunately, Hizballah, a radical Shi'a organization listed by the U.S. State Department as a Foreign Terrorist Organization, retained its weapons and control over much of southern Lebanon. In July 2006, Hizballah militia kidnapped Israeli soldiers and launched rockets and mortars into northern Israel. Israel retaliated by blockading Lebanese ports and airports and by conducting airstrikes against known or suspected Hizballah locations throughout Lebanon. Since Hizballah militia are located throughout urban areas, Israeli retaliation resulted in many civilian deaths as well. And, of course, most of the Israelis killed by Hizballah rockets were civilians. Nine hundred thousand Lebanese and three hundred thousand Israelis were displaced by warfare, and normal life was disrupted across all of Lebanon and northern Israel. A UN resolution, which was approved by both Lebanese and Israeli governments in August 2006, called for the disarming of Hizballah, for Israel to withdraw, and for the deployment of the Lebanese Army and an enlarged UN peace-keeping force in southern Lebanon. The disarming of Hizballah has proven almost impossible, and Hizballah forces continue to occupy much of southern Lebanon. The situation remains tense.

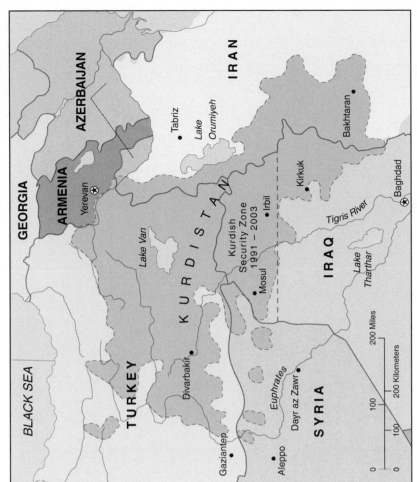

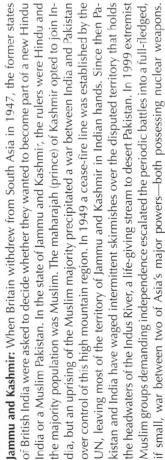

Kurdistan: Where Turkey, Iran, and Iraq meet in the high mountain region of the Tauros and Zagros mountains, a nation of 25 million people exists. This nation is "Kurdistan," but the Kurds, the occupants of this area for over 3,000 years, have no state, and receive much less attention than other stateless nations like the Palestinians. Following the 1991 Gulf War between Iraq and a U.S.-led coalition of European and Arabic states, the United Nations demarcated a Kurdish "security zone" in northern Iraq. From 1991 to 2003 the Security Zone was anything but secure as Iraqi militants from the south and Turks from the north infringed on Kurdish territory, and the internal militant extremist groups, such as the Kurdish Workers' Party, staged periodic attacks on rival villages. During the 2003 U.S.-led invasion of Iraq that eliminated the Baathist regime of Saddam Hussein, the Kurds played an important role in securing the northern portions of Iraq for the U.S.-British coalition and fought alongside American troops in expelling elements of the Iraqi army from cities like Mosul and Kirkuk. Rich in oil and history, Kurdistan will probably remain as a nation without a state, shared by Iraq, Turkey, and Iran—none of which is likely to give up substantial portions of territory for the establishment of a Kurdish state. By 2007, that portion of northern Iraq under Kurdish control was the most stable of that war-torn country.

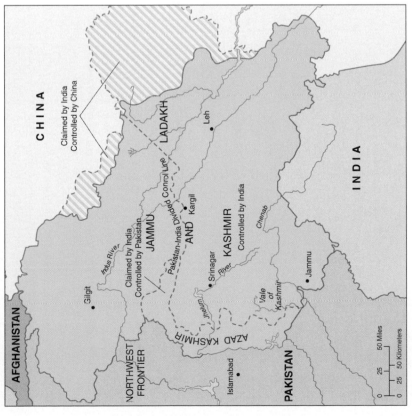

Jammu and Kashmir: When Britain withdrew from South Asia in 1947, the former states of British India were asked to decide whether they wanted to become part of a new Hindu India or a Muslim Pakistan. In the state of Jammu and Kashmir, the rulers were Hindu and the majority population was Muslim. The maharajah (prince) of Kashmir opted to join India, but an uprising of the Muslim majority precipitated a war between India and Pakistan over control of this high mountain region. In 1949 a cease-fire line was established by the UN, leaving most of the territory of Jammu and Kashmir in Indian hands. Since then Pakistan and India have waged intermittent skirmishes over the disputed territory that holds the headwaters of the Indus River, a life-giving stream to desert Pakistan. In 1999 extremist Muslim groups demanding independence escalated the periodic battles into a full-fledged, if small, war between two of Asia's major powers—both possessing nuclear weapons.

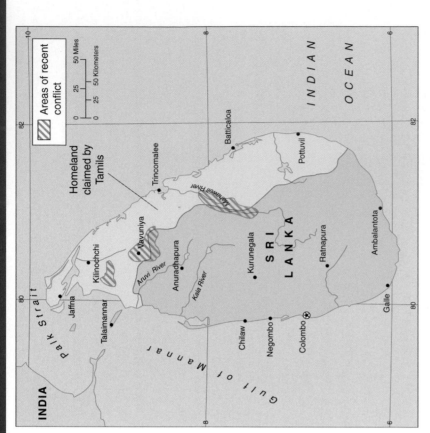

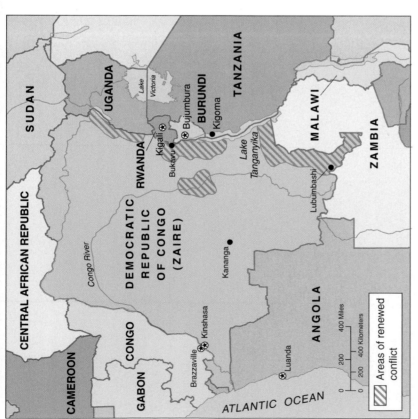

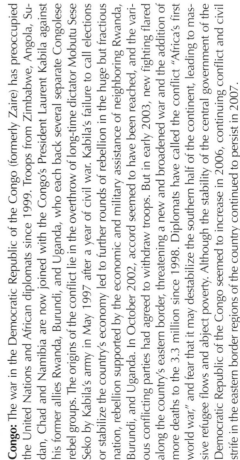

Sri Lanka: The island state of Sri Lanka, historically known as Ceylon, is potentially one of the most agriculturally productive regions of Asia. Unfortunately for plans related to agricultural development, two quite different peoples have occupied the island country: The Buddhist Sinhalese originally from northern India and long the dominant population in Sri Lanka, and the minority Hindu Tamil, a Dravidian people from south India. Since independence from Britain, Sri Lankan governments have sought to "resettle" the Tamil population in south India, actions that finally precipitated an armed rebellion by Tamils against the Sinhalese-dominated government. The Tamils at present are demanding a complete separation of the state into two parts, with a Tamil homeland in the north and along the east coast. At one time viewed as an island paradise, Sri Lanka is now a troubled country with an uncertain future. A cease fire between Sinhalese and Tamil fighters was brokered in 2001 by Norway but fell apart in late 2003 with the resumption of violence. In May 2004, Norwegian diplomats again made an attempt to negotiate a cease fire but with questionable results. 2006 and 2007 brought a renewal of terrorist attacks instigated by the Tamil faction, bringing to an end the ceasefire brokered by Norway.

Congo: The war in the Democratic Republic of the Congo (formerly Zaire) has preoccupied the United Nations and African diplomats since 1999. Troops from Zimbabwe, Angola, Sudan, Chad and Namibia are now joined with the Congo's President Laurent Kabila against his former allies Rwanda, Burundi, and Uganda, who each back several separate Congolese rebel groups. The origins of the conflict lie in the overthrow of long-time dictator Mobutu Sese Seko by Kabila's army in May 1997 after a year of civil war. Kabila's failure to call elections or stabilize the country's economy led to further rounds of rebellion in the huge but fractious nation, rebellion supported by the economic and military assistance of neighboring Rwanda, Burundi, and Uganda. In October 2002, accord seemed to have been reached, and the various conflicting parties had agreed to withdraw troops. But in early 2003, new fighting flared along the country's eastern border; threatening a new and broadened war and the addition of more deaths to the 3.3 million since 1998. Diplomats have called the conflict "Africa's first world war," and fear that it may destabilize the southern half of the continent, leading to massive refugee flows and abject poverty. Although the stability of the central government of the Democratic Republic of the Congo seemed to increase in 2006, continuing conflict and civil strife in the eastern border regions of the country continued to persist in 2007.

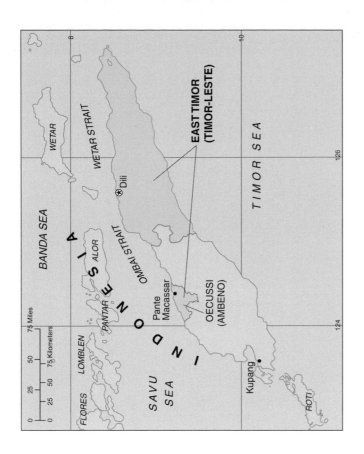

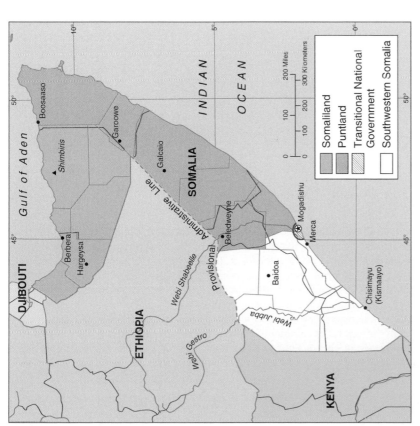

Somalia: With the ouster of the government led by Mohamed Said Barre in January 1991, turmoil, factional fighting, and anarchy have followed in Somalia, with several separate governments arising in different parts of the country. The northern clans declared an independent Republic of Somaliland. Although not recognized by any government, it has maintained a stable existence, aided by the overwhelming dominance of a ruling clan and economic infrastucture left behind by British, Russian, and American military assistance programs. Puntland, the central portion of Somalia, from the Horn of Africa to the coast of the Indian Ocean and the border with Ethiopia, has been a self-governing autonomous state since 1998. The area of Southwestern Somalia is poorly organized and more conflict-ridden than any other part of the country, with much of that conflict centered on attempts to control the nominal Somali capital of Mogadishu and ongoing famine. UN humanitarian efforts were unable to either quell guerrilla activity or alleviate famine, and the U.N. withdrew in 1995. In 2004 a new government, the Transitional Federal Government (TFG), was created for the entire country. The president and parliament of the new government have not yet moved to Mogadishu, and discussions regarding the government's establishment are ongoing in Kenya. Numerous warlords and factions are still fighting for control of the capital city as well as for other southern regions. In 2006 and 2007 a push by central government forces, backed up by units of the Ethiopian regular army, succeeded in driving Islamic extremist forces out of the Mogadishu region. But there is still no unification of the country and, by any definition, Somalia is a "disordered" or "failed" state in 2007.

East Timor: The island of Timor was incorporated into Indonesia as a province in July 1976. For two decades, Indonesian troops attempted to pacify the natives of the island, at the cost of somewhere between 100,000 to 250,000 lives. In August 1999, in a UN-supervised popular referendum, an overwhelming majority of the people of the eastern portion of Timor voted for independence from Indonesia and incorporation as a separate state of East Timor. A multinational peacekeeping force was slated to arrive in September 1999 to oversee the transition. Prior to the arrival of that force, however, anti-independence Timorese militias—most of them linked directly to the Indonesian military—carried out a large-scale campaign of retribution against the supporters of independence, killing over 1,400 Timorese and forcing more than 300,000 to flee to West Timor as refugees. During the retribution insurgency, most of the country's infrastructure (homes, irrigation systems, schools, transportation lines, public utilities) was destroyed. The violence was brought to an end with the arrival of an Australian-led peacekeeping force at the end of September 1999. East Timor was officially recognized as an independent state in May 2002. The boundary between East Timor and Indonesia continues to be in dispute, however, and Indonesia and East Timor are contesting for control of coral islands north of the island, preventing delimitation of the northern maritime boundaries. Moreover, many refugees who left East Timor in 2003 still reside in Indonesia and refuse repatriation, placing pressures on both governments. Conflicts also exist with Australia over off-shore oil deposits to the south, hampering the creation of a southern maritime boundary with Indonesia. Any country with unresolved boundaries and large numbers of disaffected populations is, by definition, a flashpoint.

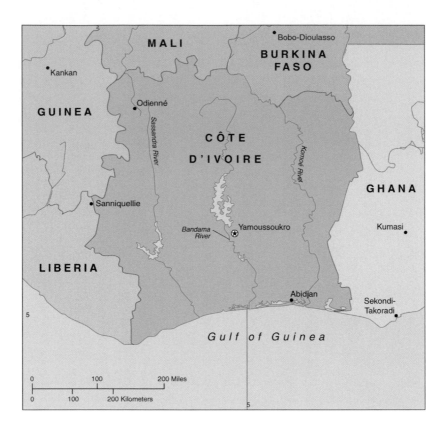

Côte d'Ivoire: Until relatively recently, its close ties to France following independence in 1960 and its development of cocoa production for export (along with significant foreign investment) made Côte d'Ivoire (Ivory Coast) one of the most prosperous of the tropical African states. Since 1999, however, political turmoil has disrupted economic development. In December 1999, the first military coup in Côte d'Ivoire's history overthrew the elected government. The leader of the coup rigged elections held in late 2000 and assumed "legitimate" power, but popular protest forced him to step aside in favor of the runner-up in the 2000 elections. Another coup, this one a failure, was launched by Ivorian dissidents and disaffected members of the military in September 2002. Rebel forces claimed the northern half of the country, and in January 2003 were granted ministerial positions in a unity government. For all practical purposes, Côte d'Ivoire has been since then in a state of civil war with the central government yet to exert control over the northern regions. In late 2006, anti-government protests intensified, leaving no apparent end in sight to a political impasse that has pitted the president against his prime minister. The international community and particularly the United Nations has been divided over how to deal with the continuing civil conflict in Côte d'Ivoire.

Colombia: Colombia was one of three countries (along with Ecuador and Venezuela) that emerged from the collapse of the newly independent country of Gran Colombia in 1830 (the former Spanish Viceroyalty of New Granada). Although possessing a rich natural resource base and agricultural abundance, Colombia has been torn apart internally for more than four decades as the result of conflict between government forces and antigovernment insurgent groups and illegal paramilitary groups. The two largest insurgent groups are the Revolutionary Armed Forces of Colombia (FARC) and the National Liberation Army (ELN). The largest illegal paramilitary group is a semi-organized array of disparate paramilitary forces called the United Self-Defense Groups of Colombia (AUC). Both insurgency and paramilitary organizations are heavily funded by the illegal trade in cocaine, the most important (but untaxed) commodity in the Colombian economy. The insurgents do not have the military or popular support necessary to overthrow the government but continue to engage in attacks against government forces and civilians, and many areas of the country are under the control of guerillas who double as drug traffickers. The insurgency groups, with a more political agenda, and the paramilitary groups, who have a fairly simple agenda of controlling the cocaine trade, not only battle the government forces but also one another. Large swaths of internal Colombia are under the control of either insurgents or paramilitary drug lords. Over the last few years, the Colombian government has increased efforts to regain control of these areas, with some mild success. However, neighboring countries remain concerned about the probability of the violence spilling into their borders. Colombian-organized illegal narcotics, guerrilla, and paramilitary activities penetrate all of its neighbors' borders and have created a serious refugee crisis with over 300,000 persons having fled the country, mostly into neighboring states. In 2006 and 2007 a "fumigation" process sponsored and funded by the United States was implemented to reduce the acres in coca cultivation. This attempt at a reduction in the coca production system has been largely unsuccessful.

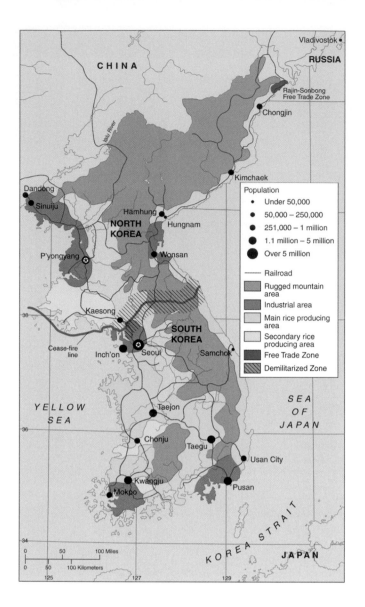

Korean Peninsula: The Korean peninsula is one of the world's most dangerous flashpoints, although active military conflict on even a minor scale has not existed since the 1950s. Throughout much of its history, Korea was an independent kingdom, although periodically a province of one of the Chinese dynasties. Beginning in the early twentieth century, Korea was annexed and occupied by Japan until the end of World War II. At that time, Korea was split into North Korea under Communist domination, and South Korea as an ostensible republic backed by the United States. Since the end of the Korean War of 1950–53—an attempt on the part of Communist North Korea, allied with China, to reunite the entire peninsula under Communist rule—South Korea has flourished economically and has become one of the most productive of the so-called Pacific Tigers with strong and profitable trading links to many different countries. North Korea, on the other hand, adopted a policy of ostensible diplomatic and economic "self-reliance" and became one of the world's most reclusive, authoritarian, and isolated states. North Korea molded its political, economic, and military policies around the core ideological objective of eventual unification of Korea and still retains that objective. While South Korea was flourishing economically, North Korea so mismanaged and misallocated its resources that, since the mid-1990s, the country has not been able to feed itself. It continues to expend resources to maintain an army of 1 million—one of the world's largest. North Korea also has active military programs, including long-range missile development as well as chemical and biological weapons programs, massive conventional armed forces, and the development of nuclear weapons with long-range missile delivery systems. All of these programs are of major concern to the international community. In 2003, North Korea announced that it would violate a 1994 agreement with the United States to freeze and ultimately dismantle its existing plutonium-based program. It also expelled monitors from the International Atomic Energy Agency (IAEA) and withdrew completely from the international Non-Proliferation Treaty. By 2006, North Korea announced the development of nuclear weapons and delivery systems that were designed to "protect" North Korea against American aggression. In 2007, the North Korean government, in exchange for the relaxing of sanctions against it, agreed unilaterally to halt its attempt to build a nuclear arsenal. Given that the United States still maintains a military presence in South Korea, the potential for destabilization of the entire peninsula exists up to and including the use of North Korean nuclear weapons against South Korea and the "American occupiers."

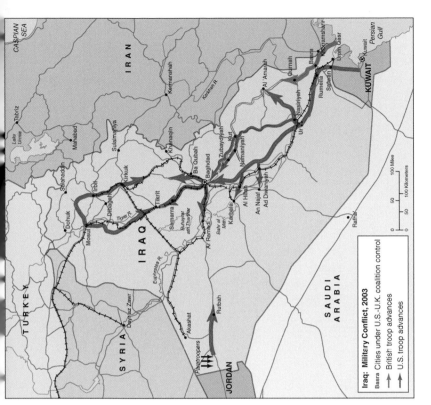

Iraq: Military Conflict, 2003: Basra Cities under U.S.-U.K. coalition control — British troop advances → U.S. troop advances

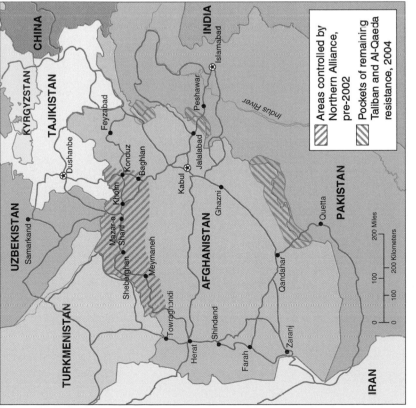

Areas controlled by Northern Alliance, pre-2002

Pockets of remaining Taliban and Al-Qaeda resistance, 2004

Afghanistan: In the aftermath of the tragic September 11, 2001, terrorist attacks on the World Trade Center and the Pentagon, the United States (backed to varying degrees by its allies) has declared a massive and global "war on terrorism" and any states that may provide "safe harbor" to terrorists. To date, the most prominent target of this U.S. declaration of war has been the Taliban regime of Islamic extremists who controlled about 95 percent of the territory of the beleaguered nation of Afghanistan. International observers believe that the Taliban regime welcomed and provided a base for the al-Qaeda terrorist network dominated by Saudi expatriate and millionaire Osama bin Laden since the late 1990s. As a result of this intelligence, the U.S. and Britain pursued a daily bombardment of key al-Qaeda and Taliban installations inside Afghanistan for several months, with key logistical support in the form of air bases and supply depots provided by the government of Pakistan (in exchange for financial considerations and political support of the non-elected Pakistani government). U.S. and allied ground troops, aided by members of the Northern Alliance of Afghan rebels opposed to the Taliban regime, expelled the Taliban government in 2002. While now under home rule and with a duly elected government, Afghanistan still is plagued by warlords in remote areas of the country who refuse to recognize the legally constituted government. In addition, along the Afghanistan-Pakistan border, significant pockets of resistance from remnants of the former Taliban regime and from al-Qaeda forces are engaged in ongoing military conflict with American and Pakistani troops. In 2006 and 2007 a marked resurgence of Taliban military activity occurred along the border between Afghanistan and Pakistan, giving rise to fears that the central government in Kabul—not strong to begin with—was beginning to lose its grasp of the peripheral areas of the country.

Iraq: Military Conflict, 2003–2004: Following the failure of the United States and allies Great Britain and Spain to secure approval from the United Nations to begin a UN-sponsored military conflict to "disarm" Iraq and effect "regime change" by removing the Baathist party dictator Saddam Hussein from power, the United States and its allies launched an independent military attack on Iraq in April 2003. The military campaign began with massive air and sea bombardments on government and military targets, then ground troops moved from Kuwait along highway routes to secure the oil fields and major urban areas. By early May 2003, virtually all of the country was under the control of the U.S.-led coalition of forces. The Iraqi military, for the most part, melted away into the general civilian population and there were no major pitched battles for territory in the short-lived war. Conflicts between British forces and paramilitary/political forces in the important southern city of Al Basrah produced casualties on both sides before the city was secured. And the U.S. troops met guerrilla resistance from political affiliates of Hussein's regime in cities such as An Najaf and Al Nasiriyah. In the northern parts of the country, U.S. troops inserted by parachute joined forces with Kurdish paramilitary groups to secure major cities like Mosul, Arbit, and Kirkuk. Although the U.S. and coalition forces controlled the country by June 2003, civil authority and infrastructure continued to be unavailable throughout large areas of Iraq by mid-2004. The spring of 2004 brought significant insurgency action against U.S. and coalition forces, who were increasingly viewed by the Iraqis as occupiers rather than liberators. A June 30, 2004, date was set to return Iraq to civilian Iraqi control. Although a civilian government, elected by the Iraqis, and with a ratified constitution has existed since 2005, Iraq is still a state that is, by nearly any definition, a disordered state and in a condition of civil war between Sunni and Shiite Muslim factions.

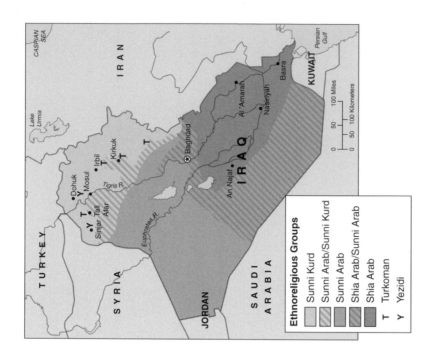

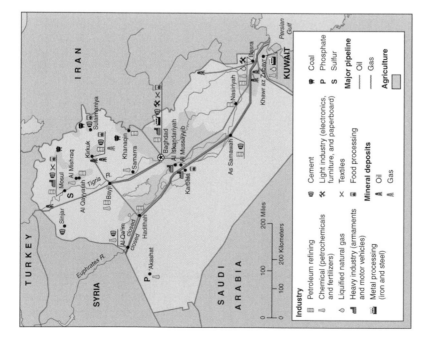

Iraq: Prior to the 1990–91 invasion of Kuwait by Iraq and the subsequent United Nations coalition's military expulsion of Iraq from its neighbor, Iraq was one of the most prosperous countries in the Middle East and the only one with full capacity to feed itself, even without the vast oil revenues generated by the country's immense reserves. Despite the inefficiencies of the Baathist dictatorship of Saddam Hussein, the country had a solid agricultural base and a burgeoning industry. The combination of military adventurism and conflict, in the form of a lengthy war with Iran and the ill-advised invasion of Kuwait, limited further economic development, however. Development was also problematic given the country's internal tensions between Arabic Sunni Muslims and Arabic Shiite Muslims, and between Arabs and Kurds and a few other minority populations in the northern parts of the country.

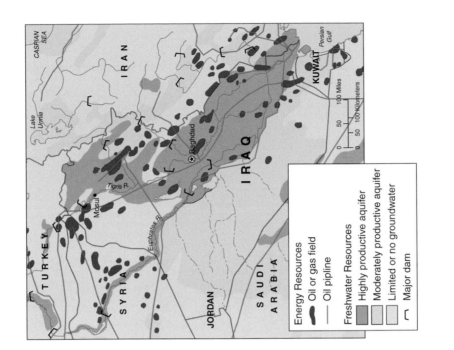

Energy Resources
- Oil or gas field
- Oil pipline

Freshwater Resources
- Highly productive aquifer
- Moderately productive aquifer
- Limited or no groundwater
- Major dam

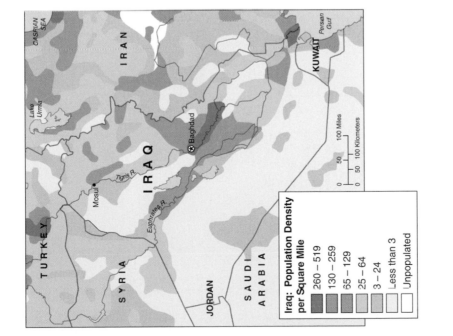

Iraq: Population Density per Square Mile
- 260 – 519
- 130 – 259
- 65 – 129
- 25 – 64
- 3 – 24
- Less than 3
- Unpopulated

Iraq: The most densely settled areas of Iraq are in the more well-watered portions of the country in the floodplains of the Tigris and Euphrates rivers, the historical center of Mesopotamian civilization since the fifth millennium BC. To the west of the floodplain region lies the northeastern portions of the great Arabian desert, and population densities here are very low. Most of Iraq's huge oil reserves are located in the areas of greatest population density and agricultural production, between the rivers and north and east of the Tigris River. The combination of the Middle East's highest potential level of agricultural production and great oil wealth make Iraq unique among states of the region in terms of potential self-sufficiency. That potential is currently being hindered by the ongoing civil conflict between the Shiite majority and the Sunni minority populations.

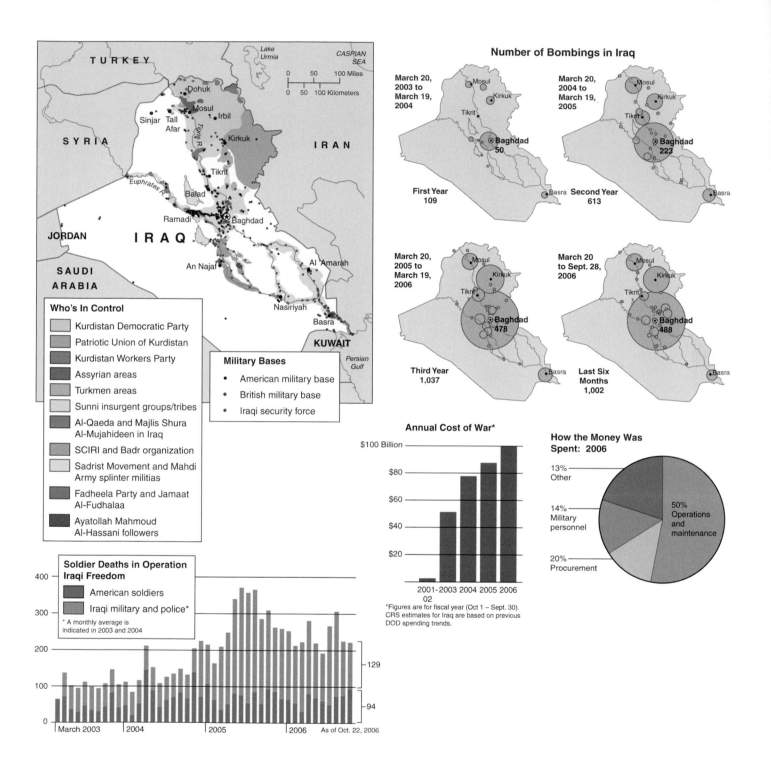

Number of Bombings in Iraq

March 20, 2003 to March 19, 2004
Mosul
Kirkuk
Tikrit
⊕ Baghdad 50
Basra
First Year 109

March 20, 2004 to March 19, 2005
Mosul
Kirkuk
Tikrit
⊕ Baghdad 223
Basra
Second Year 613

March 20, 2005 to March 19, 2006
Mosul
Kirkuk
Tikrit
⊕ Baghdad 478
Basra
Third Year 1,037

March 20 to Sept. 28, 2006
Mosul
Kirkuk
Tikrit
⊕ Baghdad 488
Basra
Last Six Months 1,002

Who's In Control

- Kurdistan Democratic Party
- Patriotic Union of Kurdistan
- Kurdistan Workers Party
- Assyrian areas
- Turkmen areas
- Sunni insurgent groups/tribes
- Al-Qaeda and Majlis Shura Al-Mujahideen in Iraq
- SCIRI and Badr organization
- Sadrist Movement and Mahdi Army splinter militias
- Fadheela Party and Jamaat Al-Fudhalaa
- Ayatollah Mahmoud Al-Hassani followers

Military Bases
- • American military base
- • British military base
- • Iraqi security force

Annual Cost of War*

$100 Billion
$80
$60
$40
$20

2001-02 2003 2004 2005 2006

*Figures are for fiscal year (Oct 1 – Sept. 30). CRS estimates for Iraq are based on previous DOD spending trends.

How the Money Was Spent: 2006

13% Other
14% Military personnel
20% Procurement
50% Operations and maintenance

Soldier Deaths in Operation Iraqi Freedom

- American soldiers
- Iraqi military and police*

* A monthly average is indicated in 2003 and 2004

400
300
200
100
0

March 2003   2004   2005   2006   As of Oct. 22, 2006

129
94

More than 3 years after the U.S.-led invasion, Iraq is in critical condition. Sectarian violence is rampant, death tolls continue to rise, and the price of Operation Iraqi Freedom has reached a staggering $318 billion. As of 2006, the maps above show the state of Iraq nearly 3 years after the end of active military conflict between the Baathist forces of Saddam Hussein and the U.S.-led coalition forces. It is a country fractured by conflicting tribal and religious loyalties, beset by a continuing Sunni insurgency against the Shiite-dominated constitutional government, and seemingly descending more deeply into the spiral of all-out civil war.

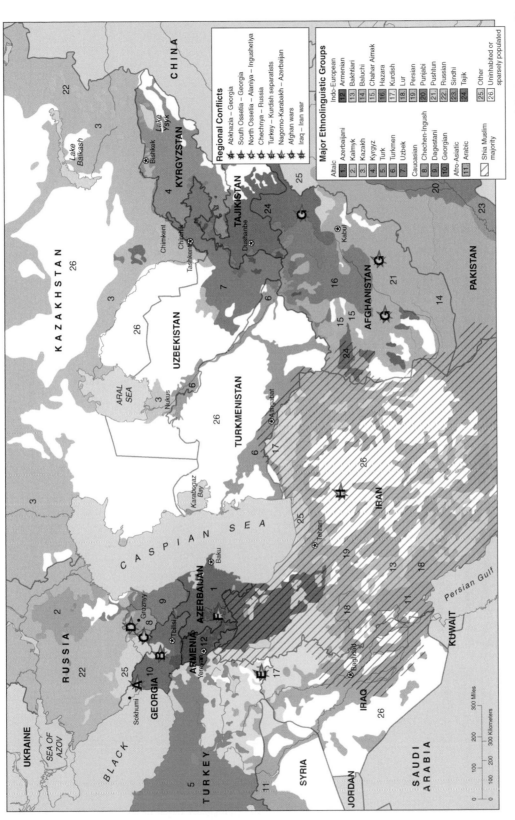

South-Central Eurasia: The area of south-central Eurasia represents what is perhaps the world's most volatile area in terms of potential military conflict. A crazy-quilt of ethnic and linguistic groups, this region contains politically defined "states," but nothing approaching "nation-states" as they are understood elsewhere. Even reasonably well-consolidated states, such as Iran, are hampered by the mixture of languages and ethnic populations within their borders. For some countries, such as Afghanistan, the ethnolinguistic mix is so historically fixed as to render any attempts at modern state building nearly hopeless. This vast area—although nearly universally Muslim—is also split between the two primary Islamic sects, Sunni and Shia, with several smaller sectarian divisions as well. The division of one of the world's global religions into two principal factions occurred in the seventh century, originally over the question of the source of authority in the religious hierarchy. But it has since come to be a theological and metaphysical separation, and Sunni and Shia Muslims now bear somewhat the same relationship to one another as did Catholics and Protestants in seventeenth- and eighteenth-century Europe—a mutual antipathy that periodically flares into civil unrest and conflict that goes far beyond the bounds of religious debate. The area is rich in natural resources, but the mixture of ethnicity, language, and religion has and will continue to produce the human conflicts that inhibit human development.

Map 34 International Terrorism Incidents, 1998–2006

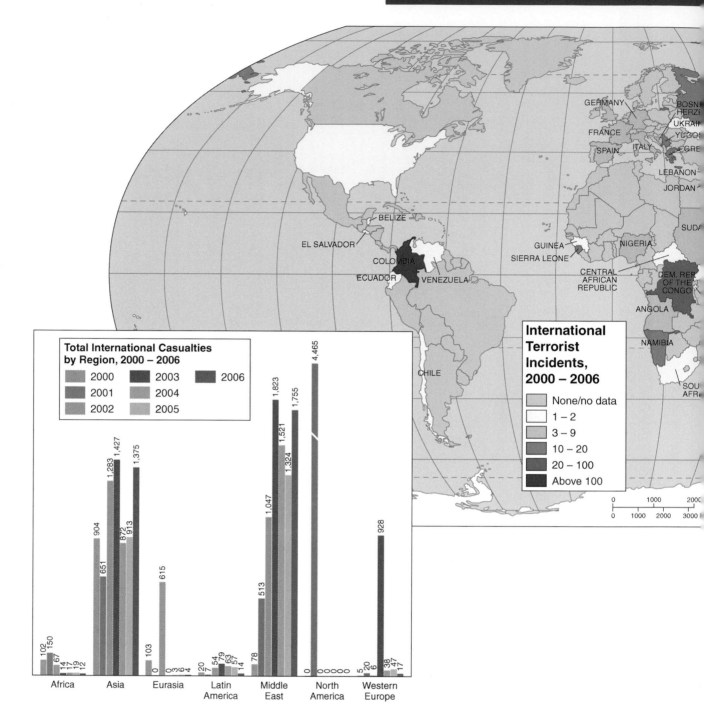

Total International Casualties by Region, 2000 – 2006

- 2000
- 2001
- 2002
- 2003
- 2004
- 2005
- 2006

Africa: 102, 150, 67, 14, 17, 19, 12
Asia: 904, 651, 1,283, 1,427, 872, 913, 1,375
Eurasia: 103, 0, 615, 0, 3, 6, 4
Latin America: 20, 7, 54, 79, 63, 57, 14
Middle East: 78, 513, 1,047, 1,823, 1,521, 1,324, 1,755
North America: 0, 4,465, 0, 0, 0, 0, 0
Western Europe: 5, 20, 6, 928, 38, 47, 17

International Terrorist Incidents, 2000 – 2006

- None/no data
- 1 – 2
- 3 – 9
- 10 – 20
- 20 – 100
- Above 100

Americans have made a mantra of the saying "the world has changed" as a consequence of the terrorist attacks on the World Trade Center and the Pentagon on September 11, 2001. As the map above and the accompanying graphs of terrorist activities before and after 9/11/01 indicate, however, the world did not change, although the focus of a major terrorist attack shifted from Africa, Asia, and the Middle East to North America. Many other areas of the world have lived with terrorism and terrorist activity for years. In 2000 and 2001, despite the enormous losses in the United States in the 9/11 attacks, more lives were lost in Asia and Africa as a result of terrorism than were lost in North America. The world did not change, but Americans' perception of that world and their place in it has certainly changed. Events subsequent to 9/11 indicate a

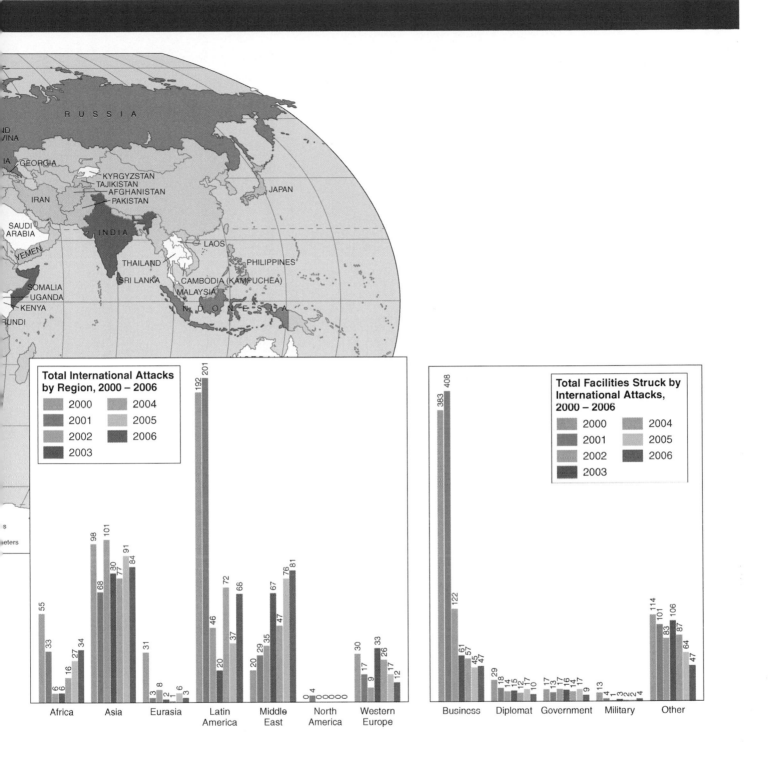

Total International Attacks by Region, 2000 – 2006

2000	2004
2001	2005
2002	2006
2003	

Africa: 55, 33, 6, 6, 16, 27, 34
Asia: 98, 68, 101, 80, 77, 91, 84
Eurasia: 31, 3, 8, 2, 1, 6, 3
Latin America: 192, 201, 46, 20, 72, 37, 66
Middle East: 20, 29, 35, 67, 47, 76, 81
North America: 0, 4, 0, 0, 0, 0, 0
Western Europe: 30, 17, 9, 33, 26, 17, 12

Total Facilities Struck by International Attacks, 2000 – 2006

2000	2004
2001	2005
2002	2006
2003	

Business: 383, 408, 122, 61, 57, 45, 47
Diplomat: 29, 18, 14, 15, 12, 17, 10
Government: 17, 13, 17, 16, 14, 17, 9
Military: 13, 4, 3, 2, 2, 4
Other: 114, 101, 83, 106, 87, 64, 47

shift back to more "normal" patterns in North America in 2002, and 2003 showed no terrorist activities—in sharp contrast to many other world regions, including Europe. Two qualifiers need to be added regarding the data presented: the term "casualties" refers to dead and wounded (the number of the dead represent a relatively small percentage of total casualties by region), and the term "terrorist attacks" does not include insurgency events in areas of military conflict and, therefore, does not include activities carried out against U.S. forces or others in places like Afghanistan or Iraq where military action continued throughout the time frame of the data. Hence, data from 2004–2006 are not directly comparable to data from 2003 and earlier, although we have attempted to adjust the data to be as comparable as possible.

Map 35   The Political Geography of a Global Religion: The Islamic World

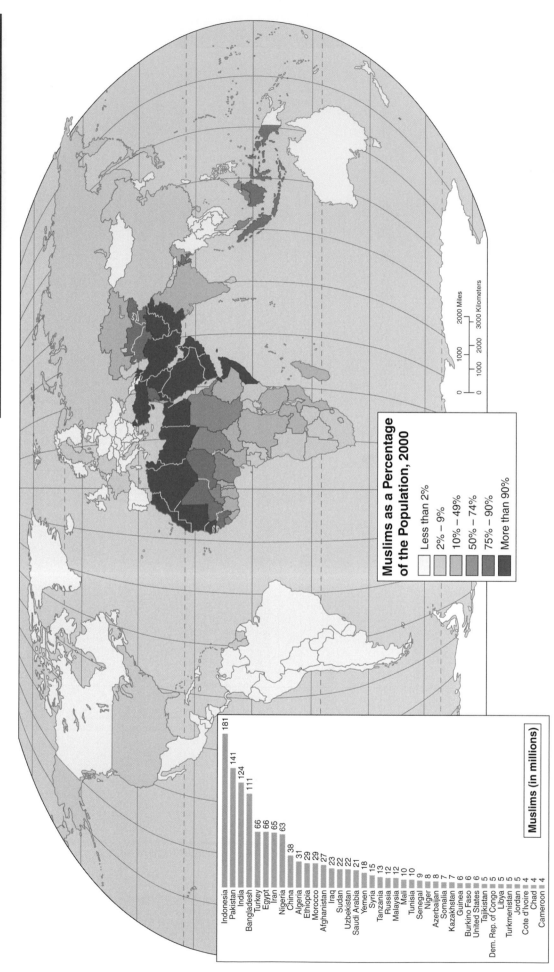

Muslims as a Percentage of the Population, 2000

- Less than 2%
- 2% – 9%
- 10% – 49%
- 50% – 74%
- 75% – 90%
- More than 90%

Muslims (in millions)

Country	Muslims
Indonesia	181
Pakistan	141
India	124
Bangladesh	111
Turkey	66
Egypt	66
Iran	65
Nigeria	63
China	38
Algeria	31
Ethiopia	29
Morocco	29
Afghanistan	27
Iraq	23
Sudan	22
Uzbekistan	22
Saudi Arabia	21
Yemen	18
Syria	15
Tanzania	13
Russia	12
Malaysia	12
Mali	10
Tunisia	10
Senegal	9
Niger	8
Azerbaijan	8
Kazakhstan	7
Guinea	6
Burkino Faso	6
United States	6
Tajikistan	5
Dem. Rep. of Congo	5
Libya	5
Turkmenistan	5
Jordan	5
Cote d'Ivoire	4
Chad	4
Cameroon	4

0   1000   2000 Miles
0   1000   2000   3000 Kilometers

Islam, as a religion, does not promote conflict. The term *jihad*, often mistranslated to mean "holy war," in fact refers to the struggle to find God and to promote the faith. In spite of the beneficent nature of Islamic teachings, the tensions between Muslims and adherents of other faiths often flare into warfare. A comparison of this map with the map of international conflict will show a disproportionate number of wars in that portion of the world where Muslims are either majority or significant minority populations. The reasons for this are based more in the nature of government, cultures, and social structure, than in the tenets of the faith of Islam. Nevertheless, the spatial correlations cannot be ignored. Similarly, terrorist incidents falling considerably short of open armed warfare are spatially consistent with the distribution of Islam and even more consistent with the presence of Islamic fundamentalism or "Islamism," which tends to be less tolerant and more aggressive than the mainstream of the religion. Terrorism is also consistent with those areas where the legacy of colonialism or the persistent presence of non-Islamic cultures intrude into the Islamic world.

Map 36   Nations with Nuclear Weapons

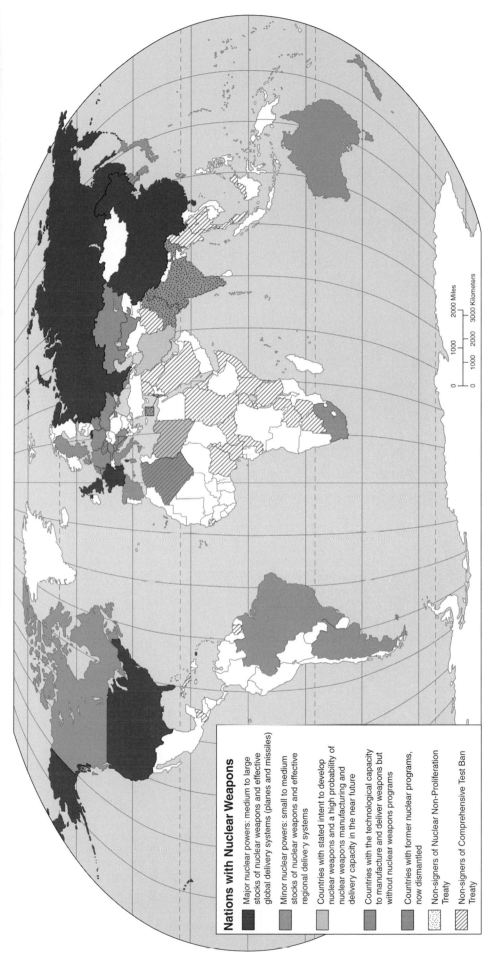

Nations with Nuclear Weapons

- Major nuclear powers: medium to large stocks of nuclear weapons and effective global delivery systems (planes and missiles)
- Minor nuclear powers: small to medium stocks of nuclear weapons and effective regional delivery systems
- Countries with stated intent to develop nuclear weapons and a high probability of nuclear weapons manufacturing and delivery capacity in the near future
- Countries with the technological capacity to manufacture and deliver weapons but without nuclear weapons programs
- Countries with former nuclear programs, now dismantled
- Non-signers of Nuclear Non-Proliferation Treaty
- Non-signers of Comprehensive Test Ban Treaty

0   1000   2000 Miles
0   1000   2000   3000 Kilometers

Since 1980, the number of countries possessing the capacity to manufacture and deliver nuclear weapons has grown dramatically, increasing the chances of accidental or intentional nuclear exchanges. In addition to the traditional nuclear powers of the United States, Russia, China, the United Kingdom, and France, must now be added Israel, India, and Pakistan as countries that, without possessing the large stocks of weapons of the major powers, nor the extensive delivery systems of the United States and Russia, still have effective regional (and possibly global) delivery systems and medium stocks of warheads. Countries such as Kazakhstan, Ukraine, Georgia, and Belarus that were created out of what had been the Soviet Union did have some nuclear capacity in the 1991–1995 period but have since had all nuclear weapons removed from their territories. However, North Korea has recently announced the re-establishment of its suspended nuclear weapons programs and may possess a small stock of nuclear warheads, along with the capacity to deliver those weapons regionally. Both Iran and Libya have nuclear ambitions,

as did Iraq until the overthrow of the Baathist regime of Saddam Hussein by a U.S.-led military coalition in 2003. The proliferation of nuclear states threatens global security, and the objective of the Nuclear Non-Proliferation Treaty was to reduce the chances for expanding nuclear arsenals worldwide. This treaty has been partially successful in that a number of countries in the developed world certainly have the capacity to manufacture and deliver nuclear weapons but have chosen not to do so. These countries include Canada, European countries other than the United Kingdom and France, South Korea, Japan, Australia, and New Zealand, and Brazil and Argentina in South America. On the other side of the coin, the intent of North Korea to develop nuclear weapons—despite the North Korean government's backing away from that intent somewhat in 2007—may ultimately force non-nuclear countries such as South Korea and Japan, both of which possess appropriate technology, to rethink their position regarding the possession of a nuclear arsenal.

-61-

Map 37 Size of Armed Forces

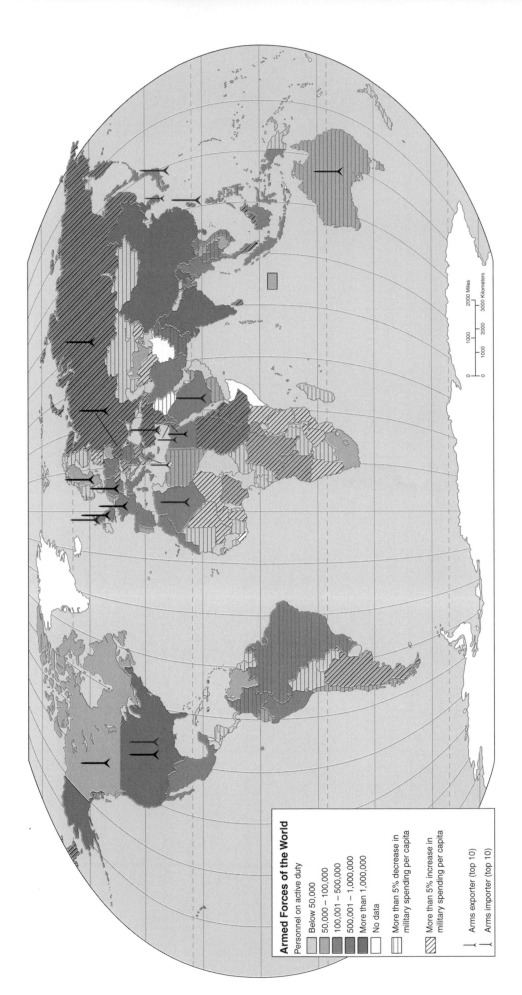

Armed Forces of the World

Personnel on active duty

- Below 50,000
- 50,000 – 100,000
- 100,001 – 500,000
- 500,001 – 1,000,000
- More than 1,000,000
- No data

More than 5% decrease in military spending per capita

More than 5% increase in military spending per capita

Arms exporter (top 10)

Arms importer (top 10)

0   1000   2000 Miles
0   1000   2000   3000 Kilometers

While the size of a country's armed forces is still an indicator of national power on the international scene, it is no longer as important as it once was. The increasing high technology of military hardware allows smaller numbers of military personnel to be more effective. There are some countries, such as China, with massive numbers of military personnel but with relatively limited military power because of a lack of modern weaponry. Additionally, the use of rapid transportation allows personnel to be deployed about the globe or any region of it quickly; this also increases the effectiveness of highly trained and well-armed smaller military units. Nevertheless, the world is still a long way from the pre-

dicted "push-button warfare" that many experts have long anticipated. Indeed, the pattern of the last few years has been for most military conflicts to involve ground troops engaged in fairly traditional patterns of operation. Even in the Persian Gulf conflict, with its highly publicized "smart bombs," the bulk of the military operation that ended the conflict was carried out by infantry and armor operating on the ground and supported by traditional air cover using conventional weaponry. Thus, while the size of a country's armed forces may not be as important as it once was, it is still a major factor in measuring the ability of nations to engage successfully in armed conflict.

Map 38   Military Expenditures as a Percentage of Gross National Product

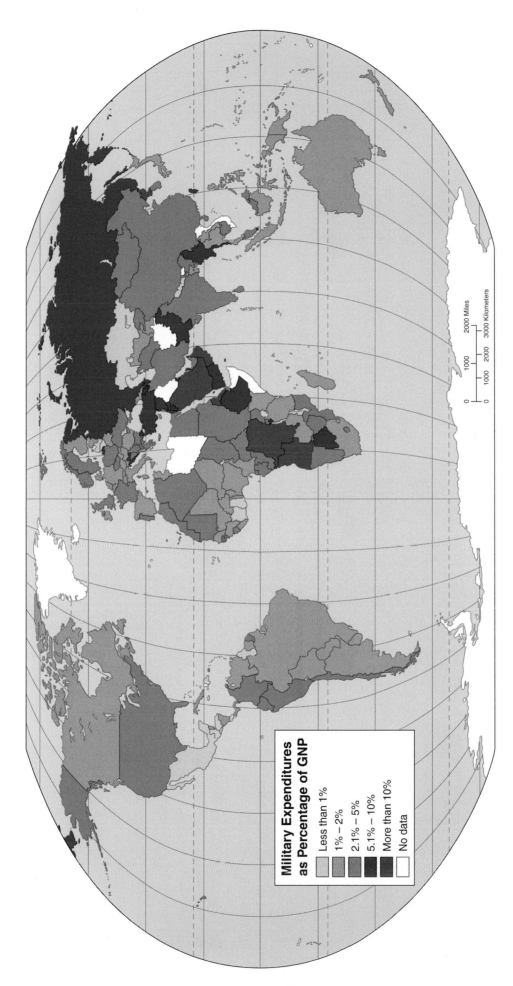

**Military Expenditures
as Percentage of GNP**

Less than 1%
1% – 2%
2.1% – 5%
5.1% – 10%
More than 10%
No data

0   1000   2000 Miles
0   1000   2000   3000 Kilometers

Many countries devote a significant proportion of their total central governmental expenditures to defense: weapons, personnel, and research and development of military hardware. A glance at the map reveals that there are a number of regions in which defense expenditures are particularly high, reflecting the degree of past and present political tension between countries. The clearest example is the Middle East. The steady increase in military expenditures by developing countries is one of the most alarming (and least well known) worldwide defense issues. Where the end of the cold war has meant a sub-

stantial reduction of military expenditures for the countries in North America and Europe and for Russia, in many of the world's developing countries military expenditures have risen between 15 percent and 20 percent per year for the past few years, averaging out to 7.5 percent per year for the past quarter century. Even though many developing countries still spend less than 5 percent of their gross national product on defense, these funds could be put to different uses in such human development areas as housing, land reform, health care, and education.

Map 39 Abuse of Public Trust

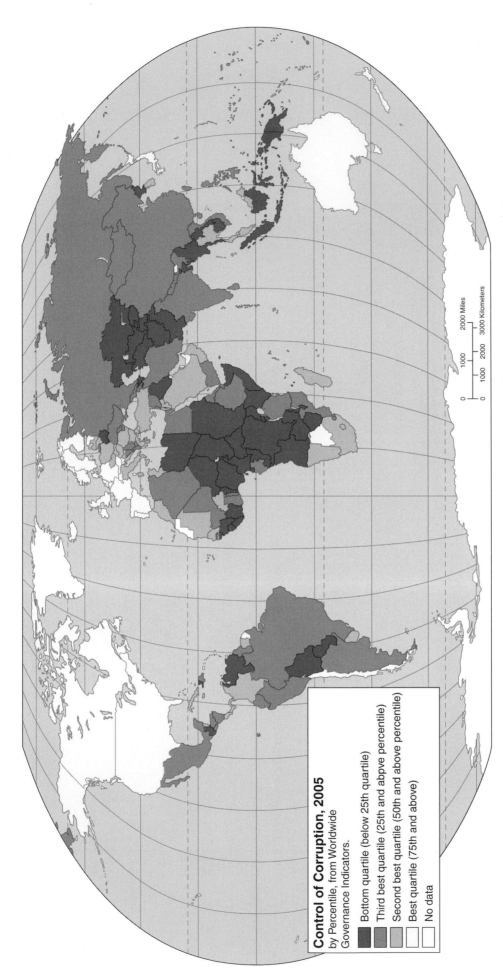

Control of Corruption, 2005
by Percentile, from Worldwide
Governance Indicators.

- Bottom quartile (below 25th quartile)
- Third best quartile (25th and abpve percentile)
- Second best quartile (50th and above percentile)
- Best quartile (75th and above)
- No data

0   1000   2000 Miles
0   1000   2000   3000 Kilometers

Abusing the public trust is simply another way of saying "corruption in government." In many parts of the world, corruption in the government is not an aberration but a way of life. Normally, although not always, governmental corruption is an indication of a weak and ineffective government, one that negatively affects such public welfare issues as public health, sanitation, education, and the provision of social services. It also tends to impact the cost of doing business and, thereby, drives away the foreign capital so badly needed in many African and Asian countries for economic development. Corruption is not automatic in poor countries, nor are rich countries free from it. But there is a general correlation between abuse of the public trust and lower levels of

per capita income—excepting such countries as the Baltic states and Chile that have reached high standards of governance without joining the ranks of the wealthy countries. Studies by the World Bank have shown that countries that address issues of corruption and clean up the operations of their governments increase national incomes as much as four or five times. In those countries striving to attain governments that function according to a rule of law—rather than a rule of abusing the public trust—such important demographic measures as child mortality drop by as much as 75%. Clearly, good government and good business and higher incomes and better living conditions for the general public all go hand-in-hand.

-64-

Unit III

Population, Health, and Human Development

Map 40   Population Growth Rates

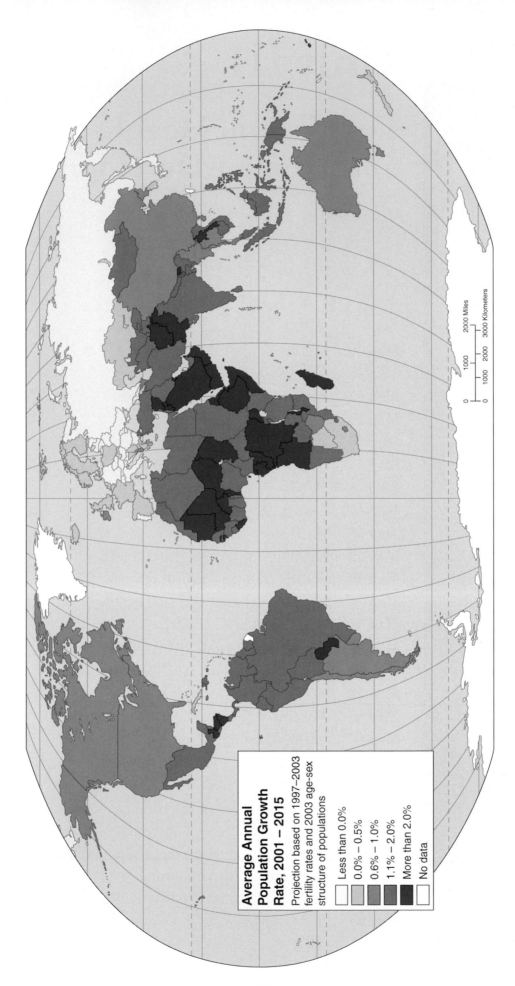

Average Annual Population Growth Rate, 2001 – 2015

Projection based on 1997–2003 fertility rates and 2003 age-sex structure of populations

- Less than 0.0%
- 0.0% – 0.5%
- 0.6% – 1.0%
- 1.1% – 2.0%
- More than 2.0%
- No data

0   1000   2000 Miles
0   1000   2000   3000 Kilometers

Of all the statistical measurements of human population, that of the rate of population growth is the most important. The growth rate of a population is a combination of natural change (births and deaths), in-migration, and out-migration; it is obtained by adding the number of births to the number of immigrants during a year and subtracting from that total the sum of deaths and emigrants for the same year. For a specific country, this figure will determine many things about the country's future ability to feed, house, educate, and provide medical services to its citizens.

Some of the countries with the largest populations (such as India) also have high growth rates. Since these countries tend to be in developing regions, the combination of high population and high growth rates poses special problems for political stability and continuing economic development; the combination also carries heightened risks for environmental degradation. Many people believe that the rapidly expanding world population is a potential crisis that may cause environmental and human disaster by the middle of the twenty-first century.

Map 41 Infant Mortality Rate

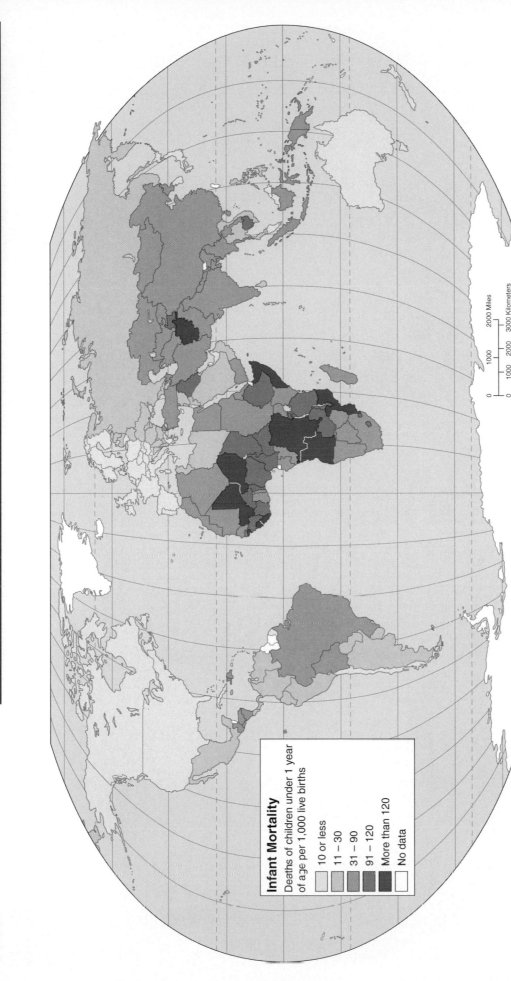

Infant Mortality

Deaths of children under 1 year
of age per 1,000 live births

- 10 or less
- 11 – 30
- 31 – 90
- 91 – 120
- More than 120
- No data

Infant mortality rates are calculated by dividing the number of children born in a given year who die before their first birthday by the total number of children born that year and then multiplying by 1,000; this shows how many infants have died for every 1,000 births. Infant mortality rates are prime indicators of economic development. In highly developed economies, with advanced medical technologies, sufficient diets, and adequate public sanitation, infant mortality rates tend to be quite low. By contrast, in less developed countries, with the disadvantages of poor diet, limited access to medical technology, and the other problems of poverty, infant mortality rates tend to be high. Although worldwide infant mortality has decreased significantly during the last two decades, many regions of the world still experience infant mortality above the 10 percent level (100 deaths per 1,000 live births). Such infant mortality rates not only represent human tragedy at its most basic level, but also are powerful inhibiting factors for the future of human development. Comparing infant mortality rates in the midlatitudes and the tropics shows that children in most African countries are more than 10 times as likely to die within a year of birth as children in European countries.

-67-

Map 42   Average Life Expectancy at Birth

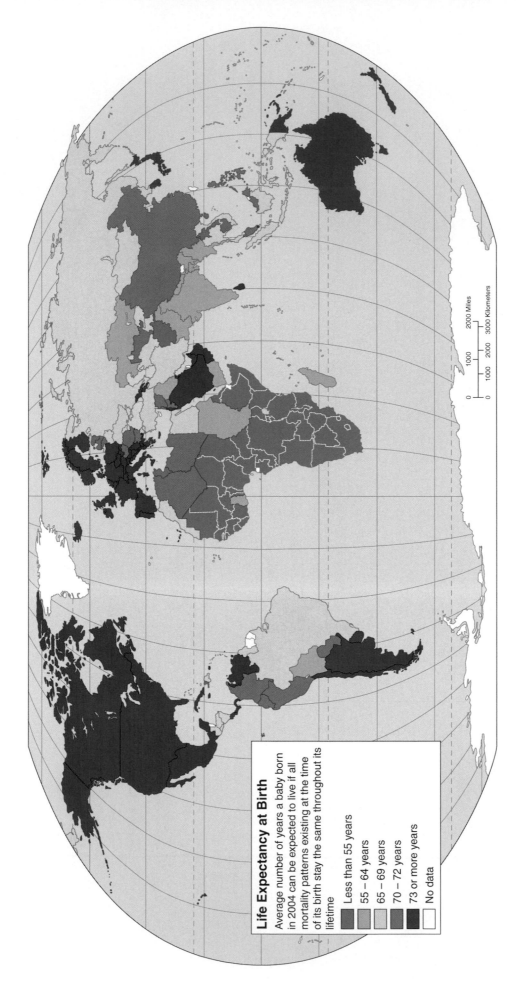

Life Expectancy at Birth

Average number of years a baby born in 2004 can be expected to live if all mortality patterns existing at the time of its birth stay the same throughout its lifetime

- Less than 55 years
- 55 – 64 years
- 65 – 69 years
- 70 – 72 years
- 73 or more years
- No data

Average life expectancy at birth is a measure of the average longevity of the population of a country. Like all average measures, it is distorted by extremes. For example, a country with a high mortality rate among children will have a low average life expectancy. Thus, an average life expectancy of 45 years does not mean that everyone can be expected to die at the age of 45. More normally, what the figure means is that a substantial number of children die between birth and 5 years of age, thus reducing the average life expectancy for the entire population. In spite of the dangers inherent in misinterpreting the data, average life expectancy (along with infant mortality and several other measures) is a valid way of judging the relative health of a population. It reflects the nature of the health care system, public sanitation and disease control, nutrition, and a number of other key human need indicators. As such, it is a measure of well-being that is significant in indicating economic development and predicting political stability.

Map 43   Population by Age Group

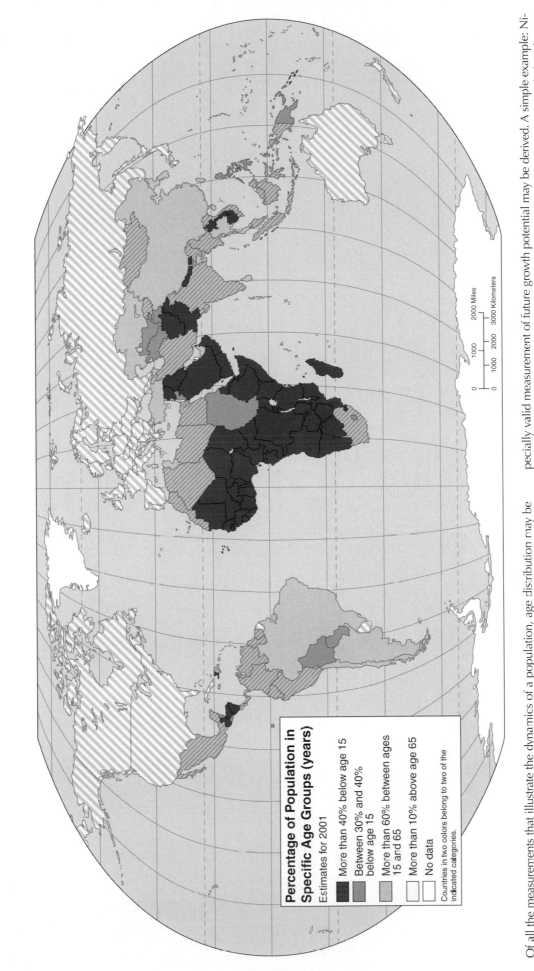

Percentage of Population in Specific Age Groups (years)

Estimates for 2001

- More than 40% below age 15
- Between 30% and 40% below age 15
- More than 60% between ages 15 and 65
- More than 10% above age 65
- No data

Countries in two colors belong to two of the indicated categories.

0   1000   2000 Miles
0   1000   2000   3000 Kilometers

Of all the measurements that illustrate the dynamics of a population, age distribution may be the most significant, particularly when viewed in combination with average growth rates. The particular relevance of age distribution is that it tells us what to expect from a population in terms of growth over the next generation. If, for example, approximately 40–50 percent of a population is below the age of 15, that suggests that in the next generation about one-quarter of the total population will be women of childbearing age. When age distribution is combined with fertility rates (the average number of children born per woman in a population), an es-

pecially valid measurement of future growth potential may be derived. A simple example: Nigeria, with a 2002 population of 130 million, has 43.6 percent of its population below the age of 15 and a fertility rate of 5.5; the United States, with a 2002 population of 280 million, has 21 percent of its population below the age of 15 and a fertility rate of 2.07. During the period in which those women presently under the age of 15 are in their childbearing years, Nigeria can be expected to add a total of approximately 155 million persons to its total population. Over the same period, the United States can be expected to add only 61 million.

-69-

Map 44 International Migrant Populations, 2005

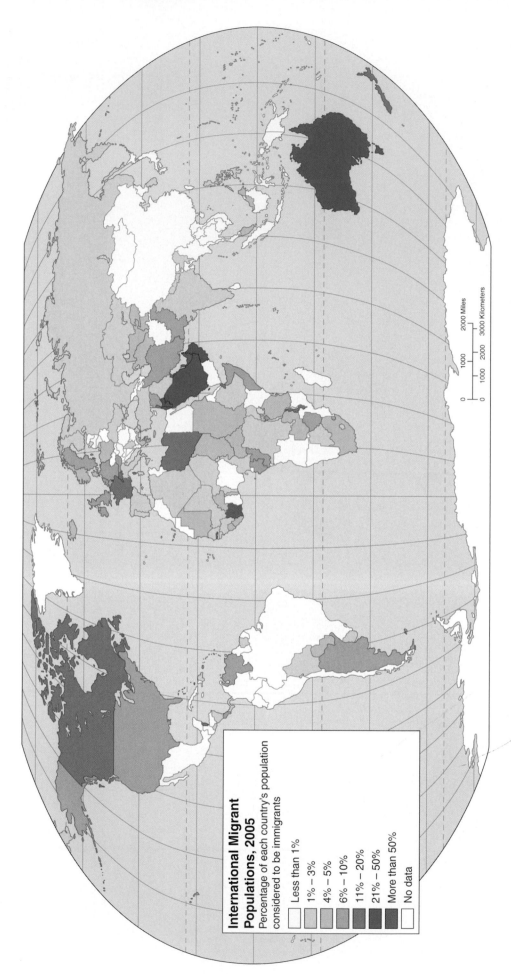

International Migrant Populations, 2005

Percentage of each country's population considered to be immigrants

Less than 1%

1% – 3%

4% – 5%

6% – 10%

11% – 20%

21% – 50%

More than 50%

No data

0 1000 2000 2000 Miles

0 1000 2000 3000 Kilometers

Migration—the movement from one place to another—takes a number of different forms. It may be a move within a country from an old job to a new one. It may also mean a migration, either forced or voluntary, from one country to another. The map here depicts international migration: migration between countries. Migration is distinguished from a refugee movement in that migrants are not defined as refugees granted a humanitarian and temporary protection status under international law. The nearly 2 million people who have fled Iraq for Iran are refugees who expect and hope to return to Iraq after the present civil war is ended. The Middle Americans who leave the Central American countries, Mexico, or the Caribbean for the United States plan to live in the United States permanently, although still retaining cultural and family ties to their native country. This map clearly shows that those countries viewed as having the most favorable opportunities for improvement in personal living conditions are those with the highest numbers of in-migrants; those countries that are overcrowded, with little economically upward mobility, or international conflict tend to be those with the greatest number of out-migrants.

Map 45　Urban Population

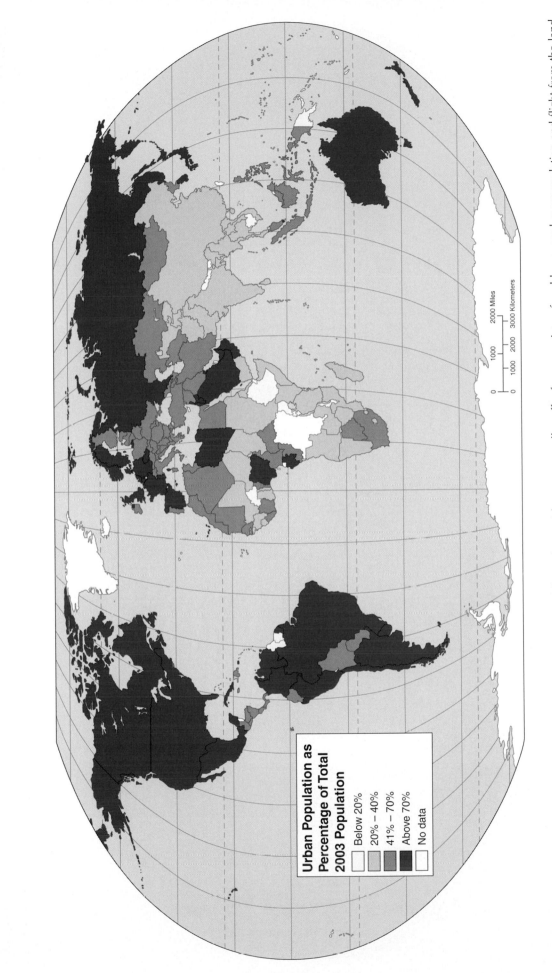

Urban Population as Percentage of Total 2003 Population

- Below 20%
- 20% – 40%
- 41% – 70%
- Above 70%
- No data

0　1000　2000　3000 Kilometers

0　1000　2000 Miles

The proportion of a country's population that resides in urban areas was formerly considered a measure of relative economic development, with countries possessing a large urban population ranking high on the development scale and countries with a more rural population ranking low. Given the rapid rate of urbanization in developing countries, however, this traditional measure is no longer so valuable. What relative urbanization rates now tell us is something about levels of economic development in a negative sense. Latin American, African, and Asian countries with more than 40 percent of their populations living in urban areas generally suffer from a variety of problems: rural overpopulation and flight from the land, urban poverty and despair, high unemployment, and poor public services. The rate of urbanization in less developed nations is such that many cities in these nations will outstrip those in North America and Europe by the end of this century. It has been estimated, for example, that Mexico City—now the world's second largest metropolis—has over 18 million inhabitants. Urbanization was once viewed as an indicator of economic health and political maturity. For many countries it is instead a harbinger of potential economic and environmental disaster.

Map 46   Illiteracy Rates

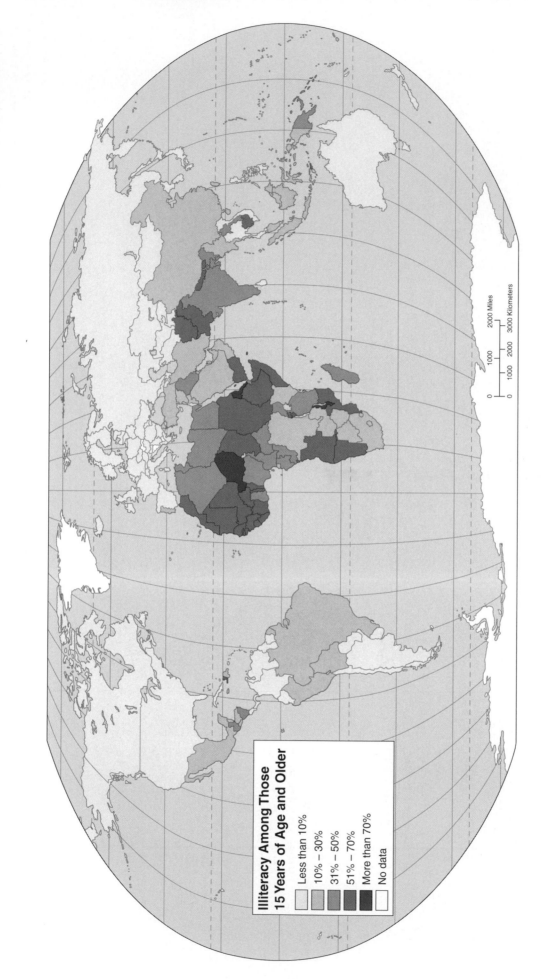

**Illiteracy Among Those
15 Years of Age and Older**

Less than 10%
10% – 30%
31% – 50%
51% – 70%
More than 70%
No data

Illiteracy rates are based on the percentages of people age 15 or above (classed as adults in most countries) who are not able to write and read, with understanding, a brief, simple statement about everyday life written in their home- or official language. As might be expected, illiteracy rates tend to be higher in the less-developed states, where educational systems are a low government priority. Rates of literacy or illiteracy also tend to be gender-differentiated, with women in many countries experiencing educational neglect or discrimination that makes it more likely they will be illiterate. In many developing countries, between five and ten times as many women will be illiterate as men, and the illiteracy rate for women may even exceed 90 percent. Both male and female illiteracy severely compromises economic development.

Map 47 Primary School Education

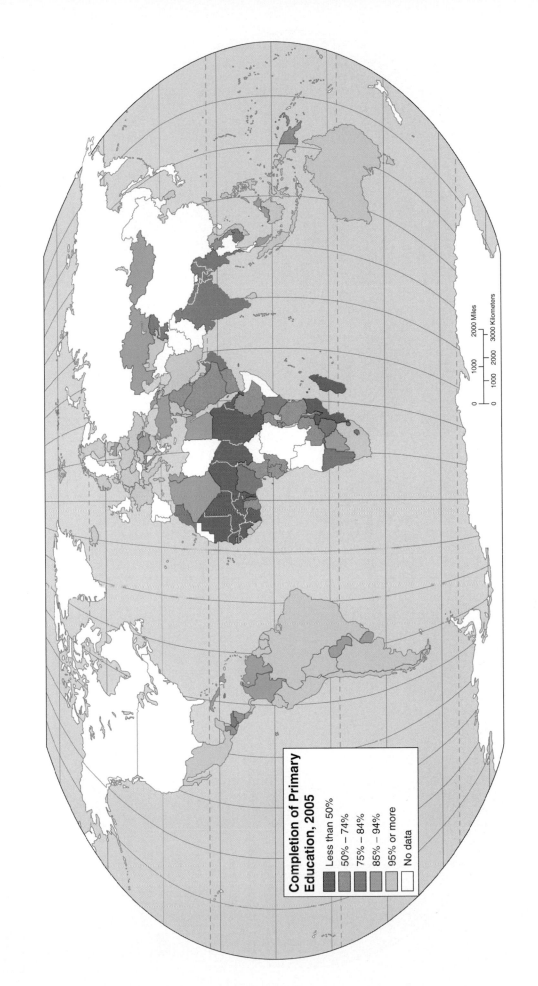

Completion of Primary Education, 2005

- Less than 50%
- 50% – 74%
- 75% – 84%
- 85% – 94%
- 95% or more
- No data

0   1000   2000 Miles
0   1000   2000   3000 Kilometers

Nearly one in five of the world's children of primary school age are not in school. Of this number, more than half are girls. The most critical area of the world in terms of primary school enrollment is sub-Saharan Africa, where 19 countries have primary school completion rates of 50 percent or less. In many of these countries, children are held out of school because of their importance in the agricultural workforce. But the global economy is changing to more knowledge-driven activities, and a lack of education will hurt those countries with low primary school enrollments the most. The need for flexible and skilled workforces, able to read and write, cannot be met unless that generation entering the workforce is educated—if only at minimal levels. Of all the measures necessary to establish sustainable economic development and to alleviate poverty, education is the most important.

Map 48 The Gender Gap: Inequalities in Education and Employment

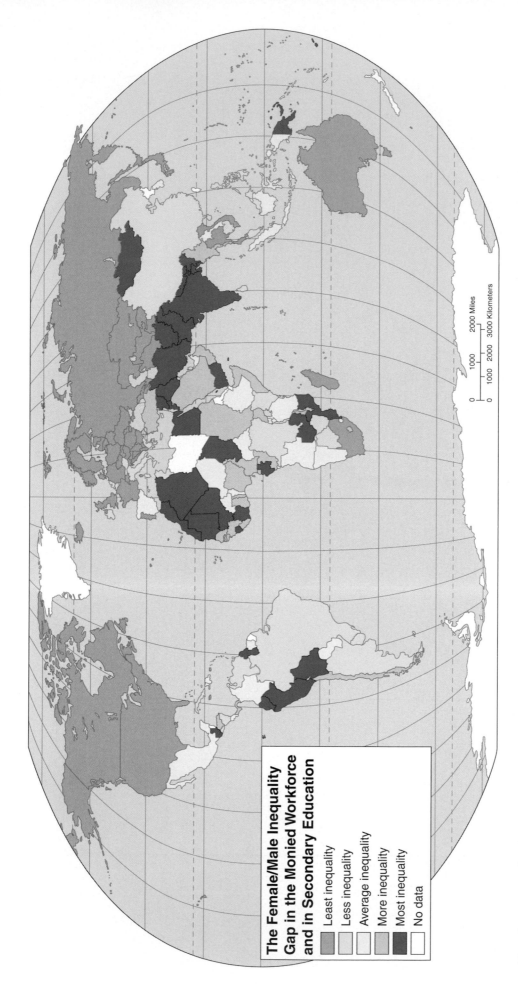

The Female/Male Inequality
Gap in the Monied Workforce
and in Secondary Education

Least inequality
Less inequality
Average inequality
More inequality
Most inequality
No data

0   1000   2000   3000 Kilometers
0   1000   2000 Miles

Although women in developed countries, particularly in North America and Europe, have made significant advances in socioeconomic status in recent years, in most of the world females suffer from significant inequality when compared with their male counterparts. Women have received the right to vote in most of the world's countries, but in over 90 percent of these countries that right has only been granted in the last 50 years. In most regions, literacy rates for women still fall far short of those for men; in Africa and Asia, for example, only about half as many women are literate as are men. Women marry con-

siderably younger than men and attend school for shorter periods of time. Inequalities in education and employment are perhaps the most telling indicators of the unequal status of women in most of the world. Lack of secondary education in comparison with men prevents women from entering the workforce with equally high-paying jobs. Even where women are employed in positions similar to those held by men, they still tend to receive less compensation. The gap between rich and poor involves not only a clear geographic differentiation, but a clear gender differentiation as well.

Map 49 Unemployment in the Labor Force

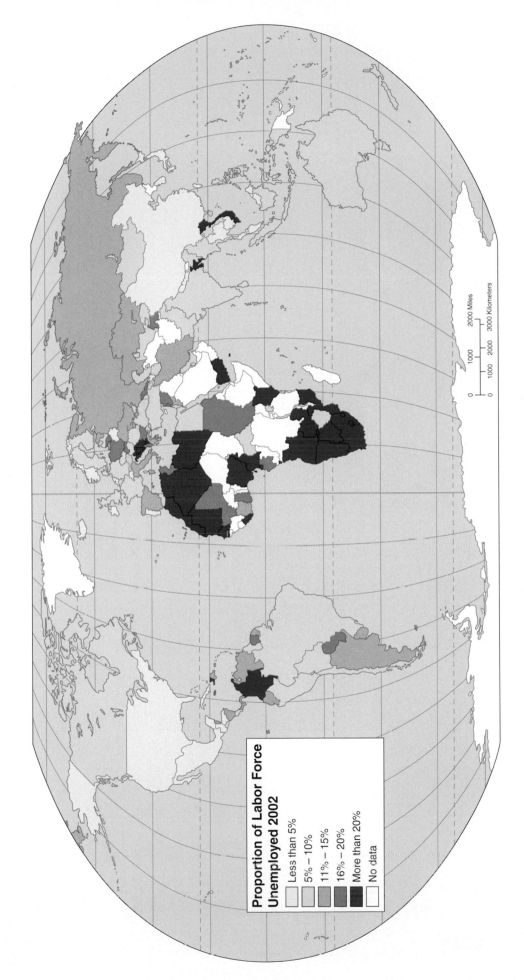

Proportion of Labor Force Unemployed 2002

- Less than 5%
- 5% — 10%
- 11% — 15%
- 16% — 20%
- More than 20%
- No data

0   1000   2000 Miles

0   1000   2000   3000 Kilometers

The percentage of a country's labor force that is classified as "unemployed" includes those without work but who are available for work and seeking employment. Countries may define the labor force in different ways, however. In many developing countries, for example, "employability" based on age may be more extensive than in more highly developed economies with stringent child labor laws. Generally, countries with higher percentages of their labor forces employed will be countries with higher levels of economic development. Where unemployment tends to be high, the out-migration of labor also tends to be high as workers unable to find employment at home cross international boundaries in search of work. Again, there tends to be a difference based on levels of economic development with the more developed countries experiencing inflows of labor while the reverse is true in the less developed world.

Map 50 Global Scourges: Major Infectious Diseases

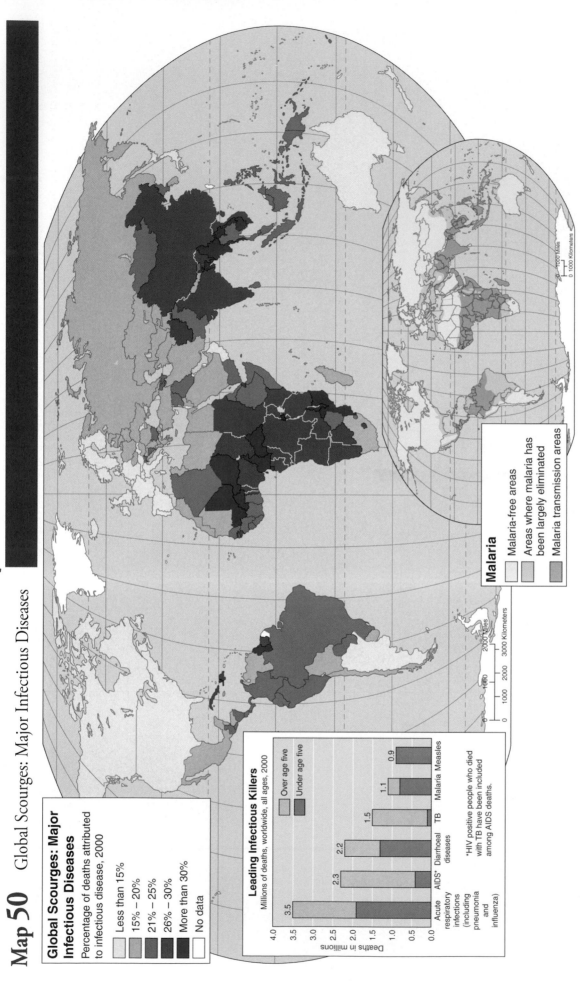

Global Scourges: Major Infectious Diseases

Percentage of deaths attributed to infectious disease, 2000

- Less than 15%
- 15% – 20%
- 21% – 25%
- 26% – 30%
- More than 30%
- No data

Malaria

- Malaria-free areas
- Areas where malaria has been largely eliminated
- Malaria transmission areas

Leading Infectious Killers
Millions of deaths, worldwide, all ages, 2000

- Over age five
- Under age five

	Deaths in millions
Acute respiratory infections (including pneumonia and influenza)	3.5
AIDS*	2.3
Diarrhoeal diseases	2.2
TB	1.5
Malaria	1.1
Measles	0.9

*HIV positive people who died with TB have been included among AIDS deaths.

Infectious diseases are the world's leading cause of premature death, and at least half of the world's population is, at any time, at risk of contracting an infectious disease. Although we often think of infectious diseases as being restricted to the tropical world (malaria, dengue fever), many if not most of them have attained global proportions. A major case in point is HIV/AIDS, which quite probably originated in Africa but has, over the last two decades, spread throughout the entire world. Major diseases of the nineteenth century, such as cholera and tuberculosis, are making a major comeback in many parts of the world, in spite of being preventable or treatable. Part of the problem with infectious diseases is that they tend to be associated with poverty (poor nutrition, poor sanitation, substandard housing, and so on) and, therefore, are seen as a problem of undeveloped countries, with the consequent lack of funding for prevention and treatment. Infectious diseases are also tending to increase because lifesaving drugs, such as antibiotics and others used in the fight against diseases, are losing their effectiveness as bacteria develop genetic resistance to them. The problem of global warming is also associated with a spread of infectious diseases as many disease vectors (certain species of mosquito, for example) are spreading into higher latitudes with increasingly warm temperatures and are spreading disease into areas where populations have no resistance to them. Infectious diseases have become something greater than simply a health issue of poor countries. They are now major social problems with potentially enormous consequences for the entire world.

Map 51 Adult Incidence of HIV/AIDS, 2005

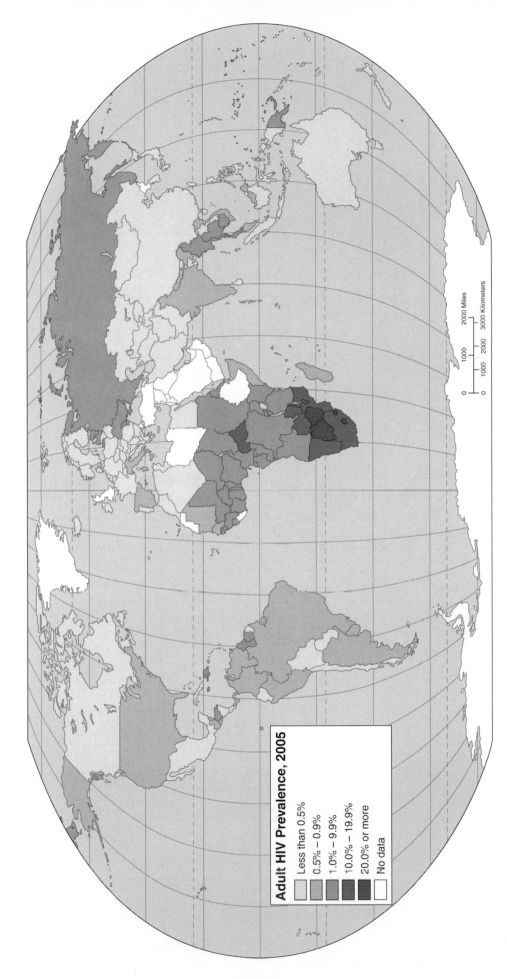

Adult HIV Prevalence, 2005

- Less than 0.5%
- 0.5% – 0.9%
- 1.0% – 9.9%
- 10.0% – 19.9%
- 20.0% or more
- No data

0 1000 2000 Miles
0 1000 2000 3000 Kilometers

Of all the infectious diseases, the one that poses the greatest risks to public health worldwide is human immune deficiency which, if untreated, progresses to the deadly autoimmune deficiency or AIDS. The highest incidence of AIDS among adult populations occurs in sub-Saharan Africa, where public health systems are too poorly funded and developed to treat HIV cases, and the medications needed to preserve health and reasonable longevity are too expensive. Since the rate of adult cases is high, large numbers of children are also infected, having been born HIV-positive. Indeed, among all the world's children living with HIV, approximately 90 percent live in sub-Saharan Africa. Other countries in the developing world also are high on the scale of HIV/AIDS incidence and the suspicion is that the official figures could go even higher if accurately reported. China, for example, may have rates that are 3 to 4 times greater than the official figures. Worldwide, HIV/AIDS has a devastating impact on family structures (many children are orphaned by both parents dying of AIDS) and on the economic growth of the developing countries.

Map 52   Undernourished Populations

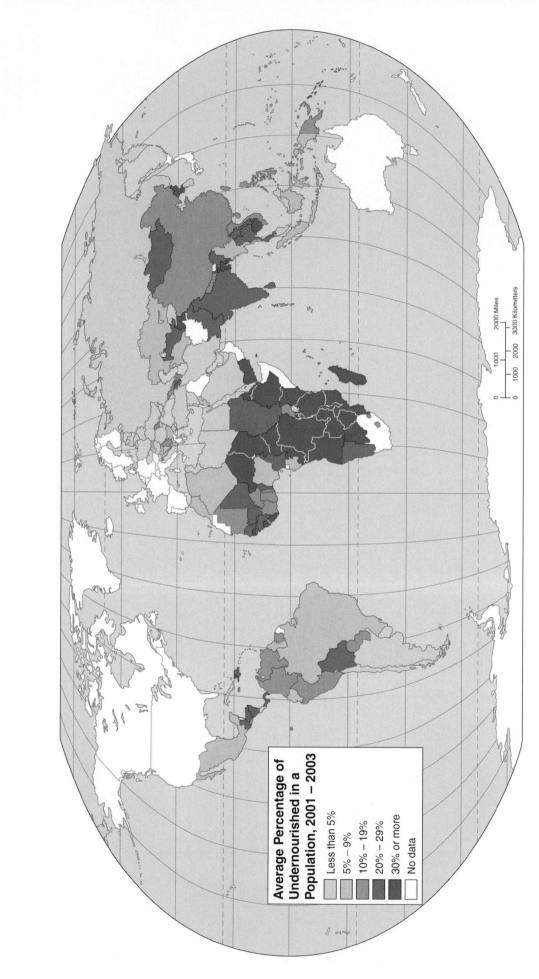

Average Percentage of Undernourished in a Population, 2001 – 2003

- Less than 5%
- 5% – 9%
- 10% – 19%
- 20% – 29%
- 30% or more
- No data

A number of international organizations, including the Food and Agriculture Organization (FAO) of the UN and the World Bank, have established a "Millenium Development Goal" of halving global hunger by 2015. Thus far, only the Latin America and Caribbean region (with several notable exceptions such as Haiti and the Dominican Republic) have succeeded in reducing hunger sufficiently to reach the goals set by the FAO. Most of the world's hungry are the rural poor—living in areas where agricultural overcrowding and the use of land for cash crops rather than food produces hunger where logic suggests there should be relative abundance. Moreover, the largest percentage of undernourished people live in areas where environmental degradation and climate change are taking the greatest toll on the ability of the land to support a human population. While people rarely starve to death, undernourishment opens up populations to a large number of wasting diseases that accompany inadequate diets. It is these wasting diseases that debilitate and, eventually, kill.

Map **53**   The World's Poorest

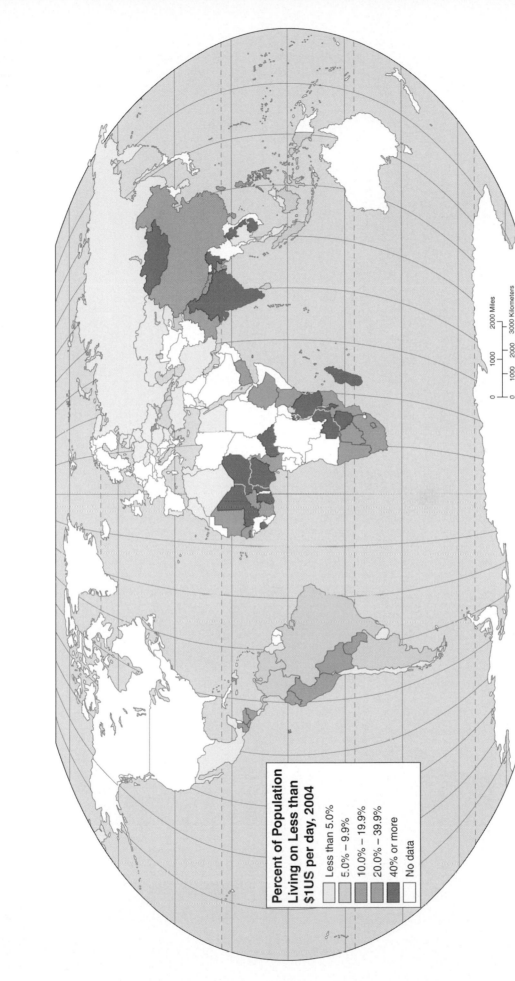

Percent of Population Living on Less than $1US per day, 2004

- Less than 5.0%
- 5.0% – 9.9%
- 10.0% – 19.9%
- 20.0% – 39.9%
- 40% or more
- No data

0   1000   2000   3000 Kilometers

0   1000   2000 Miles

Extreme poverty, represented by annual per capita incomes of approximately $300US, is found in rural areas (particularly those of subsistence rather than commercial agriculture) and in the urban slums of the developing world where rural poor have fled the countryside for the city and the hope for jobs and a better life. The greatest number of countries with high percentages of extremely poor people is in sub-Saharan Africa; the greatest populations of the extremely poor are in South Asia where nearly half a bil-

lion people live under conditions of the most severe poverty. Few developing countries are on track to halve poverty by the UN and World Bank target date of 2015. Poverty begets poverty as the poor have the lowest levels of access to education, transportation, job training, health facilities, and other "amenities" of the better well-off. As a consequence, the children of the poorest are more than likely to end up in the same classification as their parents.

-79-

Map 54 Inequality of Income and Consumption

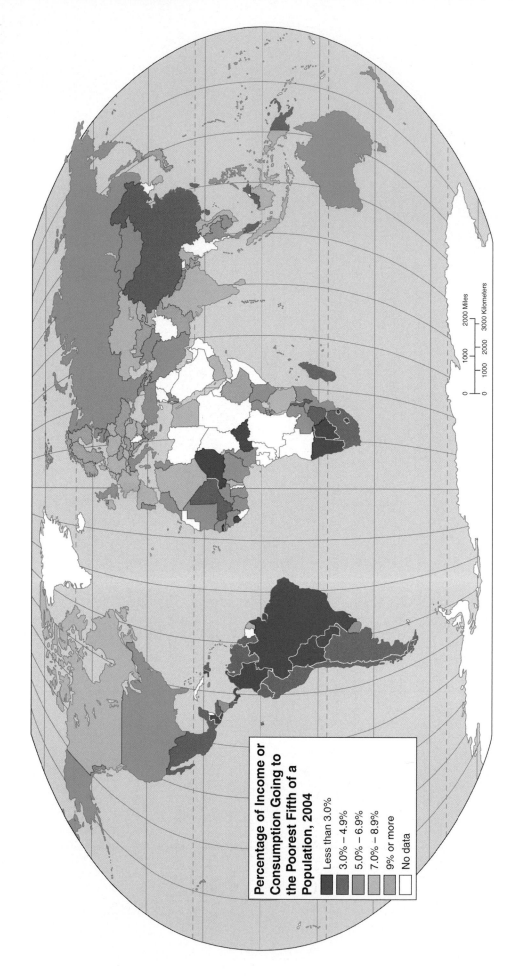

Percentage of Income or Consumption Going to the Poorest Fifth of a Population, 2004

- Less than 3.0%
- 3.0% – 4.9%
- 5.0% – 6.9%
- 7.0% – 8.9%
- 9% or more
- No data

While it is more than arguably true that the poor get poorer and the rich get richer (and that, by the way, is just as true in some highly developed areas such as the United States and the United Kingdom as it is in the lesser-developed regions), what is often ignored is the breadth of the inequality in distribution of incomes or in the levels of consumption of basic goods. In many of the world's developing countries—despite the rapid increases in economic growth of China and India over the last two decades—the poorest 20% of the population receives less than 7% of the income or consumption share. Although school participation rates have risen worldwide, in countries with the greatest inequalities of income, access to education remains low. If translated into ratios, the inequality ratio of many of the world's countries (including, as noted above, some in the highly developed world) is 8 or higher, meaning that the top 20% of the population spends and consumes at least 8 times as much per person as the bottom 20% of the population.

Map 55 Human Rights: Political Rights and Civil Liberties

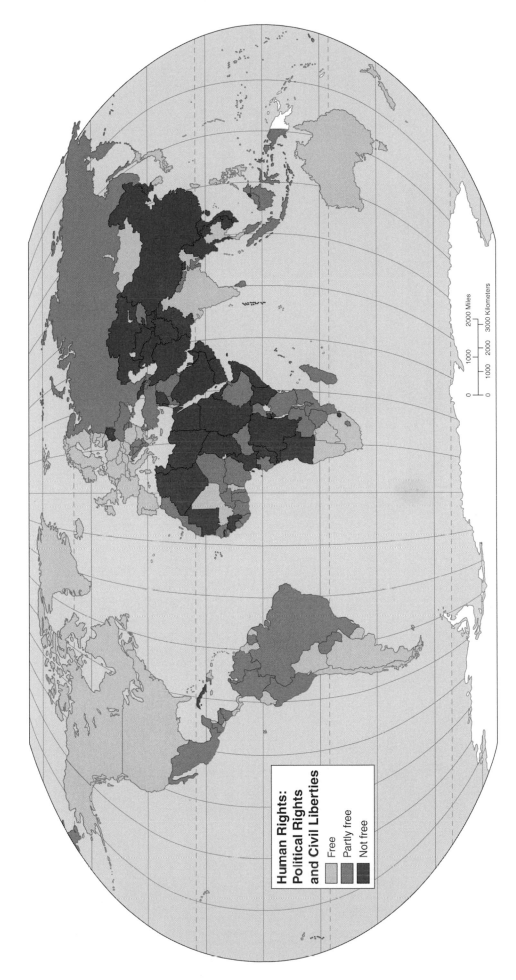

Human Rights: Political Rights and Civil Liberties

- Free
- Partly free
- Not free

Increasing contact among the world's peoples has brought to everyone more awareness of the variations in human rights from place to place. Democratic forms of government have spread to more and more countries, and public policy insists on attention to human rights. "Human rights" comprise both political rights and civil liberties. Political rights are related to democracy, which, at a minimum, involves rights of the people to choose their own authoritative leaders and to endow those chosen leaders with real power. Elections must be open and fair, and ballots must be counted honestly. Candidates may represent political parties, or families, clans, or personalities. Civil liberties are freedoms, including freedom of expression and belief, freedom of assembly and organization, rule of law (including an independent judiciary), and personal autonomy and economic rights (including privacy). Every year, Freedom House ranks all countries of the world in these two sets of rights, using a checklist of questions about real experience, not just legislation. The compilation of these scores produces the three categories shown on this map. Obviously, this process is extremely generalized, but the two sets of rights do tend to go together: countries with strong political rights also have civil liberties.

1000 2000 Miles

1000 2000 3000 Kilometers

Map 56 Women's Rights

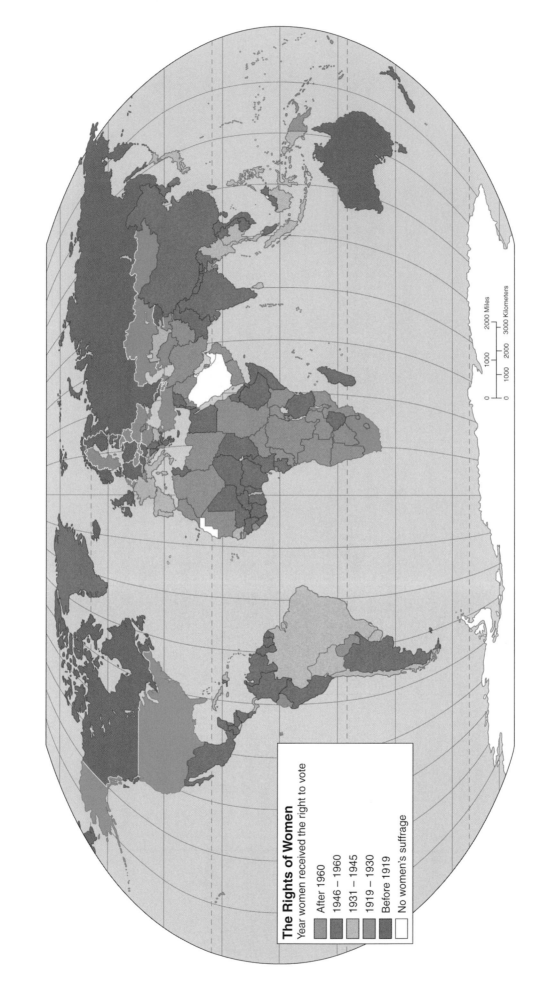

The Rights of Women
Year women received the right to vote

- After 1960
- 1946 – 1960
- 1931 – 1945
- 1919 – 1930
- Before 1919
- No women's suffrage

0   1000   2000 Miles
0   1000   2000   3000 Kilometers

The "rights" referred to in this map refer primarily to the right to vote. But where women have the right to vote in free elections, the other fundamental rights tend to become available as well: the right to own property, the right to an education, the right to leave a domestic alliance without fear of retribution, or the right to be treated as a human being rather than as property. But the time lag between women receiving the right to vote and their attainment of other fundamental human rights can be significant. On the map, the most recent countries to grant suffrage to women are in Africa and Southwest Asia. In these regions, women still do not have access to many of the basic rights of what we would consider to be a civilized life. And, of course, there are still areas where women cannot vote: Kuwait, for example. Neither men nor women are allowed to vote in Brunei, Saudi Arabia, United Arab Emirates, or Western Sahara.

Map 57 Capital Punishment

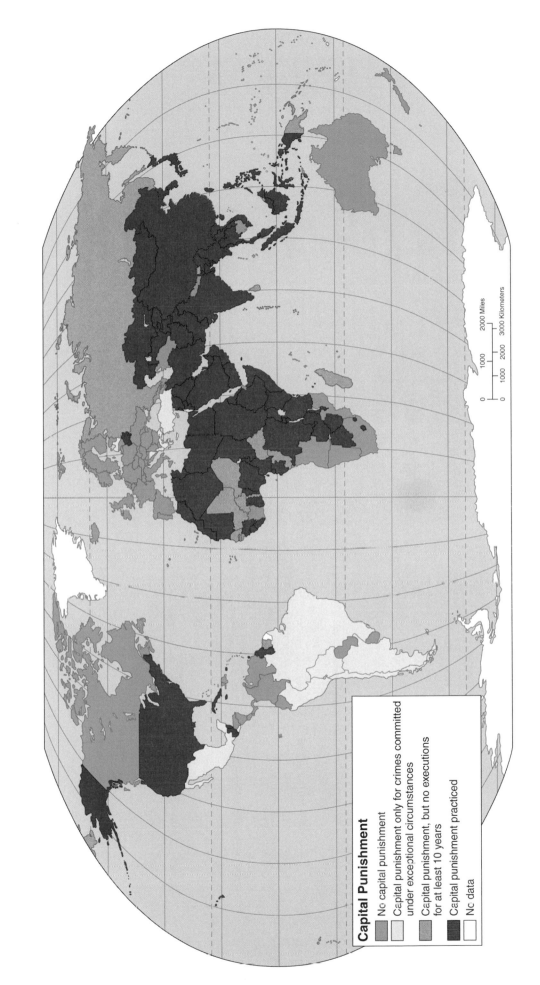

Capital Punishment

- No capital punishment
- Capital punishment only for crimes committed under exceptional circumstances
- Capital punishment, but no executions for at least 10 years
- Capital punishment practiced
- No data

0   1000   2000 Miles

0   1000   2000   3000 Kilometers

The most basic human right is life itself. More than half the countries of the world have abolished capital punishment by law or in practice. In some of these countries, capital punishment remains on the books, but no one has been executed in so long that in practice, capital punishment can be considered abolished. A few countries retain capital punishment only for crimes committed in extraordinary circumstances, such as military law. About three countries per year have abolished capital punishment in the last decade. Some states in the United States retain capital punishment; in others it has been abolished.

-83-

Map 58 The Index of Human Development

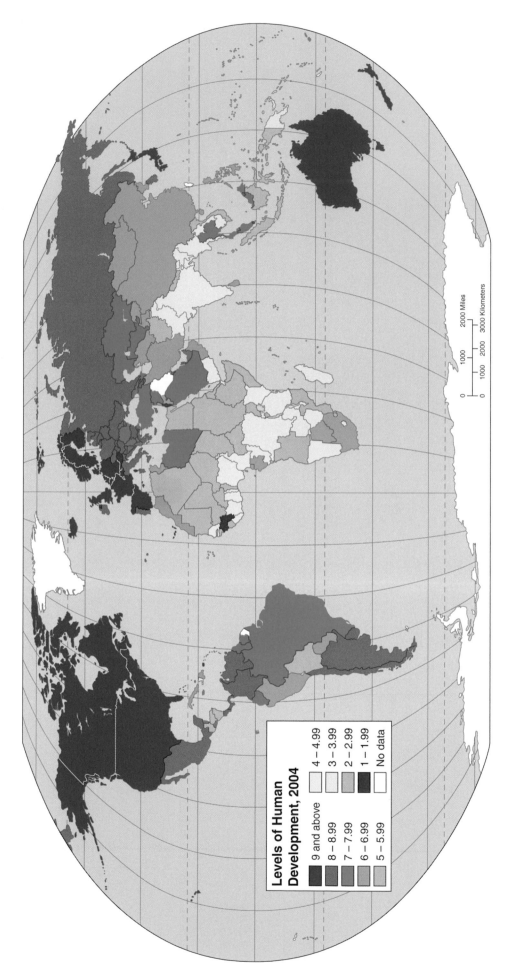

Levels of Human Development, 2004

- 9 and above
- 8 – 8.99
- 7 – 7.99
- 6 – 6.99
- 5 – 5.99
- 4 – 4.99
- 3 – 3.99
- 2 – 2.99
- 1 – 1.99
- No data

0   1000   2000 Miles
0   1000   2000   3000 Kilometers

The development index upon which this map is based takes into account a wide variety of demographic, health, and educational data, including population growth, per capita gross domestic income, longevity, literacy, and years of schooling. The map reveals significant improvement in the quality of life in Middle and South America, although it is questionable whether the gains made in those regions can be maintained in the face of the dramatic population increases expected over the next 30 years. More clearly than anything else, the map illustrates the near-desperate situation in Africa and South Asia. In those regions, the unparalleled growth in population threatens to overwhelm all efforts to improve the quality of life. In Africa, for example, the population is increasing by 20 million persons per year. With nearly 45 percent of the continent's population aged 15 years or younger, this growth rate will accelerate as the women reach childbearing age. Africa, along with South Asia, faces the very difficult challenge of providing basic access to health care, education, and jobs for a rapidly increasing population. The map also illustrates the striking difference in quality of life between those who inhabit the world's equatorial and tropical regions and those fortunate enough to live in the temperate zones, where the quality of life is significantly higher.

Map 59   Demographic Stress: The Youth Bulge

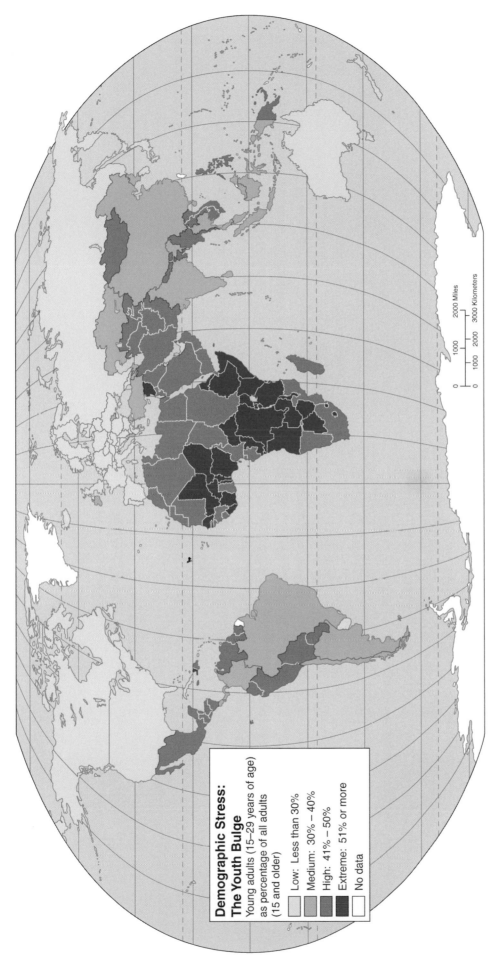

**Demographic Stress:
The Youth Bulge**

Young adults (15–29 years of age)
as percentage of all adults
(15 and older)

- Low: Less than 30%
- Medium: 30% – 40%
- High: 41% – 50%
- Extreme: 51% or more
- No data

One of the greatest stresses of the demographic transition occurs when the death rate drops as the result of better public health and sanitation and the birth rate remains high for the same reasons it has always been high in traditional, agricultural societies: (1) the need for enough children to supply labor, which is one of the few ways to increase agricultural production in a nonmechanized agricultural system, and (2) the need for enough children to offset high infant and child mortality rates so that some children will survive to take care of parents in their old age. With declining death rates and steady birth rates, population growth skyrockets—particularly among the youngest cohorts of a population (between the ages of birth and 15). While this is, on the one hand, a demographic benefit since it increases the size of the labor force in the next generation and thereby helps to accelerate economic growth, it also means more people of child-bearing age in the next generation and, hence, greater numbers of births, which continue to swell the population in the youngest, most vulnerable, and most dependent portion of the population. The literature on population and conflict suggests that the larger the percentage of a population below the age of 25, the greater the chance for political violence and warfare. The suicide bombers of the modern Middle East are not oldsters.

-85-

Map 60 Demographic Stress: Rapid Urban Growth

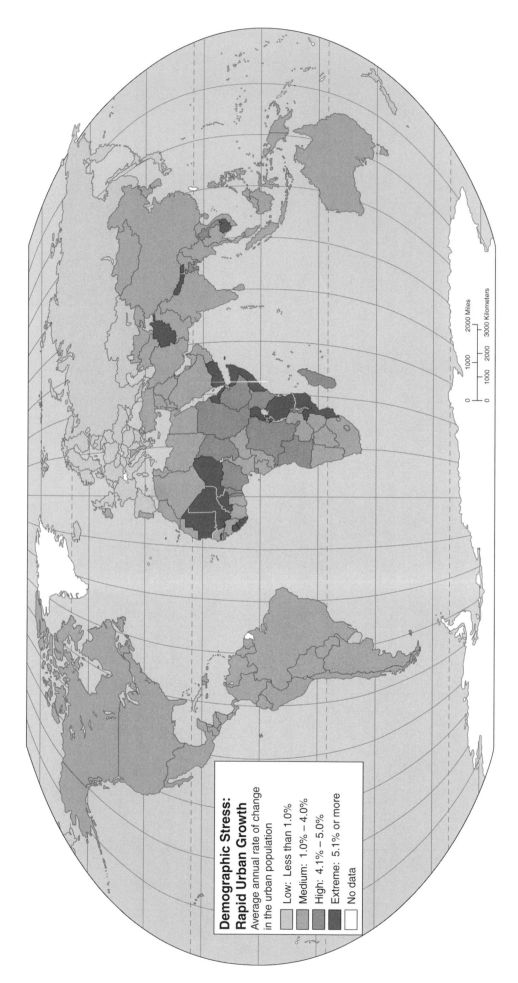

Demographic Stress: Rapid Urban Growth

Average annual rate of change in the urban population

- Low: Less than 1.0%
- Medium: 1.0% – 4.0%
- High: 4.1% – 5.0%
- Extreme: 5.1% or more
- No data

The trend toward urbanization—an increasing percentage of a country's population living in a city—is normally a healthy, modern trend. But in many of the world's developing countries, increasing urbanization is the consequence of high physiologic population densities (too many people for the available agricultural land) and the flight of poorly educated, untrained rural poor to the cities where they hope (often in vain) to find employment. High urbanization exists in many of the world's poorest countries where the urban poor live in conditions that make the worst living conditions in the inner cities of developed countries look positively luxurious. In the urban slums of South America, Africa, and South Asia, millions of people live in temporary housing of cardboard and flattened aluminum cans, with no public services such as water, sewage, or electricity. In Africa, where only 40% of the population is urbanized (in comparison with more than 90% in North America and Europe), the population of urban poor is greater than the total urban population of the United States and the European Union. This represents an increasingly destabilizing element of modern urban societies.

-86-

Map **61**   Demographic Stress: Competition for Cropland

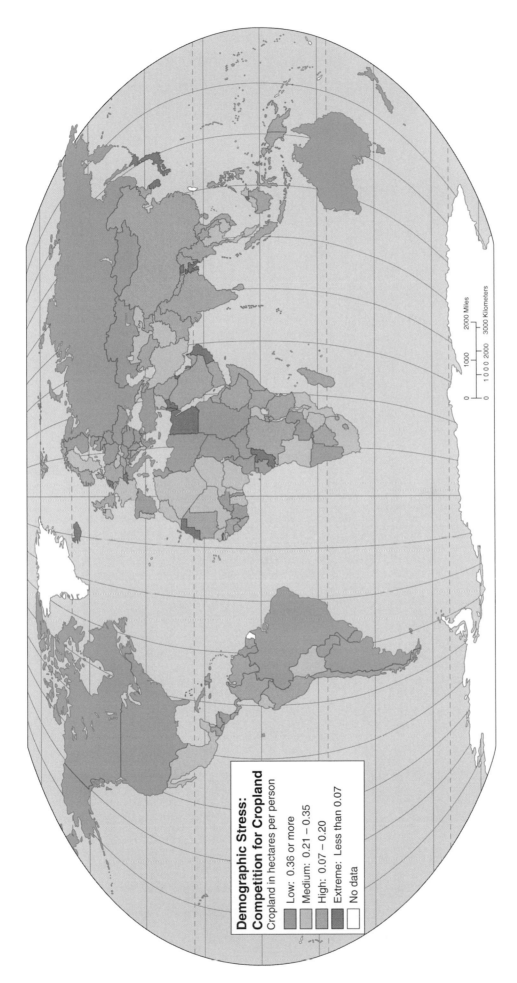

Demographic Stress: Competition for Cropland
Cropland in hectares per person

- Low: 0.36 or more
- Medium: 0.21 – 0.35
- High: 0.07 – 0.20
- Extreme: Less than 0.07
- No data

Many of the world's countries have reached the point where available acres or hectares in cropland are less than the numbers of people wishing to occupy them. For developed countries, who pay for agricultural imports with industrial exports, this is not an alarming trend, and therefore countries like Germany or Italy (where the ratio between cropland and farmers is very low) have little to worry about. But in countries in South America, Africa, and South and East Asia, the trend toward more farmers and less available land is an alarming trend. In these developing regions, farmers depend on their crops for a relatively meager subsistence diet and—if they are lucky—a few bushels of rice or corn to take to the local market to sell or exchange for the small surpluses of other farmers. Despite the broad global trends toward urbanization and more productive agriculture (and this generally means mechanized agriculture), farm occupation and subsistence cropping remain mainstays of the economy in Africa south of the Sahara, in much of western South America, and in much of South and East Asia. Here, the increasingly small margin between the numbers of farmers and the amount of available farmland can lead to conflict among tribal communities or even among members of a single family.

-87-

Map **62**   Demographic Stress: Competition for Fresh Water

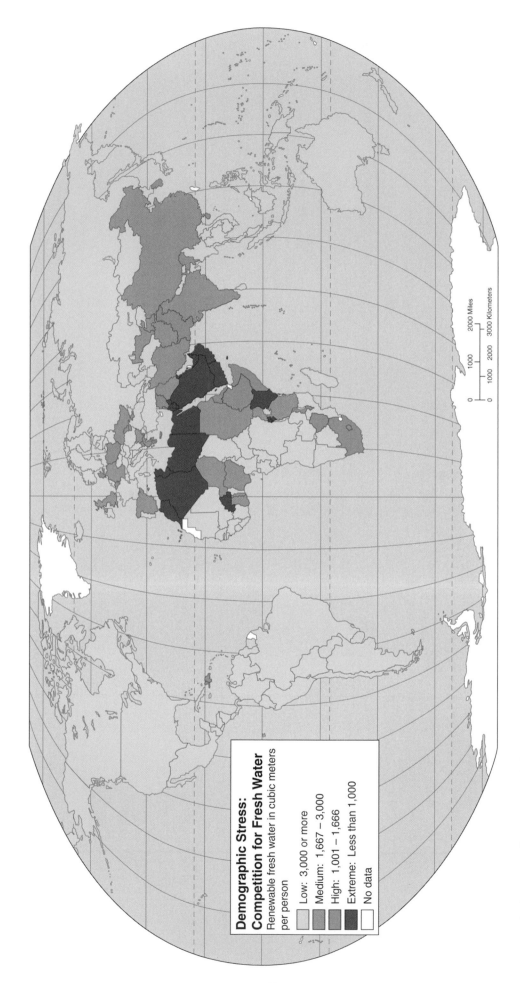

Demographic Stress:
Competition for Fresh Water
Renewable fresh water in cubic meters
per person

Low: 3,000 or more

Medium: 1,667 – 3,000

High: 1,001 – 1,666

Extreme: Less than 1,000

No data

As rates of urbanization have increased, the competition between city dwellers and farmers for water has also increased. And as the population of farmers relative to the available surface or ground water supply has accelerated, so rural competition for access to fresh water for irrigation has increased. Obviously, this trend is most obvious in the world's drier regions. On this map, the greatest stress factors relating to water availability are in North and East Africa, the Middle East, and Central and East Asia. The current conflict between Israelis and Palestinians in the West Bank goes far beyond religion or politics: Some is the result of the more affluent Israeli farmers being able to drill wells to tap ground water, which lowers the water table and causes previously accessible surface wells in Palestinian villages to go dry. And part of the horrific Hutu-Tutsi civil war in Rwanda and the taking of European farmlands by the current government of Zimbabwe have more to do with the need for access to fresh water than to racial or ethnic differences. Given that fresh water is, for all practical purposes, a nonrenewable resource, more conflicts over access to water are going to erupt in the future.

Map 63 Demographic Stress: Death in the Prime of Life

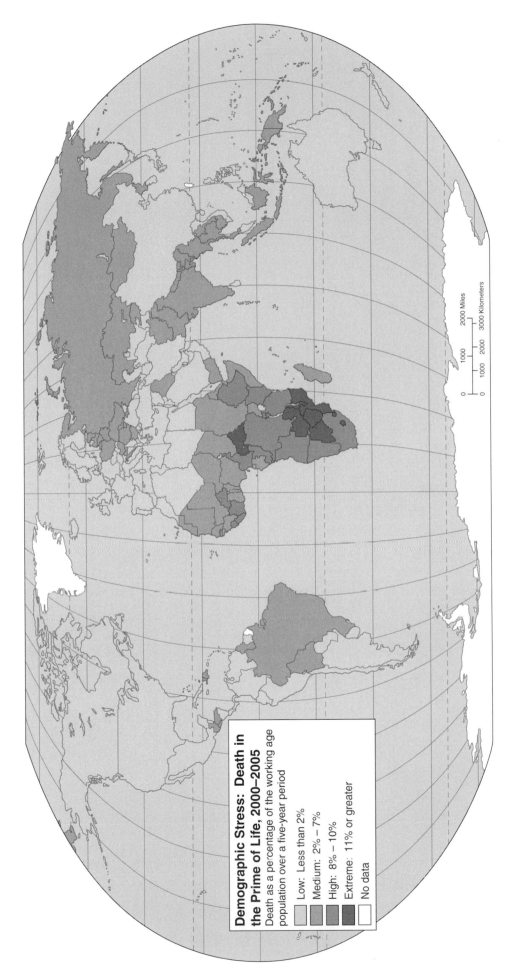

Demographic Stress: Death in the Prime of Life, 2000–2005

Death as a percentage of the working age population over a five-year period

- Low: Less than 2%
- Medium: 2% – 7%
- High: 8% – 10%
- Extreme: 11% or greater
- No data

Most infectious diseases lay waste to the oldest and the youngest sectors of a population, leaving the healthier working-age population able to reproduce itself and to continue to grow an economy. Modern infectious diseases—most particularly HIV/AIDS—impact not the youngest or oldest but those in the prime of life, in their most productive and reproductive years. Indeed, medical data from the United Nations show that 90 percent of HIV/AIDS-related deaths occur in people of working age. Some of the most severely impacted countries in southern Africa lose between 10 and 20 percent of their working age population every 5 years. Rates in the developed world are from 0.10 to 0.02 percent

of this level. A prominent fact of life in much of the developing world—particularly in sub-Saharan Africa—is the long-distance labor migration. In this pattern, a man leaves his wife and family for extended periods of time (10 or more months of the year) to work in mines, on docks, or as sailors. These men are highly vulnerable to the acquisition of HIV, which is then transmitted to wives when the husband returns home on his annual visit. Thus both the male and the female portion of the working-age population are impacted by early mortality from AIDS. None of this bodes well for economic development in those affected areas of the world.

Map 64 Demographic Stress: Interactions of Demographic Stress

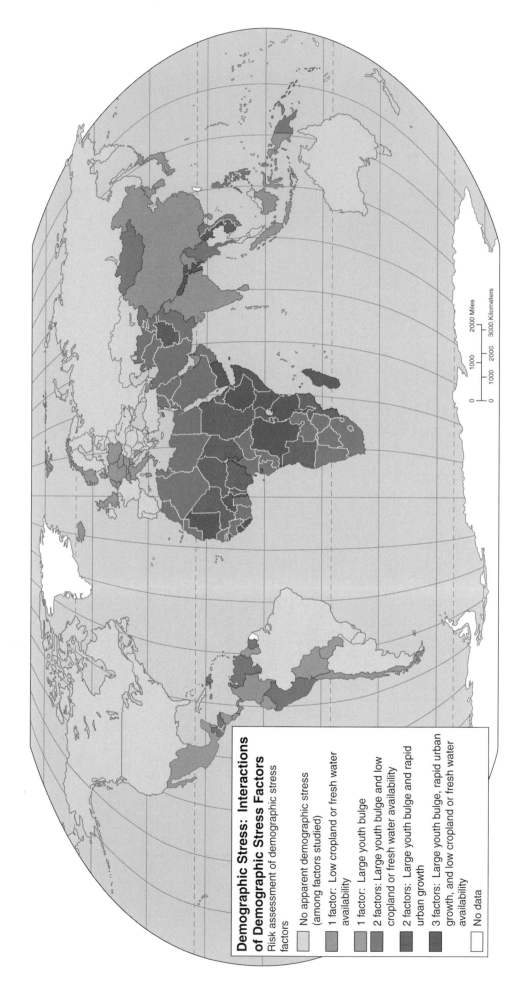

Demographic Stress: Interactions of Demographic Stress Factors

Risk assessment of demographic stress factors

- No apparent demographic stress (among factors studied)
- 1 factor: Low cropland or fresh water availability
- 1 factor: Large youth bulge
- 2 factors: Large youth bulge and low cropland or fresh water availability
- 2 factors: Large youth bulge and rapid urban growth
- 3 factors: Large youth bulge, rapid urban growth, and low cropland or fresh water availability
- No data

We have persisted in viewing internal and international conflicts as conflicts produced by religious differences, the acceptance or rejection of "freedom" or "democracy," or even, as argued by a prominent historian, a "Clash of Civilizations." While religious, political, or historical differences cannot be ignored in interpreting the causes of conflict, neither can simple demographic stresses produced by too many new urban dwellers without jobs or hopes of jobs, by too many farmers and too little farmland, by too many deaths among people who should be in the most productive portions of their lives. A massive study by Population Action International, from which these last half-dozen or so maps have been drawn, shows quite clearly that countries suffering from multiple demographic risk factors are, were, and will be much more prone to civil conflict than countries with only one or two demographic risk factors. A look at this map provides a predictor of future civil unrest, violence, and even civil war.

-90-

Map 65 Demographic Stress: A Decade of Risk of Civil Conflict, 2005–2015

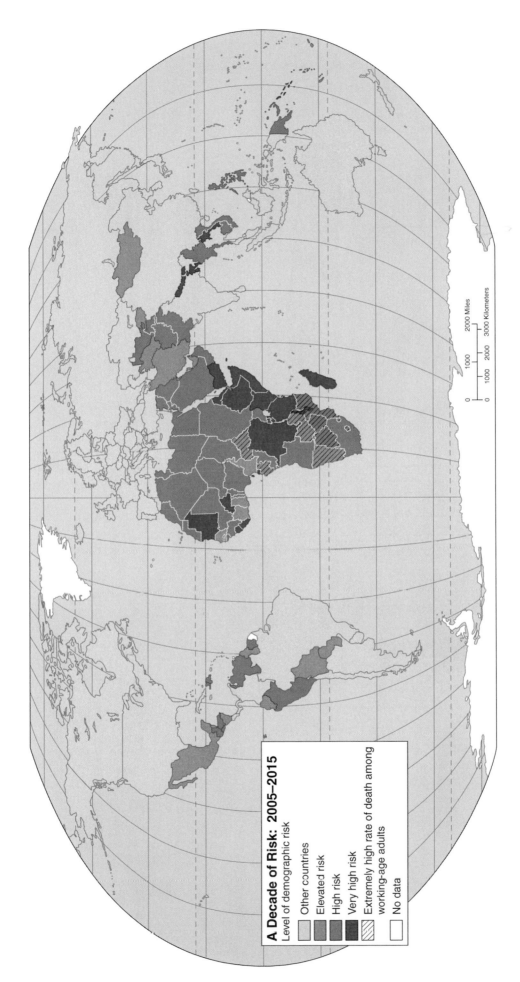

A Decade of Risk: 2005–2015
Level of demographic risk

- Other countries
- Elevated risk
- High risk
- Very high risk
- Extremely high rate of death among working-age adults
- No data

The point has been in maps 59–64 that demographic stresses enhance the risk of civil conflict, as opposed to international conflict. This map uses three demographic factors—percentage of a country's populations between the ages of 15 and 29, rate of urban population growth, and per capita availability of cropland and fresh water—to assess the risk of domestic violence and civil conflict. It needs to be noted that the data are available on a national level and that geographically large countries such as Brazil, Russia, China, or India may well have areas of demographic stress within them that are masked by the portrayal of something other than subnational data. Nevertheless, the implications of the map are striking: Those pans of the world where civil conflict is in the highest risk category are almost all in Africa and Southwest Asia. We have already seen evidences of such civil conflict: the Hutu-Tutsi civil war of Rwanda and the Shiite-Sunni chaos of Iraq. We describe those as "tribal" or "sectarian" civil conflicts. But how much of the actual conflict is the result of a combination of demographic stresses?

Unit IV

The Global Economy

Map **66**   Membership in the World Trade Organization

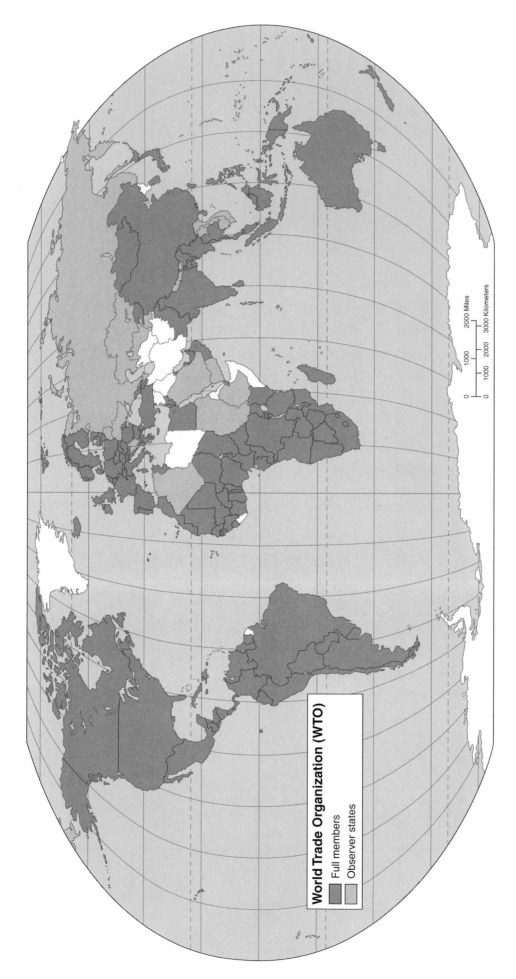

World Trade Organization (WTO)

■ Full members
□ Observer states

0   1000   2000 Miles
0   1000   2000   3000 Kilometers

After World War II, the General Agreement on Tariffs and Trade (GATT) sponsored several rounds of negotiations, especially related to lower tariffs but also considering issues such as dumping and other nontariff questions. The last round of negotiations under GATT took place in Uruguay in 1986–1994 and set the stage for the World Trade Organization (WTO), which was formally established in 1995. Today the WTO has 146 members with more than 30 "observer" governments. With the exception of the Holy See (Vatican), observer governments are expected to begin negotiations for full membership within five years of becoming observers. The objective of the WTO is to help international trade flow smoothly and fairly and to assure more stable and secure supplies of goods to consumers. To this end, it administers trade agreements, acts as a forum for trade negotiations, settles trade disputes, reviews national trade policies, assists developing countries through technical assistance and training programs, and cooperates with other international organizations. Increased globalization of the world's economy makes the administrative role of the WTO of increasing importance in the twenty-first century. The headquarters of the WTO is in Geneva, Switzerland.

Map 67 Regional Trade Organizations

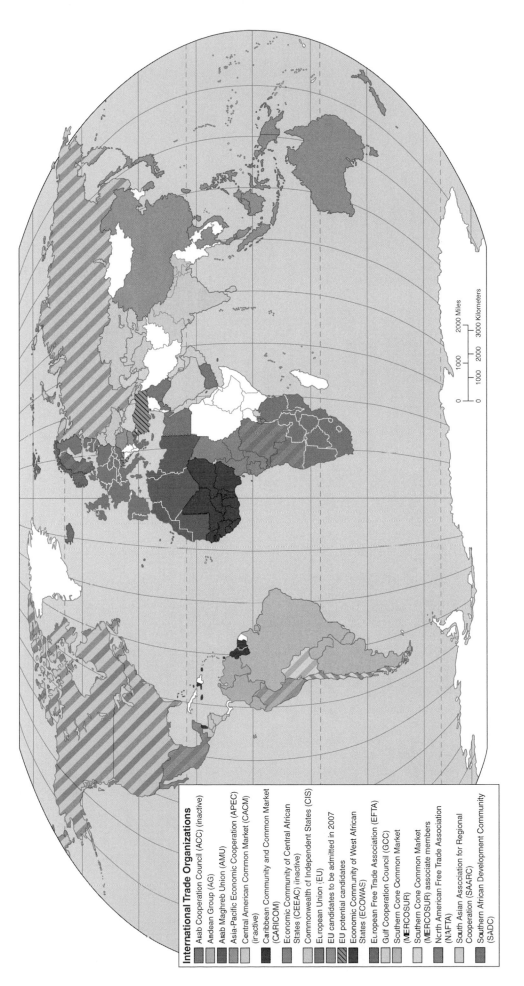

International Trade Organizations
- Arab Cooperation Council (ACC) (inactive)
- Andean Group (AG)
- Arab Maghreb Union (AMU)
- Asia-Pacific Economic Cooperation (APEC)
- Central American Common Market (CACM) (inactive)
- Caribbean Community and Common Market (CARICOM)
- Economic Community of Central African States (CEEAC) (inactive)
- Commonwealth of Independent States (CIS)
- European Union (EU)
- EU candidates to be admitted in 2007
- EU potential candidates
- Economic Community of West African States (ECOWAS)
- European Free Trade Association (EFTA)
- Gulf Cooperation Council (GCC)
- Southern Cone Common Market (MERCOSUR)
- Southern Cone Common Market (MERCOSUR) associate members
- North American Free Trade Association (NAFTA)
- South Asian Association for Regional Cooperation (SAARC)
- Southern African Development Community (SADC)

Scale bar:
0 — 1000 — 2000 Miles
0 — 1000 — 2000 — 3000 Kilometers

One of the most pervasive influences in the global economy over the last half century has been the rapid rise of international trade organizations. Pioneered by the European Economic Community, founded in part to assist in rebuilding the European economy after World War II, these organizations have become major players in global movements of goods, services, and labor. Some have integrated to form financial and political unions, such as the European Community, which has grown into the European Union. Others, like the Commonwealth of Independent States, are attempts to hold on to the remnants of better economic times. Still others, like the Asia-Pacific Economic Cooperation, are infant organizations that incorporate vastly different regions, states, and even economic systems, and are attempts to anticipate the direction of future economic growth. The role of international trade organizations is likely to grow greater in the twenty-first century. Witness the emergence of the North American Free Trade Agreement (NAFTA) that has restructured many segments of the Canadian, American, and Mexican economies (particularly in Mexico) and the probability of the adoption of the Central American Free Trade Agreement (CAFTA) that would link more closely the economies of the United States, El Salvador, Nicaragua, Guatemala, Honduras, Costa Rica, and, possibly, The Dominican Republic.

Map 68 Gross National Income Per Capita

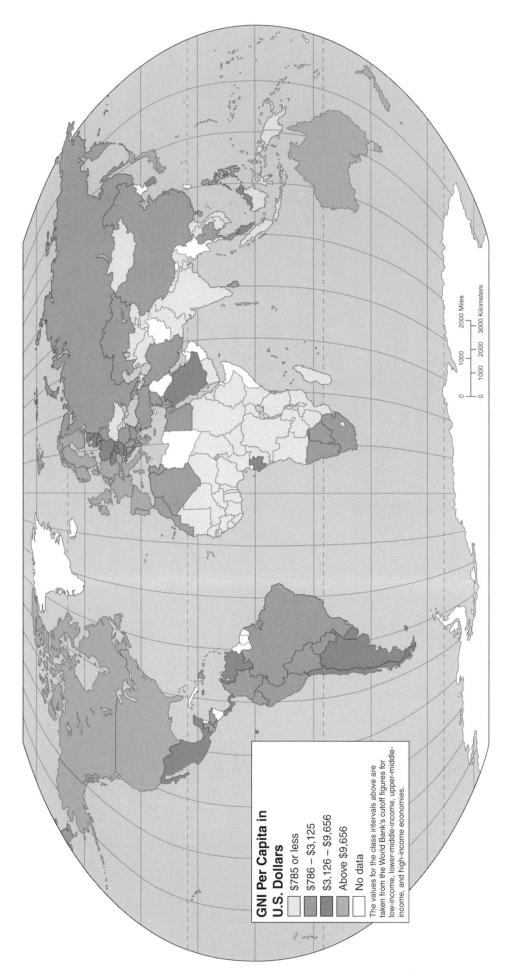

GNI Per Capita in U.S. Dollars

- $785 or less
- $786 – $3,125
- $3,126 – $9,656
- Above $9,656
- No data

The values for the class intervals above are taken from the World Bank's cutoff figures for low-income, lower-middle-income, upper-middle-income, and high-income economies.

0   1000   2000 Miles
0   1000 2000 3000 Kilometers

Gross national income (GNI) in either absolute or per capita form should be used cautiously as a yardstick of economic strength because it does not measure the distribution of wealth among a population. There are countries (most notably, the oil-rich countries of the Middle East) where per capita GNI is high but where the bulk of the wealth is concentrated in the hands of a few individuals, leaving the remainder in poverty. Even within countries in which wealth is more evenly distributed (such as those in North America or Western Europe), there is a tendency for dollars or pounds sterling or euros to concentrate in the bank accounts of a relatively small percentage of the population. Yet the maldistribution of wealth tends to be greatest in the less developed countries, where the per capita GNI is far lower than in North America and Western Europe, and poverty is widespread. In fact, a map of GNI per capita offers a reasonably good picture of comparative economic well-being. It should be noted that a low per capita GNI does not automatically condemn a country to low levels of basic human needs and services. There are a few countries, such as Costa Rica and Sri Lanka, that have relatively low per capita GNI figures but rank comparatively high in other measures of human well-being, such as average life expectancy, access to medical care, and literacy.

-96-

Map 69 Economic Growth: Change in GDP Per Capita, 2000–2005

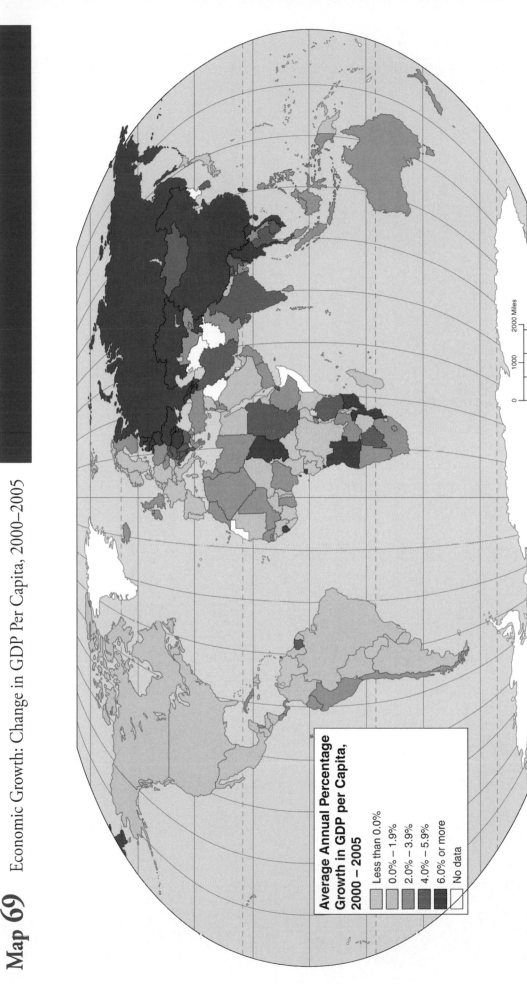

Average Annual Percentage Growth in GDP per Capita, 2000–2005

- Less than 0.0%
- 0.0% – 1.9%
- 2.0% – 3.9%
- 4.0% – 5.9%
- 6.0% or more
- No data

Gross domestic product or GDP is gross national income (GNI) less receipts of primary income from foreign sources. While the calculations of GDP growth per capita are complex, the growth rate is considered by the World Bank and international economists to be a particularly good measure of economic growth. One of the worldwide tendencies measured by GDP growth per capita is for continued economic development in Africa, and in South, Southeast, and East Asia where GDP grew at rates higher than the growth rates of "richer" countries in Europe and North and South America. This should not necessarily be viewed as a case of the poor catching up with the rich; in fact, it shows the huge impact that even relatively small production increases will have in countries with small GNIs and GDPs. Nevertheless, in spite of the continuing low economic growth through most of sub-Saharan Africa, the GDP growth rate of some of the world's poorer countries is an encouraging trend.

Map 70 Relative Wealth of Nations: Purchasing Power Parity

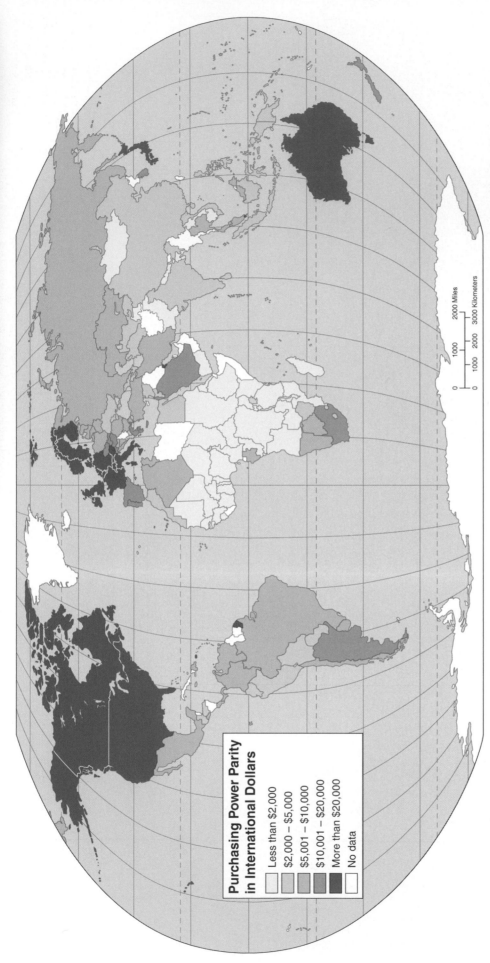

Purchasing Power Parity in International Dollars

- Less than $2,000
- $2,000 – $5,000
- $5,001 – $10,000
- $10,001 – $20,000
- More than $20,000
- No data

Of all the economic measures that separate the "haves" from the "have-nots," perhaps per capita purchasing power parity (PPP) is the most meaningful. While per capita figures can mask significant uneven distributions within a country, they are generally useful for demonstrating important differences between countries. Per capita GNP and GDP (gross domestic product) figures, and even per capita income, have the limitation of seldom reflecting the true purchasing power of a country's currency at home. In order to get around this limitation, international economists seeking to compare national currencies developed the PPP measure, which shows the level of goods and services that holders of a country's money can acquire locally. By converting all currencies to the "international dollar," the World Bank and other organizations using PPP can now show more truly comparative values, since the new currency value shows the number of units of a coun-

try's currency required to buy the same quantity of goods and services in the local market as one U.S. dollar would buy in an average country. The use of PPP currency values can alter the perceptions about a country's true comparative position in the world economy. More than per capita income figures, PPP provides a valid measurement of the ability of a country's population to provide for itself the things that people in the developed world take for granted: adequate food, shelter, clothing, education, and access to medical care. A glance at the map shows a clear-cut demarcation between temperate and tropical zones, with most of the countries with a PPP above $5,000 in the midlatitude zones and most of those with lower PPPs in the tropical and equatorial regions. Where exceptions to this pattern occur, they usually stem from a tremendous maldistribution of wealth among a country's population.

Map 71 Economic Output Per Sector

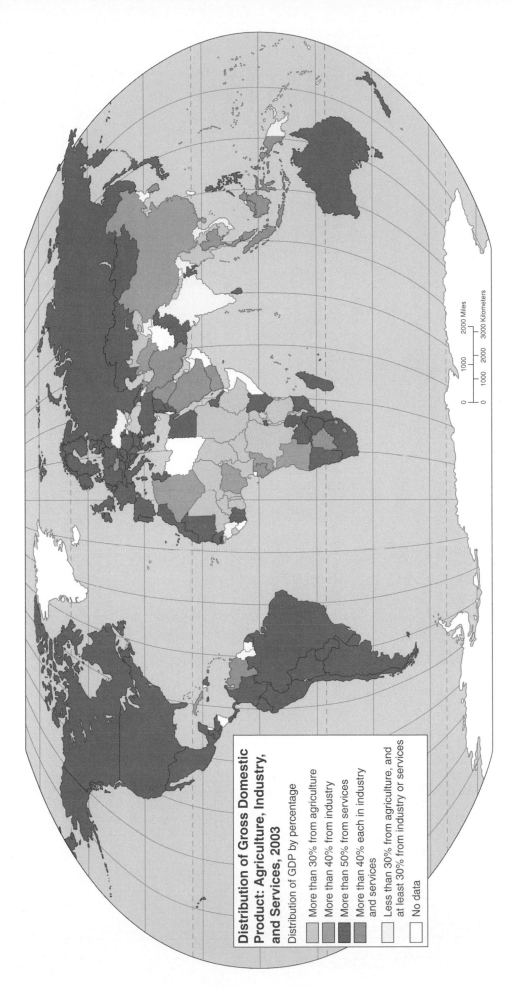

Distribution of Gross Domestic Product: Agriculture, Industry, and Services, 2003

Distribution of GDP by percentage

- More than 30% from agriculture
- More than 40% from industry
- More than 50% from services
- More than 40% each in industry and services
- Less than 30% from agriculture, and at least 30% from industry or services
- No data

0 1000 2000 Miles
0 1000 2000 3000 Kilometers

The percentage of the gross domestic product (the final output of goods and services produced by the domestic economy, including net exports of goods and nonfactor—nonlabor, noncapital—services) that is devoted to agricultural, industrial, and service activities is considered a good measure of the level of economic development. In general, countries with more than 40 percent of their GDP derived from agriculture are still in a "colonial dependency" economy—that is, raising agricultural goods primarily for the export market and dependent upon that market (usually the richer countries). Similarly, countries with more than 40 percent of GDP devoted to both agriculture and services often emphasize resource extractive (primarily mining and forestry) activities. These also tend to be

"colonial dependency" countries, providing raw materials for foreign markets. Countries with more than 40 percent of their GDP obtained from industry are normally well along the path to economic development. Countries with more than half of their GDP based on service activities fall into two ends of the development spectrum. On the one hand are countries heavily dependent upon both extractive activities and tourism and other low-level service functions. On the other hand are countries that can properly be termed "postindustrial": they have already passed through the industrial stage of their economic development and now rely less on the manufacture of products than on finance, research, communications, education, and other service-oriented activities.

-99-

Map 72 Employment by Economic Activity

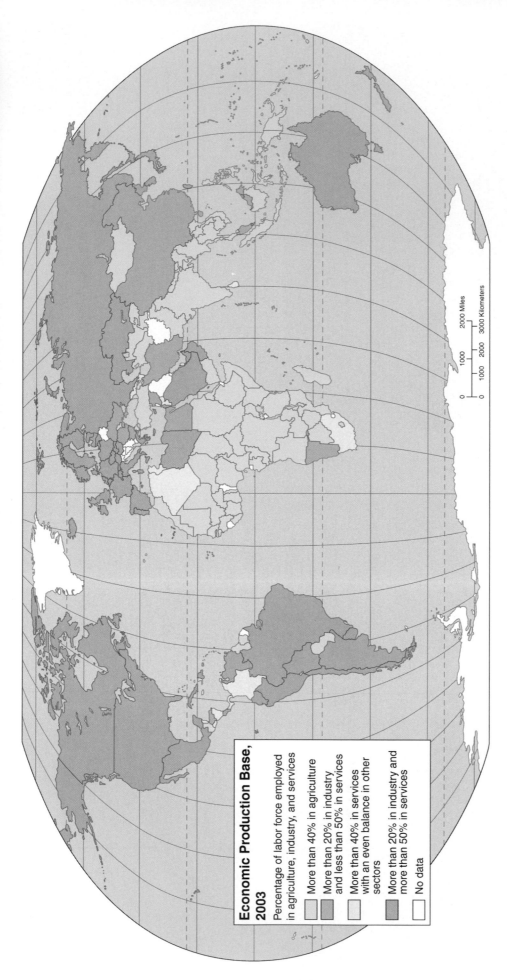

Economic Production Base, 2003

Percentage of labor force employed in agriculture, industry, and services

More than 40% in agriculture

More than 20% in industry and less than 50% in services

More than 40% in services with an even balance in other sectors

More than 20% in industry and more than 50% in services

No data

The employment structure of a country's population is one of the best indicators of the country's position on the scale of economic development. At one end of the scale are those countries with more than 40 percent of their labor force employed in agriculture. These are almost invariably the least developed, with high population growth rates, poor human services, significant environmental problems, and so on. In the middle of the scale are two types of countries: those with more than 20 percent of their labor force employed in industry and those with a fairly even balance among agricultural, industrial, and service employment but with at least 40 percent of their labor force employed in service activities. Generally, these countries have undergone the industrial revolution fairly recently

and are still developing an industrial base while building up their service activities. This category also includes countries with a disproportionate share of their economies in service activities primarily related to resource extraction. On the other end of the scale from the agricultural economies are countries with more than 20 percent of their labor force employed in industry and more than 50 percent in service activities. These countries are, for the most part, those with a highly automated industrial base and a highly mechanized agricultural system (the "postindustrial," developed countries). They also include, particularly in Middle and South America and Africa, industrializing countries that are also heavily engaged in resource extraction as a service activity.

Map 73 Central Government Expenditures Per Capita

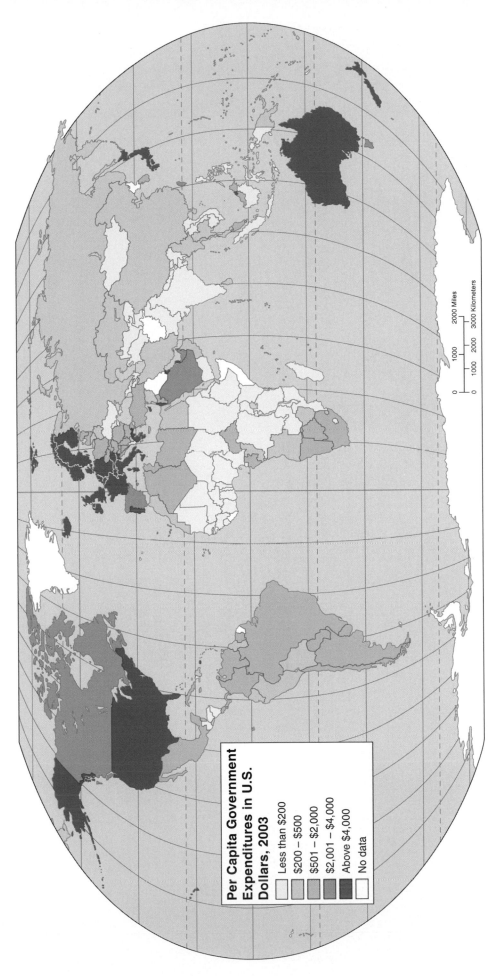

Per Capita Government Expenditures in U.S. Dollars, 2003

- Less than $200
- $200 – $500
- $501 – $2,000
- $2,001 – $4,000
- Above $4,000
- No data

The amount of money that the central government of a country spends upon a variety of essential governmental functions is a measure of relative economic development, particularly when it is viewed on a per-person basis. These functions include such governmental responsibilities as agriculture, communications, culture, defense, education, fishing and hunting, health, housing, recreation, religion, social security, transportation, and welfare. Generally, the higher the level of economic development, the greater the per capita expenditures on these services. However, the data do mask some internal variations. For example, countries that spend 20 percent or more of their central government expenditures on defense will often show up in the more developed category when, in fact, all that the figures really show is that a disproportionate amount of the money available to the government is devoted to purchasing armaments and maintaining a large standing military force. Thus, the fact that Libya spends more than the average for Africa does not suggest that the average Libyan is much better off than the average Tanzanian. Nevertheless, this map—particularly when compared with Map 83, Energy Consumption Per Capita—does provide a reasonable approximation of economic development levels.

Map 74 The Indebtedness of States

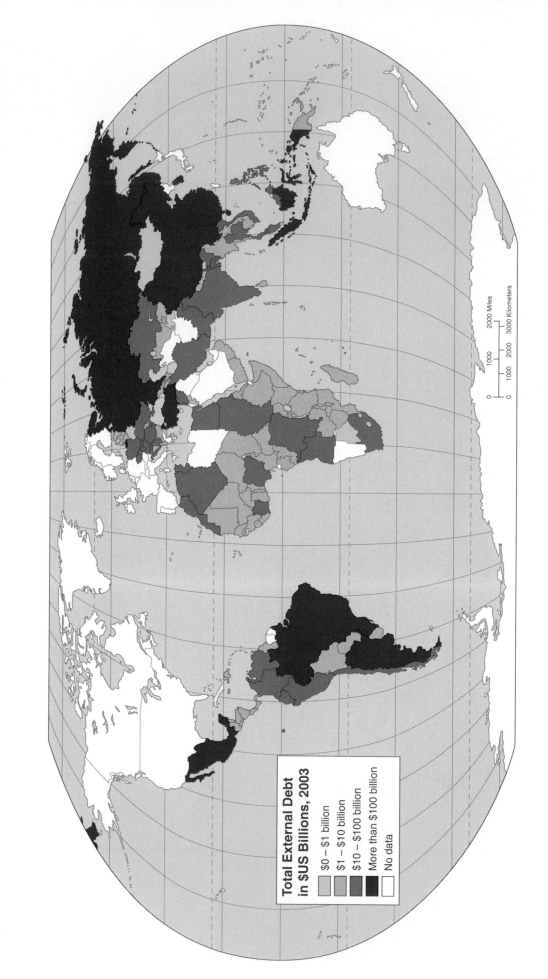

Total External Debt in $US Billions, 2003

- $0 – $1 billion
- $1 – $10 billion
- $10 – $100 billion
- More than $100 billion
- No data

2000 Miles

3000 Kilometers

Many governments spend more on a wide variety of services and activities than they collect in taxes and other revenues. In order to finance this deficit spending, governments borrow money—often from banks or other investors outside their country. Repayment of these debts, or even meeting interest payments on them, often means expending a country's export income—in other words, exchanging a country's wealth in production or, more often, resources, for debt service. Where the debt is external, as it is in most developing countries, governments become more open to outside influence in political as well as economic terms. Even internal debt service or repayment of monies owed to investors within a country gives financial establishments a measure of influence over government decisions. The amounts of debt shown on the map indicate the total external indebtedness of states.

Map 75 Exports of Primary Products

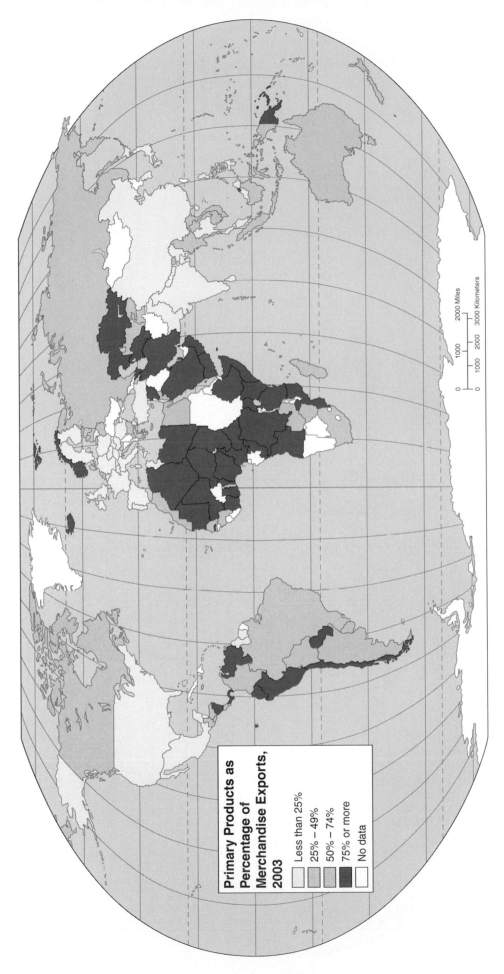

Primary Products as Percentage of Merchandise Exports, 2003

- Less than 25%
- 25% – 49%
- 50% – 74%
- 75% or more
- No data

0   1000   2000 Miles
0   1000   2000   3000 Kilometers

Primary products are those that require additional processing before they enter the consumer market: metallic ores that must be converted into metals and then into metal products such as automobiles or refrigerators; forest products such as timber that must be converted to lumber before they become suitable for construction purposes; and agricultural products that require further processing before being ready for human consumption. It is an axiom in international economics that the more a country relies on primary products for its export commodities, the more vulnerable its economy is to market fluctuations. Those countries with only primary products to

export are hampered in their economic growth. A country dependent on only one or two products for export revenues is unprotected from economic shifts, particularly a changing market demand for its products. Imagine what would happen to the thriving economic status of the oil-exporting states of the Persian Gulf, for example, if an alternate source of cheap energy were found. A glance at this map, together with Map 71, shows that those countries with the lowest levels of economic development tend to be concentrated on primary products and, therefore, have economies that are especially vulnerable to economic instability.

Map 76　Dependence on Trade

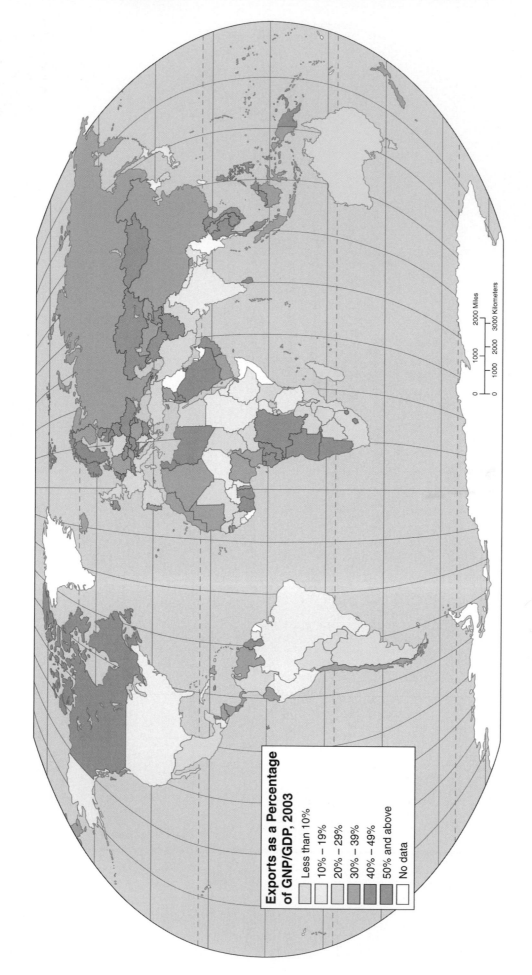

Exports as a Percentage
of GNP/GDP, 2003

Less than 10%
10% – 19%
20% – 29%
30% – 39%
40% – 49%
50% and above
No data

0   1000   2000 Miles
0 1000 2000 3000 Kilometers

As the global economy becomes more and more a reality, the economic strength of vir-tually all countries is increasingly dependent upon trade. For many developing nations, with relatively abundant resources and limited industrial capacity, exports provide the primary base upon which their economies rest. Even countries like the United States, Japan, and Germany, with huge and diverse economies, depend on exports to generate a significant percentage of their employment and wealth. Without imports, many products that consumers want would be unavailable or more expensive; without exports, many jobs would be eliminated.

Map 77 Global Flows of Investment Capital

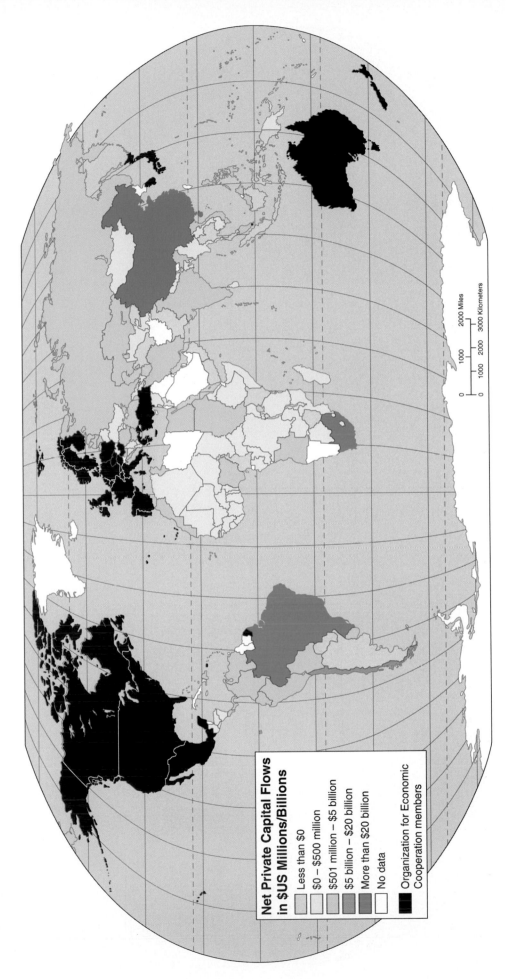

Net Private Capital Flows in $US Millions/Billions

- Less than $0
- $0 – $500 million
- $501 million – $5 billion
- $5 billion – $20 billion
- More than $20 billion
- No data
- Organization for Economic Cooperation members

0 1000 2000 Miles
0 1000 2000 3000 Kilometers

International capital flows include private debt and nondebt flows from one country to another, shown on the map as flows into a country. Nearly all of the capital comes from those countries that are members of the Organization for Economic Cooperation and Development (OECD), shown in black on the map. Capital flows include commercial bank lending, bonds, other private credits, foreign direct investment, and portfolio investment. Most of these flows are indicators of the increasing influence developed countries exert over the developing economies. Foreign direct investment or FDI, for example, is a measure of the net inflow of investment monies used to acquire long-term management interest in businesses located somewhere other than in the economy of the investor. Usually this means the acquisition of at least 10 percent of the stock of a company by a foreign investor and is, then, a measure of what might be termed "economic colonialism": control of a region's economy by foreign investors that could, in the world of the future, be as significant as colonial political control was in the past. International capital flows have increased greatly in the last decade as the result of the increasing liberalization of developing countries, the strong economic growth exhibited by many developing countries, and the falling costs and increased efficiency of communication and transportation services.

-105-

Map 78 Aiding Economic Development

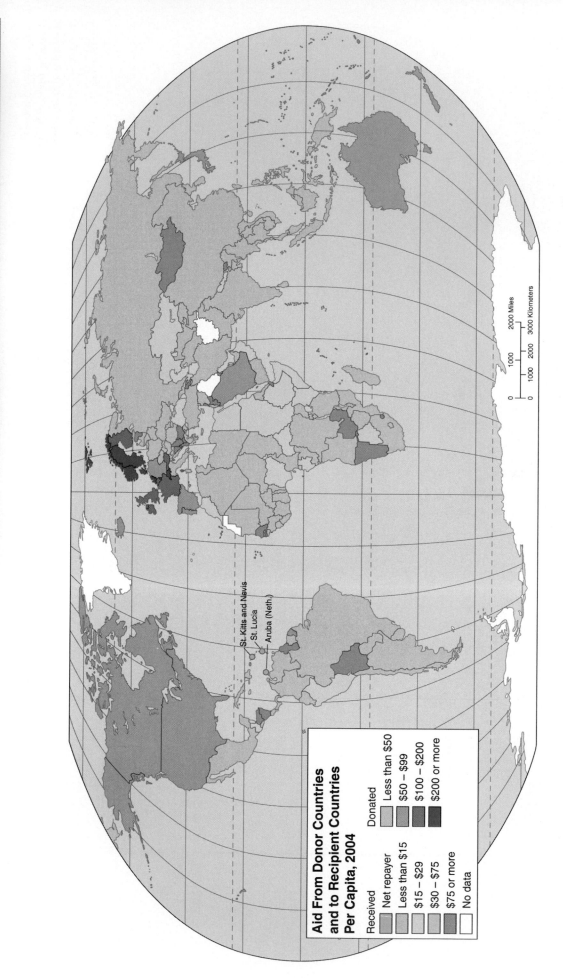

**Aid From Donor Countries
and to Recipient Countries
Per Capita, 2004**

Received
- Net repayer
- Less than $15
- $15 – $29
- $30 – $75
- $75 or more
- No data

Donated
- Less than $50
- $50 – $99
- $100 – $200
- $200 or more

St. Kitts and Nevis
St. Lucia
Aruba (Neth.)

0	1000 2000 Miles
0 1000 2000	3000 Kilometers

Over the last few years, official development assistance to developing countries from the member countries of the Organisation for Economic Co-operation and Development has risen dramatically, with the United States as the world's number 1 donor country, giving over 25 percent of the total of development assistance. Development assistance or "foreign aid" as it is sometimes called is widely recognized as benefiting both the donor and the recipient. Developing countries that increase their levels of per capita income through economic development have more money to spend on products from more highly developed countries. Increased development increases the capacity to foster not just economic but political change. In some parts of the world, such as sub-Saharan Africa, foreign aid is the largest single source of external finance, far exceeding foreign investments.

Unit V

Food, Energy, and Materials

Map 79 Agricultural Production Per Capita

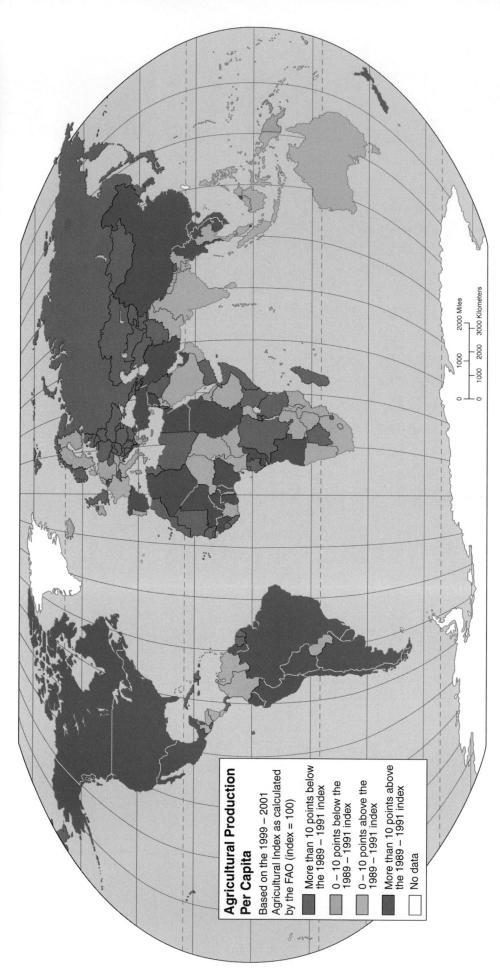

Agricultural Production Per Capita

Based on the 1999 – 2001
Agricultural Index as calculated
by the FAO (index = 100)

More than 10 points below
the 1989 – 1991 index

0 – 10 points below the
1989 – 1991 index

0 – 10 points above the
1989 – 1991 index

More than 10 points above
the 1989 – 1991 index

No data

0   1000   2000 Miles
0 1000 2000 3000 Kilometers

Agricultural production includes the value of all crops and livestock products originating within a country for the base year of 2002. The index value portrays the disposable output (after deductions for livestock feed and seed for planting) of a country's agriculture in comparison with the base period 1989–1991. Thus, the production values show not only the relative ability of countries to produce food but also show whether or not that ability has increased or decreased over a 10-year period. In general, global food production has kept up with or very slightly exceeded population growth. However, there are significant regional variations in the trend of food production keeping up with or surpassing population growth. For example, agricultural production in Africa and in Middle America has fallen, while production in South America, Asia, and Europe has risen. In the case of Africa, the drop in production reflects a population growing more rapidly than agricultural productivity. Where rapid increases in food production per capita exist (as in certain countries in South America, Asia, and Europe), most often the reason is the development of new agricultural technologies that have allowed food production to grow faster than population. In much of Asia, for example, the so-called Green Revolution of new, highly productive strains of wheat and rice made positive index values possible. Also in Asia, the cessation of major warfare allowed some countries (Cambodia, Laos, and Vietnam) to show substantial increases over the 1989–1991 index. In some cases, a drop in production per capita reflects government decisions to limit production in order to maintain higher prices for agricultural products. The United States and Japan fall into this category.

Map **80**   The Value of Agriculture

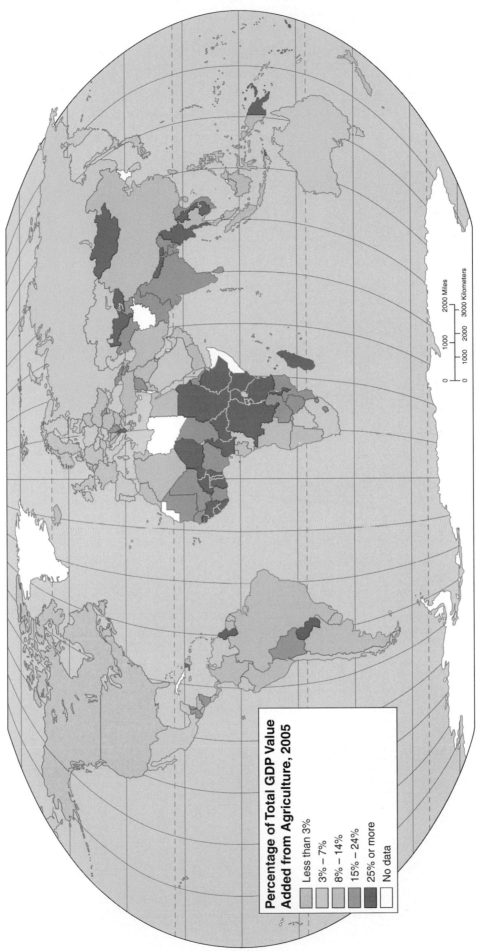

Percentage of Total GDP Value Added from Agriculture, 2005

- Less than 3%
- 3% – 7%
- 8% – 14%
- 15% – 24%
- 25% or more
- No data

```
0        1000        2000 Miles

0   1000   2000   3000 Kilometers
```

When compared with the service and industrial sectors of the global economy, agriculture grew more slowly between 1990 and 2005. The highest rates of growth were recorded in the sub-Saharan African region, where agriculture grew more than either service or industrial economies. It is clear from the sub-Saharan African figures, as well as those from Middle and South America and Asia, that agriculture is still of vital economic importance to the developing regions of the world. Not only does agriculture contribute significantly to the gross domestic product of these countries but it represents the primary source of employment in nearly two-thirds of the world's countries. Even in the rapidly expanding service and industrial economies of India and China, agriculture still counts for nearly half of all employment. This contrasts with 4 percent of total employment in the United States and Germany, and only 1 percent in the United Kingdom.

Map 81 Average Daily Per Capita Supply of Calories (Kilocalories)

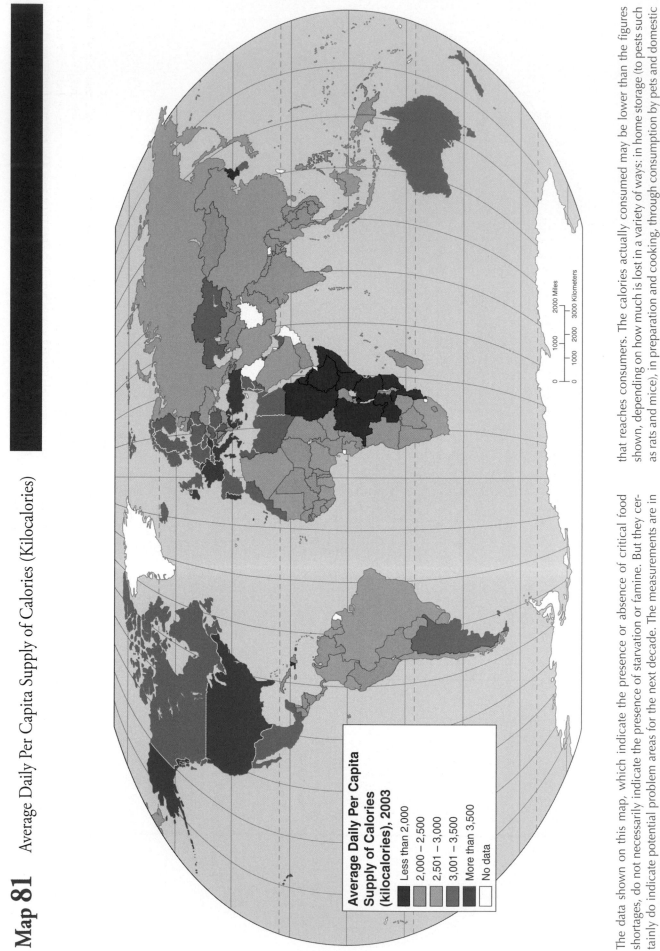

Average Daily Per Capita Supply of Calories (kilocalories), 2003

- Less than 2,000
- 2,000 – 2,500
- 2,501 – 3,000
- 3,001 – 3,500
- More than 3,500
- No data

0   1000   2000 Miles

0   1000   2000   3000 Kilometers

The data shown on this map, which indicate the presence or absence of critical food shortages, do not necessarily indicate the presence of starvation or famine. But they certainly do indicate potential problem areas for the next decade. The measurements are in calories from *all* food sources: domestic production, international trade, drawdown on stocks or food reserves, and direct foreign contributions or aid. The quantity of calories available is that amount, estimated by the UN's Food and Agriculture Organization (FAO), that reaches consumers. The calories actually consumed may be lower than the figures shown, depending on how much is lost in a variety of ways: in home storage (to pests such as rats and mice), in preparation and cooking, through consumption by pets and domestic animals, and as discarded foods, for example. The estimate of need is not a global uniform value but is calculated for each country on the basis of the age and sex distribution of the population and the estimated level of activity of the population.

Map 82   Energy Production Per Capita

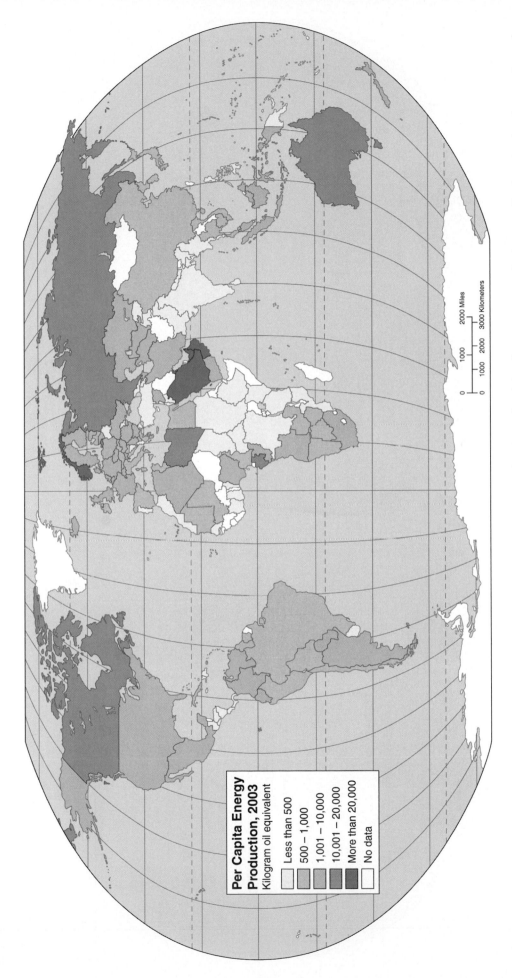

Per Capita Energy Production, 2003
Kilogram oil equivalent

- Less than 500
- 500 – 1,000
- 1,001 – 10,000
- 10,001 – 20,000
- More than 20,000
- No data

Energy production per capita is a measure of the availability of mechanical energy to assist people in their work. This map shows the amount of all kinds of energy—solid fuel (primarily coal), liquid fuel (primarily petroleum), natural gas, geothermal, wind, solar, hydroelectric, nuclear, waste recycling, and indigenous heat pumps—produced per person in each country. With some exceptions, wealthier countries produce more energy per capita than poor ones. Countries such as Japan and many European states rank among the world's wealthiest, but are energy-poor and produce relatively little of their own energy.

They have the ability, however, to pay for imports. On the other hand, countries such as those of the Persian Gulf or the oil-producing states of Central and South America may rank relatively low on the scale of economic development but rank high as producers of energy. In many poor countries, especially in Central and South America, Africa, South Asia, and East Asia, large proportions of energy come from traditional fuels such as firewood and animal dung. Indeed for many in the developing world, the real energy crisis is a shortage of wood for cooking and heating.

Map **83**   Energy Consumption Per Capita

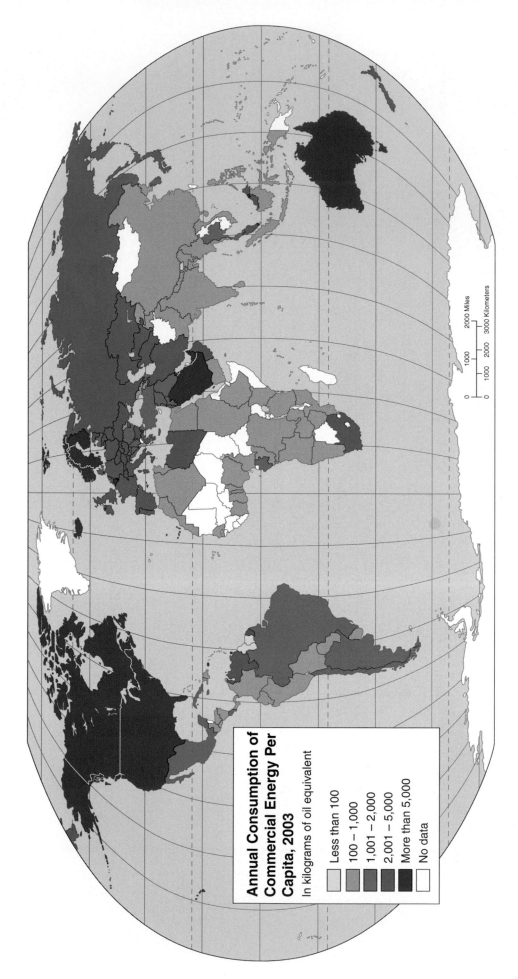

Annual Consumption of Commercial Energy Per Capita, 2003

In kilograms of oil equivalent

- Less than 100
- 100 – 1,000
- 1,001 – 2,000
- 2,001 – 5,000
- More than 5,000
- No data

0   1000   2000   3000 Kilometers
0   1000   2000 Miles

Of all the quantitative measures of economic well-being, energy consumption per capita may be the most expressive. All of the countries defined by the World Bank as having high incomes consume at least 100 gigajoules of commercial energy (the equivalent of about 3.5 metric tons of coal) per person per year, with some, such as the United States and Canada, having consumption rates in the 300 gigajoule range (the equivalent of more than 10 metric tons of coal per person per year). With the exception of the oil-rich Persian Gulf states, where consumption figures include the costly "burning off" of excess energy in the form of natural gas flares at wellheads, most of the highest-consuming countries are in the Northern Hemisphere, concentrated in North America and Western Europe. At the other end of the scale are low-income countries, whose consumption rates are often less than 1 percent of those of the United States and other high consumers. These figures do not, of course, include the consumption of noncommercial energy—the traditional fuels of firewood, animal dung, and other organic matter—widely used in the less developed parts of the world.

Map 84 Energy Dependency

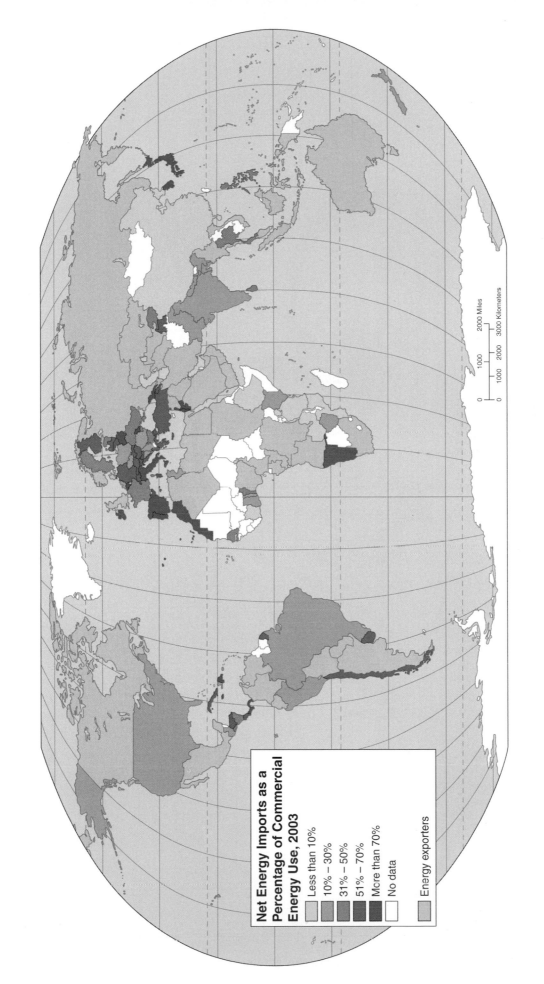

Net Energy Imports as a Percentage of Commercial Energy Use, 2003

- Less than 10%
- 10% – 30%
- 31% – 50%
- 51% – 70%
- More than 70%
- No data
- Energy exporters

0   1000   2000 Miles
0   1000   2000   3000 Kilometers

The patterns on the map show dependence on commercial energy before transformation to other end-use fuels such as electricity or refined petroleum products; energy from traditional sources such as fuelwood or dried animal dung is not included. Energy dependency is the difference between domestic consumption and domestic production of commercial energy and is most often expressed as a net energy import or export. A few of the world's countries are net exporters of energy; most are importers. The growth in global commercial energy use over the last decade indicates growth in the modern sectors of the economy—industry, transportation, and urbanization—particularly in the lesser developed countries. Still, the primary consumers of energy—and those having the greatest dependence on foreign sources of energy—are the more highly developed countries of Europe, North America, and Japan.

Map 85   Flows of Oil

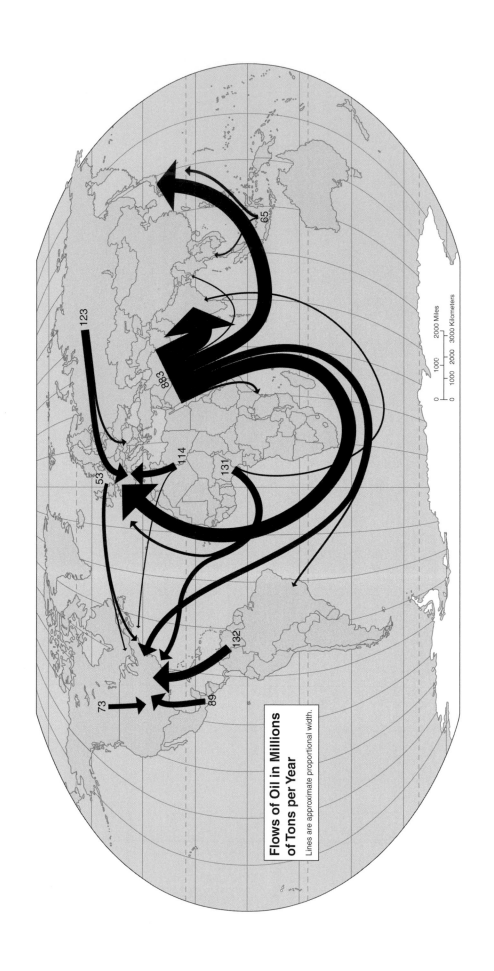

**Flows of Oil in Millions
of Tons per Year**

Lines are approximate proportional width.

123
883
114
131
53
73
89
132
65

0   1000   2000 Miles
0   1000   2000   3000 Kilometers

The pattern of oil movements from producing region to consuming region is one of the dominant facts of contemporary international maritime trade. Supertankers carry a million tons of crude oil and charge rates in excess of $0.10 per ton per mile, making the transportation of oil not only a necessity for the world's energy-hungry countries, but also an enormously profitable proposition. One of the major negatives of these massive oil flows is the damage done to the oceanic ecosystems—not just from the well-publicized and dramatic events like the wrecking of the *Exxon Valdez* but from the incalculable amounts of oil from leakage, scrubbings, purgings, and so on, which are a part of the oil transport technology. It is clear from the map that the primary recipients of these oil flows are the world's most highly developed economies.

Map 86 Production of Crucial Materials

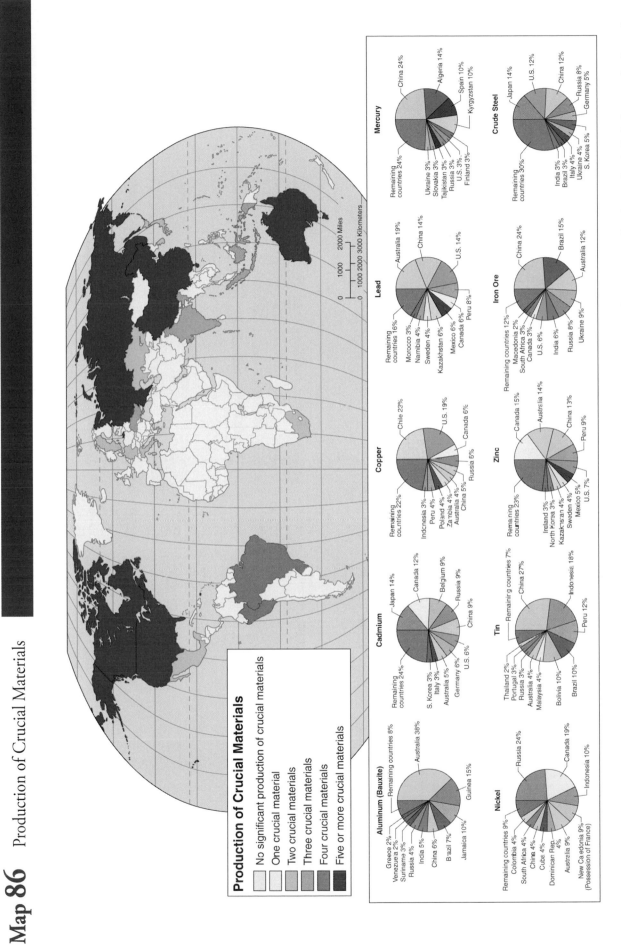

Production of Crucial Materials

- No significant production of crucial materials
- One crucial material
- Two crucial materials
- Three crucial materials
- Four crucial materials
- Five or more crucial materials

Aluminum (Bauxite)
- Remaining countries 8%
- Australia 38%
- Guinea 15%
- Jamaica 10%
- Brazil 7%
- China 6%
- India 5%
- Russia 4%
- Suriname 3%
- Venezuela 2%
- Greece 2%

Nickel
- Remaining countries 9%
- Russia 24%
- Canada 19%
- Indonesia 10%
- New Caledonia 9% (Possession of France)
- Australia 9%
- Dominican Rep. 4%
- Cuba 4%
- China 4%
- South Africa 4%
- Colombia 4%

Cadmium
- Remaining countries 24%
- Japan 14%
- Canada 12%
- Belgium 9%
- Russia 9%
- China 9%
- U.S. 6%
- Germany 6%
- Australia 5%
- Italy 3%
- S. Korea 3%

Tin
- Remaining countries 7%
- China 27%
- Indonesia 18%
- Peru 12%
- Brazil 10%
- Bolivia 10%
- Malaysia 4%
- Australia 4%
- Russia 3%
- Portugal 3%
- Thailand 2%

Copper
- Remaining countries 22%
- Chile 23%
- U.S. 19%
- Canada 6%
- Russia 6%
- China 5%
- Australia 4%
- Zambia 4%
- Poland 4%
- Peru 4%
- Indonesia 3%

Zinc
- Remaining countries 23%
- Canada 15%
- Australia 14%
- China 13%
- Peru 9%
- U.S. 7%
- Mexico 5%
- Sweden 4%
- Kazakhstan 4%
- North Korea 3%
- Ireland 3%

Lead
- Remaining countries 16%
- Australia 19%
- China 14%
- U.S. 14%
- Peru 8%
- Canada 6%
- Mexico 6%
- Kazakhstan 6%
- Sweden 4%
- Namibia 3%
- Morocco 3%

Iron Ore
- Remaining countries 12%
- China 24%
- Brazil 15%
- Australia 12%
- Ukraine 9%
- Russia 8%
- India 6%
- U.S. 6%
- Canada 3%
- South Africa 3%
- Macedonia 2%

Mercury
- Remaining countries 24%
- China 24%
- Algeria 14%
- Spain 10%
- Kyrgyzstan 10%
- Finland 3%
- U.S. 3%
- Russia 3%
- Tajikistan 3%
- Slovakia 3%
- Ukraine 3%

Crude Steel
- Remaining countries 30%
- Japan 14%
- U.S. 12%
- China 12%
- Russia 8%
- Germany 5%
- S. Korea 5%
- Ukraine 4%
- Italy 4%
- Brazil 3%
- India 3%

Scale:
0 1000 2000 Miles
0 1000 2000 3000 Kilometers

The data on this map portray world production of the metals most important for the operation of a modern industrial economy. The sector graphs across the bottom of the map show the percentage of production of crucial materials by the 10 leading countries for each of 10 materials. For copper, lead, mercury, nickel, tin, and zinc, the annual production data reflect the metal content of the ore mined. Aluminum (or bauxite ore) and iron ore production are expressed in gross weight of ore mined. Cadmium production refers to the refined metal, and crude steel production to usable ingots, cast products, and liquid steel. By comparing this map with Map 87, you will discover that some of the world's top producer nations of these critical materials are also among the world's top consumer nations.

-115-

Map 87 Consumption of Crucial Materials

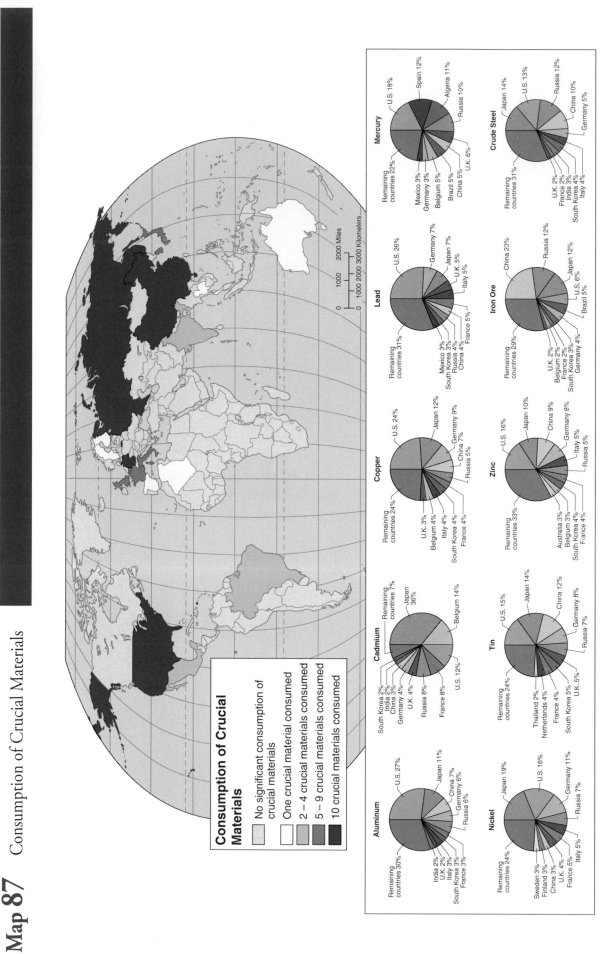

Consumption of Crucial Materials

- No significant consumption of crucial materials
- One crucial material consumed
- 2 – 4 crucial materials consumed
- 5 – 9 crucial materials consumed
- 10 crucial materials consumed

0 1000 2000 Miles
0 1000 2000 3000 Kilometers

Aluminum
- U.S. 27%
- Japan 11%
- China 7%
- Germany 6%
- Russia 6%
- France 3%
- South Korea 3%
- Italy 3%
- U.K. 2%
- India 2%
- Remaining countries 30%

Nickel
- Japan 19%
- U.S. 16%
- Germany 7%
- Russia 7%
- Italy 5%
- France 5%
- U.K. 4%
- China 3%
- Finland 3%
- Sweden 3%
- Remaining countries 24%

Cadmium
- Japan 36%
- Belgium 14%
- U.S. 12%
- France 8%
- Russia 8%
- U.K. 4%
- Germany 4%
- China 3%
- India 2%
- South Korea 2%
- Remaining countries 7%

Tin
- Japan 14%
- China 12%
- Germany 8%
- Russia 7%
- U.K. 5%
- South Korea 5%
- France 4%
- Netherlands 4%
- Thailand 2%
- U.S. 15%
- Remaining countries 24%

Copper
- U.S. 24%
- Japan 12%
- Germany 9%
- China 7%
- Russia 5%
- France 4%
- South Korea 4%
- Italy 4%
- Belgium 4%
- U.K. 3%
- Remaining countries 24%

Zinc
- U.S. 16%
- Japan 10%
- China 9%
- Germany 8%
- Italy 5%
- Russia 5%
- France 4%
- South Korea 4%
- Belgium 3%
- Australia 3%
- Remaining countries 33%

Lead
- U.S. 26%
- Germany 7%
- Japan 7%
- U.K. 5%
- Italy 5%
- France 5%
- China 4%
- Russia 4%
- South Korea 3%
- Mexico 3%
- Remaining countries 31%

Iron Ore
- China 23%
- Russia 12%
- Japan 12%
- Brazil 5%
- U.S. 5%
- Germany 4%
- South Korea 3%
- France 2%
- Belgium 2%
- U.K. 2%
- Remaining countries 29%

Mercury
- U.S. 18%
- Spain 12%
- Algeria 11%
- Russia 10%
- U.K. 6%
- China 5%
- Brazil 5%
- Belgium 5%
- Germany 3%
- Mexico 3%
- Remaining countries 22%

Crude Steel
- Japan 14%
- U.S. 13%
- Russia 12%
- China 10%
- Germany 5%
- Italy 4%
- South Korea 4%
- India 3%
- France 2%
- U.K. 2%
- Remaining countries 31%

Consumption data refer to the domestic use of refined metals (for example, the tons of steel used in the manufacture of automobiles). Some countries rank among the top in both production and consumption, and those that do are among the most highly developed nations. The United States, for example, ranks in the top 4 consumers for each metal; but the United States also ranks in the top 10 producer countries for 7 of the metals. Many countries that rank high as producers but not as consumers have colonial dependency economies, producing raw materials for an export market, often at the mercy of the marketplace. Jamaica and Suriname, for example, depend extremely heavily upon the sale of bauxite ore (crude aluminum). When the United States, Japan, or Russia cuts its use of aluminum, the economies of Jamaica and Suriname crash.

Unit VI

Environmental Conditions

Map **88** Deforestation and Desertification

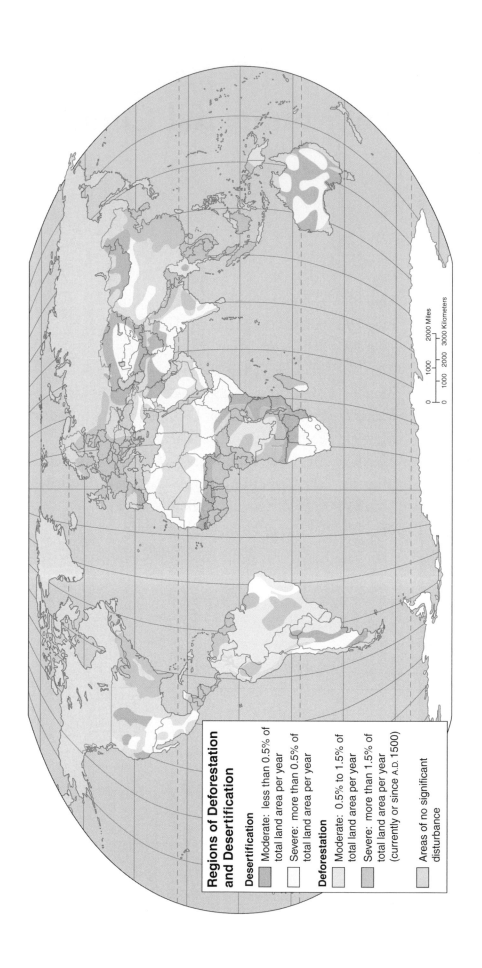

Regions of Deforestation and Desertification

Desertification

- Moderate: less than 0.5% of total land area per year
- Severe: more than 0.5% of total land area per year

Deforestation

- Moderate: 0.5% to 1.5% of total land area per year
- Severe: more than 1.5% of total land area per year (currently or since A.D. 1500)
- Areas of no significant disturbance

While those of us in the developed countries of the world tend to think of environmental deterioration as the consequence of our heavily industrialized economies, in fact the worst examples of current environmental degradation are found within the world's less developed regions. There, high population growth rates and economies limited primarily to farming have forced the increasing use of more marginal (less suited to cultivation) land. In the world's grassland and arid environments, which occupy approximately 40 percent of the world's total land area, increasing cultivation pressures are turning vulnerable areas into deserts incapable of sustaining agricultural productivity. In the world's forested regions, particularly in the tropical forests of Middle and South America, Africa, and Asia, a similar process is occurring: increasing pressure for more farmland is creating a process of deforestation or forest clearing that destroys the soil, reduces the biological diversity of the forest regions, and ultimately may have the capacity to alter the global climate by contributing to an increase in carbon dioxide in the atmosphere. This increases the heat trapped in the atmosphere and enhances the greenhouse effect.

Map **89** Forest Loss and Gain, 1990–2005

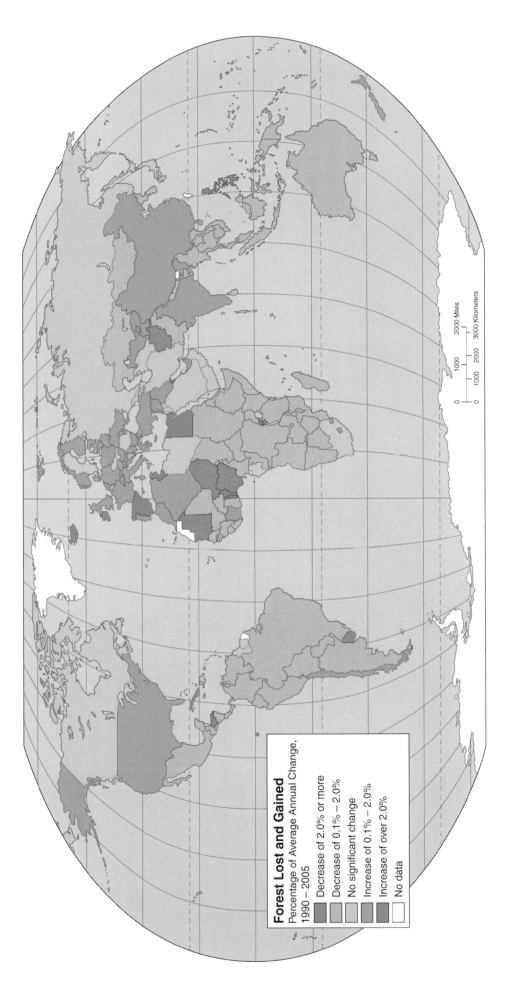

Forest Lost and Gained
Percentage of Average Annual Change,
1990 – 2005

- Decrease of 2.0% or more
- Decrease of 0.1% – 2.0%
- No significant change
- Increase of 0.1% – 2.0%
- Increase of over 2.0%
- No data

2000 Miles

1000   3000 Kilometers
0   1000   2000

0   1000   2000

During the 15 years included in this analysis, the world lost approximately 20 million acres of forest land each year or a total of 256 million acres. About 50 percent of the world's total loss came in Africa—most of this loss represented land clearance for agricultural purposes. Nearly 40 percent of the world's total loss was in Brazil and, again, the majority of this loss resulted from land clearance for agriculture. At the global level, forest clearance seems to be slowing somewhat—but it still is an area of concern for a variety of reasons. Healthy forests act as a "carbon sink" and withdraw carbon dioxide from the atmosphere, aiding in the reduction of this important greenhouse gas and helping to reduce the impact of carbon dioxide on global warming. Equally important is the fact that forest clearance disturbs all other components of an ecosystem, from soil chemistry to water quality and quantity. There is a temptation to blame countries in Africa, Middle or South America for failing to protect these forests. But the agricultural products grown on cleared land, or the livestock pastured on forests cleared and replaced by grasslands, are generally consumed by the market of the more highly developed world.

Map 90 Soil Degradation

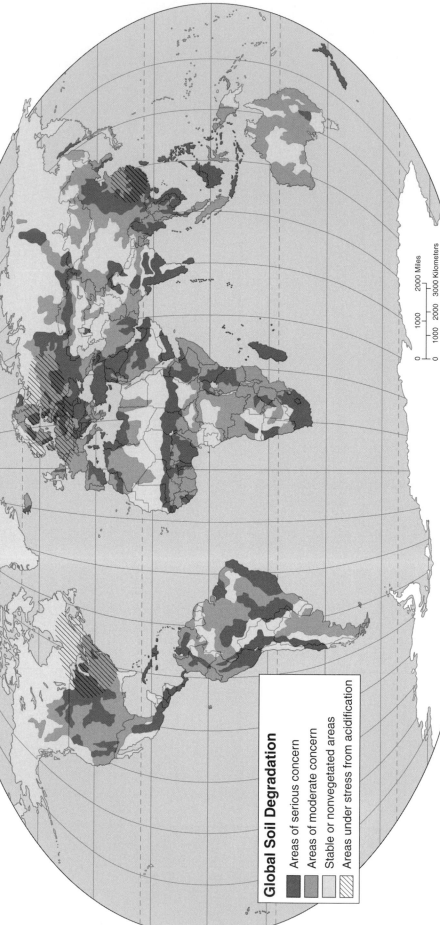

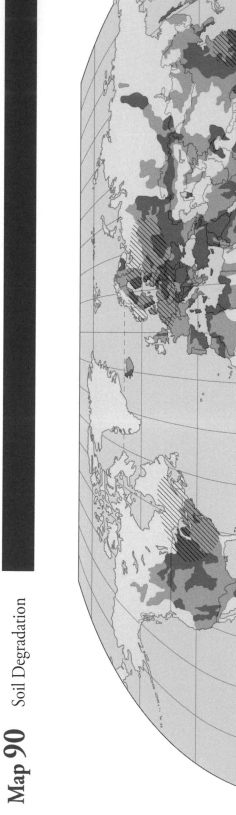

Global Soil Degradation

- ▨ Areas of serious concern
- ▨ Areas of moderate concern
- ☐ Stable or nonvegetated areas
- ▨ Areas under stress from acidification

0 1000 2000 Miles
0 1000 2000 3000 Kilometers

Recent research has shown that more than 3 billion acres of the world's surface suffer from serious soil degradation, with more than 22 million acres so severely eroded or poisoned with chemicals that they can no longer support productive crop agriculture. Most of this soil damage has been caused by poor farming practices, overgrazing of domestic livestock, and deforestation. These activities strip away the protective cover of natural vegetation—forests and grasslands—allowing wind and water erosion to remove the topsoil that contains the necessary nutrients and soil microbes for plant growth. But millions of acres of topsoil have been degraded by chemicals as well. In some instances

these chemicals are the result of overapplication of fertilizers, herbicides, pesticides, and other agricultural chemicals. In other instances, chemical deposition from industrial and urban wastes and from acid precipitation has poisoned millions of acres of soil. As the map shows, soil erosion and pollution are problems not just in developing countries with high population densities and increasing use of marginal lands but in the more highly developed regions of mechanized, industrial agriculture as well. While many methods for preventing or reducing soil degradation exist, they are seldom used because of ignorance, cost, or perceived economic inefficiency.

Map 91 Air and Water Quality

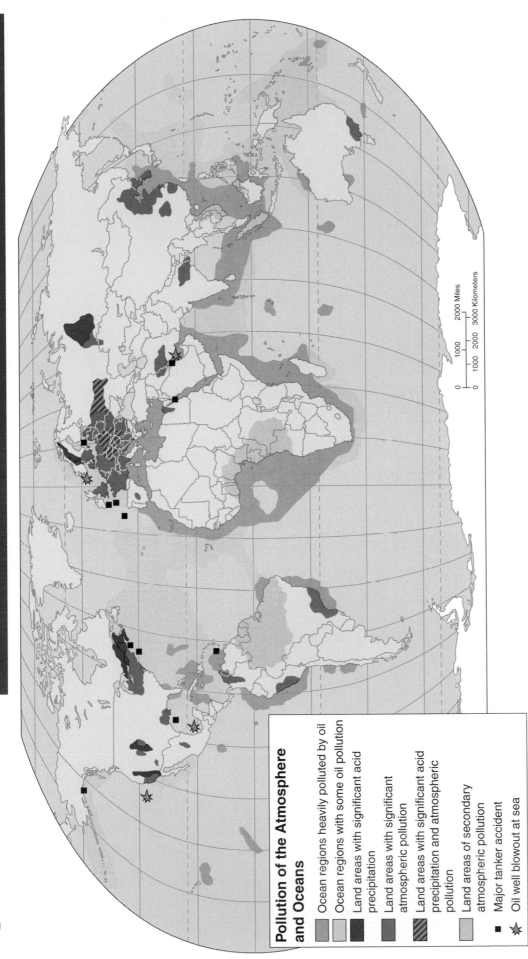

Pollution of the Atmosphere and Oceans

- Ocean regions heavily polluted by oil
- Ocean regions with some oil pollution
- Land areas with significant acid precipitation
- Land areas with significant atmospheric pollution
- Land areas with significant acid precipitation and atmospheric pollution
- Land areas of secondary atmospheric pollution
- ■ Major tanker accident
- ✦ Oil well blowout at sea

The pollution of the world's oceans and atmosphere has long been a matter of concern to environmental scientists. The great circulation systems of ocean and air are the controlling factors of the earth's natural environment, and modifications to those systems have unknown consequences. This map is based on what we can measure: (1) areas of oceans where oil pollution has been proven to have inflicted significant damage to ocean ecosystems and lifeforms (including phytoplankton—the oceans' primary food producers, the equivalent of land vegetation); (2) areas of oceans where unusually high concentrations of hydrocarbons from oil spills may have inflicted some damage to the oceans' biota; (3) land areas where the combination of sulphur and nitrogen oxides with atmospheric

water vapor has produced acid precipitation at high enough levels to have produced significant damage to terrestrial vegetation systems; (4) land areas where the emissions from industrial, transportation, commercial, residential, and other uses of fossil fuels have produced concentrations of atmospheric pollutants high enough to be damaging to human health; and (5) land areas of secondary air pollution where the primary pollutant is smoke from forest clearance. A glance at the map shows that there are few areas of the world where some form of oceanic or atmospheric pollution is not a part of our environmental system. Scientists are still debating the long-range implications of this pollution, but nearly all agree that the consequences, whatever they may be, will not be good.

Map 92 Availability of Improved Water Supply

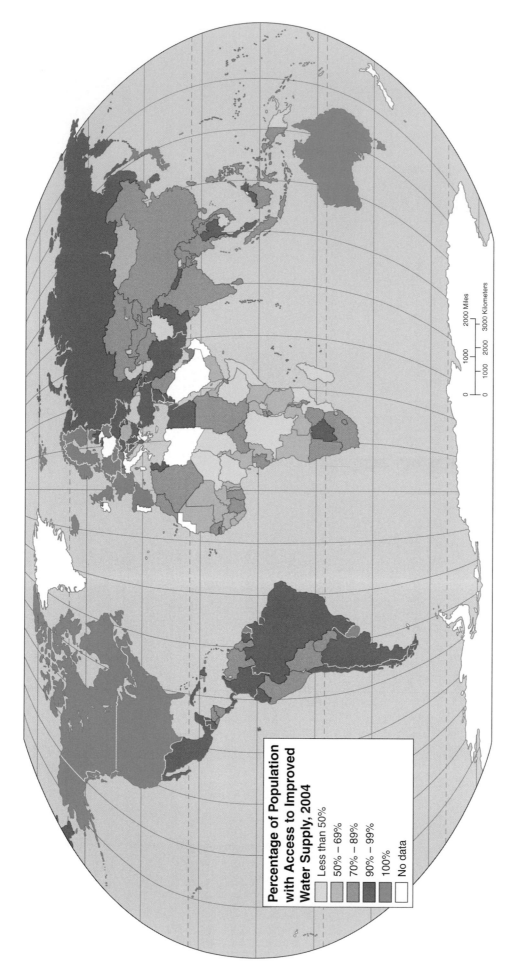

Percentage of Population with Access to Improved Water Supply, 2004

- Less than 50%
- 50% – 69%
- 70% – 89%
- 90% – 99%
- 100%
- No data

0   1000   2000 Miles

0   1000   2000   3000 Kilometers

The term "improved water supply" refers to water that does not come directly from surface water supplies or contaminated ground water supplies without being treated to remove harmful impurities. Only about 50 percent of the population of the developing countries of the world share in the luxury of treated water. This helps to explain the high incidence of water-borne diseases in these parts of the world. Fresh water—and even more particularly, improved fresh water—is a globally scarce resource. In spite of the large quantity of fresh water in the world (11 million cubic miles), most of this water is locked up in glacial ice in Greenland and Antarctica or in deep underground aquifers. Less than 1 percent of the world's fresh water is readily available for human use and of this 1 percent, less than half is treated so as to be free from chemical and biological contaminants. Nearly 1 out of every 6 people on earth does not have access to treated water within a half-mile of their dwelling. Most of these people are in rural areas, but also included in those without access to treated water are the dwellers in the urban slums of the developing world.

-122-

Map 93 Per Capita Carbon Dioxide (CO₂) Emissions

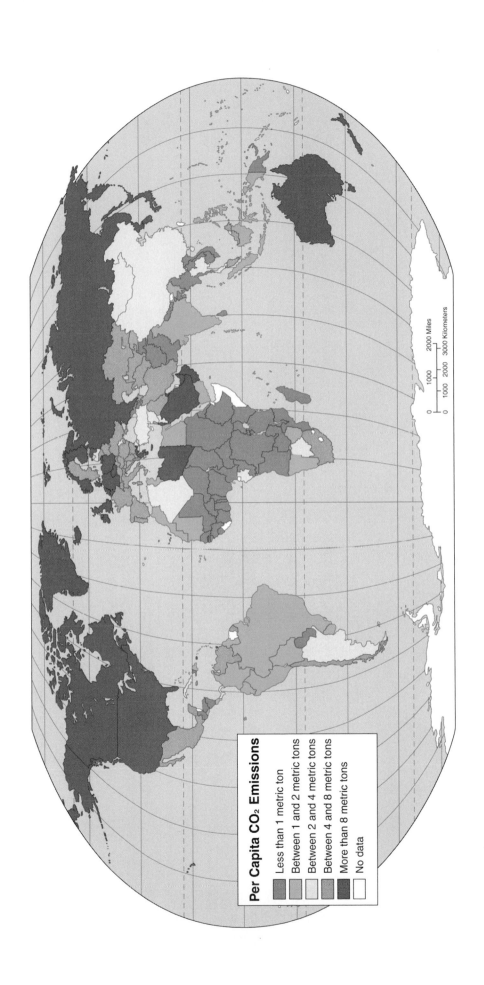

Per Capita CO₂ Emissions

- Less than 1 metric ton
- Between 1 and 2 metric tons
- Between 2 and 4 metric tons
- Between 4 and 8 metric tons
- More than 8 metric tons
- No data

Carbon dioxide emissions are a major indicator of economic development, since they are generated largely by burning of fossil fuels for electrical power generation, for industrial processes, for domestic and commercial heating, and for the internal combustion engines of automobiles, trucks, buses, planes, and trains. Scientists have long known that carbon dioxide in the atmosphere increases the ability of the atmosphere to retain heat, a phenomenon known as the greenhouse effect. While the greenhouse effect is a natural process (and life

on earth as we know it would not be possible without it), many scientists are concerned that an increase in carbon dioxide in the atmosphere will augment this process, creating a global warming trend and a potential worldwide change of climate patterns. These climatological changes threaten disaster for many regions and their peoples in both the developed and less developed areas of the world. You will note from the map that the countries of the midlatitude regions generate extremely high levels of carbon dioxide per capita.

Map 94   Potential Global Temperature Change

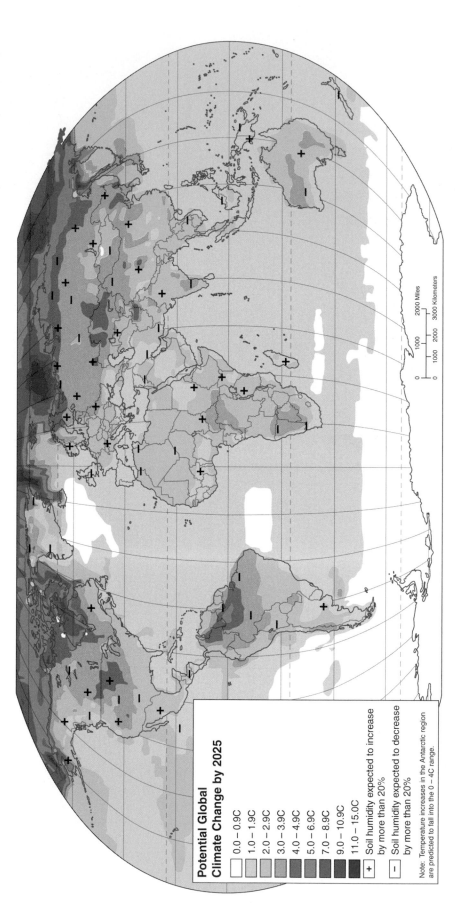

**Potential Global
Climate Change by 2025**

	0.0 – 0.9C
	1.0 – 1.9C
	2.0 – 2.9C
	3.0 – 3.9C
	4.0 – 4.9C
	5.0 – 6.9C
	7.0 – 8.9C
	9.0 – 10.9C
	11.0 – 15.0C

+   Soil humidity expected to increase by more than 20%

I   Soil humidity expected to decrease by more than 20%

Note: Temperature increases in the Antarctic region are predicted to fall into the 0 – 4C range.

According to atmospheric scientists, one of the major problems of the twenty-first century will be "global warming," produced as the atmosphere's natural ability to trap and retain heat is enhanced by increased percentages of carbon dioxide, methane, chlorinated fluorocarbons or "CFCs," and other "greenhouse gases" in the earth's atmosphere. Computer models based on atmospheric percentages of carbon dioxide resulting from present use of fossil fuels show that warming is not just a possibility but a probability. Increased temperatures would cause precipitation patterns to alter significantly as well and would produce a number of other harmful effects, including a rise in the level of the world's oceans that could flood most coastal cities. International conferences on the topic of the enhanced greenhouse effect have resulted in several international agreements to reduce the emission of carbon dioxide or to maintain it at present levels. Unfortunately, the solution is not that simple since reduction of carbon dioxide emissions is, in the short run,

expensive—particularly as long as the world's energy systems continue to be based on fossil fuels. Chief among the countries that could be hit by serious international mandates to reduce emissions are those highest on the development scale who use the highest levels of fossil fuels and, therefore, produce the highest emissions, and those on the lowest end of the development scale whose efforts to industrialize could be severely impeded by the more expensive energy systems that would replace fossil fuels. In April 2007, the Intergovernmental Panel on Climate Change—an international body of diplomats and scientists—issued the direst warning yet about the virtual certainty of human-induced global warming and the impacts it would have on water supplies, species extinction, and sea levels. The report represented the best scientific conclusions possible but was criticized by many scientists as not going far enough. As severe as the language of the IPCC report was, it was toned down by the threat of refusal to sign by China and the United States.

Map 95 The Loss of Biodiversity: Globally Threatened Animal Species

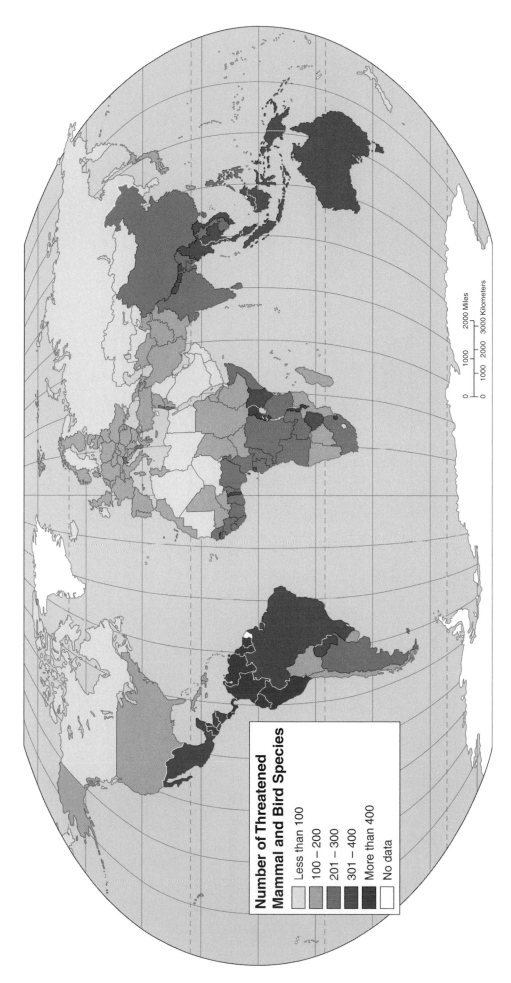

Number of Threatened Mammal and Bird Species

- Less than 100
- 100 – 200
- 201 – 300
- 301 – 400
- More than 400
- No data

0   1000   2000 Miles
0   1000   2000   3000 Kilometers

Threatened species are those in grave danger of going extinct. Their populations are becoming restricted in range, and the size of the populations required for sustained breeding is nearing a critical minimum. *Endangered species* are in immediate danger of becoming extinct. Their range is already so reduced that the animals may no longer be able to move freely within an ecozone, and their populations are at the level where the species may no longer be able to sustain breeding. Most species become threatened first and then endangered as their range and numbers continue to decrease. When people think of animal extinction, they think of large herbivorous species like the rhinoceros or fierce carnivores like lions, tigers, or grizzly bears. Certainly these animals make almost any list of endangered or threatened species. But there are literally hundreds of less conspicuous animals that are equally threatened. Extinction is normally nature's way of informing a species that it is inefficient. But conditions in the early twenty-first century are controlled more by human activities than by natural evolutionary processes. Species that are endangered or threatened fall into that category because, somehow, they are competing with us or with our domesticated livestock for space and food. And in that competition the animals are always going to lose.

Map 96   The Loss of Biodiversity: Globally Threatened Plant Species

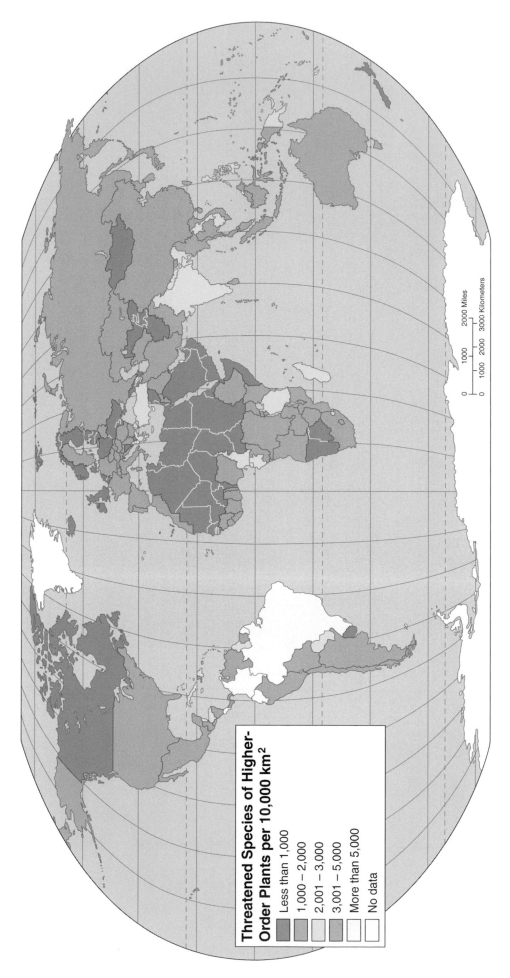

Threatened Species of Higher-Order Plants per 10,000 km²

- Less than 1,000
- 1,000 – 2,000
- 2,001 – 3,000
- 3,001 – 5,000
- More than 5,000
- No data

0   1000   2000   3000 Kilometers
0   1000   2000 Miles

While most people tend to be more concerned about the animals on threatened and endangered species lists, the fact is that many more plants are in jeopardy, and the loss of plant life is, in all ecological regions, a more critical occurrence than the loss of animal populations. Plants are the primary producers in the ecosystem; that is, plants produce the food upon which all other species in the food web, including human beings, depend for sustenance. It is plants from which many of our critical medicines come, and it is plants that maintain the delicate balance between soil and water in most of the world's regions. When environmental scientists speak of a loss of biodiversity, what they are most often describing is a loss of the richness and complexity of plant life that lends stability to ecosystems. Systems with more plant life tend to be more stable than those with less. For these and other reasons, the scientific concern over extinction is greater when applied to plants than to animals. It is difficult for people to become as emotional over a teak tree as they would over an elephant. But as great a tragedy as the loss of the elephant would be, the loss of the teak would be greater.

Map 97 Global Hotspots of Biodiversity

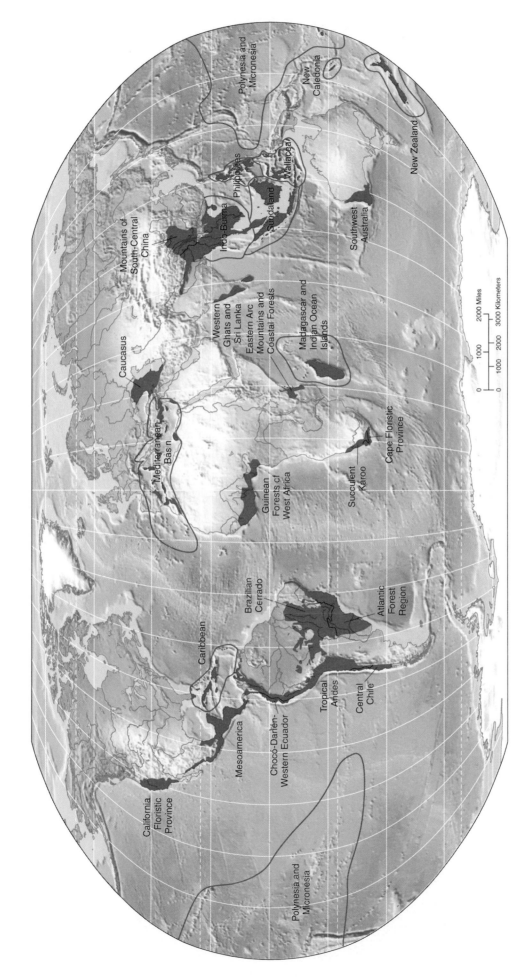

Where we have normally thought of tropical forest basins such as Amazonia as the world's most biologically diverse ecosystems, recent research has discovered the surprising fact that a number of hotspots of biological diversity exist outside the major tropical forest regions. These hotspot regions contain slightly less than 2 percent of the world's total land area but may contain up to 60 percent of the total world's terrestrial species of plants and animals. Geographically, the hotspot areas are characterized by vertical zonation (that is, they tend to be hilly to mountainous regions), long known to be a factor in biological complexity. They are also in coastal locations or near large bodies of water, locations that stimulate climatic variability and, hence, biological complexity. Although some of the hotspots are sparsely populated, others, such as "Sundaland," are among the world's most densely populated areas. Protection of the rich biodiversity of these hotspots is, most biologists feel, of crucial importance to the preservation of the world's biological heritage.

Map 98   Degree of Human Disturbance

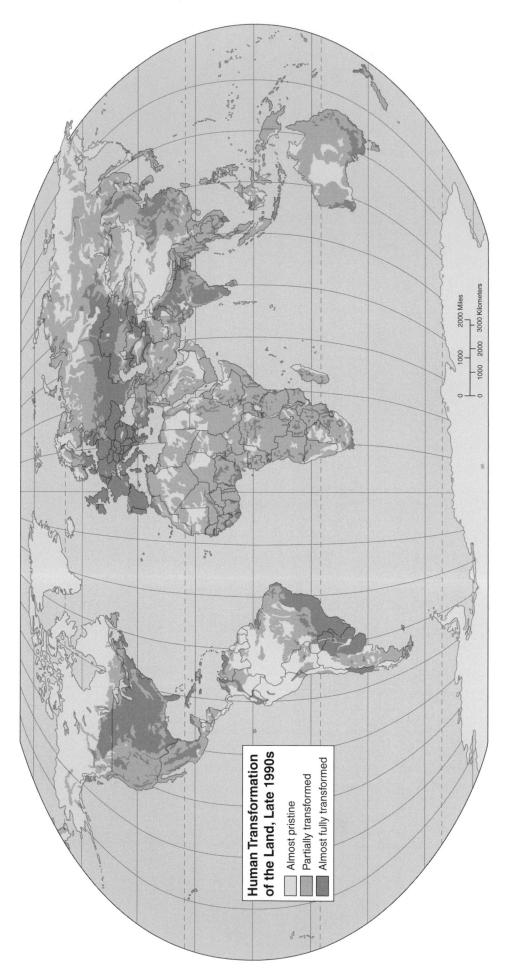

**Human Transformation
of the Land, Late 1990s**

☐ Almost pristine
◩ Partially transformed
■ Almost fully transformed

0   1000   2000 Miles

0   1000   2000   3000 Kilometers

The data on human disturbance have been gathered from a wide variety of sources, some of them conflicting and not all of them reliable. Nevertheless, at a global scale this map fairly depicts the state of the world in terms of the degree to which humans have modified its surface. The almost pristine areas, covered with natural vegetation, generally have population densities under 10 persons per square mile. These areas are, for the most part, in the most inhospitable parts of the world: too high, too dry, too cold for permanent human habitation in large numbers. The partially transformed areas are normally agricultural areas, either subsistence (such as shifting cultivation) or extensive (such as livestock grazing). They often contain areas of second-ary vegetation, regrown after removal of original vegetation by humans. They are also often marked by a density of livestock in excess of carrying capacity, leading to overgrazing, which further alters the condition of the vegetation. The almost fully transformed areas are those of permanent and intensive agriculture and urban settlement. The primary vegetation of these regions has been removed, with no evidence of regrowth or with current vegetation that is quite different from natural (potential) vegetation. Soils are in a state of depletion and degradation, and, in drier lands, desertification is a factor of human occupation. The disturbed areas match closely those areas of the world with the densest human populations.

Unit VII

Regions of the World

Map 99   North America: Physical Features

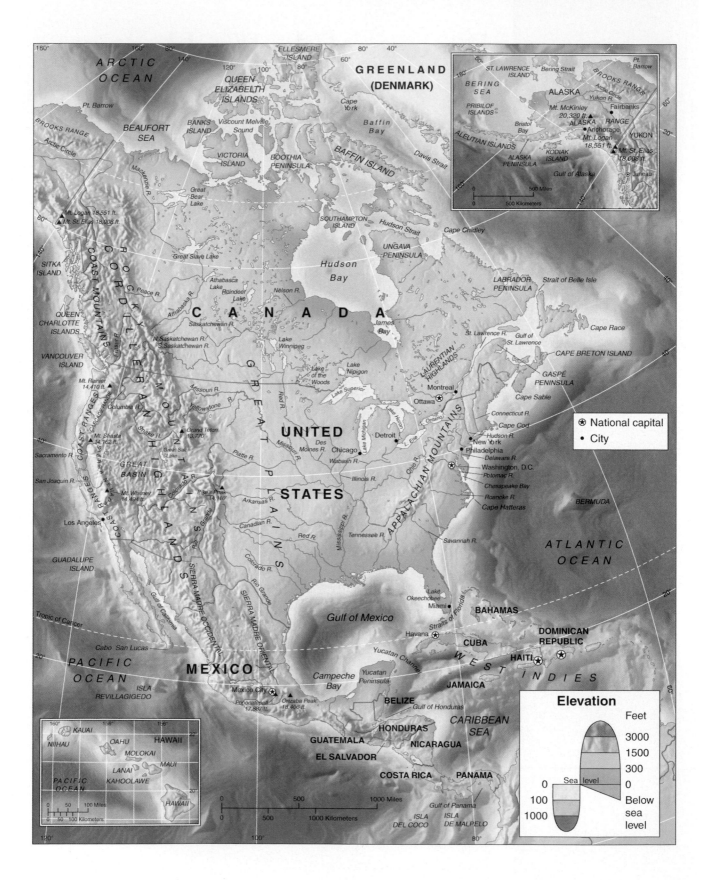

Map **100**   North America: Political Divisions

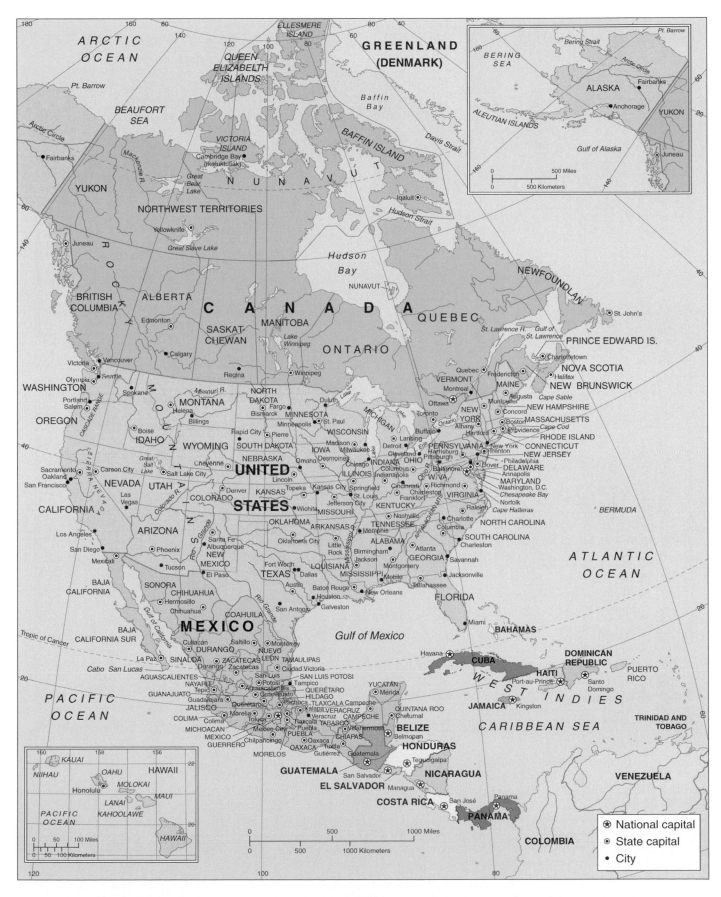

Map 101   North American Land Use

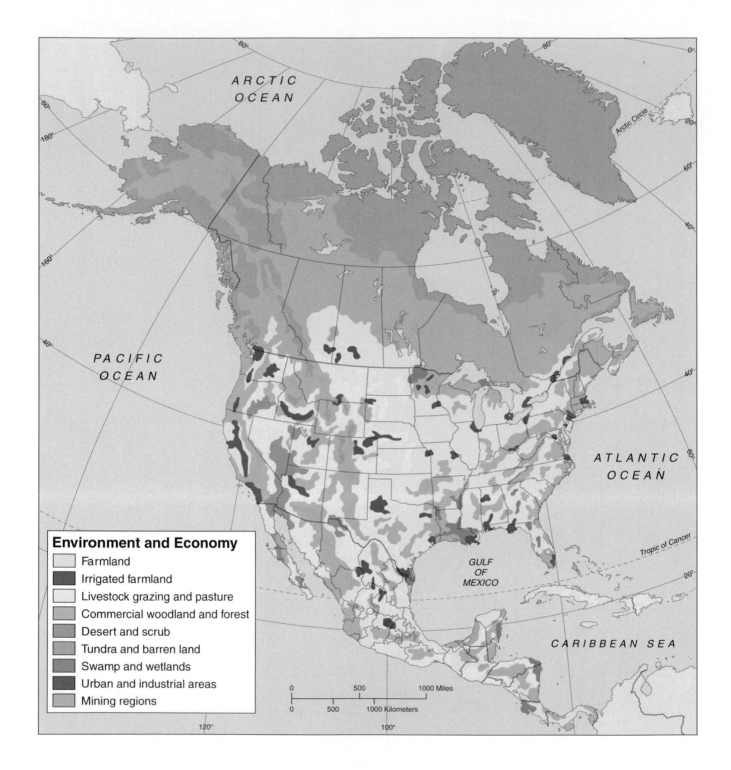

Environment and Economy

- Farmland
- Irrigated farmland
- Livestock grazing and pasture
- Commercial woodland and forest
- Desert and scrub
- Tundra and barren land
- Swamp and wetlands
- Urban and industrial areas
- Mining regions

ARCTIC OCEAN

PACIFIC OCEAN

ATLANTIC OCEAN

GULF OF MEXICO

CARIBBEAN SEA

Arctic Circle

Tropic of Cancer

The use of land in North America represents a balance between agriculture, resource extraction, and manufacturing that is unmatched. The United States, as the world's leading industrial power, is also the world's leader in commercial agricultural production. Canada, despite its small population, is a ranking producer of both agricultural and industrial products and Mexico has begun to emerge from its developing nation status to become an important industrial and agricultural nation as well.

The countries of Middle America and the Caribbean are just beginning the transition from agriculture to modern industrial economies. Part of the basis for the high levels of economic productivity in North America is environmental: a superb blend of soil, climate, and raw materials. But just as important is the cultural and social mix of the plural societies of North America, a mix that historically aided the growth of the economic diversity necessary for developed economies.

Map 102 South America: Physical Features

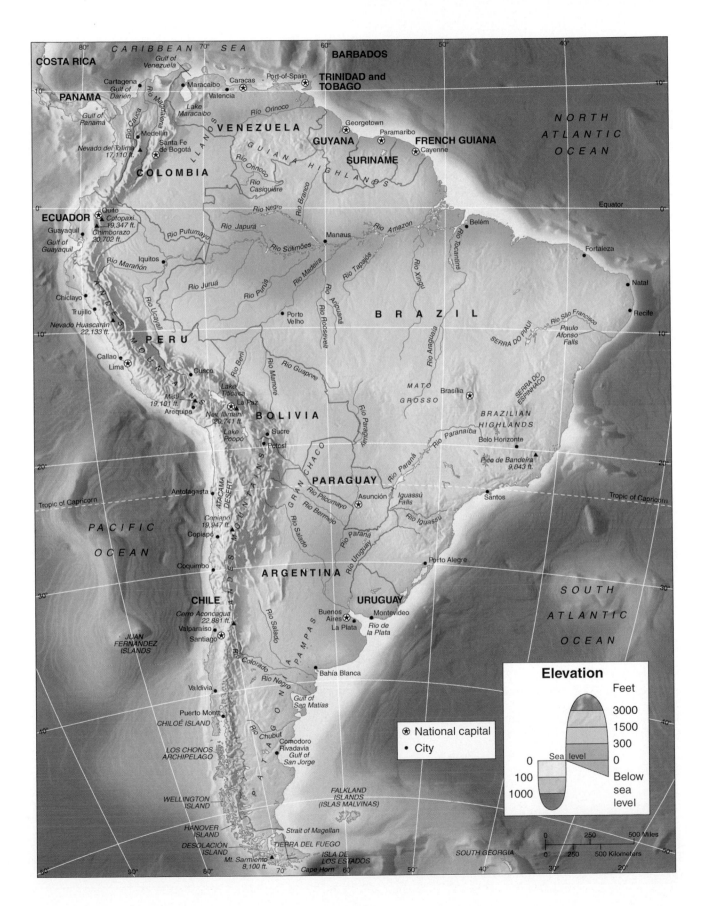

Elevation

	Feet
	3000
	1500
	300
0 Sea level	0
100	Below sea level
1000	

⊛ National capital
• City

0   250   500 Miles
0   250   500 Kilometers

Map **103** South America: Political Divisions

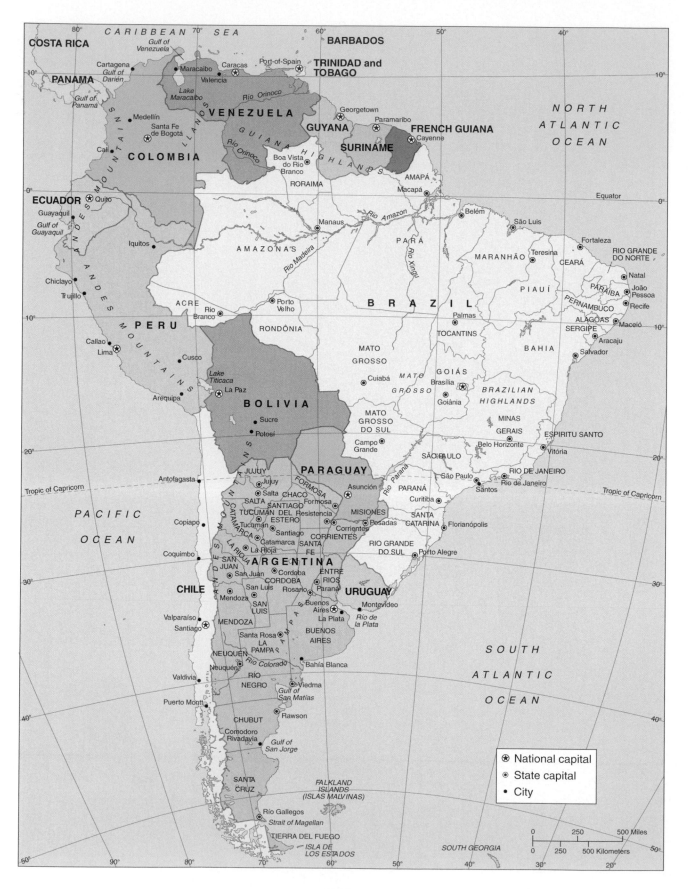

Map 104   South American Land Use

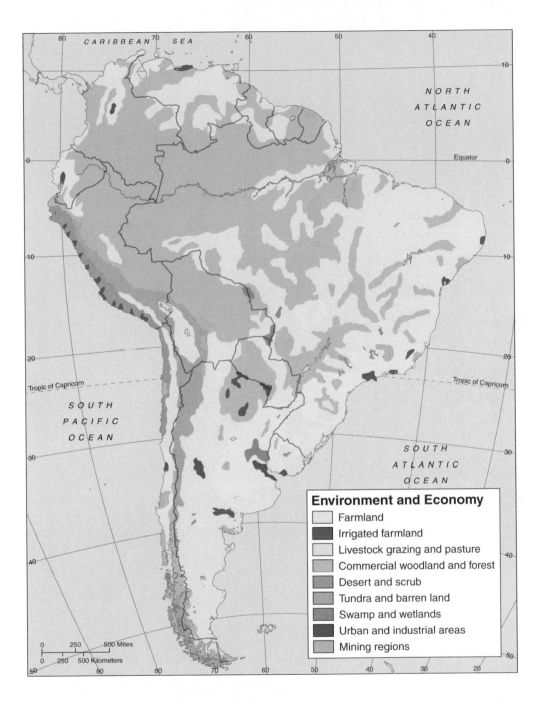

Environment and Economy

- Farmland
- Irrigated farmland
- Livestock grazing and pasture
- Commercial woodland and forest
- Desert and scrub
- Tundra and barren land
- Swamp and wetlands
- Urban and industrial areas
- Mining regions

South America is a region just beginning to emerge from a colonial-dependency economy in which raw materials flowed from the continent to more highly developed economic regions. With the exception of Brazil, Argentina, Chile, and Uruguay, most of the continent's countries still operate under the traditional mode of exporting raw materials in exchange for capital that tends to accumulate in the pockets of a small percentage of the population. The land use patterns of the continent are, therefore, still dominated by resource extraction and agricul-

ture. A problem posed by these patterns is that little of the continent's land area is actually suitable for either commercial forestry or commercial crop agriculture without extremely high environmental costs. Much of the agriculture, then, is based on high value tropical crops that can be grown in small areas profitably, or on extensive livestock grazing. Even within the forested areas of the Amazon Basin where forest clearance is taking place at unprecedented rates, much of the land use that replaces forest is grazing.

Map 105 Europe: Physical Features

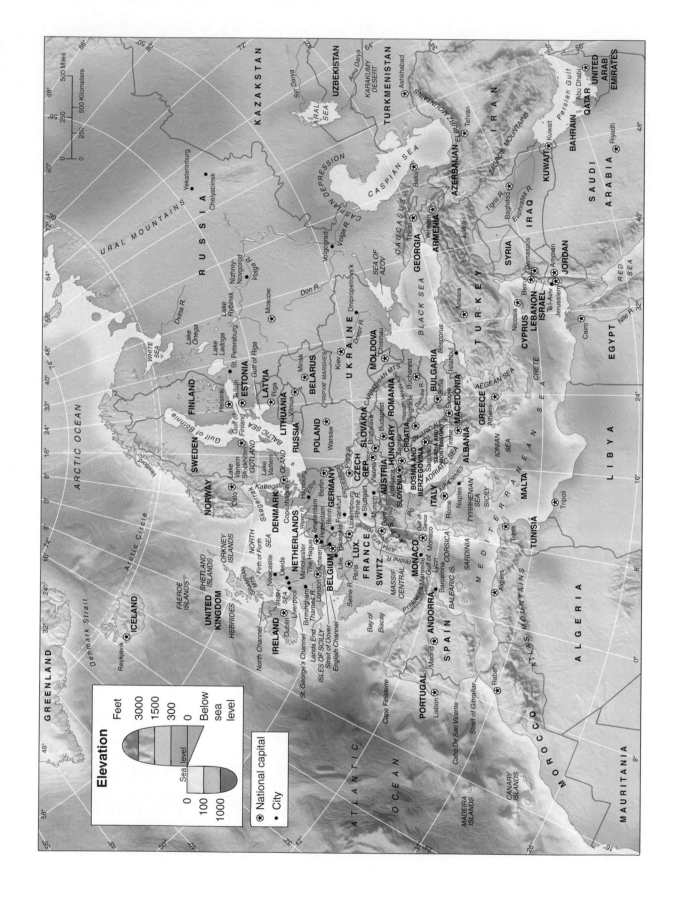

Elevation

Feet	
3000	
1500	
300	
0	Below sea level

Sea level

0	
100	
1000	

⊛ National capital

• City

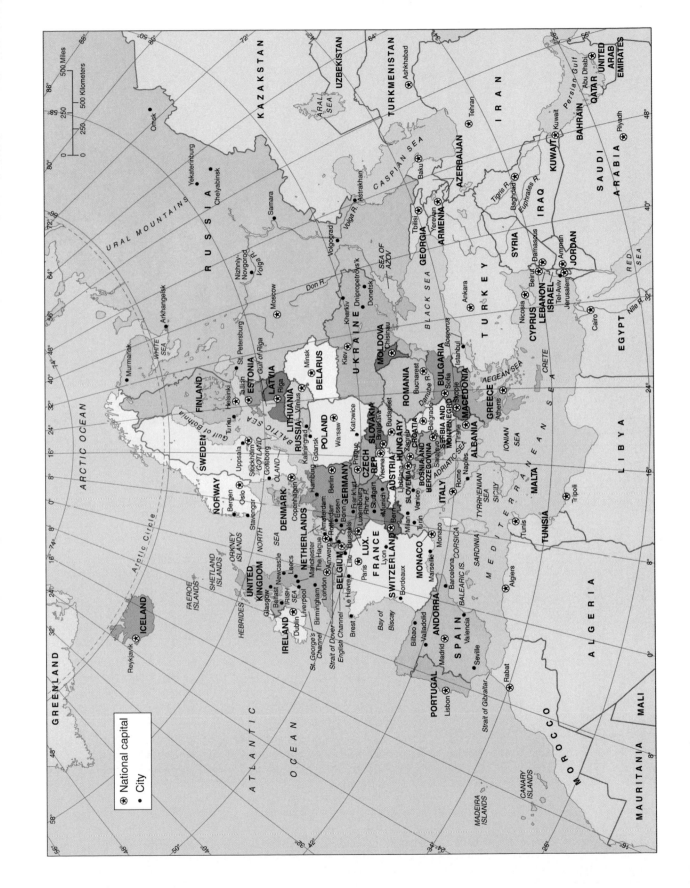

Map **106** Europe: Political Divisions

Map 107 European Land Use

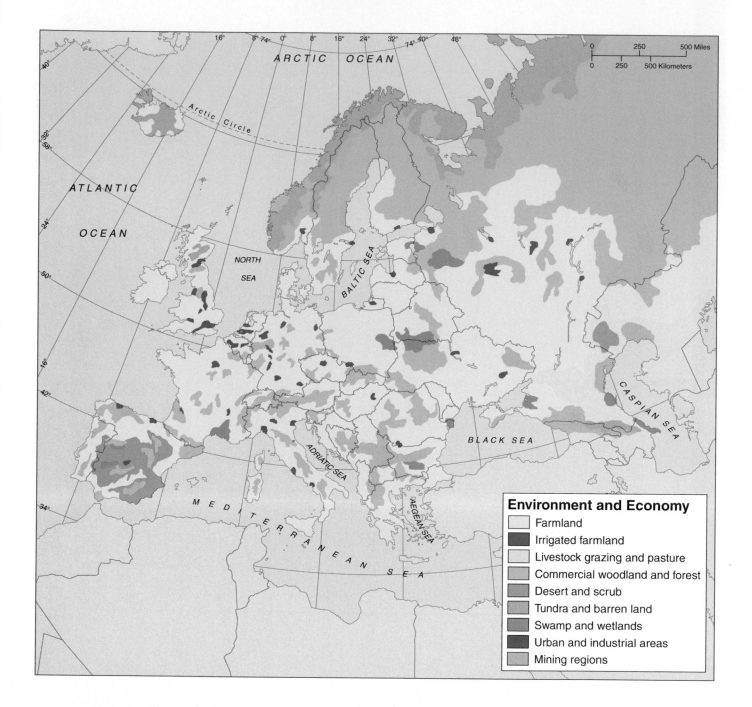

Environment and Economy
- Farmland
- Irrigated farmland
- Livestock grazing and pasture
- Commercial woodland and forest
- Desert and scrub
- Tundra and barren land
- Swamp and wetlands
- Urban and industrial areas
- Mining regions

More than any other continent, Europe bears the imprint of human activity—mining, forestry, agriculture, industry, and urbanization. Virtually all of western and central Europe's natural forest vegetation is gone, lost to clearing for agriculture beginning in prehistory, to lumbering that began in earnest during the Middle Ages, or, more recently, to disease and destruction brought about by acid precipitation. Only in the far north and the east do some natural stands remain. The region is the world's most heavily industrialized, and the industrial areas on the map represent only the largest and most significant. Not shown are the industries that are found in virtually every small town and village and smaller city throughout the industrial countries for Europe. Europe also possesses abundant raw materials and a very productive agricultural base. The mineral resources have long been in a state of active exploitation and the mining regions shown on the map are, for the most part, old regions in upland areas that are somewhat less significant now than they may have been in the past. Agriculturally, the northern European plain is one of the world's great agricultural regions but most of Europe contains decent land for agriculture.

Map **108**   Asia: Physical Features

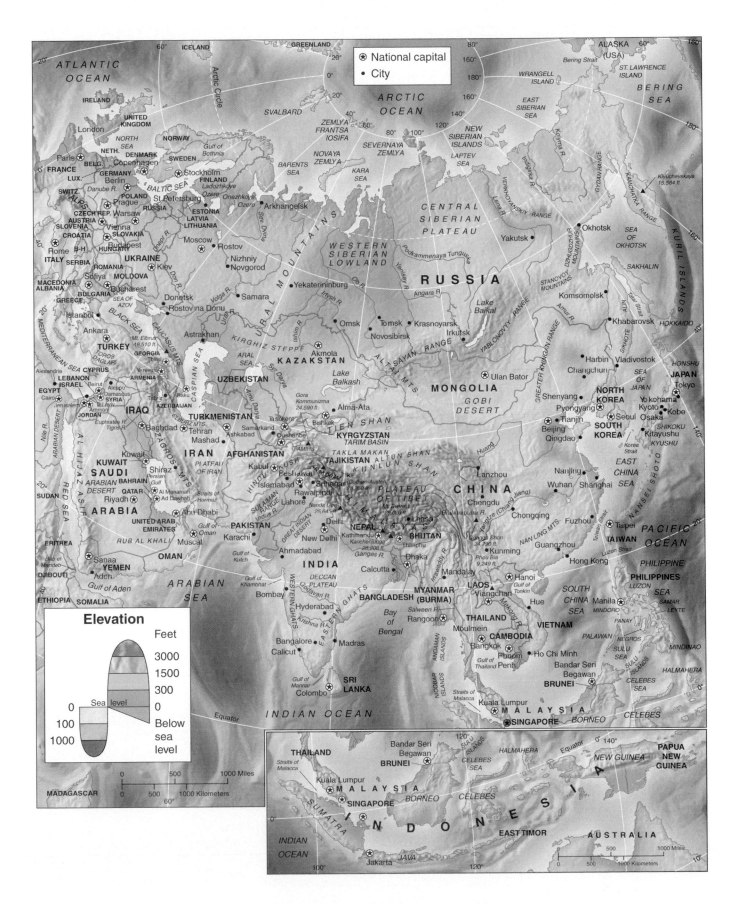

Map 109   Asia: Political Divisions

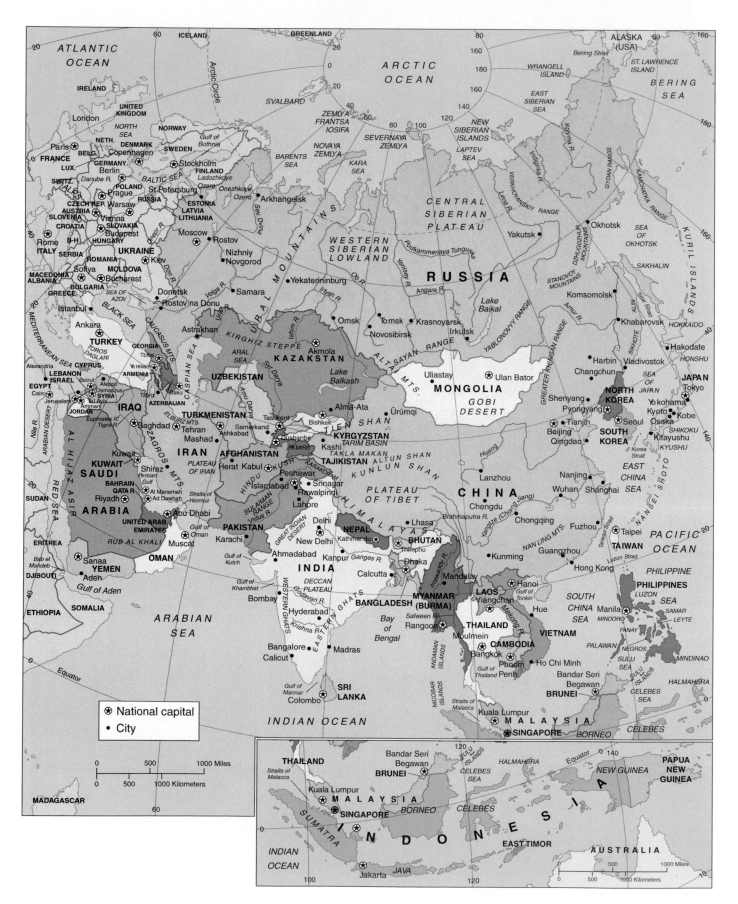

National capital
City

Map 110 Asian Land Use

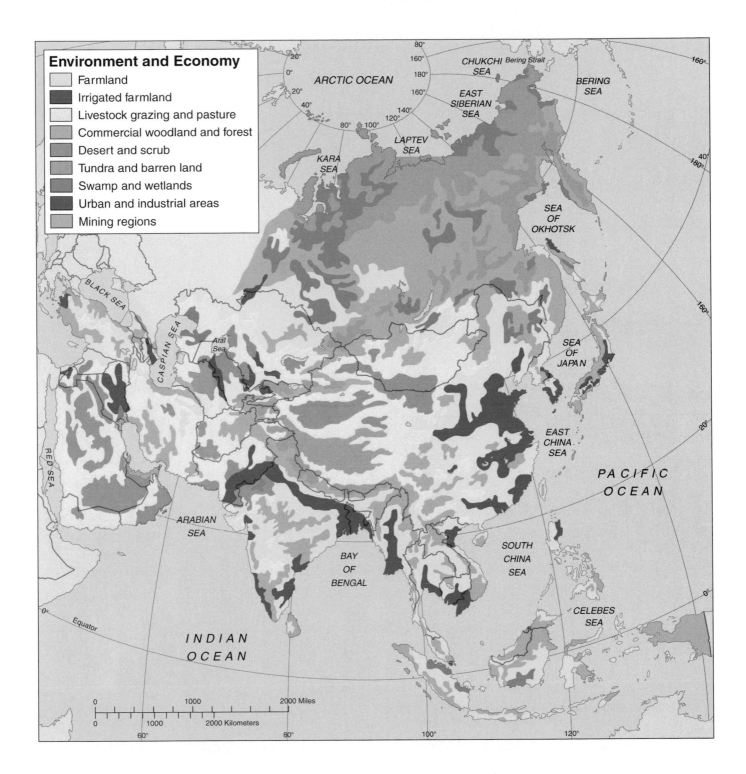

Environment and Economy

- Farmland
- Irrigated farmland
- Livestock grazing and pasture
- Commercial woodland and forest
- Desert and scrub
- Tundra and barren land
- Swamp and wetlands
- Urban and industrial areas
- Mining regions

Asia is a land of extremes of land use with some of the world's most heavily industrialized regions, barren and empty areas, and productive and densely populated farm regions. Asia is a region of rapid industrial growth. Yet Asia remains an agricultural region with three out of every four workers engaged in agriculture. Asian commercial agriculture and intensive subsistence agriculture is characterized by irrigation. Some of Asia's irrigated lands are desert requiring additional water. But most of the Asian irrigated regions have suffi-cient precipitation for crop agriculture, and irrigation is a way of coping with seasonal drought—the wet-and-dry cycle of the monsoon—often gaining more than one crop per year on irrigated farms. Agricultural yields per unit area in many areas of Asia are among the world's highest. Because the Asian population is so large and the demands for agricultural land so great, Asia is undergoing rapid deforestation, and some areas of the continent have only small remnants of a once-abundant forest reserve.

Map 111 Southwest and Central Asia: Physical Features

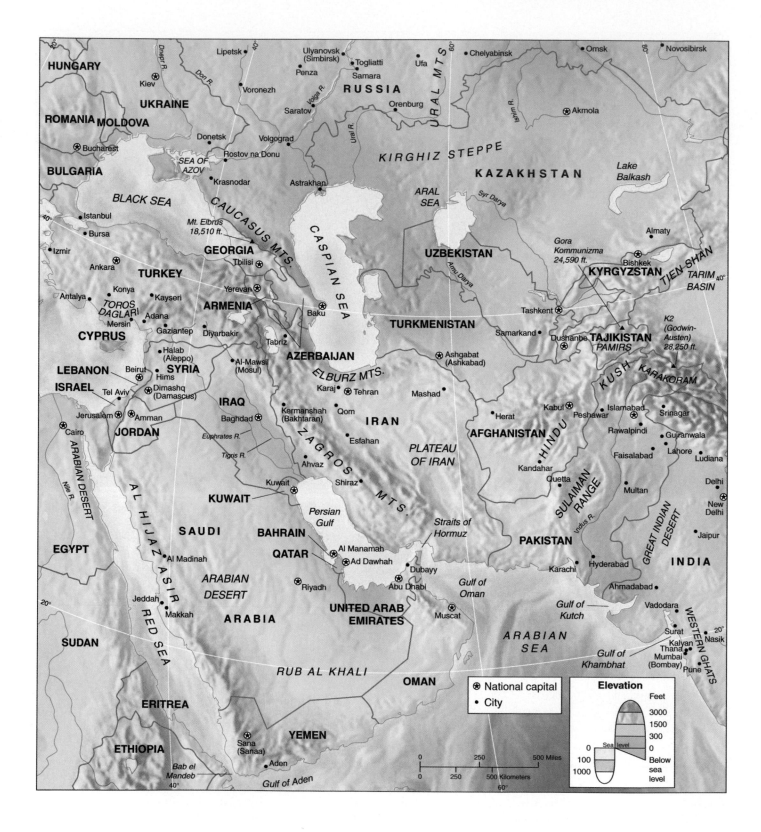

Map 112   Southwest and Central Asia: Political Divisions

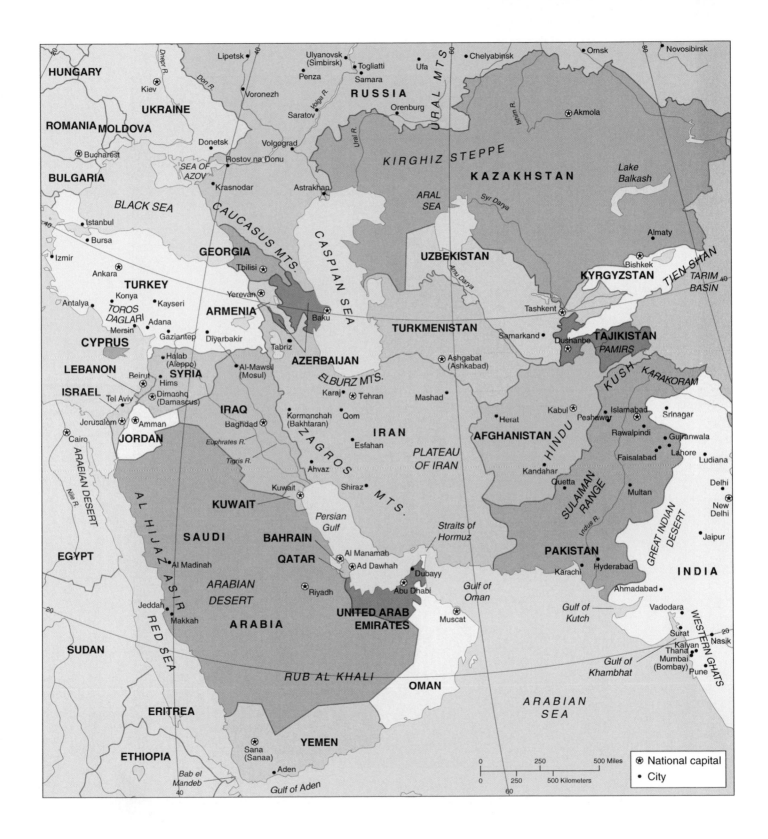

Map 113 South and Southeast Asia: Physical Features

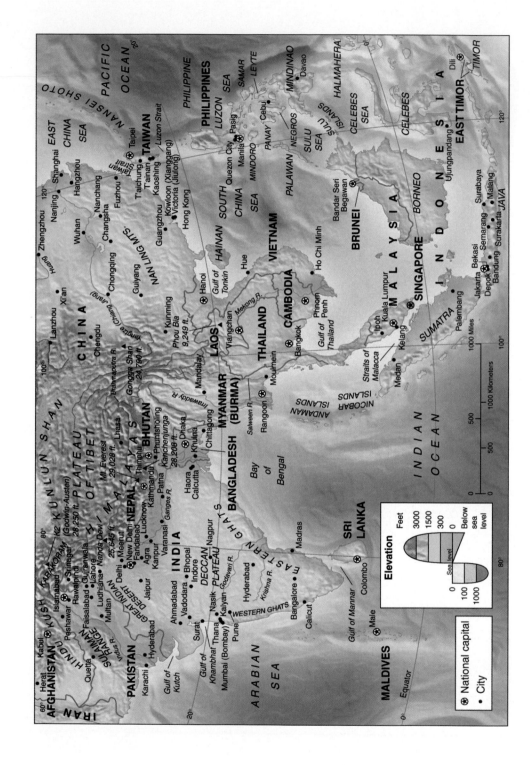

Map 114 South and Southeast Asia: Political Divisions

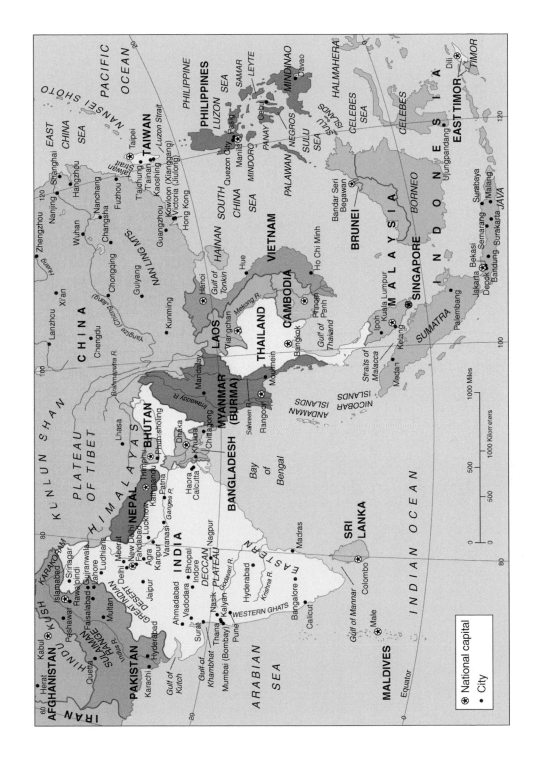

Map 115 North and East Asia: Physical Features

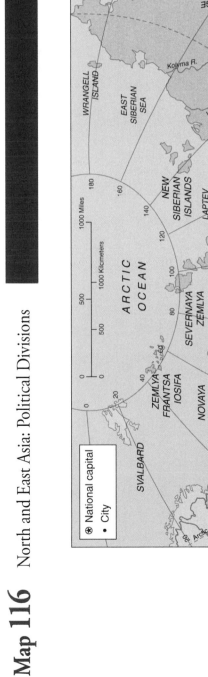

Map 116 North and East Asia: Political Divisions

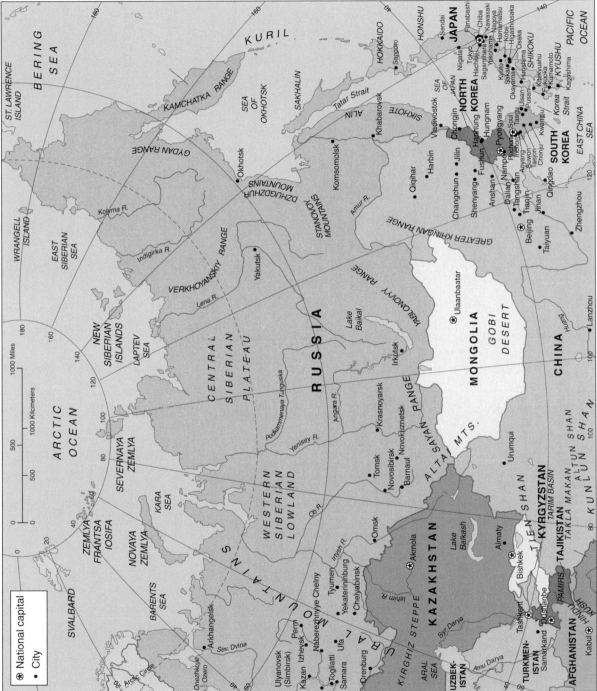

Map 117   Africa: Physical Features

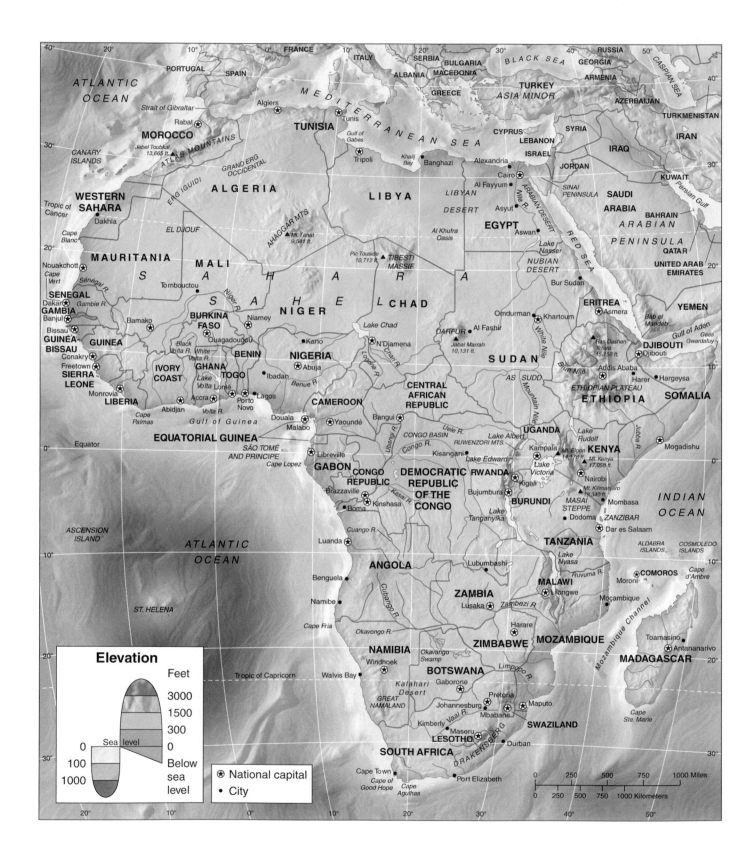

Map 118 Africa: Political Divisions

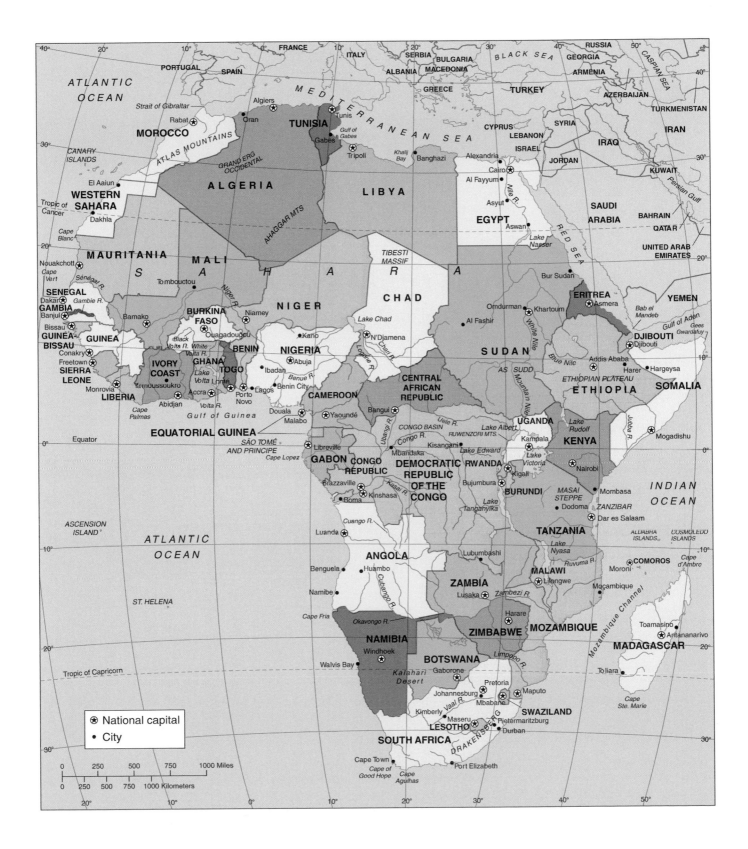

⊛ National capital
• City

0 250 500 750 1000 Miles

0 250 500 750 1000 Kilometers

Map **119**   African Land Use

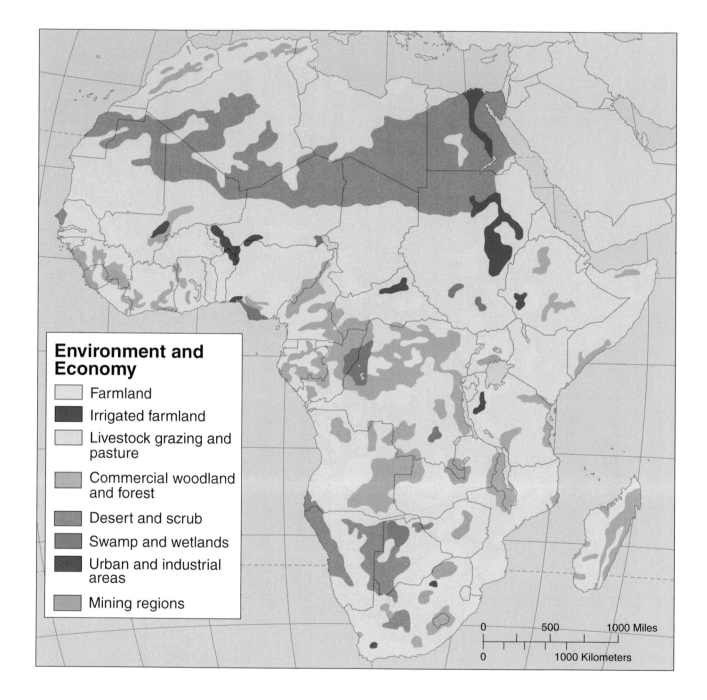

Environment and Economy

- ▢ Farmland
- ▪ Irrigated farmland
- ▢ Livestock grazing and pasture
- ▢ Commercial woodland and forest
- ▢ Desert and scrub
- ▢ Swamp and wetlands
- ▪ Urban and industrial areas
- ▢ Mining regions

0 — 500 — 1000 Miles

0 — 1000 Kilometers

Africa's economic landscape is dominated by subsistence, or marginally commercial agricultural activities and raw material extraction, engaging three-fourths of Africa's workers. Much of this grazing land is very poor desert scrub and bunch grass that is easily impacted by cattle, sheep, and goats. Growing human and livestock populations place enormous stress on this fragile support capacity and the result is desertification: the conversion of even the most minimal of grazing environments or land suitable for crop farming to virtual desert conditions. Although the continent has approximately 20 percent of the world's total land area, the proportion of Africa's arable land is small. The agricultural environment is also uncertain; unpredictable precipitation and poor soils hamper crop agriculture.

Map 120 Australia and Oceania: Physical Features

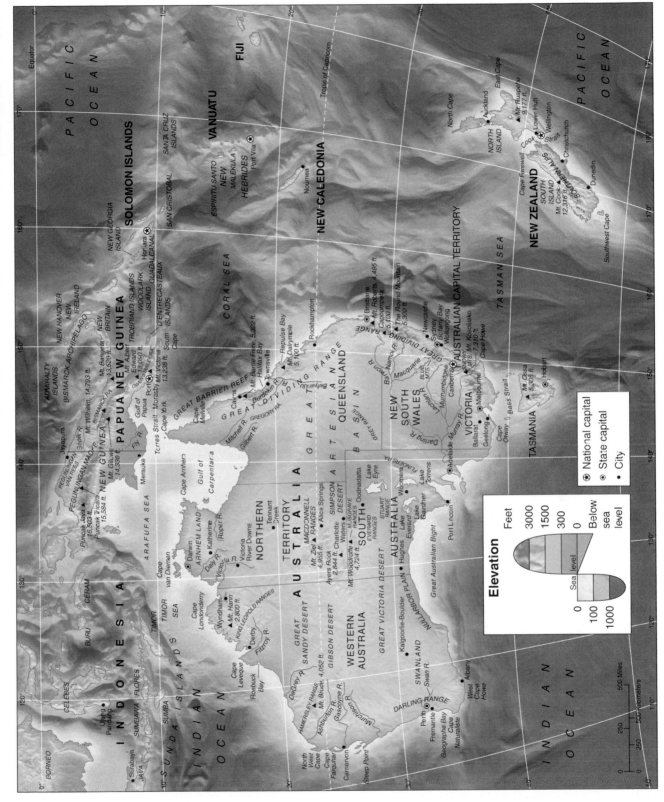

Map 121 Australia and Oceania: Political Divisions

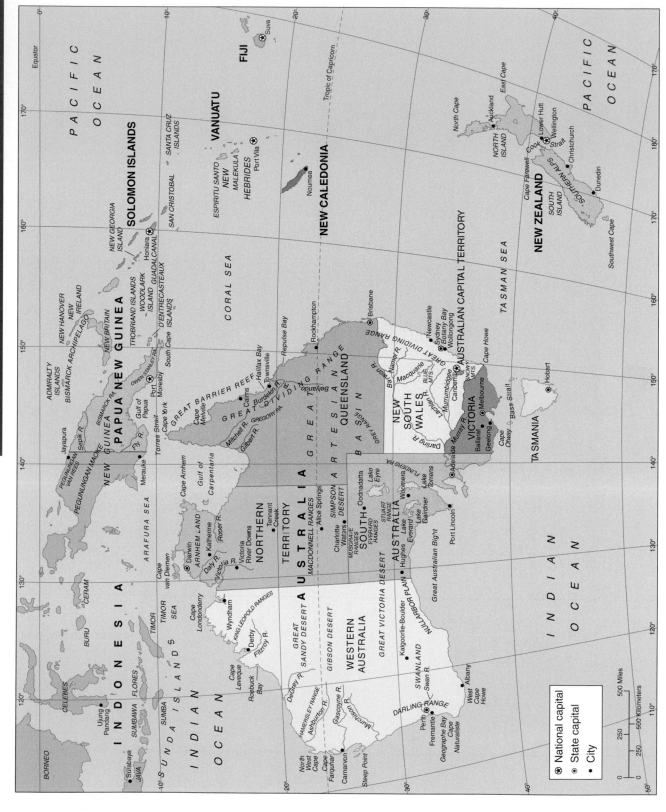

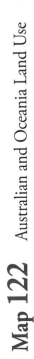

Map 122 Australian and Oceania Land Use

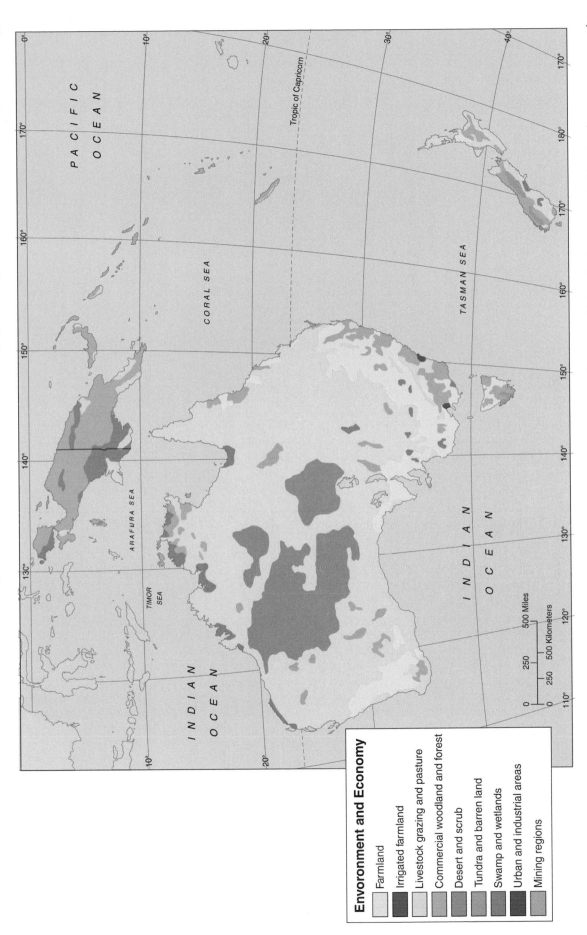

Envoronment and Economy

- Farmland
- Irrigated farmland
- Livestock grazing and pasture
- Commercial woodland and forest
- Desert and scrub
- Tundra and barren land
- Swamp and wetlands
- Urban and industrial areas
- Mining regions

Australasia is dominated by the world's smallest and most uniform continent. Flat, dry, and mostly hot, Australia has the simplest of land use patterns: where rainfall exists so does agricultural activity. Two agricultural patterns dominate the map: livestock grazing, primarily sheep, and wheat farming, although some sugar cane production exists in the north and some cotton is grown elsewhere. Only about 6 percent of the continent consists of arable land so the areas of wheat farming, dominant as they may be in the context of Australian agriculture, are small. Australia also supports a healthy mineral resource economy, with iron and copper and precious metals making up the bulk of the extraction. Elsewhere in the region, tropical forests dominate Papua New Guinea, with some subsistence agriculture and livestock. New Zealand's temperate climate with abundant precipitation supports a productive livestock industry and little else besides tourism—which is an important economic element throughout the remainder of the region as well.

-153-

Map **123**   The Pacific Rim

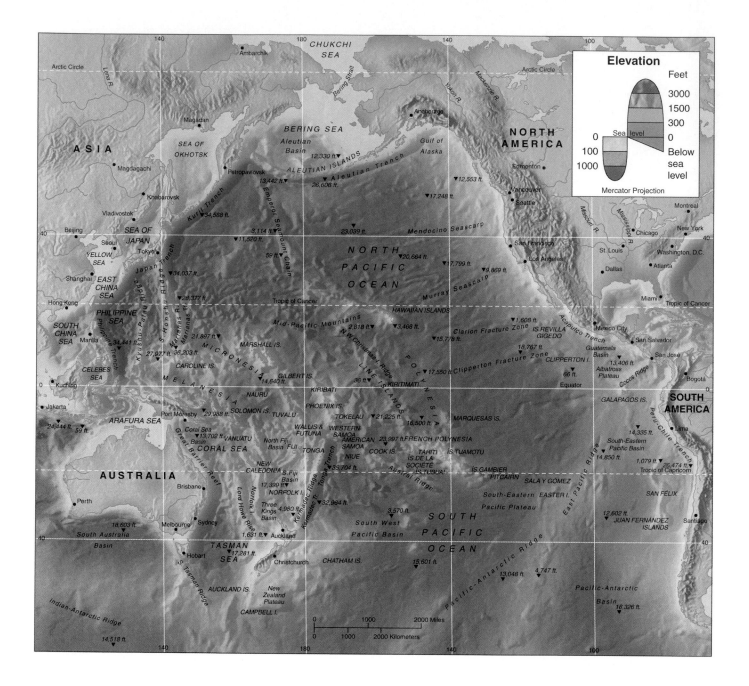

Map 124   The Atlantic Ocean

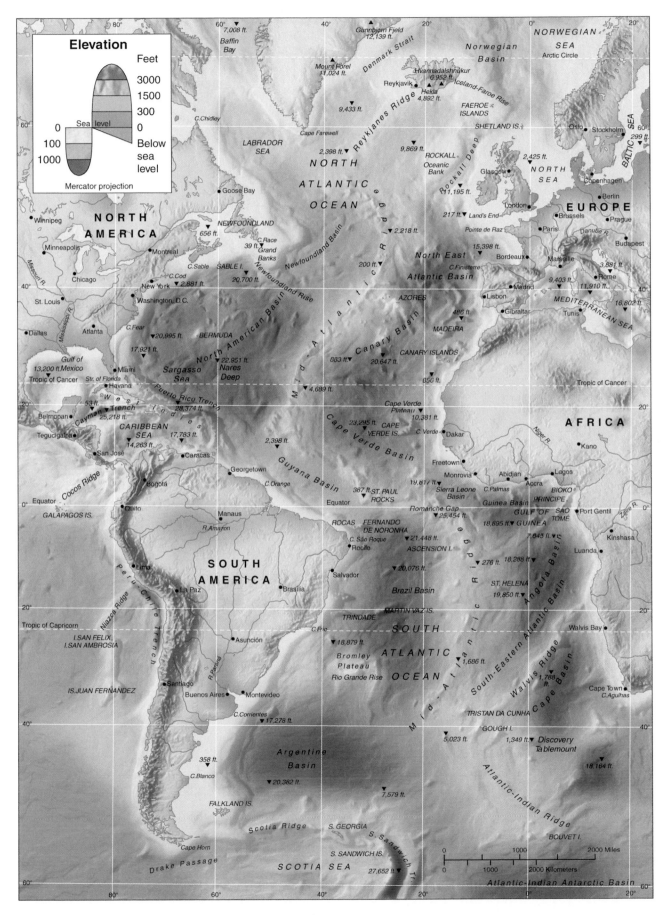

Map 125   The Indian Ocean

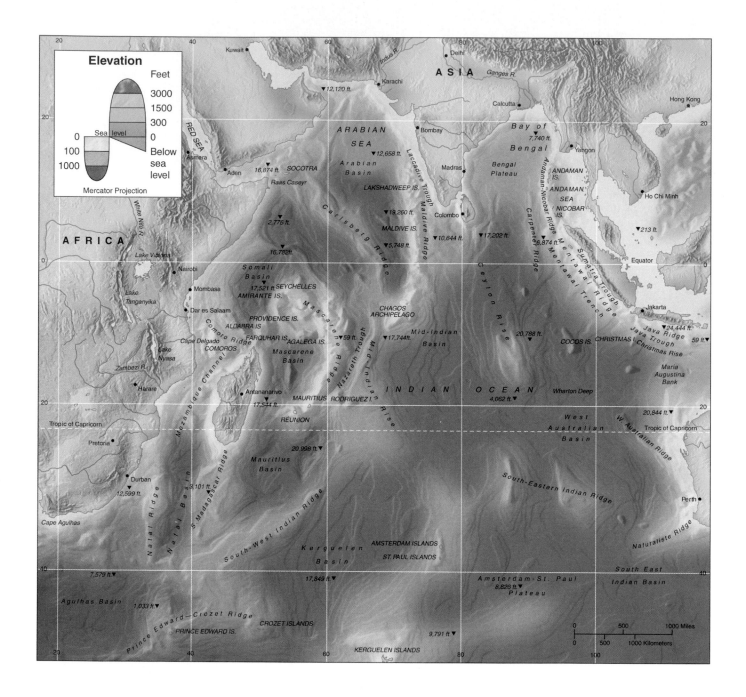

Elevation

Feet
3000
1500
300

Sea level

0	Sea level	0
100		Below
1000		sea level

Mercator Projection

Kuwait · Delhi
Indus R. · Ganges R.
ASIA
Karachi
▼12,120 ft.
Calcutta
Hong Kong

ARABIAN SEA
Bombay
Bay of
Bengal
7,740 ft.
Yangon
▼12,658 ft.
Arabian Basin
Madras
Bengal Plateau
ANDAMAN IS.
16,874 ft. SOCOTRA
Aden
Raas Caseyr
LAKSHADWEEP IS.
ANDAMAN SEA
NICOBAR IS.
Ho Chi Minh
RED SEA
Asmera
▼19,260 ft.
MALDIVE IS.
Colombo
▼10,644 ft.
▼17,202 ft.
▼213 ft.
WHITE Nile R.
2,776 ft.
▼5,748 ft.
6,874 ft.
Equator
AFRICA
Lake Victoria
16,792ft.
Somali Basin
Nairobi
17,521 ft. SEYCHELLES
AMIRANTE IS.
CHAGOS ARCHIPELAGO
Mid-Indian Basin
20,788 ft.
Jakarta
Lake Tanganyika
Mombasa
PROVIDENCE IS.
ALDABRA IS.
FARQUHAR IS. AGALEGA IS.
▼59 ft.
▼17,744 ft.
COCOS IS. CHRISTMAS I.
▼24,444 ft.
59 ft.
Dar es Salaam
Cape Delgado
COMOROS
Mascarene Basin
Maria Augustina Bank
Lake Nyasa
Zambezi R.
Antananarivo
MAURITIUS RODRIGUEZ I.
INDIAN OCEAN
Wharton Deep
4,062 ft.▼
Harare
17,544 ft.
RÉUNION
West Australian Basin
20,844 ft.▼
Tropic of Capricorn
Pretoria
20,998 ft.▼
Mauritius Basin
Tropic of Capricorn
Durban
3,101 ft.▼
South-Eastern Indian Ridge
Perth
12,599 ft.
Amsterdam Islands
ST. PAUL ISLANDS
Naturaliste Ridge
Cape Agulhas
Kerguelen Basin
South East Indian Basin
7,579 ft.▼
17,849 ft.▼
Amsterdam-St. Paul Plateau
8,826 ft.▼
Agulhas Basin
1,033 ft.▼
Prince Edward-Crozet Ridge
CROZET ISLANDS
9,791 ft.▼
PRINCE EDWARD IS.
KERGUELEN ISLANDS

| 0 | 500 | 1000 Miles |
| 0 | 500 | 1000 Kilometers |

Map 126 The Arctic

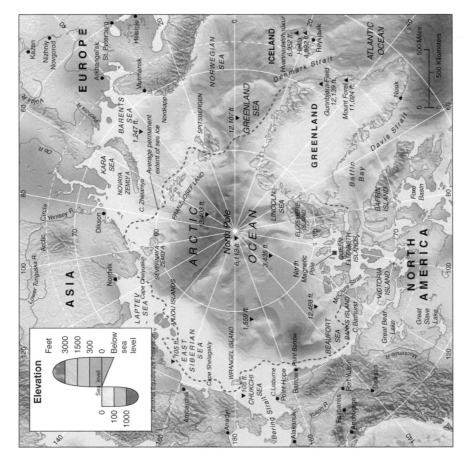

Map 127 Antarctica

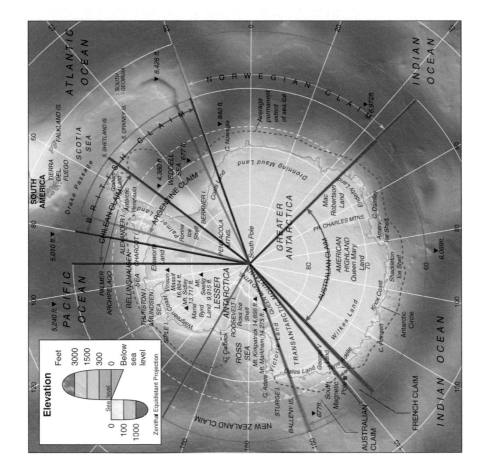

Unit VIII

World Countries: Data Tables

Table A
World Countries: Area, Population, and Population Density, 2005

COUNTRY	AREA		POPULATION	DENSITY	
	(ml²)	(km²)	(estimated 12/2005)	(pop/mi²)	(pop/km²)
Afghanistan	251,826	652,090	30,328,497	120.43	46.51
Albania	11,100	28,750	3,129,678	281.95	108.86
Algeria	919,595	2,381,740	32,853,798	35.73	13.79
Angola	481,354	1,246,700	15,941,392	33.12	12.79
Antigua and Barbuda	171	440	82,786	484.13	188.15
Argentina	1,073,400	2,780,400	38,747,148	36.10	13.94
Armenia	11,506	29,800	3,016,312	262.15	101.22
Australia	2,966,155	7,741,220	20,329,000	6.85	2.63
Austria	32,377	83,860	8,233,300	254.29	98.18
Azerbaijan	33,436	86,600	8,388,000	250.87	96.86
Bahamas, The	5,382	13,880	323,063	60.03	23.28
Bahrain	267	710	726,617	2,721.41	1,023.40
Bangladesh	55,598	144,000	141,822,272	2,550.85	984.88
Barbados	166	430	269,556	1,623.83	626.87
Belarus	80,155	207,600	9,775,591	121.96	47.09
Belgium	11,783	30,510	10,478,650	889.30	343.45
Belize	8,866	22,960	291,800	32.91	12.71
Benin	43,475	112,620	8,438,853	194.11	74.93
Bhutan	18,200	47,000	636,638	34.98	13.55
Bolivia	424,165	1,098,580	9,182,015	21.65	8.36
Bosnia and Herzegovina	19,776	51,210	3,907,074	197.57	76.30
Botswana	231,803	581,730	1,764,926	7.61	3.03
Brazil	3,286,488	8,514,880	186,404,912	56.72	21.89
Brunei	2,228	5,770	373,819	167.78	64.79
Bulgaria	42,823	110,990	7,740,000	180.74	69.74
Burkina Faso	105,869	274,000	13,227,835	124.95	48.28
Burundi	10,745	27,830	7,547,515	702.42	271.20
Cambodia	69,898	181,040	14,071,014	201.31	77.72
Cameroon	183,569	475,440	16,321,863	88.91	34.33
Canada	3,849,674	9,970,610	32,299,000	8.39	3.24
Cape Verde	1,557	4,030	506,807	325.50	125.76
Central African Republic	240,535	622,980	4,037,747	16.79	6.48
Chad	495,755	1,284,000	9,748,931	19.66	7.59
Chile	292,259	756,630	16,295,102	55.76	21.54
China	3,705,392	9,598,050	1,304,499,968	352.05	135.91
Colombia	439,734	1,138,910	45,600,244	103.70	40.04
Comoros	838	2,230	600,490	716.58	269.28
Congo, Dem. Rep.	905,564	2,344,860	57,548,744	63.55	24.54
Congo, Rep.	132,047	342,000	3,998,904	30.28	11.69
Costa Rica	19,730	51,100	4,327,228	219.32	84.68
Cote d'Ivoire	124,502	322,460	18,153,868	145.81	56.30
Croatia	21,824	56,540	4,443,350	203.60	78.59
Cuba	42,804	110,860	11,269,400	263.28	101.65
Cyprus	3,571	9,250	757,800	212.21	81.92
Czech Republic	30,387	78,870	10,234,092	336.79	129.76

Table A (continued)
World Countries: Area, Population, and Population Density, 2005

COUNTRY	AREA		POPULATION	DENSITY	
	(mi²)	(km²)	(estimated 12/2005)	(pop/mi²)	(pop/km²)
Denmark	16,629	43,090	5,415,978	325.69	125.69
Djibouti	8,494	23,200	793,078	93.37	34.18
Dominica	290	750	72,000	248.28	96.00
Dominican Republic	18,815	48,730	8,894,907	472.76	182.53
Ecuador	109,484	283,560	13,228,423	120.83	46.65
Egypt, Arab Rep.	386,662	1,001,450	74,032,880	191.47	73.93
El Salvador	8,124	21,040	6,880,951	846.99	327.04
Equatorial Guinea	10,831	28,050	503,519	46.49	17.95
Eritrea	46,842	117,600	4,401,357	93.96	37.43
Estonia	17,413	45,230	1,346,100	77.30	29.76
Ethiopia	435,184	1,104,300	71,256,000	163.74	64.53
Fiji	7,054	18,270	847,706	120.17	46.40
Finland	130,127	338,150	5,246,100	40.32	15.51
France	176,460	551,500	60,873,000	344.97	110.38
Gabon	103,347	267,670	1,383,841	13.39	5.17
Gambia, The	4,363	11,300	1,517,079	347.71	134.25
Georgia	26,911	69,700	4,474,404	166.27	64.20
Germany	137,803	357,030	82,469,400	598.46	230.99
Ghana	92,098	238,540	22,112,804	240.10	92.70
Greece	50,942	131,960	11,104,000	217.97	84.15
Grenada	131	340	106,500	812.98	313.24
Guatemala	42,042	108,890	12,599,059	299.68	115.70
Guinea	94,926	245,860	9,402,098	99.05	38.24
Guinea-Bissau	13,948	36,120	1,586,344	113.73	43.92
Guyana	83,000	214,970	751,218	9.05	3.49
Haiti	10,714	27,750	8,527,777	795.95	307.31
Honduras	43,277	112,090	7,204,723	166.48	64.28
Hungary	35,920	93,030	10,087,050	280.82	108.43
Iceland	39,768	103,000	296,750	7.46	2.88
India	1,269,340	3,287,260	1,094,583,040	862.32	332.98
Indonesia	741,097	1,904,570	220,558,000	297.61	115.80
Iran, Islamic Rep.	636,294	1,648,200	68,251,088	107.26	41.41
Iraq (2004)	168,754	438,320	24,699,540	146.36	56.47
Ireland	27,137	70,270	4,159,100	153.26	59.19
Israel	8,019	22,140	6,923,600	863.40	312.72
Italy	116,305	301,340	58,607,048	503.91	194.49
Jamaica	4,244	10,990	2,654,500	625.47	241.54
Japan	145,882	377,890	127,774,000	875.87	338.12
Jordan	35,445	89,210	5,473,000	154.41	61.35
Kazakhstan	1,049,156	2,724,900	15,146,081	14.44	5.56
Kenya	224,961	580,370	34,255,720	152.27	59.02
Kiribati	277	730	99,000	357.40	135.62
Korea, Dem. Rep.	46,540	120,540	22,487,660	483.19	186.56
Korea, Rep.	38,023	99,260	48,294,144	1,270.13	486.54
Kuwait	6,880	17,820	2,535,446	368.52	142.28

COUNTRY	AREA		POPULATION	DENSITY	
	(mi²)	(km²)	(estimated 12/2005)	(pop/mi²)	(pop/km²)
Kyrgyz Republic	76,641	199,900	5,143,500	67.11	25.73
Lao PDR	91,429	236,800	5,924,145	64.80	25.02
Latvia	24,749	64,600	2,300,500	92.95	35.61
Lebanon	4,015	10,400	3,576,818	890.86	343.92
Lesotho	11,720	30,350	1,794,769	153.14	59.14
Liberia	43,000	111,370	3,283,267	76.36	29.48
Libya	679,362	1,759,540	5,853,452	8.62	3.33
Liechtenstein	62	160	34,750	560.48	217.19
Lithuania	25,174	65,300	3,414,300	135.63	52.29
Luxembourg	998	2,586	456,710	457.63	176.61
Macedonia, FYR	9,781	25,710	2,034,060	207.96	79.12
Madagascar	226,658	587,040	18,605,920	82.09	31.69
Malawi	45,747	118,480	12,883,935	281.63	108.74
Malaysia	127,317	329,750	25,347,368	199.09	76.87
Maldives	115	300	329,198	2,862.59	1,097.33
Mali	478,767	1,240,190	13,518,416	28.24	10.90
Malta	124	320	403,500	3,254.03	1,260.94
Marshall Islands	70	181	63,266	903.80	348.96
Mauritania	397,954	1,025,520	3,068,742	7.71	2.99
Mauritius	718	2,040	1,243,253	1,731.55	609.44
Mexico	761,603	1,958,200	103,089,136	135.36	52.64
Micronesia, Fed. Sts.	271	702	110,487	407.70	157.39
Moldova	13,012	33,840	4,205,747	323.22	124.28
Monaco	1	2	33,400	27,603.31	17,128.21
Mongolia	604,427	1,566,500	2,554,000	4.23	1.63
Morocco	172,413	446,550	30,168,082	174.98	67.56
Mozambique	309,494	801,590	19,792,296	63.95	24.69
Myanmar	261,969	676,580	50,519,492	192.85	74.67
Namibia	318,259	824,290	2,031,252	6.38	2.46
Nepal	54,363	147,180	27,132,628	499.10	184.35
Netherlands	14,413	41,530	16,319,850	1,132.30	392.97
New Zealand	103,738	270,530	4,098,900	39.51	15.15
Nicaragua	49,998	130,000	5,149,311	102.99	39.61
Niger	489,191	1,267,000	13,956,977	28.53	11.02
Nigeria	356,669	923,770	131,529,672	368.77	142.38
Norway	125,182	323,760	4,623,300	36.93	14.28
Oman	82,030	309,500	2,566,981	31.29	8.29
Pakistan	310,402	796,100	155,772,000	501.84	195.67
Palau	177	460	20,100	113.56	43.70
Panama	30,193	75,520	3,231,502	107.03	42.79
Papua New Guinea	178,259	462,840	5,887,138	33.03	12.72
Paraguay	157,048	406,750	5,898,651	37.56	14.50
Peru	496,225	1,285,220	27,968,244	56.36	21.76
Philippines	115,831	300,000	83,054,480	717.03	276.85
Poland	120,728	312,690	38,165,448	316.13	122.06

Table A (continued)
World Countries: Area, Population, and Population Density, 2005

COUNTRY	AREA		POPULATION	DENSITY	
	(mi²)	(km²)	(estimated 12/2005)	(pop/mi²)	(pop/km²)
Portugal	35,552	91,980	10,549,450	296.73	114.69
Qatar	4,247	11,000	812,842	191.39	73.89
Romania	91,699	238,390	21,634,350	235.93	90.75
Russian Federation	6,592,745	17,075,400	143,113,648	21.71	8.38
Rwanda	10,169	26,340	9,037,690	888.75	343.12
Samoa	1,104	2,840	184,984	167.56	65.14
San Marino	23	61	28,200	1,226.09	466.12
Sao Tome and Principe	372	960	156,523	420.76	163.04
Saudi Arabia	756,982	2,149,690	23,118,994	30.54	10.75
Senegal	75,749	196,720	11,658,172	153.91	59.26
Serbia and Montenegro	39,517	102,170	8,064,253	204.07	78.93
Seychelles	175	450	84,494	482.82	187.76
Sierra Leone	27,699	71,740	5,525,478	199.48	77.02
Singapore	244	680	4,341,800	17,794.26	6,385.00
Slovak Republic	18,859	48,845	5,387,000	285.65	110.29
Slovenia	7,836	20,250	2,000,500	255.30	98.79
Solomon Islands	10,985	28,900	477,742	43.49	16.53
Somalia	246,201	637,660	8,227,826	33.42	12.90
South Africa	471,444	1,219,090	46,888,200	99.46	38.46
Spain	194,885	505,990	43,398,152	222.69	85.77
Sri Lanka	25,332	65,610	19,625,384	774.73	299.12
Sudan	967,500	2,505,810	36,232,944	37.45	14.46
Suriname	63,039	163,270	449,238	7.13	2.75
Swaziland	6,704	17,360	1,131,000	168.71	65.15
Sweden	173,732	449,960	9,024,040	51.94	20.06
Switzerland	15,943	41,290	7,437,100	466.48	180.12
Syrian Arab Republic	71,498	185,180	19,043,382	266.35	102.84
Taiwan	13,892	35,980	23,546,171	1,694.94	627.00
Tajikistan	55,251	143,100	6,506,980	117.77	45.47
Tanzania	364,900	945,090	38,328,808	105.04	40.56
Thailand	198,456	513,120	64,232,760	323.66	125.18
Timor-Leste	5,741	14,870	975,539	169.92	65.60
Togo	21,925	56,790	6,145,004	280.27	108.21
Tonga	290	750	102,311	352.80	136.41
Trinidad and Tobago	1,980	5,130	1,305,236	659.21	254.43
Tunisia	63,170	163,610	10,029,000	158.76	61.30
Turkey	301,382	774,820	72,065,000	239.12	93.01
Turkmenistan	188,456	488,100	4,833,266	25.65	9.90
Uganda	93,135	241,040	28,816,228	309.40	119.55
Ukraine	233,090	603,700	47,075,296	201.96	77.98
United Arab Emirates	31,696	83,600	4,533,145	143.02	54.22
United Kingdom	94,525	242,910	60,226,500	637.15	247.94
United States	3,717,797	9,629,090	296,410,400	79.73	30.78
Uruguay	68,039	176,220	3,463,197	50.90	19.65
Uzbekistan	172,742	447,400	26,167,368	151.48	58.49

			Table A *(continued)*			
		World Countries: Area, Population, and Population Density, 2005				
COUNTRY	AREA		POPULATION	DENSITY	
	(mi²)	(km²)	(estimated 12/2005)	(pop/mi²)	(pop/km²)
Vanuatu	5,699	12,190	211,367	37.09	17.34
Venezuela, RB	352,145	912,050	26,577,000	75.47	29.14
Vietnam	127,243	331,690	83,119,000	653.23	250.59
West Bank and Gaza	2,401	6,220	3,626,000	1,510.20	582.96
Yemen, Rep.	203,850	527,970	20,974,656	102.89	39.73
Zambia	290,586	752,610	11,668,457	40.15	15.50
Zimbabwe	150,803	390,760	13,009,534	86.27	33.29
World	51,715,141	133,941,600	6,437,682,176	124.48	48.06

Source: World Development Indicators database 2007

Table B
World Countries: Form of Government, Capital City, Major Languages

COUNTRY	GOVERNMENT	CAPITAL	MAJOR LANGUAGES
Afghanistan	Transitional multiparty republic	Kabul	Turkmen
Albania	Emerging multiparty democracy	Tiranë	Albanian, Greek
Algeria	Republic	Algiers	Arabic, Berber, dialects, French
Andorra	Parliamentary democracy	Andorra	Catalán, French, Spanish, Portuguese
Angola	Multiparty republic	Luanda	Portuguese; Bantu and other African
Antigua and Barbuda	Constitutional parliamentary democracy	St. John's	English, local dialects
Argentina	Federal republic	Buenos Aires	Spanish, English, Italian, German, other
Armenia	Republic	Yerevan	Armenian, Russian, other
Australia	Federal parliamentary democracy	Canberra	English, indigenous
Austria	Federal republic	Vienna	German
Azerbaijan	Republic	Baku	Azerbaijani, Russian, Armenian, other
Bahamas	Parliamentary democracy; independent commonwealth	Nassau	English, Creole
Bahrain	Constitutional hereditary	Al Manamah	Arabic, English, Farsi, Urdu
Bangladesh	Parliamentary democracy	Dhaka	Bangla, English
Barbados	Parliamentary democracy	Bridgetown	English
Belarus	Republic in name; dictatorship in fact	Minsk	Byelorussian, Russian, other
Belgium	Constitutional monarchy	Brussels	Dutch (Flemish), French, German
Belize	Parliamentary democracy	Belmopan	English, Spanish, Garifuna, Mayan
Benin	Multiparty republic	Porto-Novo	French, Fon, Yoruba
Bhutan	Absolute monarchy; special treaty relationship with India; transition to constitutional monarchy in 2008	Timphu	Dzongkha, Tibetan, Nepalese
Bolivia	Republic	La Paz, Sucre	Spanish, Quechua, Aymara
Bosnia-Herzegovina	Federal democratic republic	Sarajevo	Croatian, Serbian, Bosnian
Botswana	Parliamentary republic	Gaborone	English, Setswana
Brazil	Federal republic	Brasilia	Portuguese, Spanish, English, French
Brunei	Constitutional monarchy	Bandar Seri Begawan	Malay, English, Chinese
Bulgaria	Parliamentary democracy	Sofia	Bulgarian
Burkina Faso	Parliamentary republic	Ouagadougou	French, indigenous
Burundi	Republic	Bujumbura	French, Kirundi, Swahili
Cambodia	Multiparty democracy under a constitutional monarchy	Phnom Penh	Khmer, French, English
Cameroon	Multiparty republic	Yaoundé	English, French, indigenous
Canada	Federal parliamentary	Ottawa	English, French, other
Cape Verde	Republic	Cidade de Praia	Portuguese, Crioulu
Central African Republic	Republic	Bangui	French, Sangho
Chad	Republic	N'Djamena	French, Arabic, Sara, other indigenous
Chile	Republic	Santiago	Spanish
China	Single-party communist state	Beijing	Various Chinese dialects
Colombia	Republic/insurgency	Bogotá	Spanish
Comoros	Republic	Moroni	Arabic, French, Shikomoro
Congo, Dem. Rep. of	Republic/transitional from military dictatorship/insurgencies	Kinshasa	French, Lingala, Kingwana, Kikongo, Tshilluba

COUNTRY	GOVERNMENT	CAPITAL	MAJOR LANGUAGES
Congo Republic	Multiparty republic	Brazzaville	French, Lingala, Monokutuba, Kikongo
Costa Rica	Democratic republic	San José	Spanish
Côte d'Ivoire	Multiparty republic/insurgencies	Abidjan, Yamoussoukro	French, indigenous
Croatia	Parliamentary democracy	Zagreb	Croatian
Cuba	Single-party communist state	Havana	Spanish
Cyprus	Republic	Nicosia	Greek, Turkish, English
Czech Republic	Parliamentary democracy	Prague	Czech
Denmark	Constitutional monarchy	Copenhagen	Danish, Faroese, Greenlandic, German
Djibouti	Republic	Djibouti	French, Somali, Afar, Arabic
Dominica	Parliamentary democracy, republic within commonwealth	Roseau	English, French
Dominican Republic	Republic	Santo Domingo	Spanish
East Timor	Republic	Dili	Tetum, Portuguese, Indonesian, English
Ecuador	Republic	Quito	Spanish, Quechua, indigenous
Egypt	Republic	Cairo	Arabic
El Salvador	Republic	San Salvador	Spanish, Nahua
Equatorial Guinea	Republic	Malabo	Spanish, French, indigenous, English
Eritrea	Transitional government	Asmara	Afar, Amharic, Arabic, Tigre, other indigenous
Estonia	Parliamentary republic	Tallinn	Estonian, Russian, Ukranian, Finnish
Ethiopia	Federal republic	Addis Ababa	Orominga, Somali, Arabic, English
Fiji	Republic	Suva	English, Fijian, Hindustani
Finland	Republic	Helsinki	Finnish, Swedish
France	Republic	Paris	French
Gabon	Multiparty republic	Libreville	French, Fang, indigenous
The Gambia	Multiparty democratic republic	Banjul	English, Mandinka, Wolof, Fula
Georgia	Republic	Tbilisi	Armenian
Germany	Federal republic	Berlin	German
Ghana	Parliamentary democracy	Accra	English, indigenous
Greece	Parliamentary republic	Athens	Greek
Grenada	Parliamentary democracy	St. George's	English, French
Guatemala	Republic	Guatemala City	Spanish, Quiche, Cakchiquel, other indigenous
Guinea	Republic	Conakry	French, indigenous
Guinea-Bissau	Multiparty republic	Bissau	Portugese, Crioulo, indigenous
Guyana	Republic within commonwealth	Georgetown	English, Creole, Hindi, Urdu, indigenous
Haiti	Republic	Port-au-Prince	Creole, French
Honduras	Republic	Tegucigalpa	Spanish, indigenous
Hungary	Parliamentary democracy	Budapest	Hungarian
Iceland	Republic	Reykjavík	Icelandic
India	Federal republic	New Delhi	English, Hindi, 14 other official
Indonesia	Republic	Jakarta	Bahasa Indonesian, English, Dutch, Javanese
Iran	Theocratic republic	Tehran	Farsi, Turkish, Kurdish

Table B (continued)
World Countries: Form of Government, Capital City, Major Languages

COUNTRY	GOVERNMENT	CAPITAL	MAJOR LANGUAGES
Iraq	Parliamentary democracy; in transition following U.S.-led invasion/insurgencies	Baghdad	Arabic, Kurdish, Assyrian, Armenian
Ireland	Republic	Dublin	English, Irish Gaelic
Israel	Parliamentary	Jerusalem	Hebrew, Arabic, English
Italy	Republic	Rome	Italian
Jamaica	Parliamentary democracy	Kingston	English, Creole
Japan	Constitutional monarchy	Tokyo	Japanese
Jordan	Constitutional monarchy	Amman	Arabic
Kazakhstan	Republic	Astana	Kazakh, Russian
Kenya	Republic	Nairobi	English, Swahili, indigenous
Kiribati	Republic	Tarawa	English, I-Kiribati
Korea, North	Single-party communist state	Pyongyang	Korean
Korea, South	Republic	Seoul	Korean
Kuwait	Constitutional monarchy	Kuwait	Arabic, English
Kyrgyzstan	Republic	Bishkek	Kirghiz, Russian
Laos	Single-party communist state	Vientiane	Lao, French, English, indigenous
Latvia	Parliamentary democracy	Riga	Latvian, Lithuanian, Russian
Lebanon	Republic/insurgency	Beirut	Arabic, French, Armenian, English
Lesotho	Constitutional monarchy	Maseru	English, Sesotho, Zulu, Xhosa
Liberia	Republic	Monrovia	English, indigenous
Libya	Single party/military dictatorship	Tripoli	Arabic
Liechtenstein	Constitutional monarchy	Vaduz	German
Lithuania	Parliamentary democracy	Vilnius	Lithuanian, Russian, Polish
Luxembourg	Constitutional monarchy	Luxembourg	French, Luxembourgian, German
Macedonia	Parliamentary democracy	Skopje	Macedonian, Albanian, Turkish, Serbo-Croatian
Madagascar	Republic	Antananarivo	Malagasy, French
Malawi	Multiparty democracy	Lilongwe	Tombuka
Malaysia	Constitutional monarchy	Kuala Lumpur	Malay, Chinese, English, indigenous
Maldives	Republic	Male	Dhivehi
Mali	Republic	Bamako	indigenous
Malta	Parliamentary democracy	Valletta	English, Maltese
Marshall Islands	Constitutional government (free association with U.S.)	Majuro	English, Polynesian dialects, Japanese
Mauritania	Republic	Nouakchott	Arabic, Wolof, Pular, French, Solinke
Mauritius	Parliamentary democracy	Port Louis	English, Creole, French, Hindi, Urdu, Bojpoori, Hakka
Mexico	Federal republic	Mexico City	Spanish, indigenous
Micronesia	Constitutional government (free association with U.S.)	Palikir	English, Trukese, Pohnpeian, Yapese, others
Moldova	Republic	Chisinau	Moldavian, Russian, Gagauz
Monaco	Constitutional monarchy	Monaco	French, English, Italian, Monegasque
Mongolia	Republic	Ulaanbaatar	Khalkha Mongol, Turkic, Russian
Montenegro	Republic	Podgorica	Serbian, Bosnian, Albanian, Croatian
Morocco	Constitutional monarchy	Rabat	Arabic, Berber dialects, French
Mozambique	Republic	Maputo	Portuguese, indigenous
Myanmar (Burma)	Military regime	Rangoon	Burmese, indigenous

Table B (continued)
World Countries: Form of Government, Capital City, Major Languages

COUNTRY	GOVERNMENT	CAPITAL	MAJOR LANGUAGES
Namibia	Republic	Windhoek	Afrikaans, English, German, indigenous
Nauru	Republic	Yaren district	Nauruan, English
Nepal	Constitutional monarchy	Kathmandu	Nepali, indigenous
Netherlands	Constitutional monarchy	Amsterdam	Dutch
New Zealand	Parliamentary democracy	Wellington	English, Maori
Nicaragua	Republic	Managua	indigenous
Niger	Republic; transitional from military	Niamey	French, Hausa, Djerma
Nigeria	Federal republic/insurgencies	Abuja	English, Hausa, Fulani, Yorbua, Ibo
Norway	Constitutional monarchy	Oslo	Norwegian, Sami
Oman	Monarchy	Muscat	Urdu
Pakistan	Federal republic	Islamabad	Pashtu, Urbu, English, others
Palau	Constitutional government (free association with U.S.)	Koror	English, Palauan, Sonsolorese, Tobi, Angaur, Japanese
Panama	Constitutional democracy	Panama	Spanish, English
Papua New Guinea	Parliamentary democracy	Port Moresby	various indigenous, English, Motu
Paraguay	Constitutional republic	Asunción	Spanish, Guarani
Peru	Republic	Lima	Quechua, Spanish, Aymara
Philippines	Republic	Manila	English, Filipino, 8 major dialects
Poland	Republic	Warsaw	Polish
Portugal	Parliamentary democracy	Lisbon	Portuguese
Qatar	Traditional monarchy	Doha	Arabic, English
Romania	Republic	Bucharest	Romanian, Hungarian, German
Russia	Federation	Moscow	Russian, numerous other
Rwanda	Republic	Kigali	French, Kinyarwanda, English, Kiswahili
St. Kitts and Nevis	Constitutional monarchy	Basseterre	English
St. Lucia	Parliamentary democracy	Castries	English, French
St. Vincent/Grenadines	Parliamentary monarchy independent within	Kingstown	English, French
Samoa	Constitutional monarchy	Apia	Samoan, English
San Marino	Republic	San Marino	Italian
São Tomé and Príncipe	Republic	São Tomé	Portuguese
Saudi Arabia	Monarchy	Riyadh	Arabic
Senegal	Republic	Dakar	French, Wolof, indigenous
Serbia	Republic	Belgrade	Serbian, Albanian
Seychelles	Republic	Victoria	English, French, Creole
Sierra Leone	Constitutional democracy	Freetown	Temne
Singapore	Parliamentary republic	Singapore	Malay, Tamil
Slovakia	Parliamentary democracy	Bratislava	Slovak, Hungarian
Slovenia	Republic	Ljubljana	Slovenian, Serbo-Croatian, other
Solomon Islands	Parliamentary democracy	Honiara	English, indigenous
Somalia	No single permanent national government/failed state	Mogadishu	Arabic, Somali, English, Italian
South Africa	Republic	Pretoria	Afrikaans, English, Zulu, Xhosa, other
Spain	Parliamentary monarchy	Madrid	Castilian Spanish, Catalan, Galician, Basque

COUNTRY	GOVERNMENT	CAPITAL	MAJOR LANGUAGES
Sri Lanka	Republic/insurgency	Colombo	English, Sinhala, Tamil
Sudan	Provisional military	Khartoum	Arabic, Nubian, others
Suriname	Constitutional democracy	Paramaribo	Dutch, Sranang Tongo, English, Hindustani, Javanese
Swaziland	Monarchy within commonwealth	Mbabane	English, siSwati
Sweden	Constitutional monarchy	Stockholm	Swedish
Switzerland	Federal republic	Bern	German, French, Italian, Romansch
Syria	Republic (under military regime)	Damascus	Arabic, Kurdish, Armenian, Aramaic
Taiwan	Multiparty democracy	Taipei	Mandarin Chinese, Taiwanese, Hakka
Tajikistan	Republic	Dushanbe	Tajik, Russian
Tanzania	Republic	Dar es Salaam	Kiswahili, English, Arabic, indigenous
Thailand	Constitutional monarchy	Bangkok	Thai, English
Togo	Republic/transitional	Lomé	French, indigenous
Tonga	Constitutional monarchy	Nuku'alofa	Tongan, English
Trinidad and Tobago	Parliamentary democracy	Port-of-Spain	English, Hindi, French, Spanish, Chinese
Tunisia	Republic	Tunis	Arabic, French
Turkey	Parliamentary republic	Ankara	Turkish, Kurdish, Arabic, Armenian, Greek
Turkmenistan	Republic	Ashkhabad	Turkmen, Russian, Uzbek, other
Tuvalu	Constitutional monarchy	Funafuti	Tuvaluan, English, Samoan, Kiribati
Uganda	Republic	Kampala	English, Luganda, Swahili, Arabic, Indigenous
Ukraine	Republic	Kiev	Romanian, Polish, Hungarian
United Arab Emirates	Federated monarchy	Abu Dhabi	Arabic, English, Farsi, Hindi, Urdu
United Kingdom	Constitutional monarchy	London	English, Welsh, Scottish Gaelic
United States	Federal republic	Washington	English, Spanish
Uruguay	Republic	Montevideo	Spanish, Portunol/Brazilero
Uzbekistan	Republic	Tashkent	Uzbek, Russian, Kazakh, Tajik, other
Vanuatu	Republic	Port-Vila	English, French, Bislama (pidgin)
Venezuela	Federal republic	Caracas	Spanish, indigenous
Vietnam	Single-party communist state	Hanoi	Vietnamese, French, Chinese, English, Khmer
Yemen	Republic	San`aa	Arabic
Zambia	Republic	Lusaka	English, Tonga, Lozi, other indigenous
Zimbabwe	Parliamentary democracy	Harare	English, Shona, Sindebele, other

Republics are multi-party. "Theocratic" normally refers to fundamentalist Islamic rule. "Transitional" governments are those still in the process of change from a previous form (e.g., single-party communist state to multiparty republic or parliamentary democracy). Those states within which powerful insurgent groups disrupt the normal functioning of the government have been identified as having insurgencies.

Source: The World Factbook 2007 (CIA, Washington, DC, 2007).

Table C
Defense Expenditures, Armed Forces, Refugees, and the Arms Trade 2004–2005

COUNTRY	MILITARY EXPENDITURES (% OF GDP)		NUMBER IN ARMED FORCES		REFUGEE POPULATION By Country of Asylum		REFUGEE POPULATION By Country of Origin		ARMS TRADE 2004–2005 (IN US $ MILLIONS BASED ON 1990 PRICE) Total Exports		Total Imports	
	2004	2005	2004	2005	2004	2005	2004	2005	2004	2005	2004	2005
Afghanistan	..	..	27,000	27,000	30	32	2,414,402	2,166,149	..	..	0	22,000,000
Albania	1	1	21,500	22,500	51	56	10,470	12,722	..	..	0	31,000,000
Algeria	3	3	318,000	319,000	169,048	94,101	10,691	12,041	..	..	292,000,000	149,000,000
Angola	4	5	118,000	118,000	13,970	13,984	228,838	215,827	0	0	8,000,000	22,000,000
Antigua and Barbuda	..	..	170	170			..	..	..	..	..	..
Argentina	1	1	102,000	102,000	2,916	3,074	..	..	0	0	160,000,000	67,000,000
Armenia	3	3	49,000	49,000	235,235	219,550	13,424	13,965	..	..	151,000,000	0
Australia	2	2	52,000	53,000	63,476	64,964	..	..	2,000,000	50,000,000	360,000,000	396,000,000
Austria	1	1	39,000	40,000	17,795	21,230	..	..	3,000,000	3,000,000	55,000,000	21,000,000
Azerbaijan	2	2	81,000	82,000	8,606	3,004	250,583	233,675	..	..	0	0
Bahamas	1	1	860	860			..	..			0	0
Bahrain	4	..	21,000	21,000			..	..	0	0	10,000,000	0
Bangladesh	1	1	251,000	252,000	20,449	21,098	5,731	7,304	..	..	26,000,000	27,000,000
Barbados	..	..	610	610			..	..	..	..	..	..
Belarus	1	1	182,000	183,000	725	725	8,244	8,857	50,000,000	0	0	0
Belgium	1	1	36,000	37,000	13,529	15,282	..	..	0	173,000,000	17,000,000	0
Belize	..	..	1,000	1,000	732	624	..	..	..	..	0	0
Benin	..	..	6,000	8,000	4,802	30,294	..	..	..	..	0	0
Bhutan							105,255	106,537	..	..	0	0
Bolivia	2	2	68,000	70,000	524	535	..	..	..	..	1,000,000	9,000,000
Bosnia and Herzegovina	2	2	24,000	12,000	22,215	10,568	228,831	109,930	0	0	0	0
Botswana	3	2	10,000	11,000	2,839	3,109	..	..	..	..	9,000,000	0
Brazil	1	2	687,000	673,000	3,345	3,458	..	..	56,000,000	62,000,000	121,000,000	142,000,000
Brunei			10,000	11,000	..	..	..	..	..	..	0	0
Bulgaria	2	2	85,000	85,000	4,684	4,413	..	..	0	0	12,000,000	158,000,000
Burkina Faso			10,250	11,250	492	511	..	..	..	..	0	19,000,000
Burundi	1	1	81,000	82,000	48,808	20,681	485,773	438,706	..	..	0	0
Cambodia	6	0	192,000	191,000	382	127	18,121	17,806	0	0	0	0
Cameroon	2	2	23,000	23,000	58,861	52,042	7,629	9,101	..	..	0	0
Canada	1	1	71,000	71,000	141,398	147,171	..	..	577,000,000	365,000,000	314,000,000	112,000,000
Cape Verde	1	1	1,000	1,000	..	..	..	..	..	..	0	0
Central African Republic	1	..	2,000	3,000	25,020	24,569	31,069	42,890	..	..	0	0
Chad	1	1	34,000	35,000	259,880	275,412	52,663	48,400	0	0	0	0
Chile	1	1	116,000	116,000	569	806	1,194	938	0	0	43,000,000	456,000,000
China	4	4	3,755,000	3,755,000	299,375	301,041	134,724	124,101	146,000,000	129,000,000	2,760,999,936	2,696,999,936
Colombia	2	2	336,000	336,000	141	155	47,381	60,450	..	..	11,000,000	11,000,000
Congo, Dem. Rep.	4	4	64,000	65,000	199,323	204,341	462,208	430,929	..	..	0	14,000,000
Congo, Rep.	3	2	12,000	12,000	68,536	66,075	28,152	24,438	..	..	0	0
Costa Rica	..	..	0	0	10,413	11,253	..	..	..	..	0	0
Cote d'Ivoire	..	..	18,000	19,000	72,088	41,627	23,655	18,338	..	..	14,000,000	0
Croatia	..	..	30,000	31,000	3,663	2,927	215,475	119,148	0	0	8,000,000	0

Table C *(continued)*
Defense Expenditures, Armed Forces, Refugees, and the Arms Trade 2004–2005

COUNTRY	MILITARY EXPENDITURES (% OF GDP)		NUMBER IN ARMED FORCES		REFUGEE POPULATION By Country of Asylum		REFUGEE POPULATION By Country of Origin		ARMS TRADE 2004–2005 (IN US $ MILLIONS BASED ON 1990 PRICE)			
									Total Exports		Total Imports	
	2004	2005	2004	2005	2004	2005	2004	2005	2004	2005	2004	2005
Cuba	2	2	75,000	76,000	795	706	15,659	19,000	..	..	0	0
Cyprus	..	..	11,000	10,750	531	701	..	..	0	0	0	0
Czech Republic	1	..	27,000	28,000	1,144	1,802	4,542	3,589	0	10,000,000	9,000,000	630,000,000
Denmark	2	2	21,000	21,000	65,310	44,374	..	..	6,000,000	2,000,000	206,000,000	78,000,000
Djibouti	1	1	11,000	13,000	18,035	10,456	495	504	..	..	0	0
Dominican Republic	..	..	39,000	40,000	..	..	..	..	..	..	27,000,000	0
Ecuador	1	1	46,270	47,270	8,450	10,063	..	..	..	..	19,000,000	33,000,000
Egypt, Arab Rep.	2	2	798,000	799,000	90,343	88,946	5,376	6,291	0	0	368,000,000	596,000,000
El Salvador	3	3	15,000	16,000	235	49	4,497	4,281	..	..	0	0
Equatorial Guinea	1	1	1,000	1,000	..	..	..	..	..	..	8,000,000	0
Eritrea	..	..	201,000	202,000	4,240	4,418	131,131	144,066	0	0	202,000,000	276,000,000
Estonia	..	..	6,000	8,000	11	7	..	..	0	0	5,000,000	10,000,000
Ethiopia	2	2	182,000	183,000	115,980	100,817	63,150	65,461	0	0	162,000,000	0
Fiji	4	3	3,000	4,000	..	..	..	..	..	..	0	0
Finland	1	..	31,000	31,000	11,325	11,809	..	..	23,000,000	22,000,000	78,000,000	77,000,000
France	1	1	358,000	359,000	139,852	137,316	..	..	2,513,999,872	2,399,000,064	89,000,000	3,000,000
Gabon	3	2	6,000	7,000	13,787	8,545	..	..	..	..	5,000,000	0
Gambia, The	2	1	800	800	7,343	7,330	..	..	..	..	7,000,000	0
Georgia	0	0	22,000	23,000	2,559	2,497	6,633	7,301	7,000,000	0	12,000,000	0
Germany	1	3	284,000	285,000	876,622	700,016	..	..	837,000,000	1,855,000,064	207,000,000	216,000,000
Ghana	1	1	7,000	7,000	42,053	53,537	14,767	18,433	..	..	27,000,000	0
Greece	1	1	167,000	168,000	2,489	2,390	..	..	0	0	1,656,000,000	1,114,000,000
Guatemala	4	4	48,000	48,000	656	391	4,376	3,379	..	..	0	0
Guinea	0	0	11,000	13,000	139,252	63,525	4,782	5,820	..	..	0	0
Guinea-Bissau	..	..	9,000	9,000	7,536	7,616	1,018	1,050	..	..	0	0
Guyana	..	..	2,000	3,000	..	..	..	..	..	..	0	0
Haiti	..	..	0	0	..	..	9,208	13,542	..	..	..	..
Honduras	..	..	20,000	20,000	23	22	..	..	..	..	0	0
Hungary	1	1	46,000	44,000	7,708	8,046	..	..	0	70,000,000	3,000,000	12,000,000
Iceland	2	1	0	0	239	293	..	..	0	0	..	..
India	0	0	2,617,000	3,047,000	162,687	139,283	13,345	16,285	22,000,000	0	2,471,000,064	1,471,000,064
Indonesia	3	3	582,000	582,000	169	89	27,919	34,384	25,000,000	8,000,000	150,000,000	19,000,000
Iran, Islamic Rep.	1	1	460,000	585,000	1,045,976	974,296	115,162	99,428	1,000,000	0	321,000,000	403,000,000
Iraq	5	4	179,000	227,000	46,053	50,177	311,884	262,299	0	0	53,000,000	290,000,000
Ireland	..	..	10,000	10,000	6,542	7,113	..	..	..	..	28,000,000	4,000,000
Israel	1	1	176,000	176,000	574	609	..	..	401,000,000	160,000,000	732,000,000	1,422,000,000
Italy	9	8	445,000	445,000	15,674	20,675	..	..	204,000,000	827,000,000	439,000,000	224,000,000
Jamaica	2	2	2,000	3,000	..	..	..	..	..	..	0	0
Japan	1	1	251,000	272,000	1,967	1,941	..	..	0	0	298,000,000	250,000,000
Jordan	1	1	110,000	111,000	1,100	965	..	..	47,000,000	15,000,000	174,000,000	23,000,000
Kazakhstan	8	8	99,000	101,000	15,844	7,265	6,121	4,316	5,000,000	0	46,000,000	68,000,000

COUNTRY	MILITARY EXPENDITURES (% OF GDP)		NUMBER IN ARMED FORCES		REFUGEE POPULATION By Country of Asylum		REFUGEE POPULATION By Country of Origin		ARMS TRADE 2004–2005 (IN US $ MILLIONS BASED ON 1990 PRICE)			
									Total Exports		Total Imports	
	2004	2005	2004	2005	2004	2005	2004	2005	2004	2005	2004	2005
Kenya	1	1	29,000	29,000	239,835	251,271	3,847	4,640	..	..	0	25,000,000
Korea, Dem. Rep.	2	1	1,295,000	1,295,000	..	..	..	..	13,000,000	0	3,000,000	2,000,000
Korea, Rep.	..	..	696,000	693,000	44	69	..	..	20,000,000	38,000,000	772,000,000	544,000,000
Kuwait	2	3	21,000	23,000	1,519	1,523	..	..	0	0	0	55,000,000
Kyrgyz Republic	7	6	17,000	18,000	3,753	2,598	..	..	0	0	5,000,000	3,000,000
Lao PDR	3	..	129,000	129,000	..	..	3,292	3,122	..	..	0	0
Latvia	..	..	5,000	5,000	11	11	16,114	24,442	0	0	15,000,000	7,000,000
Lebanon	2	2	85,000	85,000	1,753	1,078	..	..	0	0	0	1,000,000
Lesotho	4	..	2,000	2,000	..	..	19,866	18,323	..	..	1,000,000	0
Liberia	2	2	0	15,000	15,172	10,168	..	..	..	..	0	0
Libya	..	..	76,000	76,000	12,166	12,166	335,467	231,139	0	0	74,000,000	0
Liechten-stein	2	..	..	..	149	150	..	..	..	..	..	..
Lithuania	..	..	28,000	29,000	470	531	..	..	0	0	48,000,000	9,000,000
Luxembourg	2	2	1,512	1,512	1,590	1,822	..	..	..	..	0	0
Macedonia, FYR	1	1	17,000	19,000	1,004	1,274	..	..	29,000,000	..	0	0
Madagascar	3	2	21,000	22,000	..	..	5,106	8,600	..	..	0	0
Malawi	..	..	6,000	7,000	3,682	4,240	..	..	0	0	0	0
Malaysia	..	..	130,000	135,000	24,905	33,693	..	..	0	0	81,000,000	467,000,000
Mali	2	2	11,000	12,000	11,256	11,233	483	520	..	..	0	0
Malta	2	2	2,000	2,000	1,558	1,939	..	..	10,000,000	0	0	18,000,000
Mauritania	1	1	20,000	21,000	473	632	31,131	31,651	..	..	0	0
Mauritius	1	1	0	2,000	..	..	..	..	..	..	0	0
Mexico	0	0	203,000	204,000	4,343	3,229	..	..	..	..	224,000,000	35,000,000
Moldova	0	0	9,000	10,000	57	84	11,937	12,064	0	4,000,000	0	0
Mongolia	0	0	15,000	16,000	..	..	..	..	..	..	0	0
Morocco	2	..	250,000	251,000	2,121	219	..	..	..	..	0	32,000,000
Mozambique	5	4	11,000	11,000	623	1,954	104	104	..	..	0	0
Myanmar	1	1	482,250	483,000	..	..	161,013	164,864	..	..	0	20,000,000
Namibia	..	..	15,000	15,000	14,773	5,307	..	..	..	..	13,000,000	0
Nepal	3	3	131,000	131,000	124,928	126,436	..	..	..	..	32,000,000	0
Netherlands	2	2	53,000	60,000	126,805	118,189	..	..	250,000,000	840,000,000	151,000,000	129,000,000
New Zealand	2	2	8,000	9,000	5,350	5,307	..	..	1,000,000	0	42,000,000	8,000,000
Nicaragua	1	1	14,000	14,000	292	227	1,822	1,463	0	0	0	0
Niger	1	1	10,000	10,000	344	301	689	655	..	..	0	0
Nigeria	1	..	160,000	161,000	8,395	9,019	23,892	22,128	0	0	10,000,000	0
Norway	1	1	25,000	47,000	44,046	43,034	..	..	64,000,000	13,000,000	6,000,000	9,000,000
Oman	2	2	45,000	46,000	7	7	..	..	0	0	41,000,000	98,000,000
Pakistan	12	..	921,000	921,000	1,290,984	1,084,694	25,949	29,913	8,000,000	9,000,000	..	..
Panama	4	3	0	12,000	1,608	1,730	..	..	..	..	0	0
Papua New Guinea	..	..	3,000	3,000	7,627	9,999	..	..	..	..	0	0
Paraguay	1	1	24,000	25,000	41	50	..	..	..	..	4,000,000	1,000,000
Peru	1	1	157,000	157,000	766	848	4,769	4,865	5,000,000	0	47,000,000	368,000,000

Table C (continued)
Defense Expenditures, Armed Forces, Refugees, and the Arms Trade 2004–2005

COUNTRY	MILITARY EXPENDI-TURES (% OF GDP)		NUMBER IN ARMED FORCES		REFUGEE POPULATION By Country of Asylum		REFUGEE POPULATION By Country of Origin		ARMS TRADE 2004–2005 (IN US $ MILLIONS BASED ON 1990 PRICE) Total Exports		Total Imports	
	2004	2005	2004	2005	2004	2005	2004	2005	2004	2005	2004	2005
Philippines	1	1	146,000	147,000	107	96	434	465	..	..	37,000,000	38,000,000
Poland	1	1	162,000	162,000	2,507	4,604	10,677	19,641	55,000,000	124,000,000	251,000,000	96,000,000
Portugal	2	2	91,000	93,000	377	363	..	..	0	0	44,000,000	406,000,000
Qatar	2	2	12,000	12,000	46	46	..	..	0	0	0	0
Romania	..	..	176,000	177,000	1,627	2,056	5,916	11,502	0	17,000,000	275,000,000	579,000,000
Russian Federation	2	2	1,452,000	1,452,000	1,852	1,523	107,975	103,037	6,440,000,000	5,770,999,808	0	0
Rwanda	4	4	53,000	53,000	50,221	45,206	63,812	100,264	..	..	0	0
Saudi Arabia	2	2	214,000	216,000	240,552	240,701	..	..	0	36,000,000	544,000,000	470,000,000
Senegal	8	8	18,000	19,000	20,804	20,712	8,332	8,671	..	..	0	0
Serbia and Montenegro	1	2	110,000	..	276,683	148,264	236,999	189,989	0	..	0	..
Seychelles	3	3	650	450	..	..	..	..	..	..	0	0
Sierra Leone	2	2	13,000	13,000	65,437	59,965	41,802	40,477	..	..	0	0
Singapore	1	1	165,000	167,000	1	3	..	..	66,000,000	3,000,000	487,000,000	423,000,000
Slovak Republic	5	5	20,000	20,000	409	368	..	..	79,000,000	0	0	0
Slovenia	2	2	10,000	12,000	304	251	..	..	..	..	15,000,000	2,000,000
Somalia	2	2	0	0	357	493	389,314	395,553	..	..	0	0
South Africa	..	..	55,000	56,000	27,683	29,714	..	..	37,000,000	39,000,000	2,000,000	606,000,000
Spain	1	1	220,000	220,000	5,686	5,374	..	..	73,000,000	113,000,000	206,000,000	281,000,000
Sri Lanka	1	1	239,000	200,000	63	106	114,050	108,139	..	..	16,000,000	8,000,000
Sudan	3	3	121,000	123,000	141,588	147,256	730,650	693,632	..	..	270,000,000	0
Suriname			1,000	2,000	..	..	..	..	..	..	0	0
Swaziland	..	..	..	..	704	760	..	..	..	..	0	0
Sweden	..	..	27,600	28,600	73,408	74,915	..	..	324,000,000	592,000,000	48,000,000	104,000,000
Switzerland	2	2	4,000	109,000	47,678	48,030	..	..	119,000,000	74,000,000	172,000,000	144,000,000
Syrian Arab Republic	1	1	415,000	416,000	15,604	26,089	21,439	16,401	0	0	13,000,000	0
Tajikistan	6	..	12,000	13,000	1,834	1,018	56,780	54,753	..	..	0	0
Tanzania	2		28,000	28,000	602,088	548,824	..	..	..	..	0	0
Thailand	1	1	419,000	421,000	121,139	117,053	..	..	5,000,000	0	103,000,000	98,000,000
Timor-Leste	1	1	1,000	0	3	3	221	251	..	..	..	..
Togo	..	..	8,750	9,750	11,285	9,287	10,819	51,107	..	..	0	0
Trinidad and Tobago			2,000	3,000	..	..	..	..	..	..	0	0
Tunisia	2	2	47,000	47,000	90	87	..	..	..	..	0	156,000,000
Turkey	2	1	616,000	617,000	3,033	2,399	174,574	170,561	28,000,000	28,000,000	224,000,000	746,000,000
Turkmeni-stan	3	3	26,000	26,000	13,253	11,963	..	..	..	..	10,000,000	0
Uganda	..	..	55,000	47,000	250,482	257,256	31,963	34,225	..	..	26,000,000	0
Ukraine	2	..	271,000	273,000	2,459	2,346	89,579	84,228	519,000,000	188,000,000	29,000,000	..
United Arab Emirates	3	2	50,000	51,000	105	104	..	..	2,000,000	10,000,000	1,323,000,064	2,380,999,936
United Kingdom	2	2	205,000	217,000	298,844	303,181	..	..	797,000,000	791,000,000	197,000,000	94,000,000

Table C (continued)
Defense Expenditures, Armed Forces, Refugees, and the Arms Trade 2004–2005

COUNTRY	MILITARY EXPENDI-TURES (% OF GDP)		NUMBER IN ARMED FORCES		REFUGEE POPULATION		REFUGEE POPULATION		ARMS TRADE 2004–2005 (IN US $ MILLIONS BASED ON 1990 PRICE)			
					By Country of Asylum		By Country of Origin		Total Exports		Total Imports	
	2004	2005	2004	2005	2004	2005	2004	2005	2004	2005	2004	2005
United States	3	3	1,473,000	1,546,000	420,854	379,340	..	..	5,817,999,872	7,101,000,192	508,000,000	387,000,000
Uruguay	4	4	24,920	24,920	97	121	..	..	0	0	0	18,000,000
Uzbekistan	1	1	75,000	91,000	44,455	43,950	7,288	8,323	170,000,000	0	0	0
Venezuela, RB	..	..	82,000	82,000	244	408	..	..	1,000,000	0	14,000,000	7,000,000
Vietnam	1	1	5,564,000	495,000	2,360	2,357	349,780	358,268	..	..	259,000,000	291,000,000
West Bank and Gaza	..	..	0	56,000	..	..	350,617	349,673	..	..	0	0
Yemen, Rep.	..	..	136,000	138,000	66,384	81,937	..	..	..	..	352,000,000	289,000,000
Zambia	6	6	16,000	16,000	173,907	155,718	..	..	0	0	0	0
Zimbabwe	3	..	50,000	51,000	6,884	13,850	9,568	11,251	..	..	0	0
World	3	2	32,645,142	30,898,442	9,574,840	8,661,988	8,982,645	8,300,585	19,858,999,296	21,941,000,192	19,509,999,616	21,803,999,232

Source: CIA Fact Book 2007

					Table D
			Major Armed Conflicts, 1990–2007		

COUNTRY	TYPE OF WAR	LOCATION OF WAR	ADVERSARIES (in interstate wars)	DATE WAR BEGAN	COMBAT STATUS (6/1/07)
Afghanistan	interstate war	general	US, UK, NATO forces, Afghanistan	2002	ended by agreement in 2003 with establishment of constitutional government, although fighting still is taking place between Afghan government forces, allied with NATO, and insurgents representing the Taliban (the former government)
Albania	civil war	southern regions		1996	order restored by UN peacekeepers 1997
Algeria	civil war	general		1992	ended by disbandment of the Islamic Salvation Army in 2000, although armed militants persist in attacking villages and confronting government forces
Angola	civil war	general		1975	ended in 2002 with establishment of single-party rule; legislative and presidential elections scheduled for 2007 and 2008, respectively
	regional civil war	Cabinda enclave		1978	continuing
Armenia	interstate war	Nagorno-Karabakh	Azerbaijan	1990	suspended by agreement 1994
Azerbaijan	interstate war	Nagorno-Karabakh	Armenia	1990	suspended by agreement 1994
Bangladesh	regional civil war	Chittagong		1973	suspended by agreement 1992
Bosnia-Herzegovina	civil and interstate war	general		1992	suspended by agreement 1995
Burundi	civil war	general		1988	ended with South African–brokered peace agreement with last insurgency group in September 2006; some local fighting still exists
Cambodia	civil war	general		1970	suspended by agreement 1992; fighting terminated by 1997-98
Cameroon	interstate war	Bakassi border region	Nigeria	1996	ended with 2006 peace agreement ceding Bakassi peninsula to Cameroon
Chad	civil war	general		1965	continuing
Colombia	civil war	general		1986	most insurgent paramilitary groups disbanded by September 2006, but large areas of country still are under the influence of guerilla forces heavily funded by the illicit drug trade
Congo, Republic of the	civil war	general		1993	suspended by agreement 1994
	civil war	general		1997	ended by agreement in 2003, although peace is tenuous
Cote d'Ivoire	civil war	general		2002	ended by agreement in 2003, but tensions in northern areas remain high; French and West African troops serve as peacekeeping force
Croatia	civil and interstate war	Slavonia/Krajina	Serbia-Montenegro	1991	suspended by agreement 1992
	regional civil war	Western Slavonia/Krajina		1995	suspended by agreement 1995
Democratic Republic of the Congo (formerly Zaire)	civil war	general		1996	suspended by agreement 1997

Table D (continued)
Major Armed Conflicts, 1990–2007

COUNTRY	TYPE OF WAR	LOCATION OF WAR	ADVERSARIES (in interstate wars)	DATE WAR BEGAN	COMBAT STATUS (6/1/07)
	interstate war	general	Uganda, Rwanda, Burundi, Chad, Angola, Zimbabwe	1998	suspended by agreement in 2002; transitional government established in 2003; successful elections for legislature and president held in 2005 and 2006; fighting continues between government and rebel forces on eastern border
Djibouti	regional civil war	Afar		1991	suspended by agreement 2000
East Timor	civil war	East Timor		1999	suspended by entry of international peacekeeping force in 1999, but conflict broke out again in 2006 and remains unresolved
Ecuador	interstate war	border region	Peru	1995	suspended by agreement 1998
Egypt	civil war	general		1992	no formal agreements established but conflicts have halted throughout the country
El Salvador	civil war	general		1979	suspended by agreement 1979
Eritrea	war of independence	Eritrea	Ethiopia	1962	suspended by agreement 1991
	interstate war	Hanish Islands	Yemen	1997	suspended by agreement 1998
	interstate war	border region with Ethiopia	Ethiopia	1998	suspended by agreement 2000
Ethiopia	against war of independence	Eritrea	Eritrea	1962	suspended by agreement 1991
	civil war	general		1974	suspended by agreement 1991
	interstate war	border region with Eritrea	Eritrea	1998	suspended by agreement 2000
France	interstate war	Kuwait/Iraq		1991	suspended by agreement 1991
Georgia	regional civil war	western region		1991	break in action 1993
	regional civil war	South Ossetia		1991	fighting suspended by agreement in 1996, but region remains outside control of central government
	regional civil war	Abkhazia		1992	fighting suspended by agreement in 1994, but region remains outside control of central government
Ghana	regional civil war	northern regions		1994	break in action 1995
Guatemala	civil war	general		1965	suspended by agreement 1996
Haiti	civil war	general		1991	suspended by US/UN intervention 1994
India	interstate war	Jammu-Kashmir	Pakistan	1982	ceasefire declared in 2004 has been maintained, but conflict remains unresolved, and Kashmir remains the site of the world's largest and most militarized territorial dispute
	regional civil war	Jammu-Kashmir		1990	continuing
	regional civil war	Andhra Pradesh		1969	continuing
	regional civil war	Punjab		1981	break in action 1993
	regional civil war	Assam		1987	continuing
Indonesia	regional civil war	Irian Jaya/West Papua		1963	continuing
	regional civil war	East Timor		1975	suspended by agreement/UN peacekeeping mission, 1999; East Timor became independent state 2002

COUNTRY	TYPE OF WAR	LOCATION OF WAR	ADVERSARIES (in interstate wars)	DATE WAR BEGAN	COMBAT STATUS (6/1/07)
	regional civil war	Ambon		1999	military action halted 2006
	regional civil war	Borneo		1999	military action halted 2005
	regional civil war	Sumatra (Aceh)		1989	suspended by agreement 2005
Iran	civil war	general		1978	break in action 1993
	regional civil war	northwestern Kurdish regions		1979	break in action 1995
Iraq	regional civil war	northern regions/ Kurdistan		1974	Iraqi governmental action suspended by U.S. invasion in 2003
	interstate war	Iraq/Kuwait	Kuwait, France, Saudi Arabia, Syria, United Kingdom, United States	1990/91	suspended by agreement 1991
	regional civil war	southern Shia regions		1991	Iraqi governmental action suspended by U.S. invasion in 2003
	interstate war	central Iraq	United States and Great Britain	1998	merged into direct military action via invasion by a coalition led by the United States and Great Britain in 2003
	interstate war	Iraq	United States, Great Britain, others	2003	interstate conflict between Iraq and coalition forces ceased in 2003; Iraqi elections restored state sovereignty in 2004; country remains in a state of civil war between sectarian factions (Sunni and Shiite Muslims); U.S. and other coalition forces remain to attempt to achieve national and regional stability
Israel	civil war	general, including occupied territories	Egypt, Syria, Lebanon, Jordan, Iraq and other Arab states including Israeli Palestinians	1948	continuing internal conflict between Israeli state and Palestinian insurgents
	interstate war	Lebanon/Israel	Israel, paramilitary forces quartered in southern Lebanon	2006	suspended by agreement in 2006
Kurdistan	regional civil war	Turkish border region		1991	continuing
	civil war	general		1993	suspended by U.S.-led coalition invasion of Iraq in 2003
Kuwait	interstate war	Kuwait/Iraq	Iraq	1990	suspended by agreement 1991
Laos	civil war	general		1975	break in action 1990
	civil war	border region		2000	continuing
Lebanon	general, then regional civil war	southern zone, from 1990		1975	continuing
	interstate war	Lebanon/Israel	Israel, paramilitary forces quartered in southern Lebanon	2006	suspended by agreement in 2006
Libya	civil war	general		1995	suspended by unilateral Libyan government action 2004
Mali	regional civil war	northern Tuareg regions		1990	suspended by agreement 1995
Mauritania	interstate war	border regions	Senegal	1989	suspended by agreement 1991
Mexico	regional civil war	Chiapas and other southern states		1994	continuing

COUNTRY	TYPE OF WAR	LOCATION OF WAR	ADVERSARIES (in interstate wars)	DATE WAR BEGAN	COMBAT STATUS (6/1/07)
					Table D (*continued*) **Major Armed Conflicts, 1990–2007**
Moldova	regional civil war	Trans-Dniestr		1991	suspended by agreement 1997
Morocco	against war of independence	western Sahara	Polisario Front (western Sahara)	1975	break in action 1991
Mozambique	civil war	general		1976	suspended by agreement 1992
Myanmar (Burma)	regional civil war	Kachin		1948	suspended by agreement 1994
	regional civil war	Shan		1948	continuing
	regional civil war	Karen		1949	continuing
	civil war	general		1991	break in action 1992
	regional civil war	Arakan		1992	suspended by agreement 1994
	regional civil war	Kaya		1992	continuing
Nicaragua	civil war	general		1970	suspended by agreement 1992
Niger	regional civil war	northern Tuareg regions		1991	continuing
	regional civil war	eastern region		1994	continuing
Nigeria	interstate war	Bakassi border region	Cameroon	1996	suspended by agreement 2006
	regional civil war	Kaduna state		1997	continuing
	interstate war	Sierra Leone	Sierra Leone	1997	suspended by agreement 1999
Pakistan	interstate war	Kashmir	India	1982	ceasefire declared in 2004 has been maintained, but conflict remains unresolved, and Kashmir remains the site of the world's largest and most militarized territorial dispute
	regional civil war	Karachi/Sind		1992	continuing
Papua New Guinea	regional civil war	Bougainville		1988	cease-fire and break in action 1998
Peru	civil war	general		1980	continuing
	interstate war	border region	Ecuador	1945	suspended by agreement 1998
Philippines	civil war	general		1969	continuing
	regional civil war	Mindanao		1974	suspended by agreement 2001
Russia	regional civil war	North Ossetia/ Ingushetia		1992	break in action 1992
	regional civil war	Moscow		1993	break in action 1993
Rwanda	civil war	general		1990	break in action 1998
	interstate war	general	Dem. Republic of the Congo; Angola, Namibia, Chad, Zimbabwe	1998	suspended by agreement 1999, although conflict is continuing
Saudi Arabia	interstate war	Kuwait/Iraq	Iraq	1991	suspended by agreement 1991
Senegal	interstate war	Border regions	Mauritania	1989	suspended by agreement 1991
	regional civil war	Casamance region		1984	suspended by agreement 2001
Serbia and Montenegro	interstate war	Slovenia	Slovenia	1991	suspended by agreement 1991
Sierra Leone	civil war	general		1991	suspended by agreement 1999; sporadic fighting continues
	interstate war	Sierra Leone	Liberia	1997	suspended and UN peacekeepers withdrawn 2005
Slovenia	interstate war	Slovenia	Serbia-Montenegro	1991	suspended by agreement 1992
Somalia	civil war	general		1991	continuing with Ethiopian government forces entering capital region in 2006 in successful attempt to expel Islamist forces

Table D (continued)
Major Armed Conflicts, 1990–2007

COUNTRY	TYPE OF WAR	LOCATION OF WAR	ADVERSARIES (in interstate wars)	DATE WAR BEGAN	COMBAT STATUS (6/1/07)
	regional civil war	Somaliland		1991	break in action 1995
South Africa	civil war	general		1948	suspended by agreement 1994
Spain	regional civil war	Basque region		1968	ongoing
Sri Lanka	regional civil war	Tamil areas/north-east		1977	continuing
Sudan	regional civil war	southern regions		1983	continuing
	regional civil war	Kassala/Darfur		2000	ongoing
Suriname	civil war	general		1986	suspended by agreement 1992
Syria	interstate war	Kuwait/Iraq	Iraq	1991	suspended by agreement 1991
Tajikistan	civil war	general		1992	ended by agreement in 1997; borders with China and Uzbekistan remain poorly defined
Togo	civil war	general		1991	break in action 1991
Trinidad and Tobago	civil war	general		1990	break in action 1990
Turkey	regional civil war	southeastern Kurdish region/northern Iraq		1977	continuing
	regional civil war	western region		1991	break in action 1992
Uganda	regional civil war	northern region		early 1980's	continuing
	regional civil war	central region		1994	break in action 1995
	regional civil war	southeastern region		1995	break in action 1995
	interstate war	general	Dem. Republic of the Congo; Angola, Namibia, Chad, Zimbabwe	1998	suspended by agreement 1999
United Kingdom	regional civil war	northern Ireland		1969	suspended by agreement 1994
	interstate war	Kuwait/Iraq	Iraq	1991	suspended by agreement 1991
	interstate war	Iraq	Iraq	2003	interstate conflict ended in 2003 with fall of Baathist government; U.K. forces remain in attempt to quell sectarian violence between Sunni and Shiite Muslims that has brought Iraq to a state of virtual civil war
United States	interstate war	Kuwait/Iraq	Iraq	1991	suspended by agreement 1991
	interstate war	Iraq	Iraq	2003	interstate conflict ended in 2003 with fall of Baathist government; U.S. forces remain in attempt to quell sectarian violence between Sunni and Shiite Muslims that has brought Iraq to a state of virtual civil war
Venezuela	civil war	general		1992	break in action 1992
Yemen	civil war	general		1994	suspended by agreement 1994
	interstate war	Croatia	Croatia	1991	suspended by agreement 1992
	interstate war	Kosovo	NATO countries	1999	suspended by agreement 1999

Source: The World Factbook 2007 (CIA).

Table E
World Countries: Basic Economic Indicators

COUNTRY	GROSS NATIONAL INCOME (GNI) 2005		PURCHASING POWER PARITY (GNI) 2005			AVERAGE ANNUAL % GROWTH IN GDP			STRUCTURE OF ECONOMIC OUTPUT (GDP) 2003 (value added in % of GDP)			
	Total ($US billions)	Per Capita ($US)	Total ($Int billions)	Per Capita ($US)	Rank	1995	2000	2005	Agriculture	Industry	Manufacturing	Services
Afghanistan		..		..		..	..	14	36	24	15	39
Albania	8.52	2,570	16.93	5,410	125	9	7	6	23	22	..	56
Algeria	97.34	2,730	220.78	6,720	107	4	2	5	8	61	6	30
Angola	28.74	1,410	32.52	2,040	168	10	3	21	7	74	4	19
Antigua and Barbuda	0.84	11,512	0.98	12,070	70	–4	3	..	4	20	2	76
Argentina	176.99	4,470	534.71	13,800	66	–3	–1	9	9	36	23	55
Armenia	4.95	1,470	15.05	4,990	128	7	6	14	21	44	21	35
Aruba		..		..		11	4	..	..	..	..	..
Australia	704.83	33,120	621.86	30,590	24	4	2	3	3	..	12	70
Austria	302.25	37,190	274.00	33,280	12	2	3	2	2	31	20	68
Azerbaijan	10.96	1,240	36.74	4,380	134	–12	11	26	10	62	8	28
Bahamas, The		..		..		0	5	..	..	..	..	..
Bahrain		14,370	10.44	18,770	49	4	5	7	..	..	..	..
Bangladesh	63.10	470	306.34	2,160	163	5	6	6	20	27	17	53
Barbados	2.94	..		..		1	..	..	4	16	7	80
Belarus	29.58	2,760	77.42	7,920	94	–10	6	9	10	41	33	49
Belgium	374.83	36,140	340.24	32,470	16	2	4	1	1	24	17	75
Belize	0.99	3,570	1.86	6,390	112	0	12	3	14	18	9	68
Benin	4.26	510	9.54	1,130	189	5	6	4	32	13	8	54
Bermuda		..		..	2	4	..	..	..	..	..	..
Bhutan	0.82	1,250		..		6	6	6	25	37	7	38
Bolivia	8.96	1,010	24.88	2,710	152	5	3	4	15	32	14	53
Bosnia and Herzegovina	10.42	2,700		..		21	6	5	10	25	12	65
Botswana	9.58	5,590	20.31	11,510	76	4	8	6	2	53	4	44
Brazil	770.75	3,550	1,517.34	8,140	91	4	4	2	8	38	..	53
Brunei		..		..		3	3	..	..	..	..	..
Bulgaria	26.95	3,450	70.74	9,140	85	3	5	6	10	32	19	59
Burkina Faso	5.16	400	16.01	1,210	185	5	2	5	31	20	13	50
Burundi	0.78	100	5.13	680	206	–8	–1	1	35	20	9	45
Cambodia	5.94	430	36.87	2,620	153	7	8	13	34	27	19	39
Cameroon	16.41	1,000	36.56	2,240	162	3	4	2	41	14	7	45
Canada	1,093.58	32,590	1,058.44	32,770	14	3	5	3	..	..	..	..
Cape Verde	0.95	1,930	2.84	5,610	122	7	7	6	..	..	..	..
Central African Republic	1.37	350	4.93	1,220	184	7	2	2	54	21	..	25
Chad	4.44	400	11.31	1,160	187	1	0	6	23	51	5	26
Chile	104.67	5,870	177.94	10,920	77	11	4	6	6	47	18	48
China	2,244.93	1,740	8,857.56	6,790	105	11	8	10	13	48	33	40
Colombia	116.78	2,290	317.83	6,970	104	5	3	5	12	34	15	53
Comoros	0.38	650	1.19	1,980	170	4	1	4	51	11	4	38
Congo, Dem. Rep.	6.79	120	39.13	680	206	1	–7	7	46	25	6	29
Congo, Rep.	3.94	950	3.92	980	195	5	8	9	6	46	6	48
Costa Rica	19.40	4,700	42.67	9,860	82	4	2	6	9	30	22	61

-180-

Table E *(continued)*
World Countries: Basic Economic Indicators

COUNTRY	GROSS NATIONAL INCOME (GNI) 2005		PURCHASING POWER PARITY (GNI) 2005			AVERAGE ANNUAL % GROWTH IN GDP			STRUCTURE OF ECONOMIC OUTPUT (GDP) 2003 (value added in % of GDP)			
	Total ($US billions)	Per Capita ($US)	Total ($Int billions)	Per Capita ($US)	Rank	1995	2000	2005	Agriculture	Industry	Manufacturing	Services
Cote d'Ivoire	15.61	870	28.50	1,570	178	7	–4	2	23	26	19	51
Croatia	37.27	8,290	56.08	12,620	72	7	3	4	7	31	20	62
Cuba		..		..		2	6	..	..	..	..	..
Cyprus		18,430	15.89	..	44	6	5	..	..	..	..	..
Czech Republic	118.43	11,220	200.18	19,560	50	6	4	6	3	37	25	60
Denmark	259.17	48,330	184.31	34,030	10	3	4	3	2	25	14	74
Djibouti	0.78	1,010	1.89	2,380	156	–3	0	3	4	17	3	79
Dominica	0.26	..	0.42	5,820	115	2	1	..	18	24	8	57
Dominican Republic	27.67	2,460	68.58	7,710	97	5	8	9	12	25	15	62
Ecuador	34.53	2,620	54.37	4,110	137	2	3	5	6	46	9	48
Egypt, Arab Rep.	89.16	1,260	320.56	4,330	135	5	5	5	15	36	17	49
El Salvador	16.40	2,450	34.96	5,080	127	6	2	3	10	30	23	60
Equatorial Guinea		..		..		14	1	..	..	..	..	..
Eritrea	0.96	170	4.84	1,100	190	3	–13	1	23	23	8	55
Estonia	12.41	9,060	19.73	14,660	61	5	8	10	4	29	19	67
Ethiopia	11.14	160	74.82	1,050	192	5	5	9	48	13	5	39
Fiji	2.70	3,170	5.08	5,990	117	3	–2	1	16	25	14	59
Finland	192.93	37,530	168.45	32,110	20	3	5	2	3	30	22	68
France	2,137.57	34,600	1,859.06	30,540	25	2	4	1	2	21	13	77
French Polynesia		..		..		0	4	..	..	..	..	..
Gabon	7.27	5,010	8.69	6,280	113	7	2	2	8	58	5	35
Gambia, The	0.45	290	2.82	1,860	173	1	6	5	33	13	5	54
Georgia	6.49	1,320	15.26	3,410	147	3	2	9	17	27	18	56
Germany	2,799.62	34,870	2,433.67	29,510	28	2	3	1	1	30	23	69
Ghana	10.59	450	54.18	2,450	155	4	4	6	37	23	8	39
Greece	221.05	19,840	254.84	22,950	43	2	4	4	5	21	11	74
Grenada		3,860	0.73	6,860	100	3	8	..	7	23	6	68
Guatemala	31.34	2,400	56.82	4,510	133	5	4	3	23	19	13	58
Guinea	3.24	420	21.44	2,280	161	6	2	3	25	36	5	39
Guinea-Bissau	0.29	180	1.25	790	201	4	8	4	60	12	9	28
Guyana	0.74	1,020	3.18	4,230	136	5	–1	–2	31	25	8	44
Haiti	4.27	450	14.16	1,660	177	–4	0	2	..	..	..	..
Honduras	7.96	1,120	23.70	3,290	148	4	6	4	14	31	20	55
Hong Kong, China	178.02	27,670	242.33	34,900	9	4	10	7	..	10	4	90
Hungary	102.47	10,070	169.26	16,780	56	1	6	4	6	32	23	65
Iceland	15.37	48,570	10.53	35,490	8	0	4	6	7	25	16	68
India	800.07	730	3,754.42	3,430	146	8	4	9	18	27	16	54
Indonesia	278.24	1,280	820.48	3,720	140	8	5	6	13	46	28	41
Iran, Islamic Rep.	186.99	2,600	535.77	7,850	95	3	5	4	10	45	12	45
Iraq		..		..		..	–4	..	..	..	..	..

COUNTRY	GROSS NATIONAL INCOME (GNI) 2005		PURCHASING POWER PARITY (GNI) 2005			AVERAGE ANNUAL % GROWTH IN GDP			STRUCTURE OF ECONOMIC OUTPUT (GDP) 2003 (value added in % of GDP)			
	Total ($US billions)	Per Capita ($US)	Total ($Int billions)	Per Capita ($US)	Rank	1995	2000	2005	Agriculture	Industry	Manufacturing	Services
Ireland	170.79	41,140	135.50	32,580	15	10	9	6	3	38	27	60
Israel	121.55	18,580	176.34	25,470	37	7	8	5	..	..	..	..
Italy	1,756.76	30,250	1,666.79	28,440	30	3	4	0	2	27	18	71
Jamaica	8.95	3,390	10.64	4,010	139	2	1	2	6	33	14	61
Japan	4,641.47	38,950	4,090.05	32,010	21	2	3	3	2	31	..	68
Jordan	13.09	2,460	31.14	5,690	120	6	4	7	3	30	19	68
Kazakhstan	51.76	2,940	107.84	7,120	102	−8	10	10	7	39	15	54
Kenya	18.62	540	42.13	1,230	183	4	1	6	27	19	11	54
Kiribati		..	0.80	8,150	87	5	2	0	8	12	1	79
Korea, Dem. Rep.		..		..		..	..	..	..	..	..	..
Korea, Rep.	786.91	15,840	1,062.95	22,010	46	9	8	4	3	40	28	56
Kuwait	89.61	30,630	74.04	29,200	29	5	5	9	..	..	..	..
Kyrgyz Republic	2.36	450	9.57	1,860	173	−5	5	−1	34	21	14	45
Lao PDR	2.60	430	10.96	1,850	175	7	6	7	45	29	21	26
Latvia	15.65	6,770	31.03	13,490	67	−1	8	10	4	22	13	74
Lebanon	21.43	6,320	19.49	5,450	124	7	2	1	6	22	14	71
Lesotho	1.78	950	7.32	4,080	138	4	1	1	17	41	18	41
Liberia	0.44	130		..		−4	26	5	64	15	12	21
Libya	37.89	5,530		..		..	1	4	..	..	..	..
Lithuania	25.00	7,210	48.28	14,140	64	3	4	7	6	33	22	61
Luxembourg		..	22.08	48,700	1	1	8	4	0	16	9	83
Macao, China		..		..		4	6	7	0	12	3	70
Macedonia, FYR	5.71	2,830	14.50	7,130	101	−1	5	4	13	29	18	58
Madagascar	4.98	290	16.93	910	197	2	5	5	28	16	14	56
Malawi	2.03	160	8.37	650	208	17	2	3	35	19	13	46
Malaysia	124.03	4,970	262.60	10,360	81	10	9	5	9	52	31	40
Maldives	0.74	2,320		..		..	4	−5	..	..	..	..
Mali	5.07	380	13.38	990	193	6	3	6	37	24	3	39
Malta	5.40	13,610	7.51	18,620	54	6	6	2	..	..	..	..
Marshall Islands	0.18	2,930		..		3	1	4	..	..	..	..
Mauritania	1.91	580	7.09	2,310	160	10	2	5	24	29	5	47
Mauritius	6.28	5,250	15.79	12,700	71	4	4	5	6	28	20	66
Mexico	755.04	7,310	1,088.62	10,560	80	−6	7	3	4	26	18	70
Micronesia, Fed. Sts.	0.24	2,300	0.84	7,580	99	3	8	0	..	..	..	..
Moldova	3.28	930	9.93	2,360	157	−1	2	7	17	24	17	58
Monaco		..		..		..	..	..	..	..	..	..
Mongolia	1.83	690	5.24	2,050	167	27	1	6	22	29	3	49
Morocco	51.30	1,740	136.66	4,530	132	−7	1	2	14	30	17	56
Mozambique	6.22	310	22.96	1,160	187	3	2	8	22	30	14	48
Myanmar		..		..		7	10	5	..	..	..	..
Namibia	6.21	2,990	15.62	7,690	98	4	3	4	10	32	13	58

Table E *(continued)*
World Countries: Basic Economic Indicators

COUNTRY	GROSS NATIONAL INCOME (GNI) 2005		PURCHASING POWER PARITY (GNI) 2005			AVERAGE ANNUAL % GROWTH IN GDP			STRUCTURE OF ECONOMIC OUTPUT (GDP) 2003 (value added in % of GDP)			
	Total ($US billions)	Per Capita ($US)	Total ($Int billions)	Per Capita ($US)	Rank	1995	2000	2005	Agriculture	Industry	Manufacturing	Services
Nepal	7.41	270	42.33	1,560	179	3	6	3	38	21	8	41
Netherlands	629.70	39,340	538.07	32,970	13	3	3	1	2	24	..	74
New Caledonia		..		..		6	2	..	..	..	..	..
New Zealand	111.28	25,920	104.32	25,450	38	4	2	2	..	..	..	..
Nicaragua	4.79	950	18.43	3,580	143	6	4	4	19	28	18	53
Niger	3.40	240	10.89	780	202	3	−1	5	..	..	..	..
Nigeria	86.75	560	130.21	990	193	3	5	7	23	57	..	20
Norway	297.14	60,890	192.56	41,650	4	4	3	2	2	43	..	55
Oman		..		..		5	5	..	..	..	8	42
Pakistan	108.34	690	361.39	2,320	159	5	4	8	22	25	18	53
Palau	0.15	7,670		..		11	0	6	3	19	0	77
Panama	14.33	4,630	22.78	7,050	103	2	3	6	8	16	8	76
Papua New Guinea		..		..	158	−3	−1	3	40	39	6	19
Paraguay	7.34	1,040	27.43	4,650	130	5	−3	3	22	19	12	59
Peru	74.30	2,650	158.02	5,650	121	9	3	6	7	35	16	58
Philippines	107.39	1,320	462.61	5,570	123	5	6	5	14	32	23	53
Poland	292.71	7,160	510.27	13,370	68	7	4	3	5	31	18	64
Portugal	180.29	17,190	211.73	20,070	48	4	4	0	3	26	..	72
Puerto Rico		..		..		5	2	..	..	..	..	..
Qatar		..		..	19	..	..	6	..	..	..	..
Romania	97.66	3,910	194.28	8,980	86	7	2	4	10	35	24	55
Russian Federation	744.98	4,460	1,514.14	10,580	79	−4	10	6	6	38	18	56
Rwanda	2.13	230	10.75	1,190	186	35	6	6	42	20	8	37
Samoa	0.38	2,020	1.08	5,820	119	7	7	5	14	27	15	59
San Marino		..		..		..	2	..	..	..	..	..
Sao Tome and Principe	0.07	440	0.33	2,090	165	2	3	3	15	13	3	72
Saudi Arabia	310.05	12,510	363.66	15,730	57	0	5	7	4	..	..	37
Senegal	8.09	700	20.52	1,760	176	5	3	5	18	19	11	63
Serbia and Montenegro	25.75	3,220		..		6	5	5	16	33	20	51
Seychelles	0.66	8,180	1.29	15,250	59	−1	5	−2	3	28	17	69
Sierra Leone	1.16	220	4.31	780	202	−8	4	8	46	24	..	29
Singapore	116.21	27,580	128.17	29,520	27	8	10	6	0	34	28	66
Slovak Republic	44.44	7,950	81.88	15,200	60	6	2	6	3	29	19	67
Slovenia	34.15	17,440	44.29	22,140	45	4	4	4	3	34	25	63
Solomon Islands	0.30	620	0.97	2,030	169	7	−14	5	..	..	..	..
Somalia		..		..		..	..	..	..	..	..	..
South Africa	234.66	4,770	510.14	10,880	78	3	4	5	3	30	19	67
Spain	1,106.62	25,250	1,160.03	26,730	34	3	5	3	3	29	16	67
Sri Lanka	23.20	1,160	89.10	4,540	131	6	6	5	17	26	15	57
St. Kitts and Nevis	0.39	..	0.53	11,360	75	4	3	..	3	28	10	69

Table E (continued)
World Countries: Basic Economic Indicators

COUNTRY	GROSS NATIONAL INCOME (GNI) 2005		PURCHASING POWER PARITY (GNI) 2005			AVERAGE ANNUAL % GROWTH IN GDP			STRUCTURE OF ECONOMIC OUTPUT (GDP) 2003 (value added in % of GDP)			
	Total ($US billions)	Per Capita ($US)	Total ($Int billions)	Per Capita ($US)	Rank	1995	2000	2005	Agriculture	Industry	Manufacturing	Services
St. Lucia	0.77	..	0.98	6,060	111	3	5	..	5	18	5	77
St. Vincent and the Grenadines	0.40	3,530	0.73	6,100	116	1	2	2	8	25	5	67
Sudan	25.61	640	70.29	1,940	172	6	6	8	34	30	7	37
Suriname	1.16	2,540	3.01	6,690	108	1	0	5	11	24	6	65
Swaziland	2.76	2,280	5.51	4,870	129	4	2	2	12	48	37	41
Sweden	356.78	40,910	292.74	32,440	17	4	4	3	1	28	..	71
Switzerland	397.66	55,320	287.15	38,610	6	0	4	2	..	..	..	..
Syrian Arab Republic	25.47	1,380	70.08	3,680	142	6	3	5	23	35	30	41
Tajikistan	2.22	330	8.46	1,300	182	−12	8	8	24	32	24	44
Tanzania	12.06	340	28.36	740	204	4	5	7	45	18	8	38
Thailand	172.44	2,720	544.05	8,470	88	9	5	4	10	44	35	46
Timor-Leste	0.55	600		..		..	14	3	30	15	..	54
Togo	2.17	350	9.09	1,480	180	8	−1	3	42	23	10	35
Tonga		..	0.80	7,860	90	4	5	2	27	15	5	56
Trinidad and Tobago	13.73	10,300	18.22	13,960	65	4	6	7	1	60	6	40
Tunisia	27.18	2,880	79.53	7,930	93	2	5	4	12	29	18	60
Turkey	361.91	4,750	604.63	8,390	89	7	7	7	12	24	14	64
Turkmeni-stan	7.50	..		..		−7	19	..	23	41	22	39
Uganda	8.56	280	41.21	1,430	181	12	6	7	33	25	9	43
Ukraine	81.89	1,520	318.70	6,770	106	−12	6	3	11	34	20	55
United Arab Emirates		..	103.64	23,990	36	8	5	9	2	56	14	42
United Kingdom	2,246.58	37,740	2,045.29	33,960	11	3	4	2	1	26	15	73
United States	12,448.41	43,560	12,449.24	42,000	3	3	4	3	1	23	14	77
Uruguay	16.21	4,360	33.32	9,620	84	−1	−1	7	9	31	22	60
Uzbekistan	13.93	520	53.90	2,060	166	−1	4	7	28	29	11	43
Vanuatu	0.33	1,560	0.66	3,120	149	0	3	3	..	..	..	..
Venezuela, RB	138.21	4,820	173.81	6,540	110	4	4	9	..	..	..	..
Vietnam	51.14	620	249.36	3,000	150	10	7	8	21	41	21	38
West Bank and Gaza	4.41	1,230		..		6	−6	6	..	..	..	..
Yemen, Rep.	13.39	600	17.41	830	200	12	4	3	13	..	4	45
Zambia	6.80	500	11.20	960	196	−3	4	5	19	25	12	56
Zimbabwe	3.22	350	25.37	1,950	171	0	−8	−7	18	23	13	59
World	44,609.79	7,011	61,085.47	9,489		3	4	3	4	28	18	69

Source: World Bank Economic Indicators (2007)

Table F
World Countries: Population Growth, 1950–2025

COUNTRY	POPULATION (thousands)			AVERAGE ANNUAL POPULATION CHANGE (percent)		AVERAGE ANNUAL INCREMENT TO THE POPULATION (mid-year population, in thousands)		
	1950	2000[a]	2025[a]	1975–1980	2001–2015[a]	1985–1990	1995–2000	2005–2010
WORLD	2,518,629.0	6,070,581.0	7,851,455.0	1.7	2.5	85,831.0		
AFRICA								
Algeria	8,753.0	30,245.0	42,429.0	3.1	1.5	631.8	566.0	539.3
Angola	4,131.0	12,386.0	19,268.0	2.7	2.6	130.2	187.2	267.5
Benin	2,046.0	6,222.0	11,120.0	2.5	2.4	135.6	184.8	204.6
Botswana	419.0	1,725.0	1,614.0	3.5	0.5	43.3	21.5	–15.4
Burkina Faso	3,960.0	11,905.0	24,527.0	2.5	2.1	233.8	307.0	360.3
Burundi	2,456.0	6,267.0	12,328.0	2.3	1.7	95.2	123.0	166.5
Cameroon	4,466.0	15,127.0	20,831.0	2.8	1.7	326.5	370.9	374.8
Central African Republic	1,314.0	3,715.0	5,193.0	2.3	1.5	57.5	62.0	60.0
Chad	2,658.0	7,861.0	15,770.0	2.1	2.9	171.2	259.8	340.4
Congo Democratic Republic	12,184.0	48,571.0	95,448.0	3.0	2.6	1,146.2	1,234.4	1,907.8
Congo Republic	808.0	3,447.0	6,750.0	2.9	2.7	56.3	62.4	67.2
Cote d'Ivoire	2,775.0	15,827.0	22,140.0	3.9	1.6	411.1	350.2	394.2
Egypt	21,834.0	67,784.0	103,165.0	2.4	1.5	1,318.5	1,199.9	1,125.0
Equatorial Guinea	226.0	456.0	812.0	–0.7	..	8.7	11.1	13.6
Eritrea	1,140.0	3,712.0	7,261.0	2.6	2.3	35.4	134.9	153.2
Ethiopia	18,434.0	65,590.0	116,006.0	2.4	2.1	1,530.7	1,670.9	1,848.4
Gabon	469.0	1,258.0	1,915.0	3.1	2.2	11.6	13.9	8.6
Gambia	294.0	1,312.0	2,177.0	3.1	2.0	33.0	42.3	48.0
Ghana	4,900.0	19,593.0	30,618.0	1.9	1.6	435.4	300.2	285.2
Guinea	2,550.0	8,117.0	13,704.0	1.5	1.9	173.7	63.1	193.9
Guinea-Bissau	505.0	1,367.0	2,774.0	4.7	2.2	22.1	28.4	35.1
Kenya	6,265.0	30,549.0	39,917.0	3.8	1.4	723.5	604.9	206.8
Lesotho	734.0	1,785.0	1,608.0	2.5	0.8	41.5	39.6	11.5
Liberia	824.0	2,943.0	6,081.0	3.1	2.3	–2.9	236.3	107.3
Libya	1,029.0	5,237.0	7,785.0	4.4	1.9	92.8	92.2	136.3
Madagascar	4,230.0	15,970.0	30,249.0	2.5	2.5	308.1	433.2	590.5
Malawi	2,881.0	11,370.0	18,245.0	3.3	1.8	416.6	169.9	103.8
Mali	3,520.0	11,904.0	25,679.0	2.1	2.1	164.0	305.1	390.7
Mauritania	825.0	2,645.0	4,973.0	2.5	2.3	47.5	65.2	94.9
Morocco	8,953.0	29,108.0	40,721.0	2.3	1.4	565.7	535.1	515.0
Mozambique	6,442.0	17,861.0	25,350.0	2.8	1.6	78.7	359.2	75.1
Namibia	511.0	1,894.0	2,350.0	2.7	1.2	58.6	33.5	7.5
Niger	2,500.0	10,742.0	25,722.0	3.2	2.8	207.6	259.7	322.0
Nigeria	29,790.0	114,746.0	192,115.0	2.8	1.9	2,530.7	3,225.5	3,161.6
Rwanda	2,162.0	7,724.0	12,509.0	3.3	1.6	187.9	311.1	49.1
Senegal	2,500.0	9,393.0	15,663.0	2.8	2.0	191.6	278.9	336.2
Sierra Leone	1,944.0	4,415.0	7,593.0	2.0	1.9	106.3	143.8	162.5
Somalia	2,264.0	8,720.0	20,978.0	7.0	3.1	45.8	192.4	266.1
South Africa	13,683.0	44,000.0	42,962.0	2.2	0.4	943.4	383.4	–419.6
Sudan	9,190.0	31,437.0	47,536.0	3.1	2.0	634.6	902.5	1,059.5

Table F (continued)
World Countries: Population Growth, 1950–2025

COUNTRY	POPULATION (thousands)			AVERAGE ANNUAL POPULATION CHANGE (percent)		AVERAGE ANNUAL INCREMENT TO THE POPULATION (mid-year population, in thousands)		
	1950	2000[a]	2025[a]	1975–1980	2001–2015[a]	1985–1990	1995–2000	2005–2010
Tanzania	7,886.0	34,837.0	53,435.0	3.1	1.7	799.7	832.1	970.9
Togo	1,329.0	4,562.0	7,551.0	2.7	1.9	122.0	160.9	115.3
Tunisia	3,530.0	9,586.0	12,843.0	2.6	1.3	168.9	124.3	104.8
Uganda	5,310.0	23,487.0	54,883.0	3.2	2.4	590.9	598.7	877.5
Zambia	2,440.0	10,419.0	14,401.0	3.4	1.2	210.9	174.1	190.9
Zimbabwe	2,744.0	12,650.0	12,857.0	3.0	0.6	308.9	78.1	−58.6
NORTH AND CENTRAL AMERICA						353.9		
Belize	69.0	240.0	356.0	1.7	..	5.0	6.3	7.2
Canada	13,737.0	30,769.0	36,128.0	1.2	0.6	369.8	331.8	289.5
Costa Rica	966.0	3,929.0	5,621.0	3.0	1.4	76.6	65.4	58.0
Cuba	5,850.0	11,202.0	11,479.0	0.9	0.3	93.2	48.4	37.3
Dominican Republic	2,353.0	8,353.0	10,955.0	2.4	1.3	141.1	136.4	147.1
El Salvador	1,951.0	6,209.0	8,418.0	2.1	1.6	87.1	110.8	117.7
Guatemala	2,969.0	11,428.0	19,456.0	2.5	2.4	255.9	317.6	366.3
Haiti	3,261.0	8,005.0	10,670.0	2.1	1.7	111.8	89.1	114.6
Honduras	1,380.0	6,457.0	10,115.0	3.4	2.1	117.2	151.1	134.9
Jamaica	1,403.0	2,580.0	3,263.0	1.2	1.1	18.3	16.8	23.9
Mexico	27,737.0	98,933.0	129,866.0	2.7	1.4	1,594.3	1,572.4	1,425.0
Nicaragua	1,134.0	5,073.0	8,318.0	3.1	2.1	91.0	107.6	100.9
Panama	860.0	2,950.0	4,290.0	2.5	1.3	44.8	39.8	32.5
Trinidad and Tobago	636.0	1,289.0	1,340.0	1.3	0.8	6.5	−4.9	−6.1
United States	157,813.0	285,003.0	358,030.0	0.9	0.8	2,296.3	2,503.8	2,429.2
SOUTH AMERICA								
Argentina	17,150.0	37,074.0	47,043.0	1.5	1.0	445.4	427.4	401.1
Bolivia	2,714.0	8,317.0	12,495.0	2.4	1.8	127.7	155.2	128.3
Brazil	53,975.0	171,796.0	216,372.0	2.4	1.1	2,756.3	1,975.6	1,285.4
Chile	6,082.0	15,224.0	19,651.0	1.5	1.0	212.2	189.7	148.3
Colombia	12,568.0	4,120.0	58,157.0	2.3	1.3	636.0	681.0	630.9
Ecuador	3,387.0	12,420.0	16,704.0	2.8	1.5	262.0	264.1	257.2
Guyana	423.0	759.0	724.0	0.7	..	−3.2	−3.5	4.1
Paraguay	1,488.0	5,470.0	9,173.0	3.2	2.1	113.5	141.6	162.8
Peru	7,632.0	25,952.0	35,622.0	2.7	1.3	472.9	491.4	432.4
Suriname	215.0	425.0	486.0	−0.5	..	3.9	3.3	1.4
Uruguay	2,239.0	3,342.0	3,875.0	0.6	0.6	19.4	23.7	26.7
Venezuela	5,094.0	24,277.0	31,189.0	3.4	1.5	465.5	397.3	351.7
ASIA								
Afghanistan	8,151.0	21,391.0	44,940.0	0.9	2.5	170.3	879.9	724.7
Armenia	1,354.0	3,112.0	2,866.0	1.8	0.3	−0.7	−13.8	7.6
Azerbaijan	2,896.0	8,157.0	10,222.0	1.6	0.7	103.6	23.6	61.8
Bangladesh	41,783.0	137,952.0	208,268.0	2.8	1.6	2,028.8	2,001.0	2,119.6
Bhutan	734.0	2,063.0	3,701.0	2.3	..	34.7	42.4	48.8
Cambodia	4,346.0	13,147.0	21,899.0	−1.8	1.5	313.1	271.6	314.6
China[b]	556,924.0	1,282,472.0	1,454,141.0	1.5	0.6	16,833.4	11,408.3	8,726.8
Georgia[b]	3,527.0	5,262.0	4,429.0	0.7	−0.7	49.9	−53.5	−14.4

Table F (continued)
World Countries: Population Growth, 1950–2025

COUNTRY	POPULATION (thousands)			AVERAGE ANNUAL POPULATION CHANGE (percent)		AVERAGE ANNUAL INCREMENT TO THE POPULATION (mid-year population, in thousands)		
	1950	2000[a]	2025[a]	1975–1980	2001–2015[a]	1985–1990	1995–2000	2005–2010
India	357,561.0	1,016,938.0	1,369,284.0	2.1	1.2	16,448.0	16,317.4	15,140.5
Indonesia	79,538.0	211,559.0	270,113.0	2.1	1.1	3,283.4	3,702.8	3,388.7
Iran	16,913.0	664,423.0	90,927.0	3.3	1.6	1,632.8	818.3	1,000.3
Iraq	5,158.0	23,224.0	41,707.0	3.3	1.9	488.2	623.7	719.5
Israel	1,258.0	6,042.0	8,598.0	2.3	1.5	87.4	107.5	73.6
Japan	83,625.0	127,034.0	123,444.0	0.9	–0.2	556.6	252.5	–30.4
Jordan	472.0	5,035.0	8,116.0	2.3	2.2	126.9	159.4	145.2
Kazakhstan	6,703.0	15,640.0	15,388.0	1.1	0.1	148.5	–42.0	85.9
Korea, North	10,815.0	22,268.0	24,665.0	1.6	0.6	307.4	27.2	4,294.4
Korea, South	18,859.0	46,835.0	50,165.0	1.6	0.4	943.5	459.2	322.0
Kuwait	152.0	2,247.0	3,930.0	6.2	2.1	81.8	70.6	90.4
Kyrgyzstan	1,740.0	4,921.0	6,484.0	1.9	1.1	76.8	30.0	80.9
Laos	1,755.0	5,279.0	8,635.0	1.2	2.2	110.7	130.3	155.3
Lebanon	1,443.0	3,478.0	4,554.0	–0.7	1.2	11.8	48.7	46.0
Malaysia	6,110.0	23,001.0	33,479.0	2.3	1.5	391.7	436.4	438.2
Mongolia	761.0	2,500.0	3,368.0	2.8	1.3	62.1	37.4	44.4
Myanmar (Burma)	17,832.0	47,544.0	59,760.0	2.1	1.0	452.8	317.4	162.3
Nepal	8,643.0	23,518.0	37,831.0	2.5	2.0	457.5	559.0	616.3
Oman	456.0	2,609.0	4,785.0	5.0	2.2	58.3	80.5	104.3
Pakistan	39,659.0	142,654.0	249,766.0	2.6	2.2	2,984.4	2,984.8	2,936.8
Philippines	1,996.0	75,711.0	108,589.0	2.3	1.6	1,450.5	1,658.1	1,666.1
Saudi Arabia	3,201.0	22,147.0	39,751.0	5.6	2.9	527.8	678.3	922.2
Singapore	1,022.0	4,016.0	4,905.0	1.3	1.1	56.1	134.2	169.1
Sri Lanka	7,483.0	18,595.0	21,464.0	1.7	1.1	234.4	186.9	153.5
Syria	3,495.0	16,560.0	26,979.0	3.1	2.1	391.1	399.2	431.5
Tajikistan	1,532.0	6,089.0	8,193.0	2.8	1.5	149.0	115.3	168.7
Thailand	19,626.0	60,925.0	73,869.0	2.4	0.6	755.5	598.8	468.5
Turkey	21,484.0	68,281.0	88,995.0	2.1	1.1	1,083.1	895.5	732.4
Turkmenistan	1,211.0	4,643.0	6,549.0	2.5	1.1	85.4	83.3	95.8
United Arab Emirates	70.0	2,820.0	3,944.0	14.0	1.8	76.1	38.6	40.0
Uzbekistan	6,314.0	24,913.0	33,774.0	2.6	1.3	473.1	381.7	485.8
Vietnam	27,369.0	78,137.0	104,649.0	2.2	1.2	1,321.7	1,178.3	1,123.4
Yemen	4,316.0	18,017.0	43,204.0	3.2	3.0	436.3	524.0	782.1
EUROPE								
Albania	1,215.0	3,113.0	3,629.0	1.9	1.0	60.3	50.7	34.4
Austria	6,935.0	8,102.0	7,979.0	–0.1	–0.1	32.1	17.8	11.3
Belarus	7,745.0	10,034.0	8,950.0	0.6	–0.5	46.7	–7.5	–1.4
Belgium	8,639.0	10,251.0	10,516.0	0.1	0.0	22.2	20.9	5.3
Bosnia-Herzegovina	2,661.0	3,977.0	4,183.0	0.9	0.5	29.7	96.0	15.5
Bulgaria	7,251.0	8,099.0	6,609.0	0.3	–0.7	–9.9	–95.1	–74.3
Croatia	3,850.0	4,446.0	4,088.0	0.5	–0.3	10.1	–34.6	11.2
Czech Republic	8,925.0	10,269.0	9,806.0	0.6	–0.2	–0.1	–10.6	–14.7
Denmark	4,271.0	5,322.0	5,469.0	0.2	0.1	5.5	20.8	12.0

Table F (continued)
World Countries: Population Growth, 1950–2025

COUNTRY	POPULATION (thousands)			AVERAGE ANNUAL POPULATION CHANGE (percent)		AVERAGE ANNUAL INCREMENT TO THE POPULATION (mid-year population, in thousands)		
	1950	2000[a]	2025[a]	1975–1980	2001–2015[a]	1985–1990	1995–2000	2005–2010
Estonia	1,101.0	1,369.0	1,017.0	0.6	−0.5	7.0	−10.5	−4.9
Finland	4,009.0	5,177.0	5,289.0	0.3	0.1	16.9	12.3	4.8
France	41,829.0	59,296.0	64,165.0	0.4	0.3	312.8	236.0	142.8
Germany	68,376.0	82,282.0	81,959.0	−0.1	−0.2	339.1	229.8	152.4
Greece	7,566.0	10,903.0	10,707.0	1.3	0.1	44.5	22.4	11.0
Hungary	9,338.0	10,012.0	8,865.0	0.3	−0.6	−55.4	−31.4	−31.1
Iceland	143.0	282.0	325.0	0.9	..	2.7	1.8	1.1
Ireland	2,969.0	3,819.0	4,668.0	1.4	0.8	−6.4	37.2	31.9
Italy	47,104.0	57,536.0	52,939.0	0.4	−0.4	4.0	74.2	−67.5
Latvia	1,949.0	2,373.0	1,857.0	0.4	−0.7	12.3	−23.5	−12.9
Lithuania	2,567.0	3,501.0	3,035.0	0.7	−0.2	22.2	−10.4	−3.6
Macedonia	1,230.0	2,024.0	2,199.0	1.4	0.4	6.9	11.0	7.2
Moldova	2,341.0	4,283.0	4,096.0	0.9	−0.2	49.9	−5.8	16.0
Netherlands	10,114.0	15,898.0	17,123.0	0.7	0.4	92.0	86.6	62.5
Norway	3,265.0	4,473.0	4,859.0	0.4	0.4	17.9	24.4	18.2
Poland	24,824.0	38,671.0	37,337.0	0.9	0.0	178.7	8.5	11.2
Portugal	8,405.0	10,016.0	9,834.0	1.4	−0.1	5.1	15.9	9.6
Romania	16,311.0	22,480.0	20,806.0	0.9	−0.3	69.0	−56.3	−49.8
Russian Federation	102,192.0	145,612.0	124,428.0	0.6	−0.5	820.8	−422.7	−281.7
Serbia-Montenegro	7,131.0	10,555.0	10,230.0	0.9	0.1	21.0	−5.2	−4.6
Slovak Republic	3,463.0	5,391.0	5,397.0	1.0	0.0	23.6	9.3	6.1
Slovenia	1,473.0	1,990.0	1,859.0	1.0	−0.2	4.6	3.6	1.2
Spain	28,009.0	40,752.0	40,369.0	1.1	0.0	163.2	49.1	−2.8
Sweden	7,014.0	8,856.0	9,055.0	0.3	0.0	40.5	9.5	0.5
Switzerland	4,694.0	7,173.0	6,801.0	−0.1	−0.1	54.8	19.2	7.9
Ukraine	37,298.0	49,688.0	40,775.0	0.4	−0.7	142.7	−432.6	−264.4
United Kingdom	49,816.0	58,689.0	63,275.0	0.0	0.0	189.0	178.9	94.6
OCEANIA								
Australia	8,219.0	19,153.0	23,205.0	0.9	0.7	246.8	209.7	167.0
Fiji	289.0	814.0	965.0	1.9	..	7.8	11.3	12.8
New Zealand	1,908.0	3,784.0	4,379.0	0.2	0.5	12.3	50.8	38.5
Papua New Guinea	1,798.0	5,334.0	8,443.0	2.5	1.9	89.3	116.4	125.1
Solomon Islands	90.0	437.0	783.0	3.5	..	11.0	13.8	14.3

a Data include projections based on 1990 base year population data

b Includes Hong Kong and Macao

Source: United Nations Population Division and International Labour Organisation. World Resources Institute, *World Resources 2000–2001* (U.S. Bureau of the Census International Data Base, 2000.

Table G
World Countries: Basic Demographic Data, 1990–2005

COUNTRY	CRUDE BIRTH RATE (births per 1,000 population)		LIFE EXPECTANCY AT BIRTH (years)		LIFE EXPECTANCY OF FEMALES AND MALES				TOTAL FERTILITY RATE		PERCENTAGE OF POPULATION IN SPECIFIC AGE GROUPS					
					Females		Males				1990			2005		
	1990	2005	1990	2005	1990	2005	1990	2005	1993	2005	0–14	15–64	65 and older	0–14	15–64	65 and older
Afghanistan	48.58	..	41.52	..	41.64	..	41.40	..	6.90	..	44.08	52.99	2.93	..	..	..
Albania	24.9	12.9	72.28	75.48	75.40	78.5	69.30	72.6	3.03	1.78	32.75	61.89	5.35	26.96	64.74	8.3
Algeria	31.12	20.82	67.37	71.73	68.80	73.13	66.00	70.4	4.49	2.44	42.00	54.44	3.56	29.65	65.81	4.55
Angola	51	47.81	45.46	41.42	47.10	42.92	43.90	39.98	7.20	6.56	46.88	50.19	2.93	46.47	51.08	2.45
Antigua and Barbuda	20.1	..	73.75	..	76.35	..	71.28	..	1.78	..	..	..	..	..	..	..
Argentina	20.96	17.72	71.64	74.83	75.26	78.68	68.20	71.18	2.90	2.29	30.63	60.44	8.94	26.42	63.38	10.2
Armenia	22.5	11.7	71.72	73.33	75.20	76.4	68.40	70.4	2.62	1.37	30.37	64.02	5.61	20.79	67.11	12.09
Australia	15.4	12.55	77.00	80.63	80.12	83.16	74.02	78.21	1.91	1.77	21.90	66.96	11.14	19.63	67.68	12.7
Austria	11.6	9.5	75.53	79.38	78.89	82.2	72.33	76.7	1.45	1.41	17.40	67.63	14.97	15.5	67.78	16.72
Azerbaijan	26.4	16.9	70.80	72.28	74.80	75.1	67.00	69.6	2.74	2.33	33.12	62.06	4.82	25.78	67.11	7.1
Bahamas, The	19.6	18.25	69.24	70.96	73.30	74.24	65.38	67.84	2.12	2.25	32.42	62.87	4.71	28.32	65.44	6.24
Bahrain	27.46	17.28	71.42	74.86	73.62	76.31	69.32	73.48	3.76	2.34	31.62	65.93	2.45	27.13	69.86	3.01
Bangladesh	32.68	26.22	54.76	63.9	54.68	64.82	54.84	63.02	4.12	2.98	44.33	52.54	3.13	35.48	60.91	3.61
Barbados	15.7	..	74.94	..	77.50	..	72.50	..	1.74	..	24.90	63.43	11.67	18.95	71.05	10
Belarus	13.9	9.47	70.84	68.48	75.60	74.38	66.30	62.86	1.91	1.24	23.06	66.29	10.65	15.18	70.15	14.67
Belgium	12.4	11.4	75.97	79.48	79.40	82.4	72.70	76.7	1.62	1.72	18.15	66.77	15.07	16.8	65.64	17.56
Belize	35.24	28.04	72.55	71.81	73.82	74.24	71.34	69.49	4.49	2.97	44.14	51.60	4.26	36.75	58.98	4.27
Benin	45.46	40.93	51.87	54.99	53.82	55.79	50.02	54.23	6.62	5.6	48.33	48.47	3.20	44.2	53.09	2.71
Bhutan	..	19.7	..	63.98	..	65.25	..	62.77	..	2.5	42.20	53.97	3.83	38.39	57.02	4.6
Bolivia	36.06	28.56	58.31	64.85	60.04	67.02	56.66	62.78	4.85	3.65	41.23	55.14	3.63	38.09	57.37	4.53
Bosnia and Herzegovina	14.2	9	71.44	74.41	74.10	77.18	68.90	71.78	1.70	1.19	23.86	69.94	6.20	16.51	69.48	14.01
Botswana	38.16	25.79	56.76	34.97	58.60	34.47	55.00	35.44	5.07	3.03	45.70	51.95	2.35	37.64	59.03	3.33
Brazil	23.56	19.79	65.60	71.24	69.42	75.2	61.96	67.47	2.74	2.29	34.75	60.93	4.32	27.86	66.02	6.13
Brunei	25.82	21.83	74.16	76.97	76.38	79.38	72.04	74.68	3.20	2.38	34.11	62.77	3.12	29.59	67.25	3.15
Bulgaria	12.1	9	71.64	72.56	75.15	76.3	68.30	69	1.81	1.31	20.42	66.59	12.99	13.76	69.43	16.81
Burkina Faso	47.38	46.46	45.39	48.48	46.50	49.27	44.34	47.73	7.02	5.9	47.47	49.80	2.72	47.18	50.1	2.73
Burundi	46.4	45.44	43.59	44.65	45.20	45.67	42.06	43.67	6.80	6.8	45.60	51.19	3.21	45.01	52.27	2.72
Cambodia	40.76	30.31	50.31	57.03	51.80	60.63	48.90	53.59	5.56	3.89	39.42	57.64	2.94	37.08	59.5	3.42
Cameroon	41.12	34.19	54.18	46.06	55.74	46.64	52.70	45.51	6.00	..	44.75	51.63	3.63	41.22	55.1	3.68
Canada	15	10.5	77.38	80.18	80.65	82.68	74.26	77.8	1.83	1.51	20.74	68.05	11.21	17.6	69.26	13.14
Cape Verde	36.4	29.8	65.29	70.71	68.00	73.88	62.70	67.69	5.50	3.53	43.28	52.03	4.69	39.54	56.17	4.29
Central African Republic	40.6	36.83	47.59	39.43	49.70	40.13	45.58	38.77	5.46	4.73	43.25	52.70	4.04	42.98	52.97	4.05
Chad	46.6	48.5	46.16	44.02	47.82	45.11	44.58	42.98	7.06	6.3	45.45	51.01	3.55	47.25	49.71	3.04
Chile	23.5	15.74	73.70	78.15	76.80	81.24	70.74	75.21	2.58	1.97	30.06	63.81	6.13	24.88	67.03	8.09
China	21.06	12.22	68.87	71.83	70.47	73.69	67.36	70.07	2.10	1.81	27.69	66.75	5.56	21.41	70.99	7.6
Colombia	27.32	21.11	68.27	72.81	72.48	75.89	64.26	69.87	3.07	2.4	36.04	59.67	4.28	31	63.9	5.1
Comoros	40.28	34.35	55.97	62.64	57.40	64.02	54.60	61.33	5.80	3.76	46.97	50.37	2.66	41.97	55.36	2.68
Congo, Dem. Rep.	47.9	49.56	51.55	44.03	53.38	45.1	49.80	43.01	6.70	6.7	47.26	49.88	2.86	47.27	50.06	2.67
Congo, Rep.	44.48	44.26	51.23	52.81	53.88	54.14	48.70	51.54	6.29	5.6	45.51	51.15	3.33	47.14	49.94	2.92
Costa Rica	27.4	16.5	76.80	78.95	79.00	81.2	74.70	76.8	3.20	2	36.46	59.34	4.20	28.36	65.82	5.82
Cote d'Ivoire	41.58	36.29	49.80	46.18	51.12	46.94	48.54	45.45	6.18	4.7	47.51	49.84	2.65	41.85	54.88	3.27

COUNTRY	CRUDE BIRTH RATE (births per 1,000 population)		LIFE EXPECTANCY AT BIRTH (years)		LIFE EXPECTANCY OF FEMALES AND MALES				TOTAL FERTILITY RATE		PERCENTAGE OF POPULATION IN SPECIFIC AGE GROUPS					
					Females		Males				1990			2005		
	1990	2005	1990	2005	1990	2005	1990	2005	1993	2005	0–14	15–64	65 and older	0–14	15–64	65 and older
Croatia	11.7	9.4	72.17	75.67	75.93	79.2	68.59	72.3	1.63	1.42	20.51	68.14	11.35	15.52	67.26	17.22
Cuba	17.6	11.3	75.03	77.25	76.94	79.2	73.22	75.4	1.69	1.5	23.05	68.54	8.41	19.07	70.13	10.81
Cyprus	18.3	10.9	76.54	79.29	78.82	81.7	74.36	77	2.42	1.42	25.99	63.13	10.88	19.88	68.05	12.07
Czech Republic	12.7	9.99	71.38	75.91	75.42	79.1	67.54	72.88	1.89	1.28	21.45	66.05	12.50	14.63	71.16	14.21
Denmark	12.3	11.9	74.81	77.84	77.73	80.2	72.02	75.6	1.67	1.8	17.04	67.36	15.60	18.81	66.17	15.02
Djibouti	40.36	34.16	47.77	53.39	49.44	54.55	46.18	52.28	5.98	4.74	42.99	54.28	2.73	41.48	55.67	2.84
Dominica	23	..	73.16	..	75.00	..	71.40	..	2.70	..	..	..	..	..	..	..
Dominican Republic	28.24	23.58	65.93	68.13	68.00	71.71	63.96	64.72	3.38	2.73	37.04	59.45	3.50	32.73	63.14	4.14
Ecuador	29.34	22.17	68.12	74.67	70.64	77.69	65.72	71.79	3.71	2.67	38.93	56.94	4.13	32.39	61.8	5.81
Egypt, Arab Rep.	31.14	25.57	62.80	70.53	64.28	72.81	61.40	68.36	3.97	3.1	39.89	56.29	3.82	33.55	61.66	4.79
El Salvador	30.04	23.95	65.62	71.31	69.86	74.45	61.58	68.33	3.85	2.76	40.78	55.00	4.23	33.98	60.66	5.36
Equatorial Guinea	43.62	43.08	47.16	42.28	48.79	42.6	45.60	41.98	5.89	5.89	42.32	53.69	3.98	44.39	51.68	3.93
Eritrea	..	38.71	48.94	54.9	50.76	56.81	47.20	53.09	6.50	5.24	44.20	53.13	2.66	44.75	52.94	2.31
Estonia	14.2	10.66	69.48	72.57	74.60	78.14	64.60	67.27	2.04	1.5	22.18	66.11	11.71	15.19	68.3	16.51
Ethiopia	50.52	39.12	45.00	42.65	46.54	43.43	43.54	41.91	6.91	5.32	45.46	51.60	2.94	44.52	52.55	2.93
Fiji	24.96	22.45	66.73	68.33	68.88	70.62	64.68	66.15	3.09	2.79	38.21	58.62	3.17	31.68	64.45	3.87
Finland	13.1	11	74.81	78.82	78.88	82.3	70.94	75.5	1.78	1.8	19.30	67.32	13.38	17.29	66.85	15.86
France	13.4	12.6	76.75	80.21	80.93	83.8	72.76	76.8	1.78	1.92	20.24	65.78	13.98	18.17	65.22	16.61
French Polynesia	26.24	18.72	69.59	73.76	72.30	76.38	67.00	71.26	3.25	2.31	34.69	61.74	3.57	27.83	67.24	4.93
Gabon	36.24	29.9	51.88	53.83	53.60	54.31	50.24	53.36	5.09	3.73	36.98	57.02	5.99	40.05	55.6	4.35
Gambia, The	44.7	33.76	49.28	56.79	51.40	58.16	47.26	55.49	5.90	4.4	42.02	55.16	2.82	40.12	56.15	3.73
Georgia	17	10.7	72.31	71.31	76.10	74.9	68.70	67.9	2.21	1.39	24.60	66.07	9.33	18.9	66.79	14.31
Germany	11.4	8.4	75.21	78.93	78.58	81.8	72.00	76.2	1.45	1.36	16.09	68.96	14.95	14.3	66.92	18.77
Ghana	39.2	30.63	57.16	57.48	58.90	57.97	55.50	57.02	5.50	4.06	45.34	51.75	2.91	39.02	57.31	3.66
Greece	10.1	9.4	76.94	78.99	79.50	81.5	74.50	76.6	1.40	1.28	19.25	67.07	13.69	14.31	67.51	18.17
Grenada	..	..	..	..	..	..	..	..	..	..	..	..	..	..	..	..
Guam	28.7	34.33	74.35	67.85	77.91	71.6	70.95	64.29	3.34	4.33	30.83	66.19	2.99	43.23	52.47	4.31
Guatemala	39.32	40.75	61.42	54.05	64.18	54.29	58.80	53.83	5.33	5.6	45.95	50.88	3.16	43.74	52.73	3.53
Guinea	46.4	49.59	43.71	45.12	44.20	46.51	43.25	43.79	5.90	7.08	46.73	50.70	2.57	47.52	49.43	3.05
Guinea-Bissau	49.76	20.27	42.35	64.26	43.98	67.39	40.80	61.29	7.10	2.18	41.73	54.16	4.11	29.34	65.49	5.16
Guyana	24.82	29.65	63.66	52.61	67.06	53.31	60.42	51.95	2.61	3.75	33.49	62.74	3.77	37.5	58.5	4
Haiti	35.78	28.47	53.10	68.57	54.98	70.69	51.30	66.55	5.42	3.47	44.34	51.85	3.81	39.2	56.95	3.85
Honduras	38.02	8.2	64.92	81.58	67.36	84.5	62.60	78.8	5.16	0.97	45.21	51.84	2.95	14.45	73.58	11.97
Hong Kong, China	12.325	9.6	77.58	72.65	80.40	76.9	74.90	68.6	1.27	1.32	21.49	70.05	8.46	15.73	69.07	15.2
Hungary	12.1	14.2	69.32	81.1	73.70	83.1	65.14	79.2	1.84	2.05	20.24	66.41	13.36	22.01	66.23	11.75
Iceland	18.7	23.8	77.94	63.5	80.30	64.32	75.70	62.72	2.31	2.84	24.89	64.52	10.59	32.06	62.67	5.27
India	30.2	19.9	59.13	67.79	59.22	69.69	59.04	65.99	3.80	2.27	36.42	59.23	4.35	28.3	66.19	5.51
Indonesia	25.42	14.53	61.71	71.13	63.50	72.76	60.00	69.57	3.06	2.07	35.69	60.45	3.86	28.7	66.77	4.52

Table G (continued)
World Countries: Basic Demographic Data, 1990–2005

COUNTRY	CRUDE BIRTH RATE (births per 1,000 population)		LIFE EXPECTANCY AT BIRTH (years)		LIFE EXPECTANCY OF FEMALES AND MALES				TOTAL FERTILITY RATE		PERCENTAGE OF POPULATION IN SPECIFIC AGE GROUPS					
					Females		Males				1990			2005		
	1990	2005	1990	2005	1990	2005	1990	2005	1993	2005	0–14	15–64	65 and older	0–14	15–64	65 and older
Iran, Islamic Rep.	30.8	..	64.65	..	65.42	..	63.92	..	4.68	..	45.47	50.97	3.56	..	..	..
Iraq	38.44	15.3	61.28	79.39	62.66	81.8	59.96	77.1	5.88	1.88	44.22	52.91	2.87	20.17	68.92	10.91
Ireland	15.1	20.8	74.58	79.72	77.40	81.82	71.90	77.72	2.12	2.82	27.35	61.32	11.33	27.77	62.09	10.14
Israel	22.2	9.5	76.09	80.33	78.00	83.2	74.28	77.6	2.82	1.32	31.28	59.64	9.08	14.02	66.01	19.97
Italy	10	15.76	76.86	70.9	80.26	72.65	73.62	69.22	1.26	2.38	15.87	68.81	15.33	31.22	61.23	7.55
Jamaica	25.2	8.41	73.24	82.08	75.16	85.63	71.42	78.69	2.94	1.26	35.15	57.46	7.39	14	66.27	19.73
Japan	10	27.82	78.84	72.02	81.91	73.61	75.91	70.51	1.54	3.29	18.40	69.62	11.99	37.15	59.64	3.21
Jordan	35.8	18.19	68.48	66.25	70.34	71.85	66.70	60.91	5.40	1.75	46.83	49.99	3.18	23.15	68.35	8.5
Kazakhstan	21.7	39.22	68.34	48.99	73.10	48.11	63.80	49.82	2.72	4.98	31.53	62.60	5.87	42.81	54.37	2.82
Kenya	38.5	..	57.11	..	58.84	..	55.46	..	5.64	..	49.13	47.88	2.98	..	..	..
Kiribati	32.18	15.17	56.80	63.92	59.10	66.92	54.60	61.05	4.04	1.96	..	..	..	25	68.18	6.82
Korea, Dem. Rep.	20.72	9	65.52	77.57	68.08	81.13	63.08	74.18	2.39	1.08	26.92	68.83	4.26	18.59	71.97	9.43
Korea, Rep.	16.28	19.12	70.28	77.54	73.88	79.73	66.86	75.44	1.77	2.39	25.84	69.16	5.00	24.31	73.92	1.77
Kuwait	24.8	21.39	74.88	68.34	76.84	72.38	73.01	64.5	3.44	2.41	36.60	62.19	1.21	31.46	62.41	6.12
Kyrgyz Republic	29.3	34.28	68.30	55.67	72.60	56.95	64.20	54.45	3.69	4.5	37.57	57.45	4.98	40.85	55.49	3.65
Lao PDR	45.16	9.3	49.72	71.36	51.00	77.4	48.50	65.6	6.00	1.31	43.64	53.38	2.08	14.69	68.38	16.93
Latvia	14.2	18.4	69.27	72.54	74.60	74.79	64.20	70.4	2.02	2.25	21.43	66.57	12.00	28.65	64.01	7.35
Lebanon	27.72	27.92	67.90	35.16	69.90	35.86	66.00	34.49	3.22	3.4	34.85	59.99	5.17	38.59	56.15	5.26
Lesotho	36.88	49.58	57.58	42.47	58.98	43.3	56.24	41.68	5.08	6.78	41.36	54.64	4.00	47.07	50.7	2.22
Liberia	47.6	22.98	45.06	74.35	46.60	76.75	43.60	72.07	6.80	2.85	46.67	50.42	2.91	30.06	65.86	4.08
Libya	30.04	8.9	68.50	71.25	70.38	77.4	66.70	65.4	4.72	1.27	45.03	52.48	2.49	16.73	67.81	15.46
Lithuania	15.3	11.5	71.16	79.18	76.17	82.3	66.39	76.2	2.03	1.7	22.61	66.43	10.97	18.91	67.26	13.83
Luxembourg	12.9	11.1	75.19	73.84	78.80	76.4	71.76	71.4	1.62	1.6	17.45	69.41	13.13	19.62	69.31	11.07
Macedonia, FYR	18.8	37.99	71.62	55.82	73.56	57.1	69.78	54.59	2.06	5.04	26.10	66.46	7.44	44	52.87	3.13
Madagascar	46.02	42.84	52.76	40.52	54.30	40.22	51.30	40.81	6.22	5.84	41.96	54.86	3.18	47.34	49.65	3.01
Malawi	50.88	21.38	44.61	73.7	45.16	76.06	44.08	71.46	7.00	2.74	47.27	50.05	2.68	32.39	63.02	4.6
Malaysia	28.9	30.38	70.51	67.64	72.73	67.35	68.40	67.93	3.77	4	36.50	59.80	3.71	40.71	55.84	3.45
Maldives	39.22	48.73	61.71	48.62	61.40	49.28	62.00	47.98	5.70	6.72	46.74	50.02	3.23	48.23	49.08	2.7
Mali	50.7	9.9	44.99	79.5	46.00	81.4	44.02	77.7	..	1.37	47.19	49.75	3.06	17.58	68.91	13.51
Malta	15.2	40.47	75.50	53.66	77.85	55.3	73.26	52.1	2.05	5.59	23.59	65.95	10.45	43.02	53.58	3.4
Mauritania	44.06	15.1	49.06	73.02	50.70	76.52	47.50	69.68	6.02	1.98	44.84	51.90	3.26	24.58	68.81	6.6
Mauritius	21.3	18.4	69.40	75.37	73.40	77.89	65.60	72.98	2.32	2.11	29.76	65.03	5.21	30.98	63.68	5.34
Mexico	28	30.46	70.79	68.07	73.90	68.81	67.82	67.36	3.31	3.65	38.55	57.49	3.96	39	57.62	3.39
Micronesia, Fed. Sts.	34.6	10.5	63.45	68.26	65.50	72.2	61.50	64.5	4.76	1.27	..	..	..	18.3	71.59	10.11
Moldova	17.7	..	68.32	..	71.80	..	65.00	..	2.39	..	27.88	63.79	8.33	..	..	..
Mongolia	30.92	17.69	62.66	66.84	64.00	68.48	61.38	65.28	4.03	2.33	41.67	54.32	4.01	30.46	65.77	3.77
Morocco	31.16	22.63	63.48	70.38	65.25	72.66	61.79	68.2	4.01	2.4	38.87	57.37	3.76	31.09	64.1	4.81
Mozambique	45.18	38.77	43.44	41.81	44.84	42.25	42.10	41.39	6.34	5.3	44.29	52.46	3.25	43.98	52.68	3.34
Myanmar	30.5	19.23	54.70	61.11	56.92	64.07	52.58	58.29	3.76	2.23	35.62	60.33	4.05	29.48	65.58	4.94
Namibia	38.7	22.45	57.52	46.93	58.94	46.81	56.16	47.04	5.39	3.66	42.84	53.52	3.64	41.51	54.99	3.5

COUNTRY	CRUDE BIRTH RATE (births per 1,000 population)		LIFE EXPECTANCY AT BIRTH (years)		LIFE EXPECTANCY OF FEMALES AND MALES				TOTAL FERTILITY RATE		PERCENTAGE OF POPULATION IN SPECIFIC AGE GROUPS					
					Females		Males				1990			2005		
	1990	2005	1990	2005	1990	2005	1990	2005	1993	2005	0–14	15–64	65 and older	0–14	15–64	65 and older
Nepal	38.54	28.81	53.58	62.65	52.94	63.15	54.18	62.18	5.26	3.46	43.13	53.32	3.55	39.03	57.32	3.65
Netherlands	13.2	11.6	76.88	79.35	80.11	81.6	73.80	77.2	1.62	1.73	18.24	68.92	12.84	18.19	67.7	14.1
Netherlands Antilles	18.9	13.74	74.46	76.39	77.56	79.52	71.50	73.41	2.29	2.07	27.13	65.96	6.91	22.87	67.64	9.49
New Caledonia	23.92	17.2	70.96	75.16	74.70	77.99	67.40	72.46	2.93	2.3	32.74	63.09	4.16	28.19	65.8	6.01
New Zealand	17.5	14.1	75.38	79.62	78.40	81.79	72.50	77.56	2.18	2	23.42	65.45	11.13	21.35	66.36	12.29
Nicaragua	38.96	27.79	64.49	70.39	67.42	72.86	61.70	68.05	4.80	3.08	46.26	50.97	2.77	38.93	57.77	3.3
Niger	55.5	53.38	42.09	44.93	42.40	44.97	41.80	44.9	7.64	7.67	47.70	49.83	2.47	49.03	49.01	1.96
Nigeria	43.82	40.51	49.05	43.83	50.68	44	47.50	43.66	6.51	5.5	45.48	51.73	2.79	44.27	52.71	3.03
Norway	14.4	12.4	76.54	80.04	79.80	82.5	73.43	77.7	1.93	1.84	18.94	64.74	16.32	19.57	65.43	15
Oman	43.72	24.79	69.00	74.76	71.00	76.29	67.10	73.31	7.38	3.44	46.39	51.20	2.41	34.49	62.96	2.55
Pakistan	41.4	26.1	59.10	64.86	60.00	65.46	58.24	64.3	5.84	4.12	42.95	54.14	2.91	38.28	57.87	3.85
Panama	25.88	21.57	72.44	75.24	74.68	77.89	70.30	72.71	3.01	2.62	35.32	59.72	4.97	30.36	63.65	5.99
Papua New Guinea	33.48	29.39	55.13	56.39	55.90	56.97	54.40	55.84	5.55	3.8	40.36	57.21	2.42	40.28	57.31	2.41
Paraguay	35.1	28.51	68.14	71.45	70.44	73.77	65.94	69.24	4.60	3.67	42.00	54.33	3.67	37.6	58.66	3.74
Peru	28.8	22.39	65.80	70.66	68.24	73.31	63.48	68.14	3.68	2.74	38.27	57.76	3.97	32.21	62.52	5.27
Philippines	32.44	24.16	65.63	71.04	67.78	73.24	63.58	68.93	4.12	3.2	40.36	56.15	3.48	35.14	60.98	3.88
Poland	14.3	9.4	70.89	75	75.50	79.4	66.50	70.8	2.04	1.24	25.11	64.83	10.05	16.34	70.73	12.93
Portugal	11.8	10.5	73.66	78.07	77.30	81.4	70.20	74.9	1.43	1.4	19.98	66.41	13.61	15.89	67.03	17.08
Puerto Rico	18.5	13	74.79	77.65	79.10	81.81	70.68	73.68	2.20	1.8	27.22	63.14	9.64	22.25	65.66	12.09
Qatar	24.66	17.68	72.22	74.1	73.72	76.57	70.80	71.75	4.34	2.89	27.85	71.33	0.82	21.75	76.99	1.26
Romania	13.7	10.2	69.74	71.71	73.05	75.4	66.59	68.2	1.84	1.32	23.57	66.04	10.40	15.44	69.8	14.76
Russian Federation	13.4	10.2	68.90	65.47	74.26	72.4	63.80	58.87	1.89	1.29	22.96	67.01	10.03	15.28	70.95	13.77
Rwanda	42.04	41	40.19	44.12	41.52	45.73	38.92	42.58	7.15	5.8	47.57	49.93	2.51	43.49	54.05	2.46
Samoa	33.2	26.65	66.29	70.74	67.92	73.91	64.74	67.72	4.76	..	40.13	56.11	3.76	40.66	54.78	4.56
Sao Tome and Principe	40.44	32.97	62.15	63.49	64.20	64.59	60.20	62.44	5.07	3.76	..	..	..	39.48	56.26	4.27
Saudi Arabia	36.28	26.9	69.00	72.56	70.48	74.57	67.60	70.64	6.56	3.83	41.99	55.45	2.56	37.28	59.8	2.92
Senegal	43.04	35.95	49.54	56.45	51.68	57.74	47.50	55.23	6.20	4.9	45.45	51.67	2.88	42.59	54.28	3.12
Serbia and Montenegro	14.9	10.7	71.64	72.79	74.30	75.5	69.10	70.2	2.08	1.61	23.40	67.05	9.55	18.3	67.63	14.08
Seychelles	23.7	..	70.30	..	73.52	..	67.22	..	2.82	..	..	..	..	..	..	..
Sierra Leone	49.1	46.3	35.20	41.36	36.64	42.78	33.82	40.01	6.50	6.48	43.87	53.05	3.08	42.82	53.84	3.34
Singapore	18.4	10	74.34	79.7	76.92	81.6	71.88	77.9	1.87	1.24	21.47	73.00	5.54	19.54	71.98	8.48
Slovak Republic	15.2	10	70.93	73.9	75.44	77.9	66.64	70.1	2.09	1.25	25.27	64.44	10.29	16.72	71.48	11.81
Slovenia	11.2	8.8	73.25	77.61	77.30	81.3	69.40	74.1	1.46	1.23	19.09	69.23	11.68	13.93	70.49	15.57
Solomon Islands	39.64	31.58	64.48	62.94	65.40	63.74	63.60	62.18	5.87	4	45.93	51.58	2.49	40.63	56.94	2.43
Somalia	51.94	44.05	41.55	47.73	42.70	48.97	40.46	46.54	7.25	6.2	47.81	49.45	2.74	44.12	53.26	2.62
South Africa	31.88	23.51	61.93	47.66	65.00	48.68	59.00	46.69	3.32	2.78	37.40	59.30	3.30	32.6	63.15	4.25
Spain	10.3	10.73	76.84	80.57	80.51	83.9	73.34	77.4	1.33	1.33	19.38	66.80	13.82	14.34	69.19	16.47
Sri Lanka	20.8	18.27	70.24	74.67	72.90	77.38	67.70	72.09	2.53	1.91	32.65	62.15	5.21	24.09	68.64	7.27

Table G (continued)
World Countries: Basic Demographic Data, 1990–2005

COUNTRY	CRUDE BIRTH RATE (births per 1,000 population) 1990	2005	LIFE EXPECTANCY AT BIRTH (years) 1990	2005	LIFE EXPECTANCY OF FEMALES AND MALES — Females 1990	2005	Males 1990	2005	TOTAL FERTILITY RATE 1993	2005	PERCENTAGE OF POPULATION IN SPECIFIC AGE GROUPS — 1990 0–14	15–64	65 and older	2005 0–14	15–64	65 and older
St. Kitts and Nevis	22.03333	..	67.15	..	69.20	..	65.20	..	2.68	..	..	..	..	..	..	..
St. Lucia	27.775	14.31	70.97	74.17	73.33	75.94	68.73	72.48	3.28	2.07	..	..	..	28.83	63.99	7.17
St. Vincent and the Grenadines	21.2	19.24	70.46	72.33	73.26	75.26	67.79	69.55	2.57	..	..	..	..	29.23	64.22	6.55
Sudan	38.3	31.7	52.17	56.66	53.60	58.07	50.80	55.32	5.42	4.15	43.31	53.92	2.77	39.24	57.15	3.6
Suriname	29.04	20.55	68.66	69.71	71.22	73.01	66.22	66.56	2.64	2.51	36.07	59.69	4.24	30.07	63.57	6.36
Swaziland	41	33.67	56.64	41.46	59.00	40.71	54.40	42.17	5.30	3.91	45.84	51.38	2.78	40.97	55.48	3.55
Sweden	14.5	10.4	77.54	80.55	80.40	82.8	74.81	78.4	2.13	1.77	17.92	64.31	17.77	17.49	65.3	17.22
Switzerland	12.5	9.6	77.24	81.24	80.71	83.9	73.94	78.7	1.59	1.42	16.89	68.75	14.36	16.49	67.56	15.95
Syrian Arab Republic	37	27.65	66.41	73.82	68.52	75.67	64.40	72.05	5.34	3.24	47.80	49.48	2.72	36.86	60	3.14
Tajikistan	38.8	28.47	69.29	64.02	71.90	66.75	66.80	61.42	5.05	3.53	43.19	53.00	3.81	38.98	57.16	3.86
Tanzania	43.76	36.4	50.05	46.3	51.56	46.65	48.62	45.98	6.25	5.2	46.47	51.02	2.51	42.6	54.17	3.23
Thailand	20.9	15.62	68.51	70.9	71.00	74.46	66.14	67.51	2.27	1.89	31.92	63.75	4.33	23.81	69.13	7.05
Timor-Leste	..	50.74	..	56.72	..	57.85	..	55.64	..	7.47	41.60	56.64	1.75	41.06	56.03	2.9
Togo	42.72	37.92	50.48	55.1	52.08	56.96	48.96	53.33	6.60	5.03	45.50	51.29	3.21	43.48	53.4	3.12
Tonga	30.12	23.41	68.75	72.65	70.80	73.99	66.80	71.36	4.16	3.31	..	..	..	36.91	58.09	5.99
Trinidad and Tobago	21.92	14.31	71.11	69.97	73.52	72.72	68.82	67.35	2.36	1.61	33.50	60.33	6.17	21.51	71.12	7.37
Tunisia	25.2	17.1	70.31	73.45	72.10	75.5	68.60	71.5	3.50	2.04	37.61	58.18	4.21	25.93	67.8	6.26
Turkey	24.8	18.9	65.69	71.29	67.96	73.8	63.52	68.9	3.00	2.19	34.99	60.73	4.28	28.4	66.7	5.9
Turkmenistan	34.2	22.26	66.22	62.86	69.70	67.21	62.90	58.71	4.17	2.6	40.49	55.75	3.76	31.78	63.55	4.67
Uganda	50.32	50.66	46.75	49.95	47.12	50.64	46.40	49.3	6.98	7.1	48.44	49.08	2.48	50.46	47.09	2.45
Ukraine	12.7	9	70.14	67.96	74.90	73.97	65.60	62.23	1.85	1.2	21.43	66.44	12.13	14.86	69	16.14
United Arab Emirates	23.76	15.59	73.53	79.18	74.70	81.55	72.42	76.93	4.12	2.43	30.31	68.24	1.44	21.99	76.95	1.07
United Kingdom	13.9	11.9	75.88	78.95	78.80	81.1	73.10	76.9	1.83	1.8	19.14	65.13	15.73	17.93	66.11	15.96
United States	16.7	14	75.21	77.71	78.80	80.67	71.80	74.89	2.08	2.05	21.91	65.70	12.39	20.77	66.92	12.31
Uruguay	18	14.9	72.62	75.61	76.46	79.4	68.96	72	2.51	2	26.04	62.43	11.53	24.25	62.52	13.23
Uzbekistan	33.7	19.88	69.17	67.37	72.40	70.71	66.10	64.19	4.07	2.22	40.91	55.08	4.00	33.18	62.08	4.74
Vanuatu	37.26	29.71	64.45	69.49	66.10	71.42	62.88	67.65	5.54	3.87	44.31	51.01	4.68	39.93	56.72	3.35
Venezuela, RB	28.56	22.04	71.25	74.22	74.22	77.2	68.42	71.38	3.43	2.65	38.16	58.19	3.65	31.2	63.74	5.06
Vietnam	28.78	17.76	64.78	70.65	66.84	73.21	62.82	68.22	3.62	1.78	38.84	56.37	4.79	29.54	65.02	5.44
Virgin Islands (U.S.)	21.4	14	74.09	78.55	77.40	79.98	70.93	77.2	2.59	2.2	..	..	..	24.12	65.22	10.65
West Bank and Gaza	..	33.08	..	73.39	..	75.78	..	71.12	..	4.6	..	..	..	45.48	51.45	3.07
Yemen, Rep.	47.2	40.03	52.18	61.73	52.60	63.16	51.78	60.38	7.53	5.87	48.83	48.66	2.51	46.35	51.36	2.29
Zambia	45.72	40.34	49.15	38.41	50.06	37.9	48.28	38.89	6.32	5.4	49.20	48.37	2.43	45.82	51.17	3.01
Zimbabwe	37.46	29.46	56.16	37.26	58.04	36.55	54.36	37.94	4.78	3.34	44.28	52.93	2.79	39.98	56.38	3.64
World	..	20.17	65.25	67.56	67.31	69.61	63.28	65.6	3.12	2.58	32.36	61.47	6.18	28.14	64.48	7.38

Source: UN Population Reference Bureau (2007), World Bank Economic Indicators (2007)

COUNTRY	MORTALITY						HEALTH			NUTRITION	
	INFANT & CHILD MORTALITY		ADULT MORTALITY								
	Infant Mortality (per 1,000 live births)	Child (under 5) Mortality (per 1,000 live births)	Male (per 1,000 live births)		Female (per 1,000 live births)		Health Expenditure per Capita ($US)	Physicians per 1,000 People	Hospital Beds per 1,000 People	Prevalence of Under-nour-ishment (% of population)	Prevalence of Child Malnutrition (% of children under 5)
	2005	2005	1990	2005	1990	2005	2004	2000–2003	1998–2002	2003	1998–2002
Afghanistan	..	..	486	..	476	..	14	0.19	..	..	49.30
Albania	16	18	..	96	..	55	157	1.39	3.26	6	13.60
Algeria	34	39	193	132	156	112	94	1.00	2.10	4	6.00
Angola	154	260	514	505	420	461	26	..	..	35	30.50
Antigua and Barbuda	11	12	142	..	85	..	485	0.76	3.88	..	..
Argentina	15	18	188	174	95	87	383	..	3.29	3	5.40
Armenia	26	29	216	204	119	92	63	3.53	4.25	24	2.60
Australia	5	6	125	..	68	..	3,123	2.49	7.90	3	0.00
Austria	4	5	154	..	74	..	3,683	3.30	8.60	3	
Azerbaijan	74	89	216	226	96	104	37	3.54	8.51	7	6.80
Bahamas, The	13	15	186	270	70	189	1,211	1.06	3.94	8	
Bahrain	9	11	201	114	147	84	620	1.60	2.90	..	8.70
Bangladesh	54	73	322	238	308	205	14	0.23	..	30	52.20
Barbados	11	12	140	157	82	81	745	1.28	7.56	3	..
Belarus	10	12	254	357	98	128	147	4.50	12.58	4	
Belgium	4	5	141	..	75	..	3,363	3.90	7.30	3	
Belize	15	17	194	194	123	121	201	1.05	2.13	4	..
Benin	89	150	447	309	369	277	24	0.06	..	12	22.90
Bhutan	65	75	..	236	..	194	15	0.16	..	..	18.70
Bolivia	52	65	307	253	250	192	66	0.73	1.67	23	7.60
Bosnia and Herzegovina	13	15	186	152	109	78	198	1.34	3.22	9	4.10
Botswana	87	120	..	841	..	853	329	..	..	32	12.50
Brazil	31	33	193	252	135	132	290	2.06	3.11	7	5.70
Brunei	8	9	149	89	98	65	473	1.01	..	4	
Bulgaria	12	15	217	..	97	..	251	3.38	7.20	8	
Burkina Faso	96	191	429	407	338	386	24	0.04	1.42	15	37.7
Burundi	114	190	460	512	379	492	3	0.05	..	66	45.10
Cambodia	68	87	392	372	319	208	24	0.16	..	33	45.20
Cameroon	87	149	430	508	361	499	51	..	..	26	22.20
Canada	5	6	127	..	70	..	3,038	2.10	3.90	3	
Cape Verde	26	35	245	185	218	109	98	..	..	..	..
Central African Republic	115	193	485	658	381	662	13	0.04	..	44	23.20
Chad	124	208	487	495	397	471	20	0.03	..	35	28.00
Chile	8	10	165	131	92	65	359	1.09	2.67	4	0.80
China	23	27	160	141	135	87	71	1.64	2.45	12	10.00
Colombia	17	21	222	182	127	103	168	1.35	1.46	13	6.70
Comoros	53	71	365	248	307	188	13	..	..	60	25.40
Congo, Dem. Rep.	129	205	..	486	..	460	5	..	..	74	31.00
Congo, Rep.	81	108	370	450	273	424	28	0.25	..	33	..

-194-

COUNTRY	MORTALITY						HEALTH			NUTRITION	
	INFANT & CHILD MORTALITY		ADULT MORTALITY								
	Infant Mortality (per 1,000 live births)	Child (under 5) Mortality (per 1,000 live births)	Male (per 1,000 live births)		Female (per 1,000 live births)		Health Expenditure per Capita ($US)	Physicians per 1,000 People	Hospital Beds per 1,000 People	Prevalence of Under-nour-ishment (% of population)	Prevalence of Child Malnutrition (% of children under 5)
	2005	2005	1990	2005	1990	2005	2004	2000–2003	1998–2002	2003	1998–2002
Cote d'Ivoire	118	195	352	474	294	461	33	..	..	13	21.20
Croatia	6	7	207	164	96	67	609	2.37	6.00	7	0.60
Cuba	6	7	125	121	83	81	230	5.91	5.13	3	3.90
Cyprus	4	5	118	97	72	45	1,109	2.98	..	3	
Czech Republic	3	4	231	..	95	..	771	3.50	8.80	3	..
Denmark	4	5	155	..	101	..	3,897	3.66	4.50	3	
Djibouti	88	133	472	383	387	355	53	0.19	..	24	18.20
Dominica	13	15	154	..	113	..	215	0.47	2.65	8	
Dominican Republic	26	31	157	267	109	145	148	1.88	1.50	29	5.30
Ecuador	22	25	205	184	141	105	127	1.48	1.55	6	14.30
Egypt, Arab Rep.	28	33	230	171	190	104	64	2.12	2.10	4	8.6
El Salvador	23	27	283	221	165	137	184	1.27	1.65	11	10.3
Equatorial Guinea	123	205	488	572	400	576	168	0.21	..	..	
Eritrea	50	78	433	455	347	384	10	..		75	39.60
Estonia	6	7	286	288	106	94	463	3.16	6.72	3	
Ethiopia	80	127	448	451	358	425	6	0.03	..	46	47.20
Fiji	16	18	220	233	161	162	148	0.36	..	5	..
Finland	3	4	183	..	70	..	2,664	3.10	7.50	3	
France	4	5	168	..	69	..	3,464	3.30	8.20	3	
Gabon	60	91	402	438	332	432	231	0.29	..	5	11.90
Gambia, The	97	137	530	320	432	281	19	..	..	29	17.20
Georgia	41	45	195	214	90	82	60	3.91	4.30	9	3.10
Germany	4	5	160	..	78	..	3,521	3.30	9.10	3	
Ghana	68	112	334	344	270	330	27	0.09	..	11	22.1
Greece	4	5	117	112	67	49	1,879	4.40	4.90	3	
Grenada	17	21	..	..	..	..	293	0.65	5.27	7	
Guatemala	32	43	..	296	..	172	127	1.10	0.98	22	22.70
Guinea	97	160	529	324	495	303	22	0.09	..	24	23.20
Guinea-Bissau	124	200	544	465	533	423	9	..	..	39	25.00
Guyana	47	63	263	293	172	211	56	0.48	3.87	8	13.60
Haiti	84	120	353	454	291	447	33	0.25	0.71	46	17.20
Honduras	31	40	202	245	141	201	77	0.65	1.06	23	16.60
Hong Kong, China	..	..	122	79	64	34	..	1.32	..	..	
Hungary	7	8	305	..	133	..	800	3.10	8.20	3	..
Iceland	2	3	109	..	63	..	4,413	3.60	14.60	3	
India	56	74	236	235	241	154	31	0.51	..	20	46.70
Indonesia	28	36	275	205	219	155	33	0.16	..	6	27.30
Iran, Islamic Rep.	31	36	170	158	174	104	158	1.05	1.60	4	10.90

COUNTRY	MORTALITY						HEALTH			NUTRITION	
	INFANT & CHILD MORTALITY		ADULT MORTALITY								
	Infant Mortality (per 1,000 live births)	Child (under 5) Mortality (per 1,000 live births)	Male (per 1,000 live births)		Female (per 1,000 live births)		Health Expenditure per Capita ($US)	Physicians per 1,000 People	Hospital Beds per 1,000 People	Prevalence of Under-nourishment (% of population)	Prevalence of Child Malnutrition (% of children under 5)
	2005	2005	1990	2005	1990	2005	2004	2000–2003	1998–2002	2003	1998–2002
Ireland	5	6	134	94	78	56	3,234	2.40	9.70	3	
Israel	5	6	120	86	72	46	1,534	3.91	6.16	3	
Italy	4	4	131	..	61	..	2,580	4.40	4.90	3	..
Jamaica	17	20	155	237	97	194	176	0.85	2.12	9	3.80
Japan	3	4	109	..	54	..	2,831	2.00	16.50	3	..
Jordan	22	26	205	165	152	123	200	2.05	1.80	6	4.40
Kazakhstan	63	73	306	343	136	152	109	3.61	7.02	6	4.20
Kenya	79	120	357	479	287	551	20	0.13	..	31	19.9
Kiribati	48	65	..	..	..	..	112	0.30	..	7	..
Korea, Dem. Rep.	42	55	223	305	116	208	0	2.97		33	27.90
Korea, Rep.	5	5	239	138	117	54	787	1.40	6.10	3	
Kuwait	9	11	130	88	80	58	633	1.53	2.76	5	1.70
Kyrgyz Republic	58	67	291	264	143	124	24	2.60	5.50	4	5.80
Lao PDR	62	79	464	318	389	269	17	..	..	19	40.00
Latvia	9	11	310	..	118	..	418	2.91	8.20	3	
Lebanon	27	30	210	151	150	99	670	3.25	2.70	3	3.00
Lesotho	102	132	..	853	..	817	49	0.05	..	13	17.90
Liberia	157	235	..	535	..	500	9	..	..	50	26.50
Libya	18	19	234	137	185	93	195	..	4.30	3	4.70
Liechtenstein	3	4		..		..	..			..	
Lithuania	7	9	288	..	107	..	424	4.03	9.22	3	
Luxembourg	4	5	165	109	85	60	5,904	2.60	8.00	3	
Macedonia, FYR	15	17	147	139	100	81	212	2.19	4.83	5	5.90
Madagascar	74	119	434	337	377	294	7	0.14	0.42	38	33.10
Malawi	79	125	479	635	436	653	19	0.01	1.34	35	25.40
Malaysia	10	12	198	154	125	89	180	0.70	2.01	3	19.00
Maldives	33	42	208	182	284	180	180	0.78	..	10	30.20
Mali	120	218	433	358	351	323	24	..	0.24	29	33.20
Malta	5	6	134	80	81	51	1,239	2.93	4.96	3	
Marshall Islands	51	58	..	..	..	..	272	0.47	..	..	
Mauritania	78	125	441	341	365	284	15	0.14	..	10	31.80
Mauritius	13	15	240	207	134	110	222	0.85	..	5	14.90
Mexico	22	27	187	155	117	86	424	1.50	1.10	5	7.50
Micronesia, Fed. Sts.	34	42	316	189	256	165	156	0.60	..	..	
Moldova	14	16	269	276	146	137	46	2.69	5.89	11	
Monaco	4	5		..		..	5,330	5.86	19.57	..	
Mongolia	39	49	251	237	211	168	37	2.67	..	27	12.70
Morocco	36	40	234	162	184	109	82	0.48	0.98	6	9.00

Table H *(continued)*
World Countries: Mortality, Health, and Nutrition, 1990–2005

COUNTRY	MORTALITY						HEALTH			NUTRITION	
	INFANT & CHILD MORTALITY		ADULT MORTALITY								
	Infant Mortality (per 1,000 live births)	Child (under 5) Mortality (per 1,000 live births)	Male (per 1,000 live births)		Female (per 1,000 live births)		Health Expenditure per Capita ($US)	Physicians per 1,000 People	Hospital Beds per 1,000 People	Prevalence of Under-nourishment (% of population)	Prevalence of Child Malnutrition (% of children under 5)
	2005	2005	1990	2005	1990	2005	2004	2000–2003	1998–2002	2003	1998–2002
Myanmar	75	105	..	301	..	200	5	0.30	..	5	28.20
Namibia	46	62	373	620	318	625	190	..		24	24.00
Nepal	56	74	350	248	376	222	14	0.05	0.17	17	48.30
Netherlands	4	5	117	..	67	..	3,442	3.10	10.80	3	
Netherlands Antilles	..	..	145	113	88	61	..	..	6.15	13	
New Zealand	5	6	143	..	93	..	2,040	2.10	6.20	3	
Nicaragua	30	37	220	219	147	146	67	1.64	1.48	27	9.60
Niger	150	256	515	368	413	339	9	0.03	0.12	32	40.10
Nigeria	100	194	476	499	401	495	23	0.27	..	9	28.7
Norway	3	4	132	..	68	..	5,405	3.56	14.60	3	
Oman	10	12	217	114	157	85	295	1.26	2.20	..	17.80
Pakistan	79	99	232	180	230	152	14	0.66	..	24	35.00
Palau	10	11		..		..	656	1.09		..	
Panama	19	24	146	152	94	83	343	1.68	2.21	23	8.10
Papua New Guinea	55	74	425	388	386	349	30	0.05	..	..	..
Paraguay	20	23	..	159	..	106	88	1.17	1.34	15	..
Peru	23	27	228	186	173	120	104	0.98	1.47	12	7.10
Philippines	25	33	273	169	208	116	36	1.16	..	18	31.80
Poland	6	7	264	189	102	75	411	2.30	4.90	3	
Portugal	4	5	164	139	82	58	1,665	3.20	4.00	3	
Qatar	18	21	194	153	135	104	992	2.21	1.65	..	5.50
Romania	16	19	237	223	114	96	178	1.89	7.49	3	3.20
Russian Federation	14	18	316	467	116	173	245	4.17	10.83	3	5.50
Rwanda	118	203	493	505	409	455	16	0.02	..	33	24.30
Samoa	24	29	262	198	202	116	109	0.33	..	4	1.90
San Marino	3	3		..		..	3,356	..	..	..	
Sao Tome and Principe	75	118	..	194	..	147	48	..	..	10	12.90
Saudi Arabia	21	26	192	148	158	101	348	1.40	2.30	4	
Senegal	61	119	488	311	399	262	39	0.10	0.40	20	22.70
Serbia and Montenegro	12	15	168	164	101	89	219	2.02	5.31	9	1.90
Seychelles	12	13	221	..	113	..	534	..	..	9	
Sierra Leone	165	282	601	432	492	379	7	..	..	51	27.20
Singapore	3	3	138	85	80	50	943	1.40	..	..	3.40
Slovak Republic	7	8	247	202	100	78	565	3.60	7.80	7	
Slovenia	3	4	211	141	91	63	1,438	2.19	5.16	3	
Solomon Islands	24	29	..	252	..	226	35	0.14	..	21	21.10
Somalia	133	225	..	395	..	341	..	..	..	..	25.80

COUNTRY	MORTALITY						HEALTH			NUTRITION	
	INFANT & CHILD MORTALITY		ADULT MORTALITY								
	Infant Mortality (per 1,000 live births)	Child (under 5) Mortality (per 1,000 live births)	Male (per 1,000 live births)		Female (per 1,000 live births)		Health Expenditure per Capita ($US)	Physicians per 1,000 People	Hospital Beds per 1,000 People	Prevalence of Under-nour-ishment (% of population)	Prevalence of Child Malnutrition (% of children under 5)
	2005	2005	1990	2005	1990	2005	2004	2000–2003	1998–2002	2003	1998–2002
South Africa	55	68	..	658	..	638	390	0.69		3	11.50
Spain	4	5	146	..	60	..	1,971	2.90	4.10	3	
Sri Lanka	12	14	182	130	122	77	43	0.43	..	22	32.90
St. Kitts and Nevis	18	20	227	..	165	..	500	1.07	6.36	10	
St. Lucia	12	14	205	171	144	135	232	0.56	3.38	5	..
St. Vincent and the Grenadines	17	20	202	170	119	103	210	0.46	1.85	10	19.50
Sudan	62	90	464	339	398	299	25	0.16	..	26	40.70
Suriname	30	39	216	242	137	137	194	0.45	3.74	8	13.20
Swaziland	110	160	260	885	196	893	146	0.18	..	22	10.30
Sweden	3	4	115	..	66	..	3,532	3.05	3.60	3	
Switzerland	4	5	127	..	62	..	5,572	3.60	17.90	3	
Syrian Arab Republic	14	15	237	130	177	90	58	1.40	1.40	4	6.90
Tajikistan	59	71	168	219	106	146	14	2.18	6.40	56	
Tanzania	76	122	444	507	373	511	12	0.02	..	44	29.40
Thailand	18	21	207	228	123	119	88	0.24	1.99	22	17.60
Timor-Leste	52	61		320		276	44			9	42.60
Togo	78	139	389	369	321	310	18	0.06	..	24	25.10
Tonga	20	24	260	148	194	120	117	0.34	..	..	
Trinidad and Tobago	17	19	182	260	148	186	329	0.79	5.11	10	5.90
Tunisia	20	24	190	134	174	77	..	0.66	1.70	3	4.00
Turkey	26	29	..	186	..	115	325	1.30	2.60	3	8.30
Turkmenistan	81	104	250	305	135	156	124	3.17	7.11	7	12.00
Uganda	79	136	526	459	461	447	19	0.05	..	19	22.90
Ukraine	13	17	268	404	105	150	90	2.97	8.74	3	3.20
United Arab Emirates	8	9	130	78	101	50	711	2.02	2.64	3	7.00
United Kingdom	5	6	126	..	76	..	2,900	2.10	4.10	3	
United States	6	7	173	..	91	..	6,096	5.49	3.60	3	..
Uruguay	14	15	178	161	90	83	315	3.65	4.39	3	..
Uzbekistan	57	68	207	247	109	145	23	2.89	5.34	25	7.90
Vanuatu	31	38	288	185	241	136	58	..	..	11	12.10
Venezuela, RB	18	21	186	184	112	93	196	1.94	1.47	18	4.40
Vietnam	16	19	215	173	153	121	30	0.53	1.67	16	33.80
Yemen, Rep.	76	102	363	267	336	222	34	0.22	0.60	38	46.10
Zambia	102	182	434	672	377	713	30	0.07	..	46	28.10
Zimbabwe	81	132	305	772	270	808	27	0.06	..	47	13.00
World	51	75	219.00	232	168.29	164	649	1.65		14	

Source: World Bank Economic Indicators (2007)

Table I
World Countries: Education and Literacy, 2003–2006

	Pupil-Teacher Ratio, Primary	Public Spending on Education (% of GDP)	Primary School Enrollment (% net)	Secondary School Enrollment (% net)	Tertiary School Enrollment (% net)	Literacy Rate, Adult Total (% of people ages 15 and above)	Literacy Rate, Adult Male (% of males ages 15 and above)	Literacy Rate, Adult Female (% of females ages 15 and above)	Literacy Rate, Youth Total (% of people ages 15–24)	Literacy Rate, Youth Male (% of males ages 15–24)	Literacy Rate, Youth Female (% of females ages 15–24)
	2003–2005	2003–2005	2003–2005	2003–2005	2003–2005	2006	2006	2006	2006	2006	2006
Afghanistan	83	..	..	..	1	28	43	13	34	51	18
Albania	22	..	94	74	19	99	99	98	99	99	100
Algeria	25	..	97	66	20	70	80	60	90	94	86
Andorra	11	2.6	80	76	8	..	..	..	..	..	..
Angola	..	..	..	..	1	67	83	54	72	84	63
Antigua and Barbuda	..	..	..	..	..	..	..	..	..	..	..
Argentina	17	3.5	99	79	64	97	97	97	99	99	99
Armenia	21	..	79	84	28	99	100	99	100	100	100
Aruba	18	5.1	99	76	34	97	98	97	99	99	99
Australia	..	4.8	96	85	72	..	..	..	..	..	..
Austria	13	5.5	..	..	50	..	..	..	..	..	..
Azerbaijan	13	2.5	85	78	15	99	99	98	100	100	100
Bahamas, The	16	..	91	84	..	..	..	..	..	..	..
Bahrain	..	..	97	90	36	87	89	84	97	97	97
Bangladesh	51	2.5	93	43	6	..	..	..	..	..	..
Barbados	15	6.9	98	96	..	..	..	..	..	..	..
Belarus	16	6.0	89	89	62	100	100	99	100	100	100
Belgium	12	6.2	99	97	63	..	..	..	..	..	..
Belize	23	5.4	96	73	2	..	..	..	..	..	..
Benin	47	3.5	78	..	..	35	48	23	45	59	33
Bermuda	8	1.9	98	..	19	..	..	..	..	..	..
Bhutan	31	..	..	..	..	60	69	49	..	..	..
Bolivia	24	6.4	94	73	41	87	93	81	97	99	96
Bosnia and Herzegovina	..	..	..	..	..	97	99	94	100	100	100
Botswana	26	10.7	83	55	5	81	80	82	94	92	96
Brazil	22	..	93	76	22	89	88	89	97	96	98
Brunei	10	..	93	87	15	93	95	90	99	99	99
Bulgaria	17	4.2	95	88	41	98	99	98	98	98	98
Burkina Faso	47	4.7	45	11	2	22	29	15	31	38	25
Burundi	49	5.1	60	..	2	59	67	52	73	77	70
Cambodia	53	1.9	99	24	3	74	85	64	83	88	79
Cameroon	48	1.8	..	..	6	68	77	60	..	..	..
Canada	..	..	..	..	..	..	..	..	..	..	..
Cape Verde	26	6.6	90	58	7	..	..	..	..	..	..
Central African Republic	..	..	..	..	2	49	65	34	59	70	47
Chad	63	2.1	61	11	1	26	41	13	38	56	23
Chile	27	3.7	..	..	43	96	96	96	99	99	99
China	21	..	..	..	19	91	95	87	99	99	99
Colombia	29	4.8	87	55	28	93	93	93	98	98	98
Comoros	35	..	..	..	2	..	..	..	..	..	..

Table I (continued)
World Countries: Education and Literacy, 2003–2006

	Pupil-Teacher Ratio, Primary	Public Spending on Education (% of GDP)	Primary School Enrollment (% net)	Secondary School Enrollment (% net)	Tertiary School Enrollment (% net)	Literacy Rate, Adult Total (% of people ages 15 and above)	Literacy Rate, Adult Male (% of males ages 15 and above)	Literacy Rate, Adult Female (% of females ages 15 and above)	Literacy Rate, Youth Total (% of people ages 15–24)	Literacy Rate, Youth Male (% of males ages 15–24)	Literacy Rate, Youth Female (% of females ages 15–24)
	2003–2005	2003–2005	2003–2005	2003–2005	2003–2005	2006	2006	2006	2006	2006	2006
Congo, Dem. Rep.	34	..	..	..	..	67	81	54	70	78	63
Congo, Rep.	83	2.2	44	..	4	..	..	..	..	..	..
Costa Rica	21	4.9	..	..	25	95	95	95	98	97	98
Cote d'Ivoire	42	..	56	..	..	49	61	39	61	71	52
Croatia	15	4.7	87	85	42	98	99	97	100	100	100
Cuba	10	9.8	97	87	61	100	100	100	100	100	100
Cyprus	18	7.4	96	93	36	97	99	95	100	100	100
Czech Republic	18	4.6	..	..	43	..	..	..	..	..	..
Denmark	..	8.4	98	92	74	..	..	..	..	..	..
Djibouti	35	7.9	33	23	2	..	..	..	..	..	..
Dominica	18	..	84	79	..	..	..	..	..	..	..
Dominican Republic	24	1.8	88	53	33	87	87	87	94	93	95
Ecuador	23	..	98	52	..	91	92	90	96	96	96
Egypt, Arab Rep.	22	..	95	..	33	71	83	59	85	90	79
El Salvador	30	2.8	93	53	19	..	..	..	..	..	..
Equatorial Guinea	32	0.6	81	..	..	87	93	80	95	95	95
Eritrea	48	5.4	47	25	1	..	..	..	..	..	..
Estonia	..	5.7	94	90	65	100	100	100	100	100	100
Ethiopia	72	5.0	61	28	3	..	..	..	..	..	..
Fiji	28	6.4	96	83	15	..	..	..	..	..	..
Finland	16	6.5	99	94	89	..	..	..	..	..	..
France	19	5.9	99	96	56	..	..	..	..	..	..
Gabon	36	..	..	..	..	..	..	..	..	..	..
Gambia, The	35	2.0	..	45	1	..	..	..	..	..	..
Georgia	14	2.9	87	72	46	..	..	..	..	..	..
Germany	14	4.7	..	..	..	..	..	..	..	..	..
Ghana	33	5.5	65	37	5	58	66	50	71	76	65
Greece	11	4.0	99	87	79	96	98	94	99	99	99
Grenada	18	5.2	84	79	..	..	..	..	..	..	..
Guatemala	31	..	94	34	10	69	75	63	82	86	78
Guinea	45	2.0	66	24	3	29	43	18	47	59	34
Guinea-Bissau	..	..	..	..	..	..	..	..	..	..	..
Guyana	28	8.5	..	..	10	..	..	..	..	..	..
Haiti	..	..	..	..	..	..	..	..	..	..	..
Honduras	33	..	91	..	16	80	80	80	89	87	91
Hong Kong, China	18	4.2	93	80	31	..	..	..	..	..	..
Hungary	10	5.9	89	91	60	..	..	..	..	..	..
Iceland	11	8.1	99	88	68	..	..	..	..	..	..
India	40	3.7	90	..	12	61	73	48	76	84	68

Table I (continued)
World Countries: Education and Literacy, 2003–2006

	Pupil-Teacher Ratio, Primary	Public Spending on Education (% of GDP)	Primary School Enrollment (% net)	Secondary School Enrollment (% net)	Tertiary School Enrollment (% net)	Literacy Rate, Adult Total (% of people ages 15 and above)	Literacy Rate, Adult Male (% of males ages 15 and above)	Literacy Rate, Adult Female (% of females ages 15 and above)	Literacy Rate, Youth Total (% of people ages 15–24)	Literacy Rate, Youth Male (% of males ages 15–24)	Literacy Rate, Youth Female (% of females ages 15–24)
	2003–2005	2003–2005	2003–2005	2003–2005	2003–2005	2006	2006	2006	2006	2006	2006
Indonesia	20	1.0	94	57	17	90	94	87	99	99	99
Iran, Islamic Rep.	19	4.7	95	77	24	77	84	70	..	..	..
Iraq	21	..	88	38	15	74	84	64	85	89	80
Ireland	18	4.5	96	87	59	..	..	..	..	..	..
Israel	12	7.3	98	89	56	97	98	96	100	100	100
Italy	11	4.9	99	92	63	98	99	98	100	100	100
Jamaica	28	4.5	91	79	..	80	74	86	..	..	..
Japan	19	3.7	100	100	54	..	..	..	..	..	..
Jordan	20	..	91	81	39	90	95	85	99	99	99
Kazakhstan	17	2.3	91	92	53	100	100	99	100	100	100
Kenya	40	6.7	80	42	3	74	78	70	80	80	81
Kiribati	25	..	..	68	..	..	..	..	..	..	..
Korea, Dem	..	..	..	..	..	..	..	..	..	..	..
Korea, Rep.	29	4.6	99	90	90	..	..	..	..	..	..
Kuwait	12	5.1	87	..	18	93	94	91	100	100	100
Kyrgyz Republic	24	4.5	87	80	41	99	99	98	100	100	100
Lao PDR	31	2.3	84	38	8	69	77	61	78	83	75
Latvia	13	5.3	..	..	74	100	100	100	100	100	100
Lebanon	14	2.6	92	..	51	..	..	..	..	..	..
Lesotho	42	13.4	87	25	3	82	74	90	..	..	..
Liberia	..	..	..	..	..	..	..	..	..	..	..
Libya	..	..	..	..	56	..	..	..	..	..	..
Lithuania	15	5.2	89	94	73	100	100	100	100	100	100
Luxembourg	12	..	91	79	12	..	..	..	..	..	..
Macedonia, FYR	20	3.4	92	..	28	96	98	94	99	99	98
Madagascar	54	3.2	92	..	3	71	77	65	70	73	68
Malawi	64	5.8	95	24	0	64	75	54	76	82	71
Malaysia	18	8.0	93	76	32	89	92	85	97	97	97
Maldives	20	7.1	79	63	0	96	96	96	98	98	98
Mali	54	4.3	51	..	3	19	27	12	24	32	17
Malta	19	..	94	88	26	88	86	89	96	94	98
Marshall Islands	17	11.8	90	..	17	..	..	..	..	..	..
Mauritania	40	2.3	72	15	3	51	60	43	61	68	55
Mauritius	22	4.5	95	82	17	84	88	81	95	94	95
Mexico	28	5.8	98	64	23	91	92	90	98	98	98
Micronesia, Fed. Sts.	..	..	..	..	..	..	..	..	..	..	..
Moldova	18	4.3	86	76	34	98	99	98	100	99	100
Monaco	14	4.5	..	..	..	..	..	..	..	..	..
Mongolia	34	5.4	89	78	41	98	98	98	98	97	98
Morocco	27	6.8	86	35	11	52	66	40	70	81	60

Table I (continued)
World Countries: Education and Literacy, 2003–2006

	Pupil-Teacher Ratio, Primary	Public Spending on Education (% of GDP)	Primary School Enrollment (% net)	Secondary School Enrollment (% net)	Tertiary School Enrollment (% net)	Literacy Rate, Adult Total (% of people ages 15 and above)	Literacy Rate, Adult Male (% of males ages 15 and above)	Literacy Rate, Adult Female (% of females ages 15 and above)	Literacy Rate, Youth Total (% of people ages 15–24)	Literacy Rate, Youth Male (% of males ages 15–24)	Literacy Rate, Youth Female (% of females ages 15–24)
	2003–2005	2003–2005	2003–2005	2003–2005	2003–2005	2006	2006	2006	2006	2006	2006
Mozambique	66	3.7	79	7	1	..	..	..	..	..	..
Myanmar	31	..	90	37	..	90	94	86	95	96	93
Namibia	33	6.9	72	38	6	85	87	83	92	91	93
Nepal	40	3.4	78	..	6	49	63	35	70	81	60
Netherlands	..	5.3	99	89	59	..	..	..	..	..	..
Netherlands Antilles	20	..	..	77	..	..	..	..	..	..	..
New Zealand	16	6.8	99	..	86	..	..	..	..	..	..
Nicaragua	34	3.1	87	43	..	77	77	77	86	84	89
Niger	44	2.3	40	8	1	29	43	15	37	52	23
Nigeria	37	..	91	27	10	..	..	..	..	..	..
Norway	11	7.7	99	96	80	..	..	..	..	..	..
Oman	..	3.6	76	75	15	81	87	74	97	98	97
Pakistan	38	2.3	68	21	5	50	63	36	66	76	55
Palau	..	..	..	..	..	..	..	..	..	..	..
Panama	24	3.8	98	64	44	92	93	91	96	97	96
Papua New Guinea	35	..	..	..	..	57	63	51	67	69	64
Paraguay	..	4.3	..	..	..	..	..	..	..	..	..
Peru	22	2.4	97	69	33	88	93	82	97	98	96
Philippines	35	3.2	94	61	29	93	93	93	95	94	96
Poland	13	5.6	97	90	61	..	..	..	..	..	..
Portugal	12	5.9	98	82	57	..	..	..	..	..	..
Qatar	11	1.6	96	90	19	89	89	89	96	95	98
Romania	17	3.6	92	81	40	97	98	96	98	98	98
Russian Federation	17	3.7	91	..	68	99	100	99	100	100	100
Rwanda	62	3.8	74	..	3	65	71	60	78	79	77
Samoa	25	..	90	66	..	..	..	..	..	..	..
San Marino	6	..	..	..	..	..	..	..	..	..	..
Sao Tome and Principe	31	..	97	32	..	..	..	..	..	..	..
Saudi Arabia	..	6.8	78	66	28	79	87	69	96	98	94
Senegal	47	5.4	76	21	5	39	51	29	49	58	41
Serbia and Montenegro	..	..	..	..	..	96	99	94	99	99	99
Seychelles	14	5.4	96	93	..	92	91	92	99	99	99
Sierra Leone	67	3.8	..	..	..	35	47	24	48	59	37
Singapore	..	..	..	..	..	93	97	89	100	99	100
Slovak Republic	18	4.4	..	..	36	100	100	100	100	100	100
Slovenia	15	6.0	98	95	74	..	..	..	..	..	..
Solomon Islands	..	..	63	26	..	..	..	..	..	..	..
South Africa	36	5.4	87	..	16	82	84	81	94	94	94
Spain	14	4.3	99	97	66	..	..	..	..	..	..

Table I (continued)
World Countries: Education and Literacy, 2003–2006

	Pupil-Teacher Ratio, Primary	Public Spending on Education (% of GDP)	Primary School Enrollment (% net)	Secondary School Enrollment (% net)	Tertiary School Enrollment (% net)	Literacy Rate, Adult Total (% of people ages 15 and above)	Literacy Rate, Adult Male (% of males ages 15 and above)	Literacy Rate, Adult Female (% of females ages 15 and above)	Literacy Rate, Youth Total (% of people ages 15–24)	Literacy Rate, Youth Male (% of males ages 15–24)	Literacy Rate, Youth Female (% of females ages 15–24)
	2003–2005	2003–2005	2003–2005	2003–2005	2003–2005	2006	2006	2006	2006	2006	2006
Sri Lanka	23	..	97	..	..	91	92	89	96	95	96
St. Kitts and Nevis	18	9.4	93	78	..	..	..	..	..	..	..
St. Lucia	24	5.8	97	68	14	..	..	..	..	..	..
St. Vincent and the Grenadines	18	8.2	90	64	..	..	..	..	..	..	..
Sudan	28	..	..	..	..	61	71	52	77	85	71
Suriname	19	..	94	75	..	90	92	87	95	96	94
Swaziland	32	6.2	80	33	4	80	81	78	88	87	90
Sweden	10	7.5	99	98	84	..	..	..	..	..	..
Switzerland	..	6.1	94	83	47	..	..	..	..	..	..
Syrian Arab Republic	..	..	..	62	..	80	86	74	92	94	90
Tajikistan	21	3.5	97	80	17	99	100	99	100	100	100
Tanzania	56	..	91	..	1	69	78	62	78	81	76
Thailand	21	4.2	..	..	43	93	95	91	98	98	98
Timor-Leste	51	..	..	..	..	..	..	..	..	..	..
Togo	34	..	78	..	..	53	69	38	74	84	64
Tonga	20	4.8	95	68	6	99	99	99	99	99	99
Trinidad and Tobago	18	..	95	75	12	..	..	..	..	..	..
Tunisia	21	8.1	97	..	29	74	83	65	94	96	92
Turkey	..	4.0	89	..	29	87	95	80	96	98	93
Turkmenistan	..	..	..	..	..	99	99	98	100	100	100
Uganda	50	5.2	..	13	3	67	77	58	77	83	71
Ukraine	19	6.4	83	79	69	99	100	99	100	100	100
United Arab Emirates	15	1.3	71	57	22	..	..	..	..	..	..
United Kingdom	18	5.5	99	95	60	..	..	..	..	..	..
United States	14	5.9	92	89	82	..	..	..	..	..	..
Uruguay	21	2.2	..	..	40	..	..	..	..	..	..
Uzbekistan	..	..	..	..	15	..	..	..	..	..	..
Vanuatu	20	9.6	94	39	5	74	..	..	..	..	..
Venezuela, RB	19	..	91	63	41	93	93	93	97	96	98
Vietnam	22	..	88	69	16	90	94	87	94	94	94
West Bank and Gaza	25	..	80	95	38	92	97	88	99	99	99
Yemen, Rep.	26	..	75	..	9	..	..	..	..	..	..
Zambia	51	2.0	89	26	..	68	76	60	69	73	66
Zimbabwe	39	..	82	34	4	..	..	..	..	..	..
World	29	4.7	..	..	24	82	87	77	87	90	84

Source: World Bank Economic Indicators (2007)

COUNTRY	Arable Land (hectares per person)	Irrigated Land (hectares)	Land Area Under Cereal Production (hectares)	Fertilizer Consumption (100 grams per hectare of arable land)	Tractors per Agricultural Worker	Tractors per 100 Hectares of Arable Land	Crop Production Index (1999–2001 = 100)	Food Production Index (1989–1991 = 100)	Food Production Index (1999–2001 = 100)	Agriculture Value Added per Worker (constant 2000 US$)
	2002	2002	2004	2003	2002	2004	2004	2004	2004	2004
Afghanistan	0.28	2,386,000	3,054,700	26.30	0.00014	1				..
Albania	0.18	340,000	153,340	611.71	0.01061	148	100.9	105.9	108.6	1,356.00
Algeria	0.24	560,000	2,901,590	127.85	0.03653	129	128	118	104.6	2,267.00
Angola	0.23	75,000	1,071,572	..	0.00240	31	119.2	112.9	100	194.00
Antigua and Barbuda	0.10		35		0.03000	300	112.9	107.8	104.9	3,435.00
Argentina	0.92	1,561,000	9,331,507	219.44	0.20522	107	104.9	101.4	94.4	9,499.00
Armenia	0.16	280,000	194,816	227.94	0.09402	287	118.7	115.2	108.3	3,254.00
Australia	2.46	2,545,000	19,922,884	471.96	0.71267	67	92.1	93.3	93.2	32,346.00
Austria	0.17	4,000	812,562	1497.48	1.87500	2,379	103.8	100.4	99.3	23,764.00
Azerbaijan	0.22	1,455,000	765,399	99.23	0.03110	164	125.5	121.3	113.7	1,131.00
Bahamas, The	0.03	1,000	160	1000.00	0.02400	150	111.8	104.9	96.3	..
Bahrain	0.00	4,000	..	500.00	0.00500	75	96	110.2	113.7	
Bangladesh	0.06	4,597,000	11,620,968	1775.28	0.00014	7	105	104.6	102.6	323.00
Barbados	0.06	1,000	100	506.88	0.09750	366	91.2	94.1	95.3	14,030.00
Belarus	0.56	131,000	2,108,493	1334.29	0.09585	106	129.6	115.1	107.7	3,233.00
Belgium			300,210			1,257	106.3	101.5	99.7	39,406.00
Belize	0.26	3,000	18,929	671.43	0.04259	164	94.7	101.3	143.6	6,632.00
Benin	0.39	12,000	907,751	187.61	0.00012	1	134.1	138	115.6	622.00
Bermuda	0.02		..	1000.00	0.04500	450				..
Bhutan	0.17	40,000	61,870	..		8	92.5	94.5	99.1	134.00
Bolivia	0.34	132,000	741,752	47.38	0.00385	20	119.9	110.7	109.2	763.00
Bosnia and Herzegovina	0.24	3,000	314,624	326.98	0.34118	289	102.1	100.5	88.5	7,303.00
Botswana	0.22	1,000	31,183	124.32	0.01700	159	75.6	102.4	107.7	430.00
Brazil	0.34	2,920,000	19,912,312	1302.48	0.06360	137	126.7	123.7	123.6	3,454.00
Brunei	0.03	1,000	690	..	0.07200	55	111.5	132.9	136.4	..
Bulgaria	0.43	592,000	1,608,437	494.61	0.12528	95	106	97.7	95.9	7,556.00
Burkina Faso	0.37	25,000	3,577,488	3.84	0.00037	4	140.5	123.6	108.8	189.00
Burundi	0.14	74,000	211,700	25.75	0.00005	2	104.2	104.4	100.2	74.00
Cambodia	0.28	270,000	2,325,989	..	0.00055	7	115.1	113.3	101.8	305.00
Cameroon	0.38	33,000	977,528	58.56	0.00013	1	103.3	103	102.4	1,180.00
Canada	1.46	785,000	18,288,300	571.39	1.97466	160	102.8	102.2	103.5	44,276.00
Cape Verde	0.09	3,000	32,053	52.38	0.00040	3	90.3	94.5	102.1	1,582.00
Central African Republic	0.51		190,500	3.11	0.00002	0	102.8	108.2	114	422.00
Chad	0.43	20,000	2,047,000	48.61	0.00006	0	112.6	111.8	107.6	214.00
Chile	0.13	1,900,000	685,127	2295.66	0.05482	272	107	106.7	107.7	5,437.00
China	0.11	54,937,000	77,111,240	2776.59	0.00181	96	115.8	117.5	120.2	402.00
Colombia	0.05	900,000	1,246,490	3015.70	0.00568	93	110.8	106.4	103.4	3,157.00
Comoros	0.14		15,700	37.50		1	102.6	103.4	109.1	419.00
Congo, Dem. Rep.	0.13	11,000	1,917,825	15.69	0.00018	4	97.3	97.7	97.1	151.00

-204-

COUNTRY				AGRICULTURAL INPUTS				AGRICULTURAL OUTPUTS AND PRODUCTIVITY		
					AGRICULTURAL MACHINERY					
	Arable Land (hectares per person)	Irrigated Land (hectares)	Land Area Under Cereal Production (hectares)	Fertilizer Consumption (100 grams per hectare of arable land)	Tractors per Agricultural Worker	Tractors per 100 Hectares of Arable Land	Crop Production Index (1999–2001 = 100)	Food Production Index (1989–1991 = 100)	Food Production Index (1999–2001 = 100)	Agriculture Value Added per Worker (constant 2000 US$)
	2002	2002	2004	2003	2002	2004	2004	2004	2004	2004
Congo, Rep.	0.05	1,000	13,000	12.42	0.00122	14	104.9	108.1	120.2	368.00
Costa Rica	0.06	108,000	53,765	6736.09	0.02147	311	91.8	94	97.1	4,426.00
Cote d'Ivoire	0.19	73,000	785,574	351.61	0.00122	12	86.4	90.4	113.2	836.00
Croatia	0.33	5,000	689,455	1176.47	0.02755	29	99.8	102.6	105.4	10,240.00
Cuba	0.24	870,000	337,417	456.90	0.10317	255	116.4	111.7	96	..
Cyprus	0.09	40,000	72,745	2139.72	0.55323	1,491	96.3	105.3	110.4	..
Czech Republic	0.30	24,000	1,462,694	1201.84	0.21367	299	109.8	104.1	95.3	5,411.00
Denmark	0.42	447,000	1,484,586	1304.93	1.20588	543	101	99.7	100.6	38,502.00
Djibouti	0.00	1,000	6	..	0.00002	60	100.4	107.1	108.5	72.00
Dominica	0.07		135	1086.00	0.01125	180	98	97.3	100	4,835.00
Dominican Republic	0.13	275,000	157,100	818.46	0.00321	17	107.8	103.2	100.4	4,369.00
Ecuador	0.13	865,000	837,201	1416.80	0.01179	113	99.7	112.5	126.8	1,602.00
Egypt, Arab Rep.	0.04	3,400,000	2,751,930	4375.18	0.01058	309	105.1	108.8	119.2	2,062.00
El Salvador	0.10	45,000	320,104	838.38	0.00440	52	89.8	100.4	104.9	1,671.00
Equatorial Guinea	0.27		..	..	0.00123	13	93.8	93.4	101.9	654.00
Eritrea	0.12	21,000	373,353	73.52	0.00031	8	70.7	84.1	95.9	59.00
Estonia	0.45	4,000	263,166	439.85	0.67232	992	110.5	108.9	100.9	3,328.00
Ethiopia	0.15	190,000	8,499,198	151.00	0.00012	3	104.8	105.9	106.9	154.00
Fiji	0.24	3,000	7,020	614.50	0.05303	282	90.3	92.5	97.7	1,868.00
Finland	0.42	64,000	1,192,900	1331.82	1.49231	878	109.2	106.7	104.9	32,340.00
France	0.31	2,600,000	8,954,210	2150.79	1.54523	685	104.3	100	97.3	47,408.00
French Polynesia	0.01	1,000	..	4346.67	0.00853	967	109	105.5	93.8	..
Gabon	0.25	15,000	19,500	9.23	0.00728	46	101.5	101.1	100.7	1,929.00
Gambia, The	0.18	2,000	169,166	32.00	0.00008	1	65.6	69.2	104.5	240.00
Georgia	0.15	469,000	347,198	355.44	0.04390	273	87	99.7	109	1,459.00
Germany	0.14	485,000	6,839,431	2200.26	1.02362	798	105.5	102.8	101	28,741.00
Ghana	0.21	11,000	1,461,530	74.22	0.00063	9	121.9	121.6	111.2	354.00
Greece	0.25	1,431,000	1,275,100	1490.62	0.33187	945	95.4	96.7	96.3	9,476.00
Grenada	0.02		300		0.00150	60	99.7	96.5	101.4	3,645.00
Guam	0.03		15		0.00400	375	108	107	98.8	..
Guatemala	0.11	130,000	665,940	1369.12	0.00215	30	103.2	104.4	93.3	2,321.00
Guinea	0.12	95,000	778,000	35.56	0.00016	5	104.7	108.9	117.6	237.00
Guinea-Bissau	0.21	17,000	120,500	80.00	0.00004	1	102.1	102.2	103.1	237.00
Guyana	0.63	150,000	133,200	372.48	0.06600	76	100.1	105.8	145.3	3,707.00
Haiti	0.09	75,000	452,500	178.59	0.00006	2	100.6	102.3	108.3	..
Honduras	0.16	80,000	390,415	470.30	0.00679	50	120.1	108.5	101.5	1,214.00
Hungary	0.45	230,000	2,885,811	1086.52	0.23996	247	119.4	110.3	99.3	6,464.00

Table J (continued)
World Countries: Agricultural Operations, 2000–2004

COUNTRY				AGRICULTURAL INPUTS				AGRICULTURAL OUTPUTS AND PRODUCTIVITY		
				AGRICULTURAL MACHINERY						
	Arable Land (hectares per person)	Irrigated Land (hectares)	Land Area Under Cereal Production (hectares)	Fertilizer Consumption (100 grams per hectare of arable land)	Tractors per Agricultural Worker	Tractors per 100 Hectares of Arable Land	Crop Production Index (1999–2001 = 100)	Food Production Index (1989–1991 = 100)	Food Production Index (1999–2001 = 100)	Agriculture Value Added per Worker (constant 2000 US$)
	2002	2002	2004	2003	2002	2004	2004	2004	2004	2004
Iceland	0.02		..	25554.29	0.83846	15,413	88.4	104.3	105.1	53,027.00
India	0.15	57,198,000	98,291,000	995.58	0.00564	159	102.1	104.1	111.2	386.00
Indonesia	0.10	4,815,000	14,835,868	1459.51	0.00189	41	113.1	114.8	125.8	594.00
Iran, Islamic Rep.	0.23	7,500,000	8,744,000	859.88	0.03718	153	116.6	111.9	103.1	2,491.00
Iraq	0.24	3,525,000	2,907,000	1110.96	0.09507	80				1,898.00
Ireland	0.29		300,000	5236.40	0.97484	1,311	102.1	98.4	98.2	..
Israel	0.05	194,000	92,430	2405.33	0.36029	725	94.2	103.2	117.2	..
Italy	0.14	2,750,000	4,147,562	1728.78	1.36066	2,111	95.6	95.5	98.1	25,467.00
Jamaica	0.07	25,000	820	1287.36	0.01171	177	97.4	98.8	101.8	1,796.00
Japan	0.03	2,607,000	1,985,665	2906.29	0.82641	4,612	95.8	97.9	99.6	36,289.00
Jordan	0.06	75,000	56,229	1135.59	0.03005	328	127.4	118.5	98.8	1,385.00
Kazakhstan	1.45	2,350,000	13,678,797	30.14	0.03807	22	98	98.8	112	1,469.00
Kenya	0.15	90,000	2,102,403	310.34	0.00105	28	96	101.1	108.7	326.00
Kiribati	0.02		..		0.00180	90	105.1	107.3	128.6	417.00
Korea, Dem. Rep.	0.11	1,460,000	1,258,996	1064.80	0.01933	238	110	109.3	113.6	..
Korea, Rep.	0.04	1,138,000	1,109,257	4096.80	0.09563	1,285	90.5	92.5	98.7	11,488.00
Kuwait	0.01	13,000	1,231	807.69	0.00657	70	109.6	124.6	120.6	..
Kyrgyz Republic	0.27	1,072,000	588,876	205.20	0.04552	163	94.9	81	69.4	995.00
Lao PDR	0.17	175,000	807,987	76.29	0.00051	11	121.9	119.8	102	460.00
Latvia	0.78	20,000	434,500	273.08	0.39167	578	123.1	118.5	108.2	2,678.00
Lebanon	0.04	104,000	61,499	2318.82	0.19302	488	95.6	99.8	117.7	28,363.00
Lesotho	0.19	1,000	169,481	342.42	0.00717	61	111.2	105.3	100	494.00
Liberia	0.12	3,000	120,000	..	0.00039	9	96.7	97.4	114.9	..
Libya	0.33	470,000	340,500	341.05	0.39356	219	94.8	100.9	100.5	..
Lithuania	0.84	7,000	864,600	662.12	0.51150	671	112.4	108.4	97.8	4,790.00
Luxembourg			28,904			..	100.8	94.2	94	32,768.00
Macedonia, FYR	0.28	55,000	194,797	393.99	0.49541	954	92.9	95.1	103.2	3,545.00
Madagascar	0.18	1,090,000	1,421,140	30.93	0.00060	12	102.8	102.5	101.3	175.00
Malawi	0.21	30,000	1,704,000	839.17	0.00031	6	91.8	95.6	101.8	137.00
Malaysia	0.07	365,000	695,800	6833.33	0.02412	241	117.1	116.9	116.7	5,170.00
Maldives	0.01		5			..	112.6	112.6		..
Mali	0.41	138,000	3,474,082	90.13	0.00055	5	108.1	106.6	118.4	229.00
Malta	0.02	2,000	2,940	777.78	0.25000	500	76.6	100.8	101.8	..
Mauritania	0.18	49,000	182,270	59.43	0.00058	8	99.5	107.3	108.4	338.00
Mauritius	0.08	22,000	27	2500.00	0.00627	37	103.4	105.8	113.4	4,967.00
Mexico	0.25	6,320,000	10,603,722	690.28	0.03818	131	105.6	107.8	108.6	2,877.00
Moldova	0.43	300,000	850,079	54.99	0.08798	221	109.8	108.9	110.5	825.00
Mongolia	0.49	84,000	206,861	37.13	0.01634	42	105	92.3	92.1	802.00
Morocco	0.28	1,345,000	5,560,400	475.23	0.01147	58	133.8	122.6	100.6	1,739.00
Mozambique	0.23	107,000	2,102,055	59.29	0.00073	13	105.9	104.2	104	158.00

Table J (continued)
World Countries: Agricultural Operations, 2000–2004

COUNTRY				AGRICULTURAL INPUTS				AGRICULTURAL OUTPUTS AND PRODUCTIVITY		
				AGRICULTURAL MACHINERY						
	Arable Land (hectares per person)	Irrigated Land (hectares)	Land Area Under Cereal Production (hectares)	Fertilizer Consumption (100 grams per hectare of arable land)	Tractors per Agricultural Worker	Tractors per 100 Hectares of Arable Land	Crop Production Index (1999–2001 = 100)	Food Production Index (1989–1991 = 100)	Food Production Index (1999–2001 = 100)	Agriculture Value Added per Worker (constant 2000 US$)
	2002	2002	2004	2003	2002	2004	2004	2004	2004	2004
Myanmar	0.20	1,996,000	7,167,482	134.14	0.00050	11	116.6	116.6	122.8	..
Namibia	0.41	7,000	244,300	3.68	0.01013	39	106.6	95.7	91.3	1,099.00
Nepal	0.13	1,135,000	3,351,325	278.24	0.00042	24	112.4	108.8	106.8	211.00
Netherlands	0.06	565,000	218,598	3668.12	0.63889	1,650	98.7	93	90.9	42,325.00
Netherlands Antilles	0.04		..		..	25				..
New Caledonia	0.02	10,000	1,580	1800.00	0.04621	3,242	104.6	101.7	99.9	..
New Zealand	0.38	285,000	131,612	5685.98	0.45238	507	105.2	115.7	115.5	26,512.00
Nicaragua	0.36	94,000	538,652	279.46	0.00742	15	117.9	127.5	134.1	2,030.00
Niger	0.39	66,000	8,078,000	11.08	0.00003	0	122.5	118.3	103.5	174.00
Nigeria	0.23	233,000	17,371,000	55.03	0.00198	10	104.6	105.1	108.8	949.00
Norway	0.19	127,000	326,890	2112.51	1.30000	1,484	103	99.9	98.3	36,202.00
Oman	0.01	62,000	2,370	3219.21	0.00042	52	88.9	91.1	96.6	1,189.00
Pakistan	0.15	17,800,000	12,481,100	1381.38	0.01249	149	105.2	109.3	112.5	697.00
Panama	0.19	35,000	205,720	524.07	0.03240	148	106.2	107.8	106.5	3,897.00
Papua New Guinea	0.04		2,900	536.36	0.00060	52	102.2	107.8	112.7	631.00
Paraguay	0.55	67,000	776,259	507.18	0.02257	54	118.8	110.9	100.7	2,077.00
Peru	0.14	1,195,000	1,138,721	740.56	0.00437	36	94.9	90.4	81.9	1,489.00
Philippines	0.07	1,550,000	6,416,200	1268.46	0.00091	20	109.5	113.5	123.2	1,081.00
Poland	0.36	100,000	8,163,257	1085.84	0.32810	1,089	95.8	107.2	106.2	2,237.00
Portugal	0.19	650,000	450,970	1040.20	0.27750	1,049	99.7	101	100.7	6,297.00
Puerto Rico	0.01	40,000	260			..	99.9	100.2	100.2	..
Qatar	0.03	13,000	1,911	..	0.02050	46	98.3	143.9	159.3	..
Romania	0.43	3,077,000	5,116,684	347.01	0.11474	180	132.6	125.4	119.1	4,735.00
Russian Federation	0.86	4,600,000	36,759,400	119.39	0.08311	48	116.9	114.3	107.7	2,526.00
Rwanda	0.14	6,000	315,218	137.09	0.00001	0	113.8	112.7	105.5	222.00
Samoa	0.34		..	583.33	0.00448	16	103.7	101.4	94.8	1,628.00
Sao Tome and Principe	0.05	10,000	1,100		0.00278	156	101.8	102	102.8	221.00
Saudi Arabia	0.16	1,620,000	697,306	1059.17	0.01460	28	99.8	108.2	104.1	15,397.00
Senegal	0.25	71,000	1,331,210	136.14	0.00022	3	81.9	85.3	101.1	259.00
Serbia and Montenegro	0.42	29,000	2,006,150	..		956	126.6	113.5	94.5	1,754.00
Seychelles	0.01		..	170.00	0.00133	400	96.8	98.9	99.5	512.00
Sierra Leone	0.10	30,000	253,000	5.61	0.00008	1	109.4	110	112.3	..
Singapore	0.00		..	24180.00	0.02167	1,083	100	66.6	70.7	58,034.00
Slovak Republic			794,125			..				4,074.00
Slovenia	0.08	3,000	100,225	4159.94		..	94.2	105.7	111.9	43,795.00
Solomon Islands	0.04		1,300		0.0005	5	107.2	107.6	112.8	..
Somalia	0.11	200,000	585,555	4.78	0.00060	16				..
South Africa	0.33	1,498,000	4,660,321	654.17	0.04355	44	98.5	104.4	109.8	2,499.00

COUNTRY				AGRICULTURAL INPUTS			AGRICULTURAL OUTPUTS AND PRODUCTIVITY		
				AGRICULTURAL MACHINERY					
	Arable Land (hectares per person)	Irrigated Land (hectares)	Land Area Under Cereal Production (hectares)	Fertilizer Consumption (100 grams per hectare of arable land)	Tractors per Agricultural Worker	Tractors per 100 Hectares of Arable Land	Crop Production Index (1999–2001 = 100)	Food Production Index (1989–1991 = 100)	Food Production Index (1999–2001 = 100)	Agriculture Value Added per Worker (constant 2000 US$)
	2002	2002	2004	2003	2002	2004	2004	2004	2004	2004
Spain	0.34	3,780,000	6,570,667	1572.06	0.77545	694	103	103.7	111	20,260.000
Sri Lanka	0.05	638,000	946,340	3102.82	0.00270	115	94.4	95.2	105.9	736.00
St. Kitts and Nevis	0.15		..	2428.57	0.03875	221	99.6	89.6	100	2,385.00
St. Lucia	0.03	3,000	..	3357.50	0.00973	365	116.4	89.3	82.4	1,873.00
St. Vincent and the Grenadines	0.06	1,000	200	3047.14	0.00667	114	106	101.2	87	2,346.00
Sudan	0.50	1,950,000	9,880,820	42.81	0.00153	7	124.4	114.1	107.1	..
Suriname	0.13	51,000	52,453	982.46	0.04290	229	105.2	105.6	105.2	3,701.00
Swaziland	0.16	70,000	68,932	393.26	0.03264	222	93.9	102.2	115.2	1,212.00
Sweden	0.30	115,000	1,153,890	1000.37	1.17021	618	108.6	101	97.2	33,016.00
Switzerland	0.06	25,000	166,558	2274.82	0.73684	2,649	90.1	99.3	101.7	21,662.00
Syrian Arab Republic	0.27	1,333,000	3,117,251	702.82	0.06631	229	116.6	119.8	107.9	3,273.00
Tajikistan	0.15	719,000	393,232	300.00	0.02437	238	133.6	121.4	122	462.00
Tanzania	0.11	170,000	2,910,000	17.87	0.00052	19	104.7	103.8	109.1	303.00
Thailand	0.26	4,957,000	11,438,044	1071.79	0.01081	156	105.3	99.8	89.3	605.00
Timor-Leste	0.08		94,000		0.00036	9	106.3	106	104.6	283.00
Togo	0.53	18,000	813,000	67.95	0.00007	0	111.9	105.3	109.6	412.00
Tonga	0.17		..	..	0.01250	100	103	102.2	99.9	3,213.00
Trinidad and Tobago	0.06	4,000	2,150	434.40	0.05510	360	80.2	117.1	142.7	1,758.00
Tunisia	0.28	381,000	1,294,600	368.10	0.03664	126	94.5	96.5	98.7	2,874.00
Turkey	0.37	5,215,000	13,406,000	672.05	0.06601	427	104.7	105.2	106.8	1,793.00
Turkmenistan	0.39	1,800,000	963,000	528.65	0.07082	227	122.6	109.2	96.8	..
Uganda	0.21	9,000	1,495,000	18.25	0.00050	9	107.6	108.9	117.1	237.00
Ukraine	0.67	2,262,000	10,633,600	180.99	0.11852	120	125.6	116.1	107.8	1,718.00
United Arab Emirates	0.02	76,000	6	4666.67	0.00535	59	59.1	53.1	119.1	39,864.00
United Kingdom	0.10	170,000	3,060,100	3130.54	0.98425	884	99.3	98.1	97.2	27,316.00
United States	0.61	22,500,000	57,888,328	1096.48	1.65176	269	110.5	106.8	102	39,126.00
Uruguay	0.39	181,000	467,623	991.76	0.17460	241	122	106.6	98.4	8,107.00
Uzbekistan	0.18	4,281,000	1,794,000	1601.92	0.05655	362	106.3	105.2	104.7	1,772.00
Vanuatu	0.15		1,300		0.00234	38	96.4	96.2	95.9	1,149.00
Venezuela, RB	0.10	575,000	971,075	1229.51	0.06218	188	93.4	99.6	103.4	7,078.00
Vietnam	0.08	3,000,000	8,366,800	2948.06	0.00577	248	118.3	118.7	118.9	304.00
West Bank and Gaza			..			..				..
Yemen, Rep.	0.08	500,000	532,293	75.42	0.00223	42	100	106.5	113	334.00
Zambia	0.51	46,000	794,400	123.89	0.00195	11	106.5	106.8	98.9	219.00
Zimbabwe	0.25	117,000	1,688,171	341.61	0.00668	75	80.2	87.8	101.7	236.00
World			668,891,456			202				919.00

Source: World Bank Economic Indicators (2007), FAO, UN (2007)

Table K
Land Use and Deforestation, 1990–2005

COUNTRY	LAND AREA	RURAL POPULATION DENSITY	LAND USE						FOREST AREA	AVERAGE ANNUAL DEFORESTATION
		(people per sq km.)	Arable Land (% of land area)		Permanent Cropland (% of land area)		Other Land Use (% of land area)		(% of total land area)	(decline in % of forest area)
	(sq km.)	2005	1990	2005	1990	2005	1990	2005	2005	1990–2005
Afghanistan	652,090	..	12.1	12.13	0.22	0.22	87.65	87.65	1.33	0.8
Albania	27,400	300	21.1	21.09	4.56	4.42	74.31	74.49	28.98	0.80
Algeria	2,381,740	161	3.0	3.17	0.23	0.25	96.79	96.53	0.96	−1.30
Angola	1,246,70	219	2.3	2.65	0.40	0.24	97.27	97.35	47.41	0.20
Antigua and Barbuda	440	617	18.2	18.18	4.55	4.55	77.27	77.27	20.45	
Argentina	2,736,690	14	10.6	10.19	0.44	0.48	89.00	87.21	12.07	0.60
Armenia	28,200	218 ..		17.55 ..		2.30 ..		80.14	10.04	0.80
Australia	7,682,300	5	6.2	6.43	0.02	0.04	93.74	93.67	21.31	0.00
Austria	82,730	199	17.2	16.82	0.95	0.86	81.81	82.33	46.84	−0.20
Azerbaijan	82,600	218 ..		22.3 ..		2.74 ..		75.68	11.32	−1.30
Bahamas, The	10,010	402	0.8	0.8	0.20	0.40	99.00	98.80	51.45	
Bahrain	710	1,503	2.9	2.82	2.90	5.63	94.20	91.55		
Bangladesh	130,170	1,296	70.2	61.11	2.30	3.15	27.50	35.25	6.69	−1.30
Barbados	430	812	37.2	37.21	2.33	2.33	60.47	60.47	4.65	
Belarus	207,480	51 ..		26.29 ..		0.60 ..		72.38	38.05	−3.20
Belgium	30,230	35		27.92					22.06	0.2
Belize	22,800	203	2.3	3.07	1.10	1.40	96.62	95.53	72.47	
Benin	110,620	181	14.6	23.96	0.95	2.40	84.45	74.55	21.25	2.30
Bermuda	50	0	20.0	20					20	
Bhutan	47,000	362	2.4	3.38	0.40	0.43	97.19	96.49	67.98	
Bolivia	1,084,38	106	1.9	2.81	0.14	0.19	97.92	97.14	54.17	0.30
Bosnia and Herzegovina	51,200	216 ..		19.53 ..		1.88 ..		78.65	42.68	0.00
Botswana	566,730	208	0.7	0.67	0.01	0.01	99.26	99.34	21.07	0.90
Brazil	8,459,420	52	6.0	6.97	0.80	0.90	93.21	92.13	56.47	0.40
Brunei	5,270	755	0.6	2.66	0.76	0.76	98.67	97.53	52.75	
Bulgaria	110,630	72	34.9	29.21	2.71	2.06	62.43	67.61	33.37	−0.60
Burkina Faso	273,600	211	12.9	17.69	0.20	0.19	86.93	83.92	24.83	0.20
Burundi	25,680	644	36.2	38.55	14.02	14.21	49.77	47.39	5.92	9.00
Cambodia	176,520	298	20.9	20.96	0.57	0.61	78.50	78.43	59.18	0.60
Cameroon	465,400	125	12.8	12.81	2.64	2.58	84.59	84.62	45.65	0.90
Canada	9,220,970	14	5.0	5.02	0.01	0.01	95.02	95.02	34.1	0.00
Cape Verde	4,030	465	10.2	11.41	0.50	0.74	89.33	88.83	20.84	
Central African Republic	622,980	127	3.1	3.1	0.14	0.15	96.78	96.75	36.53	0.10
Chad	1,259,200	191	2.6	2.86	0.02	0.02	97.38	97.12	9.47	0.60
Chile	748,800	105	3.7	2.65	0.33	0.43	95.93	96.92	21.53	0.10
China	9,327,420	766	13.3	11.09	0.83	1.22	85.91	83.49	21.15	−1.20
Colombia	1,038,700	545	3.2	1.81	1.63	1.50	95.19	96.29	54.73	0.40
Comoros	2,230	463	35.0	35.87	15.70	23.32	49.33	40.81	2.24	
Congo, Dem. Rep.	2,267,050	557	2.9	2.96	0.52	0.49	96.53	96.56	58.94	0.40
Congo, Rep.	341,500	309	0.5	1.45	0.12	0.15	99.43	99.30	65.8	0.10
Costa Rica	51,060	731	5.1	4.41	4.90	5.88	90.01	89.72	46.83	0.80

COUNTRY	LAND AREA	RURAL POPULATION DENSITY	LAND USE						FOREST AREA	AVERAGE ANNUAL DEFORESTATION
		(people per sq km.)	Arable Land (% of land area)		Permanent Cropland (% of land area)		Other Land Use (% of land area)		(% of total land area)	(decline in % of forest area)
	(sq km.)	2005	1990	2005	1990	2005	1990	2005	2005	1990–2005
Cote d'Ivoire	318,000	298	7.6	10.38	11.01	11.95	81.35	78.30	32.72	0.80
Croatia	55,920	133 ..		19.85 ..		2.25 ..		71.60	38.18	−0.10
Cuba	109,820	90	29.6	27.89	7.38	10.20	63.03	65.51	24.7	−1.30
Cyprus	9,240	195	11.5	10.82	5.52	4.44	83.01	87.77	18.83	
Czech Republic	77,280	88 ..		39.44 ..		3.05 ..		57.23	34.27	0.00
Denmark	42,430	35	60.4	52.72	0.24	0.19	39.35	46.17	11.78	−0.20
Djibouti	23,180	11,488	0.0	0.04					0.26	
Dominica	750	396	6.7	6.67	14.67	20.00	78.67	73.33	61.33	
Dominican Republic	48,380	276	21.7	22.65	9.30	10.33	69.00	67.01	28.44	0.00
Ecuador	276,840	378	5.8	4.87	4.77	4.93	89.43	89.22	39.2	1.20
Egypt, Arab Rep.	995,450	1,406	2.3	3.01	0.37	0.50	97.34	96.58	0.07	−3.40
El Salvador	20,720	410	26.5	31.85	12.55	12.07	60.91	56.08	14.38	4.60
Equatorial Guinea	28,050	226	4.6	4.63	3.57	3.57	91.80	91.80	58.18	
Eritrea	101,000	586 ..		5.56 ..		0.03 ..		95.02	15.39	0.30
Estonia	42,390	76 ..		13.94 ..		0.40 ..		85.11	53.88	−0.60
Ethiopia	1,000,000	524 ..		11.06 ..		0.74 ..		89.33	13	0.80
Fiji	18,270	209	8.8	10.96	4.38	4.65	86.86	84.40	54.73	
Finland	304,590	92	7.4	7.33	0.02	0.03	92.53	92.75	73.87	0.00
France	550,100	77	32.7	33.64	2.17	2.06	65.12	64.40	28.27	−0.40
French Polynesia	3,660	3,980	0.5	0.82	5.74	6.01	93.72	93.17	28.69	
Gabon	257,670	73	1.1	1.26	0.63	0.66	98.23	98.08	84.51	0.00
Gambia, The	10,000	219	18.2	31.5	0.50	0.50	81.30	74.50	47.1	−1.00
Georgia	69,490	271 ..		11.54 ..		3.81 ..		84.69	39.72	0.00
Germany	348,950	173	34.3	34.13	1.27	0.59	64.42	65.62	31.76	0.00
Ghana	227,540	272	11.9	18.39	6.59	9.45	81.54	72.18	24.25	1.70
Greece	128,900	168	22.5	20.38	8.29	8.76	69.22	70.16	29.11	−0.90
Grenada	340	3,622	5.9	5.88	29.41	29.41	64.71	64.71	11.76	
Guam	550	518	9.1	3.64	14.55	16.36	76.36	74.55	47.27	
Guatemala	108,430	447	12.0	13.28	4.47	5.03	83.54	82.43	36.32	1.70
Guinea	245,720	555	3.0	4.48	2.03	2.60	95.00	93.73	27.36	0.50
Guinea-Bissau	28,120	350	10.7	10.67	4.16	8.82	85.17	80.51	73.68	0.90
Guyana	196,850	112	2.4	2.44	0.11	0.15	97.45	97.41	76.73	
Haiti	27,560	664	28.3	28.3	11.61	11.61	60.09	60.09	3.81	5.70
Honduras	111,890	351	13.1	9.55	3.20	3.22	83.73	87.24	41.54	1.00
Hong Kong, China	1,042	..		..					..	
Hungary	92,100	76	54.7	51.33	2.53	2.06	42.73	47.84	22.05	−0.40
Iceland	100,250	306	0.1	0.07					0.46	
India	2,973,190	479	54.9	53.7	2.12	2.83	43.01	42.78	22.77	−0.10
Indonesia	1,811,570	507	11.2	12.7	6.47	7.29	82.35	81.40	48.85	−0.10
Iran, Islamic Rep.	1,636,200	134	9.3	9.84	0.80	1.26	89.92	89.56	6.77	0.00

Table K (continued)
Land Use and Deforestation, 1990–2005

COUNTRY	LAND AREA	RURAL POPULATION DENSITY	LAND USE						FOREST AREA	AVERAGE ANNUAL DEFORESTATION
		(people per sq km.)	Arable Land (% of land area)		Permanent Cropland (% of land area)		Other Land Use (% of land area)		(% of total land area)	(decline in % of forest area)
	(sq km.)	2005	1990	2005	1990	2005	1990	2005	2005	1990–2005
Iraq	437,370	..	12.1	13.15	0.66	0.78	87.22	86.08	1.88	0.00
Ireland	68,890	135	15.1	17.64	0.04	0.03	84.85	83.70	9.71	−3.00
Israel	21,710	168	15.8	14.65	4.05	3.96	80.15	80.47	7.9	−4.00
Italy	294,110	236	30.6	26.33	10.06	9.44	59.29	62.38	33.93	−0.30
Jamaica	10,830	717	11.0	16.07	9.23	10.16	79.78	73.78	31.3	1.50
Japan	364,500	1,000	13.1	11.96	1.30	0.94	85.62	86.94	68.22	0.00
Jordan	88,930	549	3.3	2.09	1.01	1.18	95.73	95.50	0.94	0.00
Kazakhstan	2,699,700	28 ..		8.28 ..		0.05 ..		91.97	1.24	−2.20
Kenya	569,140	561	7.4	8.17	0.88	0.99	91.74	90.93	6.19	0.50
Kiribati	730	2,620	2.7	2.74	50.68	50.68	46.58	46.58	2.74	
Korea, Dem. Rep.	120,410	321	19.0	23.25	1.49	1.66	79.50	77.58	51.38	0.00
Korea, Rep.	98,730	572	19.8	16.56	1.58	1.95	78.64	80.99	63.46	0.10
Kuwait	17,820	278	0.2	0.84	0.06	0.11	99.72	99.16	0.34	−5.20
Kyrgyz Republic	191,800	241 ..		6.69 ..		0.34 ..		92.64	4.53	−2.80
Lao PDR	230,800	463	3.5	4.33	0.26	0.35	96.27	95.66	69.94	0.40
Latvia	62,050	78 ..		17.53 ..		0.47 ..		70.01	47.21	−0.40
Lebanon	10,230	281	17.9	16.62	11.93	13.98	70.19	69.40	13.29	0.90
Lesotho	30,350	445	10.4	10.87	0.13	0.13	89.42	89.00	0.26	0.30
Liberia	96,320	366	4.2	3.97	2.23	2.28	93.62	93.77	32.75	2.00
Libya	1,759,540	49	1.0	1.03	0.20	0.19	98.78	98.78	0.12	−1.40
Lichtenstein	160	..	25.0	25					43.75	
Lithuania	62,680	75 ..		30.41 ..		0.94 ..		52.31	33.49	−0.20
Luxembourg	2,586	122		23.17					33.59	
Macedonia, FYR	25,430	117 ..		22.26 ..		1.81 ..		75.93	35.63	−0.20
Madagascar	581,540	439	4.7	5.07	1.04	1.03	94.28	93.90	22.08	0.90
Malawi	94,080	421	19.3	26.04	1.22	1.49	79.49	74.06	36.16	2.40
Malaysia	328,550	474	5.2	5.48	15.97	17.61	78.85	76.91	63.58	1.20
Maldives	300	5,581	13.3	13.33	13.33	26.67	73.33	60.00	3.33	
Mali	1,220,190	187	1.7	3.93	0.03	0.03	98.28	96.15	10.3	0.70
Malta	320	218	37.5	28.13	3.13	3.13	59.38	68.75	..	
Marshall Islands	181	1,986		11.11					..	
Mauritania	1,025,220	354	0.4	0.48	0.01	0.01	99.60	99.51	0.26	2.70
Mauritius	2,030	703	49.3	49.26	2.96	2.96	47.78	47.78	18.23	0.60
Mexico	1,908,690	100	12.6	12.99	1.00	1.31	86.43	85.70	33.66	1.10
Micronesia, Fed. Sts.	702	2,114		5.71					90	
Moldova	32,880	122 ..		56.22 ..		9.12 ..		34.82	10.01	−0.20
Mongolia	1,566,500	90	0.9	0.76	0.00	0.00	99.12	99.23	6.54	0.50
Morocco	446,300	145	19.5	19.01	1.65	1.99	78.84	79.20	9.78	0.00
Mozambique	784,090	294	4.4	5.55	0.29	0.30	95.31	94.34	24.57	0.20
Myanmar	657,550	345	14.5	15.35	0.76	1.14	84.69	83.86	49	1.40
Namibia	823,290	161	0.8	0.99	0.00	0.00	99.20	99.00	9.31	0.90

Table K (continued)
Land Use and Deforestation, 1990–2005

COUNTRY	LAND AREA	RURAL POPULATION DENSITY	LAND USE						FOREST AREA	AVERAGE ANNUAL DEFORESTATION
			Arable Land (% of land area)		Permanent Cropland (% of land area)		Other Land Use (% of land area)		(% of total land area)	(decline in % of forest area)
	(sq. km.)	(people per sq km.)								
	2005	2005	1990	2005	1990	2005	1990	2005	2005	1990–2005
Nepal	143,000	941	16.0	16.48	0.46	0.66	83.55	76.97	25.43	1.80
Netherlands	33,880	379	25.9	26.8	0.89	0.97	73.17	71.99	10.77	−0.30
Netherlands Antilles	800	672	10.0	10.0					1.25	
New Caledonia	18,280	1,393	0.5	0.33	0.33	0.22	99.18	99.51	39.22	
New Zealand	267,990	37	9.4	5.6	5.05	6.99	85.58	87.42	31	−0.50
Nicaragua	121,400	110	10.7	15.86	1.61	1.94	87.69	82.20	42.74	3.00
Niger	1,266,700	75	2.8	11.43	0.01	0.01	97.15	96.45	1	3.70
Nigeria	910,770	221	32.4	33.49	2.78	3.07	64.78	63.77	12.18	2.60
Norway	306,250	120	2.8	2.82					30.85	−0.40
Oman	309,500	1,931	0.1	0.12	0.15	0.14	99.74	99.74	0.01	0.00
Pakistan	770,880	453	26.6	27.6	0.59	0.87	72.84	71.31	2.47	1.10
Palau	460	....		8.7 ..		4.35 ..		86.96	86.96	
Panama	74,430	178	6.7	7.36	2.08	1.98	91.21	90.66	57.69	1.60
Papua New Guinea	452,860	2,179	0.4	0.5	1.28	1.44	98.30	98.08	65	0.40
Paraguay	397,300	80	5.3	7.65	0.22	0.24	94.47	92.16	46.5	0.50
Peru	1,280,000	204	2.7	2.89	0.33	0.48	96.94	96.63	53.7	0.40
Philippines	298,170	548	18.4	19.12	14.76	16.77	66.86	64.11	24.02	1.40
Poland	306,290	115	47.3	39.63	1.13	0.99	51.60	53.55	30.01	−0.10
Portugal	91,500	283	25.6	16.77	8.54	7.81	65.85	70.44	41.34	−1.70
Puerto Rico	8,870	202	7.3	8	5.64	5.52	87.03	90.53	46	0.20
Qatar	11,000	196	0.9	1.64	0.09	0.27	99.00	98.09	..	
Romania	229,870	107	41.0	40.39	2.57	2.18	56.41	56.94	27.7	−0.20
Russian Federation	16,888,500	32 ..		7.43 ..		0.11 ..		92.58	49.37	0.00
Rwanda	24,670	605	35.7	48.64	12.36	10.90	51.97	43.86	19.46	3.90
Samoa	2,830	236	19.4	21.2	23.67	24.38	56.89	54.42	60.42	
Soa Tome and Principe	960	819	2.1	8.33	40.63	48.96	57.29	43.75	28.13	
Saudi Arabia	2,149,690	119	1.6	1.8	0.04	0.09	98.38	98.24	1.36	0.00
Senegal	192,530	266	12.1	12.78	0.13	0.24	87.79	86.98	45.05	0.70
Serbia and Montenegro	102,000	115	27.5	34.36	2.81 ..		69.70 ..		26.41	0.00
Seychelles	450	3,963	2.2	2.17	11.11	13.33	86.67	84.44	86.96	
Sierra Leone	71,620	546	6.8	7.96	0.75	0.91	92.46	91.62	38.45	2.90
Singapore	670	0	1.5	0.87	1.49	1.49	97.01	97.01	2.9	0.00
Slovak Republic	48,800	167		28.92					40.1	−0.30
Slovenia	20,120	566 ..		8.74 ..		1.49 ..		90.16	62.76	−0.20
Solomon Islands	27,990	2,106	0.6	0.64	1.86	2.04	97.53	97.32	77.6	
Somalia	627,340	484	1.6	1.67	0.03	0.04	98.34	98.29	11.37	1.00
South Africa	1,214,470	129	11.1	12.15	0.71	0.79	88.23	87.06	7.58	0.10
Spain	499,440	72	30.7	27.44	9.68	9.97	59.61	62.53	35.89	−0.60
Sri Lanka	64,630	1,779	13.5	14.17	15.86	15.47	70.60	70.35	29.91	1.80

Table K (continued)
Land Use and Deforestation, 1990–2005

COUNTRY	LAND AREA	RURAL POPULATION DENSITY	LAND USE						FOREST AREA	AVERAGE ANNUAL DEFORESTATION
		(people per sq km.)	Arable Land (% of land area)		Permanent Cropland (% of land area)		Other Land Use (% of land area)		(% of total land area)	(decline in % of forest area)
	(sq km.)		1990	2005	1990	2005	1990	2005	2005	1990–2005
	2005	2005								
St. Kitts and Nevis	360	451	22.2	19.44	5.56	2.78	72.22	77.78	13.89	
St. Lucia	610	2,901	8.2	6.56	21.31	22.95	70.49	70.49	27.87	
St. Vincent and the Grenadines	390	921	12.8	17.95	17.95	17.95	69.23	64.10	28.21	
Sudan	2,376,000	125	5.5	7.15	0.10	0.18	94.43	92.99	28.43	1.40
Suriname	156,000	205	0.4	0.37	0.07	0.06	99.56	99.57	94.72	
Swaziland	17,200	473	10.5	10.35	0.70	0.70	88.84	88.95	31.45	−1.20
Sweden	411,620	53	6.9	6.59	0.01	0.01	93.08	93.48	67.09	0.00
Switzerland	39,550	462	9.9	10.25	0.53	0.61	89.58	89.05	30.52	−0.40
Syrian Arab Republic	183,780	193	26.6	26.52	4.03	4.51	69.39	70.50	2.51	0.00
Tajikistan	140,600	512 ..		6.65 ..		0.90 ..		92.48	2.93	−0.50
Tanzania	883,590	707	4.0	4.53	1.02	1.24	95.02	94.23	39.9	0.20
Thailand	510,890	305	34.2	27.66	6.09	6.85	59.67	62.09	28.42	0.70
Timor-Leste	14,870	534	4.7	8.2	3.90	4.51	91.39	90.79	53.67	
Togo	54,390	143	38.6	46.15	1.65	2.21	59.74	51.65	7.1	3.40
Tonga	720	517	23.6	20.83	43.06	43.06	33.33	33.33	5.56	
Trinidad and Tobago	5,130	1,528	14.4	14.62	8.97	9.16	76.61	76.22	44.05	0.80
Tunisia	155,360	125	18.7	17.96	12.50	13.76	68.78	68.41	6.8	−0.20
Turkey	769,630	102	32.0	30.96	3.94	3.36	64.04	62.94	13.22	−0.20
Turkmenistan	1469,930	116 ..		4.68 ..		0.14 ..		95.92	8.78	0.00
Uganda	197,100	453	25.4	26.38	9.39	10.65	65.25	63.47	18.4	2.00
Ukraine	579,350	48 ..		56.01 ..		1.58 ..		42.25	16.53	−0.30
United Arab Emirates	83,600	1,453	0.4	0.77	0.24	2.28	99.34	96.82	3.73	−2.00
United Kingdom	240,880	110	27.5	23.68	0.27	0.21	72.24	75.91	11.76	−0.80
United States	9,158,960	33	20.3	19.04	0.22	0.22	79.50	80.56	33.08	−0.20
Uruguay	175,020	21	7.2	7.83	0.26	0.23	92.54	92.34	8.6	−5.00
Uzbekistan	414,240	343 ..		11.05 ..		0.83 ..		88.35	7.75	−0.20
Vanuatu	12,190	785	2.5	1.64	7.38	7.38	90.16	90.16	36.1	
Venezuela, RB	882,050	74	3.2	2.95	0.88	0.92	95.91	96.32	54.09	0.40
Vietnam	325,490	920	16.4	21.29	3.21	6.74	80.39	72.67	41.7	−0.50
Virgin Islands (U.S.)	340	350	11.8	5.71	2.94	2.94	85.29	85.29	28.57	
Yemen, Rep.	527,970	942	2.9	2.91	0.20	0.25	96.92	96.84	1.04	1.80
Zambia	743,390	140	7.1	7.08	0.03	0.04	92.91	92.89	57.11	2.40
Zimbabwe	386.850	259	7.5	8.32	0.31	0.34	92.22	91.34	45.34	1.50

Source: World Bank Economic Indicators (2007)

Table L
World Countries: Energy Production and Use: 1990–2004

COUNTRY	COMMERCIAL ENERGY PRODUCTION		COMMERCIAL ENERGY USE			COMMERCIAL ENERGY USE PER CAPITA			NET ENERGY IMPORTS	
	Thousand Metric Tons (Kilotons) of Oil Equivalent		Thousand Metric Tons (Kilotons) of Oil Equivalent		Average Annual % Growth	Kilogram of Oil Equivalent		Average Annual % Growth	% of Commercial Energy Use	
	1990	2004	1990	2004	1980–2000	1990	2004	1980–2000	1990	2004
Albania	2,449	980	2,662	2,365.00	–5.6	812.33	760.03	–6.3	8.00	59
Algeria	104,507	165,728.00	23,874	32,895.00	3.5	954.12	1,016.61	1	–337.74	–404
Angola	28,652	57,358.00	6,280	9,488.00	2.8	672.38	612.52	–0.3	–356.24	–505
Argentina	48,456	85,446.00	46,110	63,715.00	2.2	1,428.00	1,660.48	0.8	–5.09	–34
Armenia	..	746	..	2,129.00		..	703.55		..	65
Australia	157,712	261,771.00	87,536	115,776.00	2.4	5,129.53	5,762.29	1	–80.17	–126
Austria	8,080	9,881.00	25,260	33,188.00	1.6	3,269.61	4,059.84	1.1	68.01	70
Azerbaijan		20,053.00	..	12,948.00		..	1,558.80		..	–55
Bahrain	13,437	15,842.00	4,829	7,494.00		9,600.40	10,469.11		–178.26	–111
Bangladesh	10,747	18,390.00	12,815	22,789.00	4.1	116.47	163.7	1.9	16.14	19
Belarus	..	3,624.00	..	26,776.00	1.8		2,725.44		..	86
Belgium	12,490	13,534.00	48,685	57,694.00		4,884.42	5,536.26	1.6	74.35	77
Benin	1,774	1,623.00	1,678	2,475.00	2.3	356.26	302.67	–0.8	–5.72	34
Bolivia	4,923	11,818.00	2,774	4,978.00	3.8	415.95	552.56	1.5	–77.47	–137
Bosnia and Herzegovina	..	3,249.00	..	4,704.00		..	1,203.23		..	31
Brazil	97,616	176,312.00	133,531	204,847.00	2.7	902.50	1,113.83	1	26.90	14
Brunei	15,300	20,768.00	1,459	2,695.00		5,677.04	7,369.69		–948.66	–671
Bulgaria	9,613	10,270.00	28,820	18,941.00	–2.8	3,305.80	2,434.26	–2.2	66.64	46
Cameroon	12,090	12,476.00	5,031	6,949.00	2.5	431.44	433.29	–0.2	–140.31	–80
Canada	273,680	397,489.00	209,089	269,048.00	1.6	7,523.62	8,410.64	0.4	–30.89	–48
Chile	7,640	8,390.00	13,629	27,932.00	5.7	1,040.46	1,732.34	4	43.94	70
China	902,689	1,536,782.00	879,923	1,609,348.00	3.7	775.14	1,241.63	2.4	–2.59	5
Colombia	48,479	76,233.00	25,048	27,682.00	2.5	716.27	616.32	0.5	–93.54	–175
Congo, Dem. Rep.	12,019	17,002.00	11,903	16,559.00	2.7	318.52	296.48	–0.6	–0.97	–3
Congo, Rep.	9,005	12,586.00	1,056	1,063.00	–1.1	423.42	273.76	–4	–752.75	–1,084
Costa Rica	1,032	1,737.00	2,025	3,700.00	4.2	664.15	869.97	1.5	49.04	53
Cote d'Ivoire	3,382	7,220.00	4,408	6,927.00	3.3	373.56	387.59	–0.1	23.28	–4
Croatia	..	3,872.00	..	8,820.00		..	1,985.21		..	56
Cuba	6,271	5,850.00	16,524	10,686.00	–1.6	1,555.20	950.29	–2.4	62.05	45
Cyprus	6	190	1,536	2,615.00		2,255.51	3,534.74		99.61	93
Czech Republic	38,474	34,242.00	47,379	45,527.00	–1.2	4,571.94	4,460.40	–1.2	18.80	25
Denmark	9,735	31,014.00	17,581	20,073.00	0.6	3,420.43	3,716.41	0.4	44.63	–55
Dominican Republic	1,031	1,611.00	4,139	7,656.00	4.0	586.43	873.19	2.1	75.09	79
Ecuador	16,474	29,295.00	6,128	10,082.00	2.1	597.04	773.16	–0.3	–168.83	–191
Egypt, Arab Rep.	54,869	64,662.00	31,895	56,881.00	4.6	608.20	783.03	2.3	–72.03	–14
El Salvador	1,722	2,441.00	2,535	4,487.00	2.2	496.09	663.52	0.6	32.07	46
Estonia	..	3,551.00	..	5,174.00		..	3,835.44		..	31
Ethiopia	14,158	19,370.00	15,151	21,179.00	2.6	296.03	302.73	–0.1	6.55	9
Finland	12,081	15,891.00	29,171	38,091.00	1.7	5,850.58	7,285.76	1.3	58.59	58
France	111,439	137,416.00	227,276	275,169.00	1.9	4,005.92	4,546.66	1.5	50.97	50
Gabon	14,630	12,107.00	1,242	1,693.00	–0.2	1,303.25	1,242.72	–3.1	–1,077.94	–615

-214-

Table L (continued)
World Countries: Energy Production and Use: 1990–2004

COUNTRY	COMMERCIAL ENERGY PRODUCTION		COMMERCIAL ENERGY USE			COMMERCIAL ENERGY USE PER CAPITA			NET ENERGY IMPORTS	
	Thousand Metric Tons (Kilotons) of Oil Equivalent		Thousand Metric Tons (Kilotons) of Oil Equivalent		Average Annual % Growth	Kilogram of Oil Equivalent		Average Annual % Growth	% of Commercial Energy Use	
	1990	2004	1990	2004	1980–2000	1990	2004	1980–2000	1990	2004
Georgia	..	1,287.00	..	2,828.00		..	625.94		..	54
Germany	186,159	136,009.00	356,221	348,036.00	−0.2	4,484.55	4,217.79	−0.5	47.74	61
Ghana	4,392	6,230.00	5,337	8,354.00	3.6	349.35	385.61	0.5	17.71	25
Greece	9,200	10,292.00	22,181	30,472.00	3.0	2,182.95	2,754.72	2.5	58.52	66
Guatemala	3,390	5,331.00	4,478	7,569.00	3.5	511.83	615.63	0.9	24.30	30
Haiti	1,253	1,654.00	1,585	2,205.00	0.4	244.86	262.28	−1.6	20.95	25
Honduras	1,694	1,747.00	2,416	3,859.00	2.8	496.30	547.51	−0.2	29.88	55
Hong Kong, China	43	48	10,662	17,121.00		1,869.05	2,487.58		99.60	100
Hungary	14,325	10,235.00	28,553	26,355.00	−1.0	2,754.75	2,607.57	−0.7	49.83	61
Iceland	1,400	2,519.00	2,172	3,498.00		8,524.33	11,975.51		35.54	28
India	334,056	466,873.00	365,377	572,851.00	3.8	430.10	530.55	1.8	8.57	19
Indonesia	161,308	258,009.00	94,836	174,042.00	4.8	532.09	799.87	3.1	−70.09	−48
Iran, Islamic Rep.	179,738	277,992.00	68,775	145,835.00	5.6	1,264.25	2,166.45	3.1	−161.34	−91
Iraq	106,715	103,419.00	20,841	29,748.00	4.3	1,152.84	1,060.27	1.3	−412.04	−248
Ireland	3,467	1,902.00	10,575	15,206.00	2.7	3,016.43	3,737.54	2.3	67.22	87
Israel	433	1,714.00	12,112	20,743.00	5.2	2,599.14	3,048.87	2.6	96.43	92
Italy	25,548	30,138.00	152,553	184,460.00	1.3	2,689.63	3,170.76	1.2	83.25	84
Jamaica	485	489	2,943	4,071.00	3.5	1,231.38	1,540.88	2.6	83.52	88
Japan	76,129	96,758.00	445,916	533,201.00	2.6	3,609.57	4,173.36	2.2	82.93	82
Jordan	162	292	3,499	6,519.00	4.9	1,103.79	1,218.50	0.5	95.37	96
Kazakhstan	..	118,597.00	..	54,819.00		..	3,651.47		..	−116
Kenya	10,272	13,675.00	12,479	16,920.00	2.2	534.34	505.57	−0.7	17.69	19
Korea, Dem. Rep.	28,725	19,207.00	32,874	20,373.00	1.9	1,647.32	910.17	0.5	12.62	6
Korea, Rep.	21,908	38,031.00	92,650	213,045.00	9.1	2,161.24	4,430.85	8	76.35	82
Kuwait	50,401	132,768.00	7,579	25,116.00	1.0	3,566.59	10,211.69	0.2	−565.01	−429
Kyrgyz Republic	..	1,482.00	..	2,780.00		..	545.87		..	47
Latvia	..	2,140.00	..	4,598.00		..	1,988.07		..	53
Lebanon	143	230	2,309	5,397.00	4.8	635.21	1,524.45	2.8	93.81	96
Libya	73,173	85,378.00	11,541	18,193.00	3.6	2,680.21	3,169.43	1	−534.03	−369
Lithuania	..	5,212.00	..	9,159.00		..	2,665.92		..	43
Luxembourg	31	72	3,571	4,751.00		9,350.62	10,480.99		99.13	98
Malaysia	48,727	88,520.00	22,455	56,735.00	7.7	1,233.66	2,279.02	4.9	−117.00	−56
Malta		..	774	908		2,150.00	2,262.65			..
Mexico	194,482	253,859.00	124,057	165,475.00	2.1	1,490.60	1,621.51	0.2	−56.77	−53
Moldova	..	84	..	3,384.00		..	802.29		..	98
Morocco	773	659	6,725	11,452.00	4.3	279.71	383.99	2.2	88.51	94
Mozambique	6,846	8,236.00	7,203	8,571.00	−0.8	509.01	441.26	−2.6	4.96	4
Myanmar	10,651	18,985.00	10,683	14,144.00	1.3	263.74	282.86	−0.4	0.30	−34
Namibia	..	321	..	1,337.00		..	665.42		..	76
Nepal	5,501	8,066.00	5,806	9,055.00	2.7	320.03	340.53	0.4	5.25	11
Netherlands	60,316	67,900.00	66,491	82,147.00	1.4	4,446.96	5,045.35	0.8	9.29	17
Netherlands Antilles		..	1,493	1,718.00		7,878.63	9,498.54			..

Table L (continued)
World Countries: Energy Production and Use: 1990–2004

COUNTRY	COMMERCIAL ENERGY PRODUCTION		COMMERCIAL ENERGY USE			COMMERCIAL ENERGY USE PER CAPITA			NET ENERGY IMPORTS	
	Thousand Metric Tons (Kilotons) of Oil Equivalent		Thousand Metric Tons (Kilotons) of Oil Equivalent		Average Annual % Growth	Kilogram of Oil Equivalent		Average Annual % Growth	% of Commercial Energy Use	
	1990	2004	1990	2004	1980–2000	1990	2004	1980–2000	1990	2004
New Zealand	12,153	12,978.00	13,914	17,644.00	3.8	4,035.38	4,344.31	2.7	12.66	26
Nicaragua	1,495	1,930.00	2,118	3,296.00	2.7	553.87	643.39	0	29.41	41
Nigeria	150,453	229,440.00	70,905	98,989.00	2.6	737.04	769.09	−0.4	−112.19	−132
Norway	120,304	238,629.00	21,492	27,661.00	1.8	5,067.08	6,023.80	1.3	−459.76	−763
Oman	38,312	58,094.00	4,562	11,826.00	11.0	2,803.93	4,667.22	6.6	−739.81	−391
Pakistan	34,360	58,993.00	43,424	74,371.00	4.8	402.17	489.09	2.2	20.87	21
Panama	612	753	1,490	2,544.00	2.7	621.35	801.17	0.7	58.93	70
Paraguay	4,578	6,628.00	3,083	4,019.00	4.2	742.89	694.36	1.2	−48.49	−65
Peru	10,596	9,474.00	9,952	13,198.00	0.2	461.40	478.84	−1.8	−6.47	28
Philippines	13,701	23,391.00	26,159	44,268.00	3.9	428.56	542.39	1.5	47.62	47
Poland	99,228	78,815.00	99,847	91,742.00	−1.4	2,619.36	2,402.74	−1.8	0.62	14
Portugal	3,393	3,901.00	17,746	26,549.00	4.7	1,793.25	2,528.00	4.7	80.88	85
Qatar	26,113	75,954.00	6,454	18,061.00		13,307.22	23,246.45		−304.60	−321
Romania	40,834	28,110.00	62,403	38,565.00	−3.1	2,688.97	1,778.43	−3.2	34.56	27
Russian Federation	..	1,158,465.00	..	641,532.00		..	4,459.74		..	−81
Saudi Arabia	372,985	556,212.00	65,538	140,413.00	5.0	4,147.19	6,232.45	1	−469.11	−296
Senegal	1,362	1,106.00	2,238	2,751.00	2.4	305.45	241.61	−0.3	39.14	60
Serbia and Montenegro	..	..	..	..		..	..		..	..
Singapore	..	..	13,357	25,586.00	8.7	4,383.66	6,034.01	6	..	..
Slovak Republic	5,273	6,456.00	21,426	18,336.00	−1.4	4,055.65	3,406.63	−1.7	75.39	65
Slovenia	..	3,439.00	..	7,171.00		..	3,590.89		..	52
South Africa	114,534	155,998.00	91,229	131,137.00	2.1	2,591.73	2,828.64	−0.2	−25.55	−19
Spain	34,648	32,532.00	91,209	142,203.00	3.2	2,348.57	3,330.93	2.9	62.01	77
Sri Lanka	4,191	5,161.00	5,516	9,439.00	2.5	339.09	485	1.4	24.02	45
Sudan	8,775	29,330.00	10,627	17,638.00	3.1	426.32	496.52	0.7	17.43	−66
Sweden	29,754	35,088.00	46,658	53,937.00	1.0	5,451.34	5,998.34	0.6	36.23	35
Switzerland	9,831	11,822.00	25,106	27,133.00	1.4	3,740.47	3,671.79	0.7	60.84	56
Syrian Arab Republic	22,570	29,516.00	11,928	18,443.00	5.4	984.48	992.51	2.2	−89.22	−60
Tajikistan	..	1,517.00	..	3,335.00		..	518.64		..	55
Tanzania	9,063	17,530.00	9,808	18,749.00	2.0	385.08	498.29	−1	7.60	7
Thailand	26,496	50,103.00	43,860	97,071.00	7.4	788.92	1,524.03	6	39.59	48
Togo	778	1,910.00	1,001	2,688.00	3.8	289.73	448.87	0.8	22.28	29
Trinidad and Tobago	12,612	29,356.00	5,795	11,289.00	3.3	4,769.55	8,675.12	2.4	−117.64	−160
Tunisia	6,127	6,805.00	5,536	8,703.00	3.7	678.90	876.22	1.6	−10.68	22
Turkey	25,857	24,111.00	53,005	81,905.00	4.6	943.92	1,151.16	2.7	51.22	71
Turkmenistan	..	58,151.00	..	15,560.00		..	3,264.79		..	−274
Ukraine	..	76,287.00	..	140,333.00		..	2,958.05		..	46
United Arab Emirates	109,446	163,981.00	17,839	43,813.00	8.2	10,061.48	10,141.90	2.8	−513.52	−274
United Kingdom	207,007	225,211.00	212,176	233,689.00	1.0	3,686.11	3,905.60	0.8	2.44	4

Table L (continued)
World Countries: Energy Production and Use: 1990–2004

COUNTRY	COMMERCIAL ENERGY PRODUCTION		COMMERCIAL ENERGY USE			COMMERCIAL ENERGY USE PER CAPITA			NET ENERGY IMPORTS	
	Thousand Metric Tons (Kilotons) of Oil Equivalent		Thousand Metric Tons (Kilotons) of Oil Equivalent		Average Annual % Growth	Kilogram of Oil Equivalent		Average Annual % Growth	% of Commercial Energy Use	
	1990	2004	1990	2004	1980–2000	1990	2004	1980–2000	1990	2004
United States	1,650,474	1,641,044.00	1,927,638	2,325,887.00	1.5	7,722.20	7,920.46	0.4	14.38	29
Uruguay	1,149	850	2,251	2,863.00	1.7	724.73	832.39	1	48.96	70
Uzbekistan	..	56,867.00	..	53,994.00		..	2,087.58		..	–5
Venezuela, RB	148,854	196,064.00	43,918	56,158.00	2.9	2,223.70	2,149.42	0.1	–238.94	–249
Vietnam	24,711	65,271.00	24,324	50,218.00	3.2	367.43	611.21	1.2	–1.59	–30
Yemen, Rep.	9,384	20,609.00	2,708	6,370.00	4.2	228.02	313.34	0.3	–246.53	–224
Zambia	4,923	6,360.00	5,470	6,943.00	1.3	702.72	604.85	–1.6	10.00	8
Zimbabwe	8,500	8,600.00	9,334	9,301.00	2.6	911.43	718.98	–0.3	8.94	8
World	8,801,246	11,171,230.00	8,616,766	10,196,820	2.9	1,686.26	1,792.95	0.9	–2.31	–2

Source: World Bank Economic Indicators (2007), CIA Fact Book 2007

Part IX

Geographic Index

GEOGRAPHIC INDEX

NAME/DESCRIPTION	LATITUDE & LONGITUDE	PAGE	NAME/DESCRIPTION	LATITUDE & LONGITUDE	PAGE
Abidjan, Côte d'Ivoire (city, nat. cap.)	5N 4W	149	Albuquerque, NM	35N 107W	131
Abu Dhabi, U.A.E. (city, nat. cap.)	24N 54E	140	Aldabra Islands	9S 44E	148
Accra, Ghana (city, nat. cap.)	64N 0	149	Aleppo, Syria (city)	36N 37E	140
Aconcagua, Mt. 22,881	38S 78W	133	Aleutian Islands	55N 175W	130
Acre (st., Brazil)	9S 70W	134	Alexandria, Egypt (city)	31N 30E	149
Addis Ababa, Ethiopia (city, nat. cap.)	9N 39E	149	Algeria (country)	28N 15E	149
Adelaide, S. Australia (city, st. cap., Aust.)	35S 139E	152	Algiers, Algeria (city, nat. cap.)	37N 3E	149
Aden, Gulf of	12N 46E	139	Alice Springs, Aust. (city)	24S 134E	152
Aden, Yemen (city)	13N 45E	140	Alma Ata, Kazakhstan (city, nat. cap.)	43N 77E	140
Admiralty Islands	1S 146E	151	Alps Mountains	46N 6E	136
Adriatic Sea	44N 14E	136	Altai Mountains	49N 87E	139
Aegean Sea	39N 25E	136	Altun Shan	45N 90E	139
Afghanistan (country)	35N 65E	140	Amapa (st., Brazil)	2N 52W	134
Aguascalientes (st., Mex.)	22N 110W	133	Amazon (riv., S. Am)	2S 53W	133
Aguascalientes, Aguas (city, st. cap., Mex.)	22N 102W	133	Amazonas (st., Brazil)	2S 64W	134
Agulhas, Cape	35S 20E	148	Amman, Jordan (city, nat. cap.)	32N 36E	140
Ahaggar Range	23N 6E	148	Amsterdam, Netherlands (city)	52N 5E	137
Ahmadabad, India (city)	23N 73E	140	Amu Darya (riv., Asia)	40N 62E	139
Astana, Kazakhstan (city)	51N 72E	140	Amur (riv., Asia)	52N 156E	139
Al Fashir, Sudan (city)	14N 25E	149	Anchorage, AK (city)	61N 150W	131 inset
Al Fayyum, Egypt (city)	29N 31E	149	Andaman Islands	12N 92E	140
Al Hijaz Range	30N 40E	139	Andes Mountains	25S 70W	133
Al Khufra Oasis	24N 23E	148	Angara (riv., Asia)	60N 100E	139
Alabama (st., US)	33N 87W	131	Angola (country)	11S 18E	149
Alagoas (st., Brazil)	9S 37W	134	Ankara, Turkey (city, nat. cap.)	40N 33E	140
Alaska (st., US)	63N 153W	131 inset	Annapolis, Maryland (city, st. cap., US)	39N 76W	131
Alaska, Gulf of	58N 150W	131 inset	Antananarivo, Madagascar (city, nat. cap.)	19S 48E	149
Alaska Peninsula	57N 155W	130 inset A	Antofagasta, Chile (city)	24S 70W	134
Alaska Range	60N 150W	130 inset	Antwerp, Belgium (city)	51N 4E	137
Albania (country)	41N 20E	137	Appalachian Mountains	37N 80W	130
Albany, Australia (city)	35S 118E	152	Appenines Mountains	32N 14E	136
Albany, New York (city, st. cap., US)	43N 74W	131	Arabian Desert	25N 33E	136
Albert Edward, Mt. 13,090	8S 147E	151	Arabian Peninsula	23N 40E	151
Albert, Lake	2N 30E	148	Arabian Sea	18N 61E	139
Alberta (prov., Can.)	55N 117W	131	Aracaju, Sergipe (city, st. cap., Braz.)	11S 37W	134
Arafura Sea	9S 133E	151	Baku, Azerbaijan (city, nat. cap.)	40N 50E	137
Araguaia, Rio (riv., Brazil)	13S 50W	133	Balearic Islands	29N 3E	137

The geographic index contains approximately 1,500 names of cities, states, countries, rivers, lakes, mountain ranges, oceans, capes, bays, and other geographic features. The name of each geographical feature in the index is accompanied by a geographical coordinate (latitude and longitude) in degrees and by the page number of the primary map on which the geographical feature appears. Where the geographical coordinates are for specific places or points, such as a city or a mountain peak, the latitude and longitude figures give the location of the map symbol denoting that point. Thus, Los Angeles, California, is at 34N and 118W and the location of Mt. Everest is 28N and 87E.

The coordinates for political features (countries or states) or physical features (oceans, deserts) that are areas rather than points are given according to the location of the name of the feature on the map, except in those cases where the name of the feature is separated from the feature (such as a country's name appearing over an adjacent ocean area because of space requirements). In such cases, the feature's coordinates will indicate the location of the center of the feature. The coordinates for the Sahara Desert will lead the reader to the place name "Sahara Desert" on the map; the coordinates for North Carolina will show the center location of the state since the name appears over the adjacent Atlantic Ocean. Finally, the coordinates for geographical features that are lines rather than points or areas will also appear near the center of the text identifying the geographical feature.

Alphabetizing follows general conventions; the names of physical features such as lakes, rivers, mountains are given as: proper name, followed by the generic name. Thus "Mount Everest" is listed as "Everest, Mt." Where an article such as "the," "le," or "al" appears in a geographic name, the name is alphabetized according to the article. Hence, "La Paz" is found under "L" and not under "P."

GEOGRAPHIC INDEX

GEOGRAPHIC INDEX

NAME/DESCRIPTION	LATITUDE & LONGITUDE	PAGE	NAME/DESCRIPTION	LATITUDE & LONGITUDE	PAGE
Birmingham, AL (city)	34N 87W	131	Burdekin (riv., Australasia)	19S 146W	151
Birmingham, UK (city)	52N 2W	137	Burkina Faso (country)	11N 2W	149
Biscay, Bay of	45N 5W	136	Buru (island)	4S 127E	151
Bishkek, Kyrgyzstan (city, nat. cap.)	43N 75E	140	Burundi (country)	4S 30E	149
Bismarck Archipelago	4S 147E	151	Cairns, Aust. (city)	17S 145E	152
Bismarck, North Dakota (city, st. cap., US)	47N 101W	131	Cairo, Egypt (city, nat. cap.)	30N 31E	149
Bismarck Range	6S 145E	151	Calcutta, (Kolkota) India (city)	23N 88E	140
Bissau, Guinea-Bissau (city, nat. cap.)	12N 16W	149	Calgary, Canada (city)	51N 114W	131
Black Sea	46N 34E	136	Calicut, India (city)	11N 76E	140
Blanc, Cape	21N 18W	148	California (st., US)	35N 120W	131
Blue Nile (riv., Africa)	10N 36E	148	California, Gulf of	29N 110W	131
Blue Mountains	33S 150E	151	Callao, Peru (city)	13S 77W	134
Boa Vista do Rio Branco, Roraima (city, st. cap., Braz.)	3N 61W	134	Cambodia (country)	10N 106E	140
Boise, Idaho (city, st. cap., US)	44N 116W	131	Cameroon (country)	5N 13E	149
Bolivia (country)	17S 65W	134	Campeche (st., Mex.)	19N 90W	131
Boma, Congo Republic (city)	5S 13E	149	Campeche Bay	20N 92W	130
Bombay, (Mumbai) India (city)	19N 73E	140	Campeche, Campeche (city, st. cap., Mex.)	19N 90W	131
Bonn, Germany (city, nat. cap.)	51N 7E	137	Campo Grande, M.G.S. (city, st. cap., Braz.)	20S 55W	134
Boothia Peninsula	71N 94W	130	Canada (country)	52N 100W	131
Borneo (island)	0 11E	140	Canadian (riv., N.Am.)	30N 100W	130
Bosnia-Herzegovina (country)	45N 18E	137	Canary Islands	29N 18W	148
Bosporus, Strait of	41N 29E	136	Canberra, Australia (city, nat. cap.)	35S 149E	152
Boston, Massachusetts (city, st. cap., US)	42N 71W	131	Cape Breton Island	46N 60W	130
Botany Bay	35S 153E	152	Cape Town, South Africa (city)	34S 18E	149
Bothnia, Gulf of	62N 20E	136	Caracas, Venezuela (city, nat. cap.)	10N 67W	134
Botswana (country)	23S 25E	149	Caribbean Sea	18N 75W	134
Brahmaputra (riv., Asia)	30N 100E	139	Carnarvon, Australia (city)	25S 113E	152
Branco, Rio (riv., S.Am.)	3N 62W	131	Carpathian Mountains	48N 24E	136
Brasilia, Brazil (city, nat. cap.)	16S 48W	134	Carpentaria, Gulf of	14S 140E	151
Bratislava, Slovakia (city, nat. cap.)	48N 17E	137	Carson City, Nevada (city, st. cap., US)	39N 120W	131
Brazil (country)	10S 52W	134	Cartagena, Colombia (city)	10N 76W	134
Brazilian Highlands	18S 45W	133	Cascade Range	45N 120W	130
Brazzaville, Congo (city, nat. cap.)	4S 15E	149	Casiquiare, Rio (riv., S.Am.)	4N 67W	133
Brisbane, Queensland (city, st. cap., Aust.)	27S 153E	152	Caspian Depression	49N 48E	136
Bristol Bay	58N 159W	130 inset	Caspian Sea	42N 48E	136
British Columbia (prov., Can.)	54N 130W	131	Catamarca (st., Argentina)	25S 70W	134
Brooks Range	67N 155W	130	Catamarca, Catamarca (city, st. cap., Argen.)	28S 66W	134
Bruce, Mt. 4,052	22S 117W	151	Cauca, Rio (riv., S.Am.)	8N 75W	133
Brussels, Belgium (city, nat. cap.)	51N 4E	137	Caucasus Mountains	42N 40E	136
Bucharest, Romania (city, nat. cap.)	44N 26E	137	Cayenne, French Guiana (city, nat. cap.)	5N 52W	134
Budapest, Hungary (city, nat. cap.)	47N 19E	137	Ceara (st., Brazil)	4S 40W	134
Buenos Aires, Argentina (city, nat. cap.)	34S 58W	134	Celebes (island)	0 120E	139
Buenos Aires (st., Argentina)	36S 60W	134	Celebes Sea	2N 120E	139
Buffalo, NY (city)	43N 79W	131	Central African Republic (country)	5N 20E	149
Bujumbura, Burundi (city, nat. cap.)	3S 29E	149	Ceram (island)	3S 129E	152
Chaco (st., Argentina)	25S 60W	134	Columbia, South Carolina (city, st. cap., US)	34N 81W	131
Chad (country)	15N 20E	149	Columbus, Ohio (city, st. cap., US)	40N 83W	131
Chad, Lake	12N 12E	149	Comodoro Rivadavia, Argentina (city)	68S 70W	134

GEOGRAPHIC INDEX

GEOGRAPHIC INDEX

GEOGRAPHIC INDEX

GEOGRAPHIC INDEX

NAME/DESCRIPTION	LATITUDE & LONGITUDE	PAGE	NAME/DESCRIPTION	LATITUDE & LONGITUDE	PAGE
Hartford, Connecticut (city, st. cap., US)	42N 73W	131	Iowa (st., US)	43N 95W	131
Hatteras, Cape	32N 73W	130	Iquitos, Peru (city)	4S 74W	134
Havana, Cuba (city, nat. cap.)	23N 82W	131	Iran (country)	30N 55E	140
Hawaii (st., US)	21N 156W	130 inset	Iraq (country)	30N 50E	140
Hebrides (island)	58N 8W	136	Ireland (country)	54N 8W	137
Helena, Montana (city, st. cap., US)	47N 112W	131	Irish Sea	54N 5W	137
Helsinki, Finland (city, nat. cap.)	60N 25E	137	Irkutsk, Russia (city)	52N 104E	140
Herat, Afghanistan (city)	34N 62E	140	Irrawaddy (riv., Asia)	25N 95E	139
Hermosillo, Sonora (city, st. cap., Mex.)	29N 111W	131	Irtysh (riv., Asia)	50N 70E	139
Hidalgo (st., Mex.)	20N 98W	131	Ishim (riv., Asia)	48N 70E	139
Himalayas	26N 80E	139	Isla de los Estados (island)	55S 60W	133
Hindu Kush	30N 70E	139	Islamabad, Pakistan (city, nat. cap.)	34N 73E	140
Ho Chi Minh City, Vietnam (city)	11N 107E	140	Isles of Scilly	50N 8W	136
Hobart, Tasmania (city, st. cap., Aust.)	43S 147E	152	Israel (country)	31N 36E	137
Hokkaido (island)	43N 142E	139	Istanbul, Turkey (city)	41N 29E	137
Honduras (country)	16N 87W	131	Italy (country)	42N 12E	137
Honduras, Gulf of	15N 88W	130	Jabal Marrah 10,131	10N 23E	148
Honiara, Solomon Islands (city, nat. cap.)	9S 160E	152	Jackson, Mississippi (city, st. cap., US)	32N 84W	131
Honolulu, Hawaii (city, st. cap., US)	21N 158W	131 inset	Jacksonville, FL (city)	30 N 82W	131
Honshu (island)	38N 140E	139	Jakarta, Indonesia (city, nat. cap.)	6S 107E	140 inset
Hormuz, Strait of	25N 58E	139	Jalisco (st., Mex.)	20N 105W	131
Horn, Cape	55S 70W	133	Jamaica (country)	18N 78W	131
Houston, TX (city)	30N 95W	131	James Bay	54N 81W	130
Howe, Cape	37S 150E	151	Japan (country)	35N 138E	140
Huambo, Angola (city)	13S 16E	149	Japan, Sea of	40N 135E	139
Huang (riv., Asia)	30N 105E	139	Japura, Rio (riv., S.Am.)	3S 65W	133
Huascaran, Mt. 22,133	8N 79W	133	Java (island)	6N 110E	139 inset
Hudson (riv., N.Am.)	42N 76W	131	Jaya Peak 16,503	4S 136W	151
Hudson Bay	60N 90W	130	Jayapura, New Guinea (Indon.) (city)	3S 141E	140 inset
Hudson Strait	63N 70W	130	Jebel Toubkal 13,665	31N 8W	148
Hue, Vietnam (city)	15N 110E	140	Jefferson City, Missouri (city, st. cap., US)	39N 92W	131
Hughes, Aust. (city)	30S 130E	152	Jerusalem, Israel (city, nat. cap.)	32N 35E	137
Hungary (country)	48N 20E	137	Joao Pessoa, Paraiba (city, st. cap., Braz.)	7S 35W	134
Huron (lake, N.Am.)	45N 85W	130	Johannesburg, South Africa (city)	26S 27E	149
Hyderabad, India (city)	17N 79E	140	Jordan (country)	32N 36E	137
Ibadan, Nigeria (city)	7N 4E	149	Juan Fernandez (island)	33S 80W	133
Iceland (country)	64N 20W	137	Jubba (riv., Africa)	3N 43E	148
Idaho (st., US)	43N 113W	131	Jujuy (st., Argentina)	23S 67W	134
Iguassu Falls	25S 55W	133	Jujuy, Jujuy (city, st. cap., Argen.)	23S 66W	134
Illimani, Mt. 20,741	16S 67W	133	Juneau, Alaska (city, st. cap., US)	58N 134W	131
Illinois (riv., N.Am.)	40N 90W	130	Jura Mountains	46N 5E	136
Jurua, Rio (riv., S.Am.)	6S 70W	133	Korea Strait	32N 130W	139
Kabul, Afghanistan (city, nat. cap.)	35N 69E	140	Kosciusko, Mt. 7,310	36S 148E	151
Kalahari Desert	25S 20E	148	Krasnoyarsk, Russia (city)	56N 93E	140
Kalgourie-Boulder, Australia (city)	31S 121E	152	Krishna (riv., Asia)	15N 76E	139
Kaliningrad, Russia (city)	55N 21E	137	Kuala Lumpur, Malaysia (city, nat. cap.)	3N 107E	140
Kamchatka Range	55N 159E	139	Kunlun Shan	36N 90E	139
Kampala, Uganda (city, nat. cap.)	0 33E	149	Kunming, China (city)	25N 106E	140
Kanchenjunga, Mt. 28,208	30N 83E	139	Kuril Islands	46N 147E	139

GEOGRAPHIC INDEX

NAME/DESCRIPTION	LATITUDE & LONGITUDE	PAGE	NAME/DESCRIPTION	LATITUDE & LONGITUDE	PAGE
Kano, Nigeria (city)	12N 9E	149	Kutch, Gulf of	23N 70E	139
Kanpur, India (city)	27N 80E	140	Kuwait (country)	29N 48E	137
Kansas (st., US)	40N 98W	131	Kuwait, Kuwait (city, nat. cap.)	29N 48E	137
Kansas City, MO (city)	39N 95W	131	Kyoto, Japan (city)	35N 136E	140
Kara Sea	69N 65E	139	Kyrgyzstan (country)	40N 75E	140
Karachi, Pakistan (city)	25N 66E	140	Kyushu (island)	30N 130W	139
Karakorum Range	32N 78E	139	La Pampa (st., Argentina)	36S 70W	134
Karakum Desert	42N 52E	136	La Paz, Baja California Sur (city, st. cap., Mex.)	24N 110W	131
Kasai (riv., Africa)	5S 18E	148	La Paz, Bolivia (city, nat. cap.)	17S 68W	134
Kashi, China (city)	39N 76E	140	La Plata, Argentina (city)	35S 58W	134
Katherine, Aust. (city)	14S 132E	152	Laptev Sea	73N 120E	139
Kathmandu, Nepal (city, nat. cap.)	28N 85E	140	La Rioja (st., Argentina)	30S 70W	134
Katowice, Poland (city)	50N 19E	137	La Rioja, La Rioja (city, st. cap., Argen.)	29S 67W	134
Kattegat, Strait of	57N 11E	136	Labrador Peninsula	52N 60W	134
Kazakhstan (country)	50N 70E	140	Lachlan (riv., Australasia)	34S 145E	151
Kentucky (st., US)	37N 88W	131	Ladoga, Lake	61N 31E	136
Kenya (country)	0 35E	149	Lagos, Nigeria (city, nat. cap.)	7N 3E	149
Kenya, Mt. 17,058	0 37E	148	Lahore, Pakistan (city)	34N 74E	140
Khabarovsk, Russia (city)	48N 135E	140	Lake of the Woods	50N 92W	130
Khambhat, Gulf of	20N 73E	139	Lands End	50N 5W	136
Kharkiv, Ukraine (city)	50N 36E	137	Lansing, Michigan (city, st. cap., US)	43N 85W	131
Khartoum, Sudan (city, nat. cap.)	16N 33E	149	Lanzhou, China (city)	36N 104E	140
Kiev, Ukraine (city, nat. cap.)	50N 31E	137	Laos (country)	20N 105E	140
Kigali, Rwanda (city, nat. cap.)	2S 30E	149	Las Vegas, NV (city)	36N 115W	131
Kilimanjaro, Mt. 19,340	4N 35E	148	Latvia (country)	56N 24E	137
Kimberly, South Africa (city)	29S 25E	149	Laurentian Highlands	48N 72W	130
King Leopold Ranges	16S 125E	151	Lebanon (country)	34N 35E	137
Kingston, Jamaica (city, nat. cap.)	18N 77W	131	Leeds, UK (city)	54N 2W	137
Kinshasa, Congo Republic (city, nat. cap.)	4S 15E	149	Le Havre, France (city)	50N 0	137
Kirghiz Steppe	40N 65E	139	Lena (riv., Asia)	70N 125E	139
Kisangani, Congo Republic (city)	1N 25E	149	Lesotho (country)	30S 27E	149
Kitayushu, Japan (city)	34N 130E	140	Leveque, Cape	16S 123E	151
Klyuchevskaya, Mt. 15,584	56N 160E	139	Leyte (island)	12N 130E	139
Kobe, Japan (city)	34N 135E	140	Lhasa, Tibet (China) (city)	30N 91E	140
Kodiak Island	58N 152W	130 inset	Liberia (country)	6N 10W	149
Kolyma (riv., Asia)	70N 160E	139	Libreville, Gabon (city, nat. cap.)	0 9E	149
Kommunizma, Mt. 24,590	40N 70E	139	Libya (country)	27N 17E	149
Komsomolsk, Russia (city)	51N 137E	140	Libyan Desert	27N 25E	148
Korea, North (country)	40N 128E	140	Lille, France (city)	51N 3E	137
Korea, South (country)	3S 130W	140	Lilongwe, Malawi (city, nat. cap.)	14S 33E	149
Lima, Peru (city, nat. cap.)	12S 77W	134	Malta (island)	36N 16E	136
Limpopo (riv., Africa)	22S 30E	148	Mamore, Rio (riv., S.Am.)	15S 65W	133
Lincoln, Nebraska (city, st. cap., US)	41N 97W	131	Managua, Nicaragua (city, nat. cap.)	12N 86W	131
Lisbon, Portugal (city, nat. cap.)	39N 9W	137	Manaus, Amazonas (city, st. cap., Braz.)	3S 60W	134
Lithuania (country)	56N 24E	137	Manchester, UK (city)	53N 2W	137
Little Rock, Arkansas (city, st. cap., US)	35N 92W	131	Mandalay, Myanmar (city)	22N 96E	140
Liverpool, UK (city)	53N 3W	137	Manila, Philippines (city, nat. cap.)	115N 121E	140
Ljubljana, Slovenia (city, nat. cap.)	46N 14E	137	Manitoba (prov., Can.)	52N 93W	131
Llanos	33N 103W	133	Mannar, Gulf of	9N 79E	139

GEOGRAPHIC INDEX

GEOGRAPHIC INDEX

GEOGRAPHIC INDEX

NAME/DESCRIPTION	LATITUDE & LONGITUDE	PAGE	NAME/DESCRIPTION	LATITUDE & LONGITUDE	PAGE
Northern Territory (st., Aust.)	20S 134W	151	Pachuca, Hidalgo (city, st. cap., Mex.)	20N 99W	131
Northwest Territories (prov., Can.)	65N 125W	131	Pacific Ocean	20N 115W	130
Norway (country)	62N 8E	137	Pakistan (country)	25N 72E	140
Nouakchott, Mauritania (city, nat. cap.)	18N 16W	149	Palawan (island)	10N 119E	139
Noumea, New Caledonia (city)	22S 167E	152	Palmas, Cape	8N 8W	148
Nova Scotia (prov., Can.)	46N 67W	131	Palmas, Tocantins (city, st. cap., Braz.)	10S 49W	134
Novaya Zemlya (island)	72N 55E	139	Pamirs	32N 70E	139
Novosibirsk, Russia (city)	55N 83E	140	Pampas	36S 73W	133
Nubian Desert	20N 30E	148	Panama (country)	10N 80W	133
Nuevo Leon (st., Mex.)	25N 100W	131	Panama, Gulf of	10N 80W	131
Nullarbor Plain	34S 125W	151	Panama, Panama (city, nat. cap.)	9N 80W	131
Nyasa, Lake	10S 35E	148	Papua, Gulf of	8S 144E	151
Oakland, CA (city)	38N 122W	131	Papua New Guinea (country)	6S 144E	151
Oaxaca (st., Mex.)	17N 97W	131	Para (st., Brazil)	4S 54W	134
Oaxaca, Oaxaca (city, st. cap., Mex.)	17N 97W	131	Paraguay (country)	23S 60W	134
Ob (riv., Asia)	60N 78E	139	Paraguay, Rio (riv., S.Am.)	17S 60W	133
Ohio (riv., N.Am.)	38N 85W	130	Paraiba (st., Brazil)	6S 35W	134
Ohio (st., US)	42N 85W	131	Paramaribo, Suriname (city, nat. cap.)	5N 55W	134
Okavongo (riv., Africa)	18S 18E	148	Parana (st., Brazil)	25S 55W	134
Okavango Swamp	21S 23E	148	Parana, Entre Rios (city, st. cap., Argen.)	32S 60W	134
Okeechobee (lake, N.Am.)	28N 82W	130	Parana, Rio (riv., S.Am.)	20S 50W	133
Okhotsk, Russia (city)	59N 140E	140	Paris, France (city, nat. cap.)	49N 2E	137
Okhotsk, Sea of	57N 150E	139	Pasadas, Misiones (city, st. cap., Argen.)	27S 56W	134
Oklahoma (st., US)	36N 95W	131	Patagonia	43S 70W	133
Oklahoma City, Oklahoma (city, st. cap., US)	35N 98W	131	Paulo Afonso Falls	10S 40W	133
Oland (island)	57N 17E	136	Peace (riv., N.Am.)	55N 120W	130
Olympia, Washington (city, st. cap., US)	47N 123W	133	Pennsylvania (st., US)	43N 80W	131
Omaha, NE (city)	41N 96W	131	Pernambuco (st., Brazil)	7S 36W	134
Oman (country)	20N 55E	140	Persian Gulf	28N 50E	139
Oman, Gulf of	23N 55E	139	Perth, W. Australia (city, st. cap., Aust.)	32S 116E	152
Omdurman, Sudan (city)	16N 32E	149	Peru (country)	10S 75W	134
Omsk, Russia (city)	55N 73E	140	Peshawar, Pakistan (city)	34N 72E	140
Onega, Lake	62N 35E	136	Philadelphia, PA (city)	40N 75W	131
Ontario (lake, N.Am.)	45N 77W	130	Philippine Sea	15N 125E	139
Ontario (prov., Can.)	50N 90W	130	Philippines (country)	15N 120E	140
Oodnadatta, Aust. (city)	28S 135E	152	Phnom Penh, Cambodia (city, nat. cap.)	12N 105E	140
Oran, Algeria (city)	36N 1W	149	Phoenix, Arizona (city, st. cap., US)	33N 112W	131
Phou Bia 9,249	24N 102E	139	Queen Elizabeth Islands	75N 110W	130
Piaui (st., Brazil)	7S 44W	134	Queensland (st., Aust.)	24S 145E	152
Piaui Range	10S 45W	133	Querataro (st., Mex.)	22N 96W	131
Pic Touside 10,712	20N 12E	148	Querataro, Querataro (city, st. cap., Mex.)	21N 100W	131
Pierre, South Dakota (city, st. cap., US)	44N 100W	131	Quintana Roo (st., Mex.)	18N 88W	131
Pietermaritzburg, South Africa (city)	30S 30E	149	Quito, Ecuador (city, nat. cap.)	0 79W	134
Pike's Peak 14,110	36N 110W	130	Rabat, Morocco (city, nat. cap.)	34N 7W	149
Pilcomayo, Rio (riv., S.Am.)	23S 60W	133	Race, Cape	46N 52W	130
Pittsburgh, PA (city)	40N 80W	131	Rainier, Mt. 14,410	48N 120W	130
Plateau of Iran	26N 60E	139	Raleigh, North Carolina (city, st. cap., US)	36N 79W	131
Plateau of Tibet	26N 85E	139	Rangoon, Myanmar (Burma) (city, nat. cap.)	17N 96E	140
Platte (riv., N.Am.)	41N 105W	130	Rapid City, SD (city)	44N 103W	131

GEOGRAPHIC INDEX

GEOGRAPHIC INDEX

GEOGRAPHIC INDEX

NAME/DESCRIPTION	LATITUDE & LONGITUDE	PAGE	NAME/DESCRIPTION	LATITUDE & LONGITUDE	PAGE
Sonora (st., Mex.)	30N 110W	131	Sweden (country)	62N 16E	137
South Africa (country)	30S 25E	149	Sydney, N.S.Wales (city, st. cap., Aust.)	34S 151E	152
South Australia (st., Aust.)	30S 125E	152	Syr Darya (riv., Asia)	36N 65E	139
South Cape, New Guinea	8S 150E	151	Syria (country)	37N 36E	137
South Carolina (st., US)	33N 79W	131	Tabasco (st., Mex.)	16N 90W	131
South China Sea	15N 115E	151	Tabriz, Iran (city)	38N 46E	140
South Dakota (st., US)	45N 100W	131	Tahat, Mt. 9,541	23N 8E	148
South Georgia (island)	55S 40W	133	Taipei, Taiwan (city, nat. cap.)	25N 121E	140
South Island (NZ)	45S 170E	151	Taiwan (country)	25N 122E	140
Southampton Island	68N 86W	130	Taiwan Strait	25N 120E	139
Southern Alps (NZ)	45S 170E	151	Tajikistan (country)	35N 75E	140
Southwest Cape (NZ)	47S 167E	151	Takla Makan	37N 90E	139
Spain (country)	38N 4W	137	Tallahassee, Florida (city, st. cap., US)	30N 84W	131
Spokane, WA (city)	48N 117W	131	Tallinn, Estonia (city, nat. cap.)	59N 25E	137
Springfield, Illinois (city, st. cap., US)	40N 90W	131	Tamaulipas (st., Mex.)	25N 95W	131
Sri Lanka (country)	8N 80E	140	Tampico, Mexico (city)	22N 98W	131
Srinagar, India (city)	34N 75E	140	Tanganyika, Lake	5S 30E	148
St. Elias, Mt. 18,008	61N 139W	130	Tanzania (country)	8S 35E	149
St. George's Channel	53N 5W	136	Tapajos, Rio (riv., S.Am.)	5S 55W	133
St. Helena (island)	16S 5W	149	Tarim Basin	37N 85E	139
St. John's, Nwfndlnd (city, prov. cap., Can.)	48N 53W	131	Tashkent, Uzbekistan (city, nat. cap.)	41N 69E	140
St. Louis, MO (city)	39N 90W	131	Tasman Sea	38S 160E	151
St. Lawrence (island)	65N 170W	130 inset	Tasmania (st., Aust.)	42S 145E	152
St. Lawrence (riv., N.Am.)	50N 65W	130	Tatar Strait	50N 142E	139
St. Lawrence, Gulf of	50N 65W	130	Tbilisi, Georgia (city, nat. cap.)	42N 45E	137
St. Marie, Cape	25S 45E	149	Teguicigalpa, Honduras (city, nat. cap.)	14N 87W	131
St. Paul, Minnesota (city, st. cap., US)	45N 93W	131	Tehran, Iran (city, nat. cap.)	36N 51E	140
St. Petersburg, Russia (city)	60N 30E	137	Tel Aviv, Israel (city)	32N 35E	137
St. Vincente, Cape of	37N 10W	136	Tennant Creek, Aust. (city)	19S 134E	152
Stanovoy Range	55N 125E	139	Tennessee (st., US)	37N 88W	131
Stavanger, Norway (city)	59N 6E	137	Tennessee (riv., N.Am.)	32N 88W	130
Tepic, Nayarit (city, st. cap., Mex.)	22N 105W	131	Tunisia (country)	34N 9E	149
Teresina, Piaui (city, st. cap., Braz.)	5S 43W	134	Turin, Italy (city)	45N 8E	137
Texas (st., US)	30N 95W	131	Turkey (country)	39N 32E	137
Thailand (country)	15N 105E	140	Turkmenistan (country)	39N 56E	137
Thailand, Gulf of	10N 105E	139	Turku, Finland (city)	60N 22E	137
Thames (riv., Europe)	52N 4W	136	Tuxtla Gutierrez, Chiapas (city, st. cap., Mex.)	17N 93W	131
The Hague, Netherlands (city, nat. cap.)	52N 4E	137	Tyrrhenian Sea	40N 12E	136
The Round Mountain 5,300	29S 152E	151	Ubangi (riv., Africa)	0 20E	148
Thimphu, Bhutan (city, nat. cap.)	28N 90E	140	Ucayali, Rio (riv., S.Am.)	7S 75W	133
Tianjin, China (city)	39N 117E	140	Uele (riv., Africa)	3N 25E	148
Tibest Massif	20N 20E	148	Uganda (country)	3N 30E	149
Tien Shan	40N 80E	139	Ujungpandang, Celebes (Indon.) (city)	5S 119E	140 inset
Tierra del Fuego	54S 68W	133	Ukraine (country)	53N 32E	137
Tierra del Fuego (st., Argentina)	54S 68W	134	Ulaanbaatar, Mongolia (city, nat. cap.)	47N 107E	140
Tigris (riv., Asia)	37N 40E	136	Uliastay, Mongolia (city)	48N 97E	140
Timor (island)	7S 126E	139	Ungava Peninsula	60N 72W	130
Timor Sea	11S 125E	152	United Arab Emirates (country)	25N 55E	140
Tirane, Albania (city, nat. cap.)	41N 20E	137	United Kingdom (country)	54N 4W	137

GEOGRAPHIC INDEX

GEOGRAPHIC INDEX

Sources

Amnesty International. Online access at www.amnesty.org.

Asia-Pacific Economic Organization (APEC). Online access at www.apecsec.org.

Bercovitch, J., and R. Jackson. (1997). *International conflict: A chronological encyclopedia of conflicts and their management 1945–1995*. Washington, DC: Congressional Quarterly.

BP Statistical Review of World Energy. Online access at: http://www.bp.com/bpstats.

Canadian Forces College, Information Resources Centre. Online access at: http://www.cfcsc.dnd.ca/links/wars/index.html.

CIA. *World Factbook, 2002*. Online access at: www.cia.gov/cia/publications/factbook.

Cohen, Saul. (2002). *Geopolitics of the world system*. Lanham, MD: Rowman & Littlefield.

Commonwealth of Independent States (CIS). Online access at: www.cis.minsk.by/english.

Crabb, C. (1993, January). Soiling the planet. *Discover, 14* (1), 74–75.

DeBlij, H. J., & Muller, P. (1998). *Geography: Realms, regions and concepts* (8th ed.). New York: John Wiley.

Domke, K. (1988). *War and the changing global system*. New Haven, CT: Yale University Press.

Economic Community of West African States (ECOWAS). Online access at: www.state.gov.

European Free Trade Association (EFTA). Online access at www.efta.int.

The European Union (EU). Online access at: www.europa.eu.int.

Food and Agricultural Organization of the United Nations (FAO). Online access at www.fao.org.

Freedom House. Online access at www.freedomhouse.org.

Goode's world atlas. (1995, 19th ed.). New York: Rand McNally.

The Greater Caribbean Community (CARICOM). Online access at: www.caricom.org.

Gunnemark, Erik V., *Countries, peoples and their languages*. Gothenburg, Sweden: The Geolinguistic Handbook (n.d., early 1990s).

Hammond atlas of the world. (1993). Maplewood, NJ: Hammond.

Information please almanac, atlas, and yearbook 2002. (2002). Boston & New York: Houghton Mifflin.

International Energy Agency. (2001). *Key world energy statistics 2000*. Paris. Online access: http://www.iea.org/statist/keyworld/keystats.htm.

Johnson, D. (1977). *Population, society, and desertification*. New York: United Nations Conference on Desertification, United Nations Environment Programme.

Köppen, W., & Geiger, R. (1954). *Klima der erde* [Climate of the earth]. Darmstadt, Germany: Justus Perthes.

Lindeman, M. (1990). *The United States and the Soviet Union: Choices for the 21st century*. Guilford, CT: Dushkin Publishing Group.

Murphy, R. E. (1968). Landforms of the world [Map supplement No. 9]. *Annals of the Association of American Geographers, 58* (1), 198–200.

National Oceanic and Atmospheric Administration. (1990–1992). Unpublished data. Washington, DC: NOAA.

North Atlantic Treaty Organization (NATO). Online access at: www.nato.int.

The *New York Times*. Online access at: http://archives.nytimes.com/archives/.

The Peace Corps. Online access at www.peacecorps.gov.

Population Reference Bureau (2001). *World population data sheet*. New York: Population Reference Bureau.

Rourke, J. T. (2003). *International politics on the world stage* (9th ed.). Guilford, CT: McGraw-Hill/Dushkin.

Southern African Development Community (SADC). Online access at www.sadc.int.

Southern Cone Common Market (Mercosur). Online access at http://www.infoplease.com/ce6/history/A0846059.html.

Spector, L. S., & Smith, J. R. (1990). *Nuclear ambitions: The spread of nuclear weapons*. Boulder, CO: Westview Press.

Time atlas of world history. (1978). London.

United Nations Development Programme (UNDP, 2001). *Human development indicators, human development report 2001*. New York: Oxford University Press. Online access at: http://www.undp.org/hdr2001/back.pdf.

United Nations Food and Agriculture Organization. *FAOSTAT database*. Online access at: http://apps.fao.org/page/collections?subset=agriculture.

United Nations High Commissioner on Refugees (UNHCR), Population Data Unit, Population and Geographic Data Section. (2000). Online access at: http://www.unhcr.ch/cgibin/texis/vtx/home. *Provisional statistics on refugees and others of concern to UNHCR for the year 2000.* Geneva.

United Nations Population Division. *World population prospects: The 2002 revision.* Online access at: http://www.un.org/esa/population/unpop.htm.

United Nations Population Fund. (2000). *The state of the world's population.* New York: United Nations Population Fund.

United Nations Statistics Division, Department of Economic and Social Affairs. (2001). *Social indicators.* Online access at: http://www.un.org/depts/unsd/social/index.htm.

Uranium Institute. Online access at: http://www.uilondon.org/safetab.htm.

U.S. Arms Control and Disarmament Agency. (1993). *World military expenditures and arms transfers.* Washington, DC: U.S. Government Printing Office.

U.S. Census Bureau. (2000). *International database, United States Census Bureau.* Online access at: http://www.census.gov/ipc/www/idbnew.html.

U.S. Central Intelligence Agency, Office of Public Affairs. 2001. *The world factbook.* Washington, DC. Online access at: http://www.odci.gov/cia/publications/factbook/.

U.S. Department of State, (1999) Undersecretary for Arms Control and International Security. *World military expenditures and arms transfers.* Online access at: http://www.state.gov/www/global/arms/bureau_ac/wmeat98/wmeat98.html.

USDA Forest Service. (1989). *Ecoregions of the continents.* Washington, DC: U.S. Government Printing Office.

Watts, Ronald K. (1999). *Comparing federal systems*, 2nd ed. Queens University Press, Kingston, Ont.

The world almanac and book of facts 2001. (2000). Mahwah, NJ: World Almanac Books.

World Bank. *World development indicators, 2003.* Washington, DC.

World Bank. *World development indicators 2001.* Washington, DC. World Bank. Online access at: http://www.worldbank.org/data/.

World Bank. (2001). *World development report 2000/2001: Attacking poverty.* New York: Oxford University Press.

World Health Organization. (1998). *World health statistics annual.* Geneva: World Health Organization.

World Resources Institute. (2000). *World resources 2000–2001. People and ecosystems: The fraying web of life.* Washington, DC: World Resources Institute: Online access at: http://www.wri.org.

World Trade Organization (WTO). Online access at: www.wto.org.

Wright, John W., ed. 2003. *The New York Times almanac 2003.* New York: Penguin Reference.